The International Library of Sociology

MARX
HIS TIME AND OURS

I0104474

Founded by KARL MANNHEIM

The International Library of Sociology

SOCIAL THEORY AND METHODOLOGY
In 22 Volumes

MARX
HIS TIME AND OURS

by

RUDOLF SCHLESINGER

ROUTLEDGE

ROUTLEDGE

Taylor & Francis Group

First published in 1950
by Routledge

Reprinted 1998, 2001, 2002
by Routledge
2 Park Square, Milton Park, Abingdon, Oxon, OX14 4RN
or
270 Madison Avenue, New York, NY 10016

First issued in paperback 2010

Routledge is an imprint of the Taylor & Francis Group

British Library Cataloguing in Publication Data
A CIP catalogue record for this book
is available from the British Library

Marx: His Time and Ours
ISBN 978–0–415–17510–4 (hbk)
ISBN 978–0–415–60500–7 (pbk)
Social Theory and Methodology: 22 Volumes
ISBN 978–0–415–17818–1
The International Library of Sociology: 274 Volumes
ISBN 978–0–415–17838–9

Publisher's Note
The publisher has gone to great lengths to ensure the quality of this
reprint but points out that some imperfections in the original
may be apparent

CONTENTS

CONTENTS

CONTENTS

PART V. THE SOCIETY TO COME

CONTENTS

PREFACE

The events of the present world find a preconceived framework in Marx's forecast of social transformations. The fit is quite loose enough to accommodate whatever changes may have occurred and may yet occur in revolutionary Russia, and whatever her influence may be on the development of other countries. It is clear, at least since the Stalingrad battle, that the Soviet Union will constitute one of the political forms of the new society. But the adaptation of the diverse national civilisations to the conditions of survival in the times to come may proceed in diverse ways. A society changes faster than its ideology : during prolonged international conflict, ideologies originally expressing the fundamental differences of the competing systems may come to lose any relevance except for self-assertion because only those systems can survive which adapt themselves to certain general patterns of structure. Only in the event of collaboration and mutual assimilation, the characteristics common to the new societies may receive expression in a universal ideology with local differences arising from national conditions. In spite of all the tribute paid by competing sects to theological and political creeds originated from past periods of social conflict, our generation is no longer exposed to the risk of periodical butcheries about the respective merits of papal authority and the Bible, or of republic and monarchy. Everyone who takes up the job of a sociologist in times like ours is likely to have done so because he considers that thereby he is making his contribution to the development of society ; but, being a scientist, he should clearly realise that he is making his contribution in a quite definite way, namely, by establishing the elements of truth approached from different starting points in different ways and by fighting the spirit of self-assertion that rejects what is deemed un-Ruritanian and repudiates forms of expression unfamiliar to the group thus asserted. Whether the fulfilment of that task may be described as a " reception of the definite achievements of Marxism into academic theory" or as "purging Marxism from Utopian elements conditioned by the specific conditions of its origin" depends very much on the respective sociologist's personal background. Naturally, my contribution is conditioned by my personal background in the continental Labour movement and by my various attempts at analysing the development of Soviet society. But if most of my criticism is devoted to those who approach the common task from various starting points this is done because I regard theirs as the only work which is relevant. The respective value of our different backgrounds will be measured by the contribution each of us can make to the synthesis to come; but the dangers of eclecticism cannot be avoided except by mutual criticism inspired not by any desire to assert the infallibility of the creed which we have been taught, but by the need to distinguish the relevant contents of theories from the ideological by-products conditioned by the circumstances of their origin. In this, and only in this sense, this book has been written from the Marxist point of view. But I do not think that the historical importance of a theory that has inspired the Russian revolution and the bulk of the modern Labour movement, and without whose impact modern historiography and sociology were inconceivable, depends on the truth of its individual tenets.

As the title of this book indicates, I am dealing far less with the internal coherence of Marx's argument in the conditions of its origin than with the issue of how far questions and answers conditioned by that setting are relevant for our, very different, days. The great World-religions provide conspicuous examples of ideologies whose motive power was, and is, being exercised in conditions very different from those in which they were shaped; but a scientific ideology should be measured, if not by its capacity to forecast the conditions of its realisations, at least, by the possibility of deriving from its basic tenets the reasons for its modifications.

I am indebted to Mr. Andrew Pearse, whose suggestions far exceeded the sphere of mere stylist revision, and to all my other friends whose criticism in the various stages of the formation of this work has helped me better to formulate my point of view even when I could not agree with them. To all of them my sincere thanks are due.

RUDOLF SCHLESINGER.

INVEREOCH, KILMUN, ARGYLLSHIRE,

March, 1949.

CHAPTER I

SOME INTRODUCTORY OBSERVATIONS ON THE SUBJECT OF THIS BOOK

Of the existing books on Marxism, some deal with the subject in terms of the historical background of the middle of the Nineteenth Century, while others interpret Marx and his teaching in the light of the Russian Revolution. The former seek to demonstrate that Marxism, despite its contribution to the progress of thought, has followed the rest of the Victorian output into obsolescence. The latter try to establish not only the Marxist ancestry of Bolshevism, which is hardly questioned since the time when Social Democracy was laying claims to Marxist orthodoxy, but also the existence of all the fundamental Bolshevist tenets in original Marxism. Most writers who have attempted this show a marked tendency to stress the self-assertion of Bolshevism within an ideological pattern of Marxist orthodoxy, but there are also attempts to prove that Marxism, just because it fits the twentieth century Russian pattern, does not fit the fundamentally different pattern of present Western civilisation.[1] Apparently such an approach supposes interpretation of the present Western Labour movement as necessarily sectional and reformist, and of the Russian Revolution as bourgeois-democratic.

A third approach to the problem may be entertained. An investigation may concentrate upon the modifications of the Marxist system made by the further evolution of the social formation investigated by Marx, including attempts at the realisation of his system. Such an approach involves inherent criticism of Marx's original system but takes the continuing relevance of that system for granted ; it is based not upon the finality of Marx's system but rather on his success in achieving a critical synthesis of all the relevant material available in his day, which enabled him to overcome the limitations of that material.

In his funeral address for Marx, Engels defined the subject of Marxism as being the laws of evolution of human history.

[1] Comp. A. Rosenberg's *History of Bolshevism*, engl. ed., London, 1934.

If one adds the rider that human societies are characterised by distinct socio-economic structures on which their other aspects depend and that there are specific laws governing the dynamics of every distinct social formation, we have a definition sufficient to distinguish Marxism from alternative approaches. Since Aristotle's days social change has been explained by alleged cyclical movement in political structures or else by the formal concept which Pareto has defined as an " exchange of elites." Marxism need not deny those elements of truth contained in such concepts, nor indeed such truisms as that " power " in the broadest sense is obviously the agent in social relations. But the formalist cannot explain even such phenomena of social change as he describes. Aristotle was right in stating that Greek city-state democracy was likely to end in dictatorship ; but Marxists will point to his failure to analyse the social conditions laying the field open for a dictator, and the policies he would be bound to pursue for survival. And they may insist that these are the things which really matter, whether they happen to us in our time, or to the common man in Athens. Similarly revolutions may imply some replacement of one elite by another ; but what matters is : why the former elite failed, how the new one originated, what social forces support its operation, etc.

Much current criticism of Marxism is directed against the dynamic approach itself; objective laws of social development are said to be incompatible with the fact that the men making history find themselves confronted with various alternatives. The choice of any group of abstractions from among an infinite number implies a basic evaluation, and pre-supposes a political decision in making that choice—a political decision which, it can be claimed, is of unscientific character.

Marx's " historicism " is intended to mean that human actions are conditioned by the historical circumstances under which men have to make decisions and does not deny the importance of those decisions as the factor immediately shaping human history.[2] To reject it is simply another way of excluding the development of society from the realm of exact scientific investigation. (This implication is admitted by some,[2] but not by all of those who utter that criticism.) But if the Marxist method achieves certain results which, though, as in all sciences,

---

[2] See below, pp. 18 and 45. The above argument has to be reiterated against a recurring misunderstanding by critics of Marxism, most recently in K. Popper's book *The Open Society* (two vols., London, 1946), which is based upon it.

they may be incomplete and even occasionally faulty, have an actual and verifiable connection with social reality, the attempt to establish laws of social dynamics cannot be inherently faulty.

Marx rejected the quest for a general trend of History as irrelevant : the scientific value of a theory should be measured by its relation not to some possible future developments but to those social transformations which are sufficiently near to the elaboration of the theory for their growth to enable the shaping of the theory just as their accomplishment serves as the test of its " this-sidedness and reality." [3] Engels published one of his works under the title *The Development of Socialism, from Utopia to Science*, and a bolshevist author added a study *From Science to Action*. But it is the obvious task of our time to confront the outcome of that action with the starting point. To a Marxist, that starting point is the second link in Engels' chain, but, being a scientist, he should not take for granted that the second link was completely free of the first. The Marxist system in which we are interested is the work of the Nineteenth Century Marx, plus the work of his Twentieth Century disciples who had to transform his thought into action. Ideological elements whose Utopian character can be proved by the historical conditions of their growth may be safely deducted without impairing the homogeneity of the system.

Our approach does not set out to test the Marxist system by comparison with the results of the Russian revolution. The French revolution played an important (Marxists will say, decisive) part in the overthrow of feudal society, but capitalist society cannot be identified with the results of the French revolution. In its day, the American revolution—itself to a large extent an aftermath of the English Civil War (and separated from it in time as the French from the Russian revolution)—was regarded as an interesting, though distant, phenomenon, comparable with the Spanish civil war in our days. Yet the American revolution, not the French, has produced the strongest power of the capitalist period. After the French revolution, thirty years passed before revolutions in the smaller countries with similar demands became a familiar phenomenon, forty years passed before the British Reform Bill which carried over the basic concepts of the French revolution to its leading opponent, three-quarters of a century passed before the abolition of serfdom in U.S.A. and Tsarist Russia, and an even longer period before Japan had to transform herself into a constitutional capitalist country in order to retain political independence. Even if the results of the Russian revolution take effect in a similar way (and up to now the timetable holds good) so that it remains the only large-scale application of Marxist principles in a revolutionary transition to socialism, it cannot be proved that a thorough application of Marxist principles in important countries other than Russia was *a priori* impossible. That the system has a large degree of inherent truth is proved by the success of its application in Russia, but in being narrowed down and made concrete it has perhaps undergone a limitation of its inherent possibilities. The failure of the German Communists to achieve socialism in their country does not necessarily demonstrate limitations of the Marxist system though it may prove the limitations of the form in which that system was bound to be represented by German Communists in the 'twenties. We must, however, preserve the standpoint that Marxism is to be verified by comparison if not with the actual, then at least with the possible. The behaviour of those Socialists who are inclined " to write off " the Russian revolution because it fails to comply with their pet Utopia, which some of them prefer to describe as " Marxism ", is truly contrary to the Marxist point of view.

PART I

THE PHILOSOPHICAL FOUNDATIONS

CHAPTER II

SOME OBSERVATIONS ON DIALECTICS

(a) Revolution as the Typical Form of Social Change.

Marx belonged to the generation whose minds had been moulded by the French revolution ; amongst his contemporaries, Germany's need for a similar revolution was accepted as a foregone conclusion ; and he appealed to the class which had stood visibly in the background of all major upheavals, a class whose conditions seemed so hopeless in his days that it might hardly expect emancipation from anything short of a very thorough revolution. This is sufficient to explain why his analysis concentrated upon the background of revolutions and the type of course they followed. It explains too why that analysis could be hailed by Lenin as the theory of the proletarian revolution. But in itself it does not justify the description of Marxism as the theory of social change in general. Nor does it explain how Marx could receive his basic methodological armour from Hegel who, though his thinking certainly centred round the phenomenon of change, was anything but a revolutionary.

There are at least three characteristic types of thorough social change which could be claimed as " revolution " :

(1) Social structures may change because of the ("gradualist") accumulation of small changes confined within the limits of the given framework none of which are intended to change that framework. A typical instance is the Industrial Revolution. At its end, British society differed fundamentally from what it had been at its start, though no individual invention or investment in itself can be described as intentionally overthrowing the existing framework. Nevertheless, the social position of whole groups was very different at the end from what it was at the beginning ; and groups with completely new characteristics, such as employers and workers in large-scale industries, originated. Even those institutions which *formally* remained unchanged did in fact suffer a change in social function. Laws, for example,

which on the eve of the industrial era restricted access to mastership to journeymen duly accepted by the guild to fill vacancies and which were meant to protect the established craftsmen against excessive competition by persons who were their equals in educational and technical equipment, now turned into obstacles against the application of advanced technical methods.

Another example for this type of change in the class-structure of society is the rise of feudalism by the submission of many free peasants to their more powerful neighbours. In all these cases the step of change, though prolonged through generations, may be elementary and "revolutionary" in comparison with the modes of life current in the preceding and in the subsequent society.

(2) Action may be taken with the intention of changing the social framework (or, if some "gradual" change in the existing framework has taken place, to adapt the institutional framework to the changed needs). Such action is usually described as a "revolution" only when it originates from groups other than the ruling one, so that its success results not only in a change of institutions, but also of that ruling group. Marxism argues that ruling groups are characterised by their very place in economic structure and therefore unlikely to initiate changes in the structure from which they profit. However, we must allow ample space for possibilities of "revolution from above" where such procedure provides the only chance for the ruling group to survive as such. Such alternatives may arise in some typical cases :

(a) In his letter to Kautsky, of February 7, 1882, Engels remarked that the actual, as distinct from the delusionary, tasks of every revolution were bound to be solved, if necessary by its "executors." Thus Bonaparte, Cavour and Bismarck solved the national issue for Italy, Hungary and Germany, the solution of which had formed one of the real tasks of the respective revolutions from below. It is difficult to overlook the circular character of an argument in which the actual tasks of a revolution are described as issues so urgent that even in the event of its defeat they have to be solved by its conquerors, so that the actual task of the revolutionary movement as such is restricted to preventing the old order lingering on by pure inertia. Lenin was not satisfied with such a restricted function of the revolutionary movement : in his concept, there is a fundamental difference between the fate of Russia with the problem of the transition from feudal to capitalist agriculture solved by Stolypin functioning as the "executor" of the defeated revolution of 1905-6 and its solution by a victorious revolution.[1] However, even the transformation consequent on the political defeat of the revolution may be thorough enough to justify the change being regarded as a "revolution from above" in the economic sphere.

(b) Without waiting for the realisation of a revolutionary threat the rulers—especially if warned by similar events in other countries—may carry out changes such as the abolition of serfdom in Russia in 1861. In such cases the possibility of getting away with a moderate amount of reform and carrying as much of the substance of traditional power as possible into the new age, formed the main incentive for the supporters of the "revolution from above," and the main argument by which they defeated the opposition within their own class against changes in the traditional order.

(c) Once a certain social structure has proved conducive to national strength in the international field, a ruling class may itself initiate the changes necessary to maintain the power of the nation, and at the same time to limit the scope of the change to this particular purpose. In 19th Century Japan, fundamental social changes were carried out by a group which had won political power by relying on traditionalist opposition to more moderate adaptations of the country to the Western model as planned by the Shogunate. The element "from below" was hardly represented, unless the support given to the Choshu-Satsuma rising (that is, to one of the competing feudal groups) by the old established commercial magnates, very comparable to the part played by the Fuggers and other great merchants in the crises of 16th century Germany, be described in such terms. But even in such cases a change in the social structure of the ruling group is likely to ensue in the wake of the "revolution from above." In the above case, many lesser samurais, if not commoners, rose to positions of influence and power by becoming capitalists.

Thus the line between "revolutions from below" and "revolutions from above" is not easy to draw. The element represented by the former is obvious in our case (a), noticeable in case (b), and may still be represented by the impact of events

[1] cf. His alternative between the "Prussian" and the "American" way of solving the agrarian problems of 1906 Russia, *Sel. Works*, vol. III, espec. pp. 180, 217 ff. and 279 ff.

abroad combining with the realisation of existing social tensions in case (c). On the other hand, if a direct change in the ruling group during the revolution is an essential element of revolution " from below," then the semi-abortive revolutions of Central Europe in 1848 are excluded while all " national revolutions " might be admitted as true revolutions even in the absence both of mass-movements and of fundamental changes in the social structure. If, with Lenin,[2] revolution is defined in terms of new political machinery originating from the mass-movement, full development and at least temporary success of those movements is essential to their appreciation as the " locomotives of history."

(3) The balance of different social structures within international society may be altered radically by the capacity of those national societies whose structure is best adapted to contemporary technical, etc., conditions to restrict or even to destroy the power of more backward ones. Where the earlier development of a society precludes its adaption to the needs of the time, it will be destroyed or absorbed by the more successful, whose external expansion thus may be regarded as the fruition of their successful internal transformation.

Of these types of social changes a subspecies of one (2), namely, " revolutions from below " in which mass-initiative is clearly predominant, is described by Marxism as fundamental. This is a hypothetical assumption, to be verified in exactly the same way in which at various stages of the development of physics the conception of mechanics, or thermodynamic energy, or electricity, or of nuclear forces as the basic physical agency has been tested and verified. Such generalisations are not based upon the assertion that the alleged basic force is the sole force in actual experience. If such were the case, there would be no scientific merit in the hypothesis. They are based on the statement that the other forces can be derived from that which is considered as basic. Marxism makes such a statement in respect of " revolutions from below " ; resort to group (1) is made mainly in order to explain the reasons why revolutions are bound to arise in consequence of the gradual accumulation of quantitative changes, resulting in society's need for a qualitatively changed setting, that is, a new structure. The gradualist counterclaim is based not on the obvious fact that there are gradual changes but on the assertion that they, in themselves, are sufficient to

[2] See below, p. 239.

adapt society to changing needs. There are obvious examples of societies which for considerable periods have managed without revolutions, and yet their international position has not been thereby impaired ; so the Marxist's task consists in demonstrating that, in those circumstances, the underlying revolutionary forces worked through the desire of ruling classes to preserve their rule and through a competition on the international stage. However, Marxism derives its general concept of social dynamics from a generalisation of a scheme characteristic of revolutions from below.

(b) THE TYPICAL STAGES OF REVOLUTIONARY DEVELOPMENTS.

Major revolutions, such as the English, the French, and the Russian revolution show certain common features in spite of the enormous variety of the conditions under which they arose. Therefore, these traits seem to be inherent in the revolutionary mode of development of human society. In every revolution, during its first stages, power is transferred, or appears to be transferred, to a comparatively moderate opposition group which had the opportunity to develop during the preceding decomposition of the *ancien regime*. Behind this " legal opposition " all the revolutionary forces rally. But if the revolution fails to overthrow that temporary leadership, it becomes abortive, like those of 1848 and 1918 in Germany, because of the inability of the moderates actually to liquidate the strongholds of power of the *ancien regime* in the framework of which they fitted. In those revolutions which have a chance to rank amongst the milestones of history, moderate leadership is eventually replaced by a radical group formed during the revolutionary process. That group has to fight other radical[3] groups, Levellers, Hebertists, Kronstadt anarchists and followers of the " Workers' Opposition " (in the Russian revolution), who defend some of the original ideological aspects of the movement, without at any time being able to proceed to their realisation. (It is thus clearly untrue to suggest that, in every revolution, power tends to be temporarily transferred to the most radical group.) After having solved its immediate task[4]—from the viewpoint of the historical perspective,

[3] " Radical " is to be understood merely at its face value. The description does not exclude the justifiable allegation by the revolutionary dictatorship that its left-wing opponents may become the rallying point for counter-revolutionaries who dare not operate under their own flag.

[4] See above, p. 6.

not necessarily from that of its own ideology[5]—the revolutionary dictatorship is faced with the danger of counter-revolution in consequence of its threatened break with those classes that, though not interested in its more thorough measures, supported it hitherto as the only efficient means of getting rid of the *ancien regime*, and in order to preserve national independence in view of the international complications hitherto connected with any major revolution. Only in the Russian revolution did the revolutionary regime succeed in adapting its policies so as to preserve the alliance of those classes and thus to make possible fundamental changes in their economic conditions by a second revolution " from above."[5a]   Whether there is a counter-revolution, whose hopeless attempts at restoring the *ancien regime* are followed by minor revolutions carried through with less energy against less resistance, like those of 1688, 1830 and 1848, or whether the revolutionary dictatorship succeeds in adapting itself to the needs of establishing a stable regime, the outcome may be very similar to what the original moderate wing of the revolutionaries dreamed of, but could not realise. The parliamentarians of 1642, the Girondists of 1792, and the Chernishevsky and Plekhanov of pre-revolutionary Russia would not have been dissatisfied with the fruits harvested by methods they disapproved of.

In the spirit of the Hegelian system,[6] this process may be described as the synthesis between the *ancien regime* and its first negation by the revolution. This statement goes far beyond the primitive concept that " the pendulum swings back." During the revolution, various emergency measures are applied, perhaps under the delusion that they are not mere emergency

---

[5] The case of the Bolsheviks in 1921, when introducing the N.E.P., is particular. Their pre-1917 ideology had prepared them for the eventuality of having to carry through a bourgeois-democratic revolution which could not proceed beyond this framework unless supported by socialist revolutions in the West (see below, pp.296-7) ; and their approach to the 1917 revolution itself (as expressed in Lenin's *Can the Bolsheviks Retain State Power?*) did provide for a gradual transition to socialism which in no way was excluded by their 1921 concessions. But these concessions certainly contradicted the ideology developed during the War Communist regime.

[5a] cf. *History of the C.P. of the U.S.S.R.*, engl. ed. of 1939, p. 305. In an attempt to assert the identity of Marxism since its earliest days, Mr. Andrew Rothstein (in his critique of my *Spirit of post-War Russia*, in *The Modern Quarterly*, Autumn, 1948) has submerged this very important characteristic by a reference to truisms such as the emphasis always laid by Marxists on the use of the State machine by the victorious working class. Though there is a fundamental difference between " revolutions from above " started by a new ruling class in order to stabilise its power and, on the other hand, those started by the old ruling class in order to avoid its overthrow (in the

measures but imply the creation of a new social order. Less of the " ancien regime " will be destroyed than appeared or was intended to be doomed at the heights of the revolutionary crisis. But to state that the synthesis resulting from the revolution preserves some elements of the *ancien regime* means more than this : the English middle-classes were actually to rule with an Established Church and with a House of Lords, and the remainder of the French nobility became one of the main elements of Conservativism in what was ultimately to become a capitalist republic. The Russian revolution had destroyed private owner-ship in land and industrial enterprises so thoroughly that it could appease the remnants of the old ruling classes only as individuals admitted to the new order. But, apart from the individuals, it also admitted much of their old ideologies, which thus became elements of the nationalism of a society completely different from that in which they had originated. Thus, the concept of syn-thesis involves not only partial preservation but also a change of function of preserved social groups, institutions and ideas, for the very reason that the revolution has thoroughly altered the frame-work within which they work.

What is the function of the revolutionary theory in this process ? First of all, if it is to become the ideology of the radical movement, it has to exercise a thorough criticism of the existing order, so that an appeal is made to all existent social tensions and that all the implications of the social order in all fields of human life are included in the criticism. A criticism of latifundia as being irrational from the agricultural viewpoint and unlikely to ease social tensions, is likely to mobilise only medium land-owners, and even they will hardly be inspired to those exertions and sacrifices necessary to carry through a serious revolution.

circumstances described in the text above), there is also an important difference between the mechanism of changes carried out during a revolutionary upheaval (including the use of a new State machine emerging from the upheaval, see below, pp. 242-4) and administrative action by a consolidated State.

⁶ In his latest period, having already become distinctly right wing, Hegel (German *Jubilaeumsausgabe*, vol. XIX, p. 516) regarded as the main shortcoming of the French Revolution the abstractness of its criticism of the *ancien regime* and its failure to realise its ideas in concrete institutions, which should certainly be described as a synthesis in the sense of the Hegelian system. He still claimed (Ibid., pp. 534-5 and 553) for contemporary German philosophy, including his own, the merit of having expressed the abstract ideas of the Revolution in their proper place, in the world of Thought. Marx (*M.E.G.A.*, vol. I/3, p. 251) reacted to this claim by demonstrat-ing the analogy between Hegel's absolute Mind and the teachings of the French " doctrinaires " " who opposed the sovereignty of the people by proclaiming the sovereignty of Reason."

Happily, from the viewpoint of the revolutionary ideologist, in every society all social relations tend to be expressed in terms of the existing order. When, on the eve of a bourgeois-democratic revolution, " privilege " is criticised, the criticism hits not only the feudal strata but also the great bourgeoisie which, in such a state of society, is likely to be protected by means of privileges fitting their condition. So also all craftsmen and workers without whose support a consistent revolutionary policy would hardly be applicable, can be mobilised. As the irrational argument needed in support of feudalism permeates the whole life of such a pre-revolutionary society, appeals to reason will attack the Church not only in its rôle as feudal latifundia-owner (a rôle which is mainly of interest to the peasants on the ecclesiastical estates) but also as the main propagandist agency of the *ancien regime* and will appeal to all who honestly strive for overcoming prejudice. Institutions and social classes not ripe for liquidation because they have a legitimate place in every type of society which may follow the *ancien regime*, will thus be included amongst the objects of the revolutionary criticism. This explains why the Utopias of today are the actual revolutionary programmes of tomorrow, and the commonplaces of the day after tomorrow. Parliamentary democracy, the Utopia of the extreme left-wing of the English Civil War, became the actual programme of the radical wing of the French revolution (in which religious tolerance, the apple of discord in 17th Century England, was regarded as a commonplace even by the most moderate elements). After the downfall of Tsarism parliamentary democracy became such a commonplace that the Russian bourgeoisie tried to rally round it against the Bolshevist revolution. From such general acceptance of a slogan at a time when it could not be realised in the event of either possible outcome of the Russian Civil War, cynics may conclude it had ceased to be actually relevant. In fact, after having been transferred from the dreams of the Levellers to the defeated political platform of the Chartists, it has been realised by evolution in the country of its origin, though it may be suggested that the Chartists—not to speak of the Levellers—might feel as much sympathy with its overthrow in Russia as with its realisation in England.

In criticising exploitation and oppression, the revolutionary theorist criticises not a mere specific form of oppression, thus leaving room for compromise with part of the existing vested interests, but exploitation and oppression in general. This distinguishes his attitude from that, say, of the average German worker who, living in a country where lordship, but not ownership of capital, was regarded as obsolete, described his struggle against his employer, " the baron of the furnace," as " defending his only capital, his labour power." Doubtless, once capitalism is in process of obsolescence in reality, though not necessarily in traditional ideology, such an attitude on the part of the average worker may enable him to slip from a revolution " against feudal privileges " to one against " lords of the furnaces " too ; but this pre-supposes revolutionary leadership which cannot emerge except from broad generalisations. It was the greatness of Marx that, on the eve of 1848, he was able to understand the problems of 1917, and even of a future which may still lie ahead of us.

(c) DIALECTICS AS A GENERAL APPROACH TO THE WORLD.

As long as we work on Herzen's conception of Dialectics as " the Algebra of Revolution " and, in a larger sense, as a key to the understanding of social changes, there is little difficulty in understanding its meaning. Hegel's Dialectics originated in an intellectual evolution that can only be understood as an ideological reflection of the development of, and reaction to, the French revolution.[7] The statement that " the history of mankind is a history of class-struggles " had to be subjected to restrictive interpretations as regards primitive and post-capitalist society, but it is not too difficult for a historian to find patterns familiar to modern revolutionary developments when he follows the history of late 14th Century England, of the German reformation—or even of Rome in the times of the Gracchi. Marxist-influenced historians have been able, more than others, to contribute to the study of the Ancient Orient and China : once we conceive evolution as a necessary element in the dialectical process there is, indeed, no reason why the pattern should not work in analysing even very slowly moving types of society provided only they fulfil the fundamental condition that the groups forming such a society can be distinguished by their different position in the social production process.[8]

But new problems arise once the Dialectical approach is applied outside the sphere from whose conditions it was derived,

[7] See below, pp. 22-4.
[8] See below, pp. 216ff.

especially in the analysis of Nature. Engels[9] noticed that Mendeleyev, in establishing his periodical system of the chemical elements, unconsciously applied the law of Dialectics as regards the transition from quantity into quality. Already at its face-value Mendeleyev's law clearly states such a transition in the field with which the law is concerned, i.e., in the only field where the scientist is within his rights to make such a statement. Of what had Mendeleyev been unconscious? Of the fact that Hegel and Marx had regarded similar transitions as characteristic of the World in general? A member of the Russian intelligentsia in the 'sixties was not likely to be quite unfamiliar with Hegel; but would he, as a scientist, have been within his rights in drawing any parallel between his scientific discovery and the structure of the World asserted by Dialectics? And what would such a parallel mean?

The actual reason for the Marxist, and even the Hegelian interest in Dialectics in general (as distinct from a helpful generali-sation in studying transformations of Society) was the quest for a "world-outlook," i.e., for a scientific substitute for the religious myths. All philosophy has originated from such a quest, whether it was politically compromising, like the Hegelian, in that it looked for an interpretation of religious dogma acceptable to contemporary educated opinion, or else politically radical, like the Marxist, in order to give the revolutionary class a new "world outlook," by replacing the religious set of interpretations and values by a new one, fitting the task it had to fulfil. But Engels himself[10] noticed that the progress of science had absorbed more and more of what before had been deemed the realm of philosophy. Once we accept science, that is to say, the body of concrete knowledge achievable at a certain time, as the new "world out-look," there is no place for Dialectics or any other statement about general qualities of Nature unless it forms a generalisation from actual observations. The assertion that quantitative changes, at a certain point, turn into qualitative ones is a mere negation of the assertion that *natura non facit saltum*. This dia-lectical statement is completely legitimate as a denial of ideo-logical restrictions of the range of possible experience, and especially of possible social change; but it is misleading to describe it as "a law of Nature." It is obviously impossible to

---

[9] *Dialectics of Nature*, ed. Haldane and Dutt, p. 33.
[10] *Ludwig Feuerbach*, etc., ed. cit., p. 69.

predict by mere Dialectics that at some concrete point a leap from mere quantitative into qualitative change will occur, or to predict the new quality.

Recently, Stalin[11] gave a summary of the essential characteristics of Dialectics that has the great advantage of avoiding the pitfalls connected with specific Hegelian language :

(a) phenomena are originally connected with, dependent on, and limited by, each other ;

(b) phenomena should be considered from the standpoint of their movement, change, and development ;

(c) change is no mere quantitative change, but at certain stages leaps in quality arise, as the natural result of an accumulation of gradual, quantitative changes ;

(d) internal contradictions are inherent in all things and phenomena, for all things have a past and a future, something dying away and something developing. The struggle between these opposites constitutes the internal content of the process of development and of the transformation of quantitative changes into qualitative.

Marx had received the term " contradictions " from Hegel, in whose system the concept made sense because Mind was supposed to develop through thesis and anti-thesis, argument and counter-argument. As against the current assertion that only one argument can be correct and that contradiction in itself is a proof of logical mistake, Hegel showed that the thesis as well as the anti-thesis contain elements of truth, in that they reflect different stages in the development of human society and human thought or of " Mind," to use Hegel's mystical expression. Transferred into the objective system of Marx, the statement that contradictions are implied in some social phenomenon or institution means that within it antagonistic social forces are developing, and that its progress implies growth of both antagonist forces which exercise their impact upon one another until their mutual relations are settled in open conflict. Even in original Marxism emphasis is laid upon the objective causes making for the ultimate triumph of one of the opposite forces, so that it may be regarded as being in ascendance ; but Marx would never have derived, for example, the contradictions existing between the two main classes growing in the midst of ascending capitalism, from the expectation that capitalism was ultimately dying away.

---

[11] On Dialectical and Historical Materialism, in *Leninism* (ed. 1942), p. 591 ff.

In Engels' exposition of Dialectics,[12] Stalin's two first characteristics of a dynamic approach are taken for granted but, along with point (c) in the above statement (in Engels' terms " the law of the transformation of quantity into quality and *vice versa* ") and (d) (" the law of the interpenetration of opposites ") " the negation of the negation " is mentioned as an additional law of Dialectics. In the only sense in which it can rationally be interpreted, it means no more than the accumulation of a plurality of qualitative leaps, just as the latter are accumulations of quantitative changes. Engels obviously intended it to mean more, namely, the assumption of some synthesis arising out of two consecutive " negations," leaps in quality. Such a scheme of development can be derived from the study of revolutionary changes in Society,[13] but not in Nature. The biological example used in Engels' explanation in *Anti-Duehring*[14] is distinctly weak : certainly the fundamental characteristics of a plant, together with new qualities acquired in consequence of the grower's activities, are preserved in the seeds resulting from the biological cycle, but the transition from seed to plant and from plant to seed is only very formally a " negation of the negation." Actually the statement implies no more than that no charge affects *all* the qualities of its subject. For good reasons Stalin has left that element out of his description of Dialectics.

The transformation of quantitative changes into qualitative ones can be explained without reference to the " struggle of opposites " as a general characteristic of Nature : a very vague conception of that struggle would be needed in order to explain the fact that, say, adding consecutive electrons to an atom nucleus

[12] *Dialectics of Nature*, ed. cit., p. 26. The sketchy character of the work should be kept in mind.

[13] See above, pp. 9-10.

[14] Ed. cit., pp. 152 ff. Engels' argument is made in defence, against Duehring, of Marx's statement, in *Capital*, that the Society to Come would preserve the capitalist achievement of large-scale " socialised " production, but restore the producers' ownership in the produced means of consumption which had been destroyed by the rise of capitalist production. As Marx and Engels knew (see below, pp. 73-5) the Society to Come will not be able, nor wish to distribute the whole of the social net product amongst the producers. But some ideological reactions are likely to be preserved in various forms through the life-time of the social formation against the establishment of which they were directed (see below, pp. 73-5); and a capitalist society may actually be abolished to the satisfaction of ideologies demanding " restoring to the small man what the capitalists have stolen from him," " the workers' right to the whole proceeds of his work," etc. Such demands can never be satisfied except in some ideological paraphrase, such as the property of the capitalists and the national output being restored to the nation, including the grandchildren of those whom the capitalists once have expropriated.

results in gradual changes in the chemical characteristics of the element up to the point when a completely new layer of external electrons is formed, with a leap in chemical quality resulting from the addition of a further electron (i.e., the first of the next layer). If we regard the World dynamically, i.e., in a permanent state of change (Stalin's statement (b)) ; and if we regard things as mutually connected with one another (statement (a)), which is merely another way of saying that they have " qualities," it follows that gradual change, at a certain point, will involve different relations to connected things, that is to say, new qualities. From the point of view of Dialectics our example falls short in that even the addition of the first electron resulted in different chemical reactions to other elements, i.e. in qualitative changes, and that our " leap " was privileged merely by being much larger than the preceding and subsequent ones ; and this shortcoming may be shared by the whole outlook of modern physics which suppose an " elementary quantum " as the minimum amount of *any* change. Possibly there is no such thing as "quantitative change " pure and simple. But this remark deals with mere mathematic abstractions ; for all practical purposes the consideration of small changes as gradual and merely quantitative will meet the case.

But the more we succeed in explaining qualitative change without resort to the " struggle of opposites," the greater the need for the latter to stand on its own merits. Engels' proof of the existence of contradictions in the very essence of things is a mere materialist re-interpretation of Hegel's statement that any concept implicitly contains its negation. Certainly it does; but the corresponding statement as regards the actual structure of Nature is involved in Stalin's statements (a) and (b), though not (d), namely, that things do not exist in isolation, cannot be conceived except in relation to other things and that all things are subject to change. To describe their correlatives as " negations " is somewhat artificial even in Logic ; but there, at least, it derives an actual meaning from the anti-thetical structure of thought and of ideological developments which reflect actual struggles in Society.

In dealing with social and economic problems, Engels[15] explained the dialectical approach as a successive analysis of (a)

[15] *On Marx's Critique of Political Economy*, in Marx-Engels *Sel. Works*, vol. I, p. 369. See also *M.E.G.A.*, vol. I/3, p. 205, and the example quoted below p. 37.

18 THE PHILOSOPHICAL FOUNDATIONS

the social relation involved in some concept, for example, that of commodity, (b) the laws governing the development of each side of the relation, and (c) resulting contradictions which demand a solution, to be found in the actual world. Obviously even in Society such an approach works only on condition that there is a tendency towards polarisation on either side of the social relation, each side being represented by a different social group whose conditions are developing in different directions. For example, in the exchange of commodities between the craftsmen of a mediaeval town, assuming approximately equal conditions in all trades, contradictions outside the mere competition of barter need not arise. But the antagonism is clear in the exchange of goods between the small craftsmen and the merchants on whom they depend for raw materials and marketing. In this case actual class-struggle and finally qualitative changes (the transformation of the craftsmen into wage-earners in manufactories owned by the former merchants) will result from a gradual accumulation of " mere quantitative changes " (a long chain of bargains to the advantage of the economically stronger). It is the merit of Marxism to emphasize this type of development, as opposed to orthodox academic economics which prefers to deal even with the marketing of labour as if it were an exchange between equals who may be regarded as mere atoms in an amorphous equilibrium. But Marxists are generally proud of noticing that Darwin's concept of the " struggle for existence " as a universal competition contained unjustified generalisations from economic theories current in his day. Therefore they should refrain from giving the social phenomenon of class-struggle a similar universal significance.

Engels[16] correctly noticed that there is a fundamental difference between Nature and Society in that in the latter the agents act consciously, though they may not be fully conscious of the actual results of their actions. But he has failed to draw all the implications of this statement in regard to the concept of Dialectics. Whatever the intentions of the small craftsman opposing the powerful merchant before and after being turned into an employee, it is only the existence of *some* intentions opposed to those of his opposite number in the economic relation, which makes it possible to describe the latter as a struggle. Stalin's description of the struggle between the past and the future, that which

---

[16] *Ludwig Feuerbach*, ed. cit., p. 58.

is dying away and that which is developing, makes impressive reading because it smacks of the struggle carried on in the most varied fields of the social world of today, with religious, philosophical, aesthetic and even mathematical disputes hanging upon cleavages caused by the great social and political issues. But, though it is easy enough to produce in embryology many examples of " leaps " from quantitative to qualititive changes, it is impossible to associate any scientific meaning with the concept of a " struggle " carried on between, say, the blastula-like past and the primate-like future of a human embryo.

It is impossible to interpret concepts like " struggle between the opposites " or " negation of the negation " except as attempts to apply to the whole of Nature concepts that have their origin and their *raison d'être* in the specific field of sociology ; recent trends in Soviet ideology to ascribe to Dialectics the rôle of the " new World-outlook," in connection with the emphasis laid on what is called " the partisan character of philosophy " [16a] should be interpreted as elements of social mythology rather than as contributions to Science.

The first applications of Dialectics in pre-socratic[17] philosophic thought deal with the conspicuous element of change in Nature, on the basis of a general world-outlook that was not then sufficiently emancipated from primitive animism to find fundamental difficulties in the way of accepting qualitative changes without quantitative basis or of preserving elements of teleology within the naturalist outlook. With the first rise of class-struggles amongst people who could express their views in, or could be influenced by, philosophic considerations, metaphysical abstractions arose which, from the Pythagoreans and Plato onwards, were intended as ideological justifications for the presumedly natural social framework. Through Christianity, their derivations have dominated the world outlook of two millenia. With the Renaissance, new classes interested in contesting the traditional outlook entered the historical scene and their new outlook, too, was expressed in metaphysical abstractions. These abstractions

[16a] See below, p. 63.

[17] Possibly one ought to say "pre-eleatic"—but this issue is for professional historians of ancient philosophy. Certainly the Pythagoreans belong definitely to the metaphysical and consciously reactionary pattern, whilst, in the sum total, the inclusion of Aristotle amongst the naive dialecticians may be justified (which would result in regarding classical ancient philosophy as essentially Dialectic, and the metaphysical counter-current as a mere preparation for another age, to last from about 300 B.C. to about A.D. 1500).

became progressively teleological and " godless " in order to be subject to mathematical treatment, as a necessary condition of modern mechanical science in which the new classes were interested, and also in order to deprive the feudal powers of their metaphysical foundations. The further development of class-struggles in a society of which all educated classes had already accepted a rationalised outlook, put the concept of a changing World within the scope of philosophical generalisation about a century before biology and physics were advanced enough to allow its serious scientific application[18]. Under the specific conditions which we are to discuss in the next Chapter, the task of understanding the dynamics of History was tackled with the tool of concept-analysis, a tool which, in Socrates' days, had served the opposite purpose of divorcing abstractions from reality. Occasional applications of Dialectics in classical German philosophy to the study of Nature were bound to result in mysticism, but we should keep in mind that in the field of Science Lamarckism was the counterpart to Schelling's *Philosophy of Nature*. Before Darwin, the theory of evolution did not reach a truly scientific level. Darwin himself did not emphasise the qualitative aspects of the changes by variations, and his concepts of the " struggle for survival " were obvious generalisations from sociological concepts of the Benthamite and Malthusian type. Social struggle gave birth to Dialectics, conditioned the form it was to take, and the way in which it was " turned upside down." It has preserved Dialectics up to our days, though by forces other than those which invented it.

[18] The evolutionist fashions in late 18th and early 19th century scientific thought, in view of their extremely poor foundations in available knowledge, should be regarded rather as reflections of contemporary historical interest in non-sociological fields. There is certainly a Marxist explanation for the time-lag : the French revolution, which supplied the thought-material for Dialectics in Sociology, has created the preliminary conditions for modern developments in Science.

CHAPTER III

THE SOURCES OF MARXIST PHILOSOPHY

(a) THE BACKGROUND OF HEGELIANISM

With pride, Engels described the German workers as the heirs of German classical philosophy. Within the framework of Germany's intellectual revival this statement is incontestable ; but it is another question whether it forms a clear recommendation of that ideology in the international sphere.

On the one hand, Marxism derived from its origins methodological foundations much more clearly elaborated than those of any competing labour ideology. Mr. Churchill's description at the eve of the 1945 general election, of Socialism as "a continental ideology," and Mr. Attlee's rejoinder that Socialism had been elaborated a generation before Marx by the British industrialist and philanthropist, Robert Owen, are not likely to upset the concepts of anyone who attempts a serious comparison between British and continental Socialism. Unless, to use Engels' term, we wish to return " from science to Utopia,"[1] the comparative merits of the two contemporaries, Hegel and Owen, appears as a rather subordinate issue to Marxists who share with Robert Owen at least his belief in human progress, and his hatred of nationalistic narrow-mindedness.

But if we accept Marx's description of the development of German classical philosophy as a substitute for the political revolution that could not be attempted in view of the backwardness of German conditions, the Marxist himself is bound to ask whether, in view of this backwardness, German philosophy could produce methodological foundations for the theory of the progressive movement in countries much more advanced than was early 19th Century Germany.

In order to answer the question, we have first to put the historical setting in its true perspective. Marx and Engels

[1] The wish for such a return backs K. Popper's book mentioned in note 2 on p. 2 above.

B

have been widely regarded as direct pupils of Hegel. Actually, there was no more direct contact between Hegel and Marx than there was, say, between Engels and Stalin. But between Engels and Stalin, Leninism developed in opposition to the intermediate period of German Social Democracy ; whilst the night of reaction covered Central Europe for a generation after Waterloo, and Hegel paid his tribute to it.

The actual development of German classical philosophy belongs to a much earlier period, namely, from the publication of Kant's *Critique of Pure Reason* in 1781 to that of Hegel's *Phenomenology of the Mind* in 1807. In terms of contemporary French developments they correspond to the period between Necker's first ministership and the culmination of Napoleon's Empire. The most outspoken statements of German classical philosophy, from Kant's statement that Practical Reason demands the realisation of the programme of the French Revolution and Fichte's assertion that absolute idealism involves atheism, to Hegel's description of the demands of objective reason as developing with the needs of the time, belong to a brief period of about 15 years. This period opened with the culmination of the French Revolution and the deep impression made by it on the few German intellectuals who, like Kant, were not afraid when facing the reality of " human emancipation." It closed with the reforms enforced by Napoleon's victories upon the German states, ideologically reflected in Hegel's demand for a " synthesis." This connection is somewhat veiled by the consequences of the reaction after the Napoleonic wars, which prevented German classical philosophy from playing its part as the ideological prelude to a revolutionary upheaval, as the French 18th Century philosophers had done. Fichte and Schelling found time to abandon the position within the general trend that had made them important, for mystical reaction. Hegel, when completing his system (especially the *Philosophy of Law*) in the years of reaction paid it his ample tribute, though hardly beyond accepting pre-Reform English standards of government. The final product of the development, Hegelian philosophy in its systematized form, served as Prussian State philosophy. It served as ideological inspiration to the servants of a state which tried to win political power by achieving economic progress in the sense of *bourgeois* economics within the framework of a political system that excluded the *bourgeoisie* from a share in power. This is important for the personal development of Marx.

and especially for his theory of the State, but not for his general philosophy which was intended to continue the general development where Hegel had left it when evolving his system.

If we make our comparisons where they should be made, namely, between Kant, Rousseau, and Burke, it is quite obvious that the backwardness of the Germans is reduced to two connected traits : (a) they dealt with very general concepts of thought implying that the German middle-classes were not advanced enough to consider concrete political action, and (b) the idea, the creative motions of which they discussed, dwelt at the universities, as the only place where people were interested in it, and where there was comparative freedom of discussion. The universities were the place where future civil servants were educated ; and the civil servants, etc., plus the people who educated them, were conspicuously the most developed section of the German middle-classes. This consideration throws some light on the kind of progress to be expected from them as long as they were left to their own efforts ; and it also dispels the delusions of Marxists who drew conclusions as to the realisation of Marxism in Germany from the role played by German classical philosophy in its evolution. But it does in no way impair the suitability of German classical philosophy as a starting point for the ideology of other people who were not satisfied with the role of the lightning preceding the thunder[2].

German classical philosophy was shaped by people whose only opportunity of shaping human history was by moulding minds, and whose basic study was the way in which the development of thought might shape human society. Hence their idealist outlook. Certainly it had another aspect, namely, the need of the state for ministers of the Established Church who should be educated in a way neither completely divorcing them from the spirit of the age, nor conspicuously contradicting the basic metaphysical assumptions of Christian religion. But the German classical philosophers did not completely compromise the logic of their thought with the practical needs of their employers and masters. Kant's attitude to those issues corresponds to that later taken by Robespierre ; Fichte (who had not, like the latter, to take responsibility for a revolutionary state with an illiterate peasantry) went to the length of proclaiming the incompatibility

---

[2] The role ascribed to German philosophy by Heine (*Zur Geschichte der Religion und Philosophie in Deutschland*).

of his philosophy with the belief in a personal God[3]. Hegel, it is true, compromised even before the time when Fichte and Schelling left philosophy in favour of religion. But already young Marx[4] noticed that this was due to certain fundamental characteristics of Hegelian philosophy that allowed of such compromises.

The positive value of German classical philosophy as a building-stone of Marxism cannot be derived from its positive teaching, its systematic side ; for this teaching was rather backward in comparison with contemporary Western thought. Distinct elements of late 18th Century ideology are elevated in Kant's transcendental cognition to the dignity of eternal truths within the limits of possible human knowledge. They comprise a mechanist concept of exact science (biology being left aside for teleological—or theological—reasons), the corresponding concepts of time and of (Euclidian) space, the Deist theology, the French Republic according to the Girondists (with due restrictions of suffrage), and a cosmopolitan outlook. Fichte proceeded in domestic politics to the Jacobin concept of Rousseau's ideals of equality and of nationalism, whilst Hegel receded to the standards of the Orleanist monarchy, watered down to the Prussian taste. All of them recognised social evolution, but, so far as the immediate content of their system is concerned, only to the point of gradually realising the definite and rational pattern of human society as demonstrated in their own respective philosophic system. There evolution stops, for the simple reason that there is no sense in idealism unless it can conceive distinct ideals. In seeking the permanent importance of German classical philosophy we have to discuss the ways it approached the World, not the results which it believed it could achieve. We may summarise the main characteristics of that approach in three points.

(1) The classical German philosophers interpreted the world in an idealistical manner. They found actual reality in thought and its development. The existence of a material world independent of the human mind was left open by Kant, but was directly denied (i.e., reduced to a reflection of the working of

[3] His conflict with Goethe, described by Heine l, c., well illustrates the difference between the active fighter against religious prejudices and the aristocrat who, though possibly personally more emancipated from the basic religious concepts, did not deem it worth while to risk princely disfavour by destroying them.

[4] *M.E.G.A.*, vol. I/1, p. 65.

Mind) by his followers. This was due partly to the above-mentioned sociological setting in which German philosophy evolved, but partly also to its intended function as a guide to action. The naturalist materialism that preceded (and followed) German idealist philosophy was unable to evolve anything more than a theoretical, purely receptive approach to the world[5], and so consistent a materialist as Lenin found it necessary to emphasize that idealism, by emphasizing the immediate motives of human action, contains a certain, though rather one-sided, element of truth.[6]

(2) As distinct from those of its successors who did not turn to materialism (consistent young Hegelians like Stirner, the Neo-Kantians, Machists, etc.), German classical idealism was objective idealism ; that is, it ascribed to the assumed substance, though described as " Mind," an existence outside the individual mind. Kant did not make any definite statement as regards the nature of the objective world ; but his transcendental cognition, from which philosophical categories as well as moral standards emerge, cannot be rationally interpreted in any other sense but as the accumulated experience of mankind.[7] Fichte completely dropped the concept of transcendental objects ; he regarded the transcendental cognition as the working of a supra-individual Ego[8], and the World as its creation. This supra-individual Ego can hardly be understood except as a spiritual continuity of the *genus humanum*. Therefore Fichte would have been defenceless against the pertinent question in Lenin's *Empirio-criticism*, whether and how the World had existed when Dinosaurian minds were the only ones available to create it. More topical difficulties arose

---

[5] Marx's first Thesis on Feuerbach, *M.E.G.A.* I/3, p. 533.
[6] *Coll. Works*, vol. XIII, Annex.
[7] Max Adler, one of the representatives of the so-called Austro-Marxist school, tried to introduce the Kantian (or rather Neo-Kantian) theory of knowledge into the Marxist fold, and what he called Marxism (but was rather left-wing Hegelianism) into the Neo-Kantian fold by asking " How is Society possible ?" He tried to answer this problem by adding a " social *a priori*" of his own to Kant's original *a prioris*. Sociologically, this meant (in Max Adler's days, that is in the early Twentieth Century) an attempt to introduce the concept of Society into the liberal-individualist concepts of Neo-Kantianism. But for Kant this would have been no discovery ; he started in the Cartesian way from the individual, but his philosophy does not make sense unless interpreted as starting from Man who *is a zoon politikon*, and therefore has evolved certain forms in which he conceives reality, or whatever may be behind it. The emphasis on the forms of cognition, which may be explained as subject to evolution according to Hegel and Marx as distinct from " eternal truths " as regards the " true nature " of space, time, etc., is the only element of classical Kantianism relevant for our time. I do not know such elements in Neo-Kantianism.
[8] For this interpretation see his *Tatsachen des Bewusstseins*, passim, and espec. pp. 99 and 123 ff. in the edition of 1817.

once it was recognised, as a reaction to the Natural Law concepts preceding the French Revolution, that the very ideals inspiring human action were subject to historical evolution. Hegel solved the problem by conceiving " Mind " as being in continuous dialectical evolution, the lowest stages of which would certainly fit dinosaurs. In this form, the borderline between the Hegelian and, say, the Spinozist Pantheism becomes rather fluid ; as an explanation of the World, idealism is actually reduced to the assertion that we can better approach the substance of the developing world by studying our minds than by studying elementary matter. In the development beyond Hegel the realist element in this concept was so strongly emphasized that young Engels[9] reproached the old Schelling for dropping " the basis of all modern Philosophy, the *Cogito ergo sum*," by questioning the real and objective existence of the Mind (in order to have an occasion to assert its reality by the help of Grace). At that stage there were only two sensible objections to the spiritual structure of Substance alleged by Hegel, namely (a) the difficulty of conceiving ascending evolution (which was clear to Hegel as to all his contemporaries) on the basis of a substratum derived from the higher instead of from the lower end of the existing scale and (b) the actual difficulties involved in the application of the idealist concept to its most proper field, the evolution of ideologies. The first difficulty was overcome by Hegel's theo-logical concept of Mind, which allowed for an initial downwards movement in order to create the conditions of further evolution ; and this solution earned Hegel Feuerbach's reproach of having constructed two scales of development. From the second difficulty arose the further development through the Young-Hegelians to Marxism.

(3) German classical philosophy was dialectical and actually made its greatest progress in this field. Even Kant did not regard logical contradiction as a proof of a logical mistake ; like the ancient Eleatics he regarded it as a proof that the real essence of the World was inaccessible to the investigating mind. Fichte used the play of contradictions inherent in concepts in order to create the World out of the motion of Mind, in the Neo-Platonic way. But only Hegel succeeded in explaining by Dialectics a real phenomenon, the evolution of ideologies. A glance at the chapter on Enlightenment in *Phenomenology*—and also its immediate predecessors—is sufficient to see the strength of Hegel's

---

[9] Schelling on Hegel, *M.E.G.A.* I/2, p. 179.

approach and the motive behind it : he wanted to explain to himself, and to those of his contemporaries who did not like reacting to the French Revolution by mere Romantic mysticism, what were the relative merits of their former outlook, and why it was insufficient. The section on Terror might have been, and indeed has been written as well, though in less complicated language, by Burke ; and to follow that Chapter with two on Morals (a hint at Kant) and Religion respectively, the latter seeming to take over the place of Enlightenment,[10] reeks of the Holy Alliance. However, in the *Phenomenology* (as distinct from expositions of the Hegelian system made later, when the Holy Alliance had been realised), the Philosophy of Mind appears as the consummation of human development, which seems to reduce religion and reaction to mere temporary truths.

The first theory of evolution we have, apart from young Kant's brilliant study on the evolution of the solar system, and the only possible in view of the state of Science in Hegel's days, is Dialectics. It deals with a historical phenomenon, the evolution of ideologies ; and it has been fruitful for the general Marxist theory of social history because the evolution of ideologies is an important element in general social development. In the preceding Chapter we saw the limitations of the "dialectical" approach to Nature. But in sociology, German classical philosophy had advantages as a starting point for Marxism. Its intentionally general character rendered it applicable to the most varied fields of social science. Its obvious connection with religion, that is, with an element of the established State-ideology, enforced the revision of the philosophy as soon as the political movement opposed the State ideology. The very backwardness of German conditions created a unique background for a revolutionary philosophy ; in none of the more developed Western countries was " No bishop, no King " still such a topical issue of social struggle nor was critical thought so much concerned with very broad generalisations. On the other side, Marxism has inherited from German classical philosophy not only a special terminology which is both recondite and mystical to the non-adept, but also that specific quest for the " world-outlook " which tends towards totalitarianism and pragmatism in that the defence of the system as a whole becomes more important than

[10] Hegel deals with Enlightenment as the antithesis to " superstition," which is one of his many compromises.

its ceaseless verification and correction by using it to get correct answers to concrete questions. But the first is already in the process of being dropped, and the second can be dropped as soon as the new shape of society has ceased to be a contested matter. Perhaps, at that point, all the inheritance of German classic philosophy may be dropped, but it is difficult to see how a general and thorough criticism of a social setting would have been possible at all without it.

(b) THE YOUNG HEGELIAN MOVEMENT AND THE GROWTH OF MARXISM.

For twenty years the civil servants of the Prussian state and the ministers of its Established Church had been educated by teachers of the " philosophy of reaction," when the literary representatives of the German middle-classes, disappointed by the failure to transfer the Paris July revolution[11] and the British reform movement to Germany, noticed that Hegelian philosophy might have other uses. In 1834, Heine, writing for a French public[2] rediscovered the function that had been a secret science during the preceding decades. In the next year Strauss, in his *Life of Jesus*, started the attack against what the Prussian State philosophy was erronously assumed to protect. Actually he said no more than could be read between the lines of the Hegelian *Logic* and of *Phenomenology*: if anything could be understood by the dialectical process in which Mind had shaped Christianity, it was that the latter had evolved by the formation of myths in the original Christian community. Its " truth " in the Hegelian sense, namely, as the highest stage then reached in the development of Mind, depended on its ability to meet the concrete needs of the human soul and to express certain fundamental characteristics of Mind, rather than on the historical truth or otherwise of the allegedly revealed myth. But it is sufficient to compare the corresponding sections in *Phenomenology*[12] with the concluding paragraphs of the *Life of Jesus* to see the fundamental difference in emphasis—which, in Hegelian philosophy, means everything, because the function of a statement is more important than its logical content. Hegel had said that Christianity was religious Truth independently of the historical truth of its foundations ; but

[11] Of which Hegel disapproved, though he recognised the need for a synthesis proceeding beyond the regime of the Restoration. See his *Philosophy of History*, in the German ed. of his Works (Lasson), vol. IX, pp. 935 ff.

[12] Ibid., vol. II, pp. 394-5.

Strauss asked : What of the religious and philosophical meaning of Christianity can still be preserved, after we have seen that the contradictory evangelical stories *cannot* be historical truth. Strauss[13] reproached Hegel for his belief that, when all the form of Christian tradition had to be dropped as another example of oriental mythological religion, the essence of traditional dogma could still be accepted, or re-interpreted[14] as true for modern man ; but against Feuerbach, who as early as in the late 'thirties had explained the content of the myths as a reflection of human needs and desires, he defended the old Hegelian concept that a supra- individual Mind had expressed its evolution, that is to say, the progress of human consciousness, by creating the myth.[15]

German academic youth at once realised that to attack the Prussian State religion on the basis of the Prussian State philosophy became the easiest way for intellectuals to attack the existing order.[16] By doing so, they sapped the position of Hegelianism, as the philosophy of a state whose control after 1840 fell into the hands of extremist reactionaries increasingly afraid of middle-class activities in this and other fields. Criticism and repression grew until the more consistent of the Young Hegelians despaired of the prospects of academic writing on the origins of Christianity and began general ideological criticism in publications outside the range of the censorship.

Bruno Bauer, whose criticism of the narratives of the Evangelists caused his dismissal from a lecturership at Bonn University, proceeded beyond Strauss by clearly stating that the gospels were the products of individual authors (explained in the rather

[13] *Christliche Glaubenslehre* (Leipzig, 1840), vol. I, pp. 13 ff.
[14] As Strauss himself had done in the conclusive paragraph of the *Life of Jesus*, Besides, even Feuerbach's materialist interpretation of Christianity as the reflection of the needs and wishes of Man in general involved its recognition as the correct reflection. In this regard he differed from idealist Hegelians like Strauss merely verbally.
[15] Op. cit., pp. 19–20.
[16] The best expression of that trend was the pamphlet *Die Posaune des juengsten Gerichtes gegen Hegel den Antichristen und Atheisten*, published 1841, by Bruno Bauer with at least collaboration of Marx (on the joint authorship see the letters by Jung and Bauer to Ruge in *M.E.G.A.* I/1/II, pp. 262–4). Under the mantle of a pietist attack on Hegel, which could easily be lifted by any critical reader, the pan-theist or rather atheist implications of Hegel's teaching were shown by ample quotations from his writings, with due emphasis on the element of individual self-consciousness then embraced by the authors. (Also Marx's *Thesis for his Doctorate*, of the same period, shows distinct traces of that element, including siding with Epicurus against Democritus for allowing a place for Free Will). The method became popular amongst the radical youths and was not only applied by young Engels against Schelling, but even by Marx in an anonymous writing published outside the reach of the Prussian censorship, in the same volume of Ruge's *Anecdota* where the secret of the *Posaune* was divulged.

lofty formula of the " human self-consciousness ") whose works should be submitted to literary criticism like any other writings, and who expressed a " movement of Mind " just as other outstanding artists did. Again, there was a difference rather in expression and emphasis between Hegel, for whom aesthetic creation had been no less an expression of the absolute Mind than religion, and Bruno Bauer, who defended his point of view against the reproach of implying a defamation of the Evangelists by asking whether Phidias had been a forger. Neither Hegel nor Bruno Bauer believed in supra-natural revelation ; but the former tried to compromise with those who did (or who regarded such belief as useful for the existing political order), whilst the latter explained all the implications of the objective Mind's working through ordinary human beings, in order to fight that order. Strauss simply confronted each gospel narrative with the others instead of investigating their historical origin and order, i.e., the material available for every successive gospel-writer. Therefore, the spirit of the community that produced the myths remained a somewhat metaphysical substance for him. Bauer criticised the " Substance theory " for its failure to answer the question why the Community produced a certain myth at a certain stage of its development.[17] But he himself could only answer that, after the Roman Empire had destroyed all the traditional, tribal and national settings in which human minds had evolved, human individuality became conscious of itself, but in abstract religious forms, and constructed the ideal type of the Messiah because of its inability to conceive its own all-embracing power.[18] All further progress, up to the winning of full self-consciousness by the individual in the Young Hegelian philosophy, followed the ordinary, old-Hegelian dialectical pattern with the only difference

[17] Preface to the *Kritik der evangelischen Geschichte der Synoptiker*, Leipzig, 1841, vol. I, pp. VIII-IX.
[18] Ibid., vol. III, p. 310. It may be interesting to note that modern Soviet authors (R. J. Wipper, *The Origins of the Christian Literature*, Moscow, Academy of Science, 1946, in Russian) support Bauer's interpretation of the origin of the gospels, as the more consistent criticism. Their sociological interpretation of the background is naturally different, and the substance of Strauss' theory is recognised, to a large extent by the reception of W. B. Smith's theory of the " pre-Christian Jesus." In Wipper's conception all the fundamental teachings of Christianity originated in the anonymous community-life of a Jewish Diaspora sect, possibly before our era ; and only after the crisis of the Jewish community in connection with the insurrection of 66-70 A.D. the need for a personal Messiah, as represented in the Apocalypse, arose. In the literary development of the following century that need was satisfied by activities of individual writers which would broadly conform with Bauer's pattern. Thus Strauss would prove right as to the origins of Christianity, though Bauer as to those of Jesus Christ.

that finally, in Bauer's friend Stirner, it embraced Solipsism and anarchism, instead of a somewhat reformed Prussian state and Christian religion, as with Hegel. Marx[19] did injustice to Fichte when he described Hegelian philosophy as a synthesis of Fichte and Spinoza and asserted that the Young Hegelians re-emphasized the Fichtean element. This statement fitted a certain stage in Bruno Bauer's development (that, in which Marx had collaborated with him) ; but while Fichte's thought was a transitional element in the evolution of objective idealism, the Young Hegelians dropped Hegel's objectivism only in order to drive idealism to its most fantastic subjectivist consequences.

In order properly to appreciate the dispute between Bruno Bauer and Strauss, and the attitude taken by young Marx in that dispute, we should not neglect the two-fold aspect which that dispute assumes in the circumstances of the time as well as in the historical perspective. The Christian religion was the main ideology of reaction in the days of the Holy Alliance ; but for any Hegelian (as for any Marxist) it was also the outstanding example of an ideology profoundly influencing the course of History. The more the concept that the ideology originated beyond human minds was dropped, the harder was the blow to contemporary reaction. And certainly, in this respect Bruno Bauer went further than Strauss, with his concept of the myth-shaping mind of the community. But this implied the danger of dropping Hegel's great advance on the 18th Century Enlightenment. Where the 18th Century had seen mere contradictions to sound reasoning and explained them away as deception by greedy priests, Hegel had conceived society as an entity which could not be explained away by dissolving it into a plurality of individual minds but which was nevertheless open to rational analysis. Strauss preserved that concept. But, though more honest than his master, he failed to develop it any further. Bauer, however, dissected the concept away to nothing. Enlightened by Bauer, modern men would have stood exactly in the position of his original Christians : as atoms confronted with the overwhelming power of social forces which could not be understood the better now that they had become anonymous instead of being called by Caesar's name. A myth, admittedly produced by social needs, does not become superfluous by the mere explanation that it has originated from the activities of certain individual writers.

[19] In *Die Heilige Familie*, *M.E.G.A.* I/3, p. 316. See above, note 8.

Both parties—including young Marx—disputed on the basis of Hegelian idealism ; and within the limits of idealism, Bauer's reduction of ideas to the output of certain individual minds was certainly the more rational approach. But from the perspective of today, we find that Strauss has told us the more relevant things about the facet of reality within the limits of which both of them were confined. Once the formation of myths within the original Christian community is put into the general setting of the socio-economic conditions of the period and of the classes to which original Christianity appealed, it becomes clear that pre-Christian myth-production and the kind of formal demands made on any new developments (for instance, the ideological demands to which a Messiah had to comply) are more important for the understanding of the formation of the gospels than the individual artistic gifts of the gospel-writers. They are more important, too, than the remains of the historical background after the application of the test of historical criticism.

Feuerbach[20] made the decisive step beyond Hegelianism by stating that the mere description of Man as " Self-consciousness " implied " an interpretation of the new philosophy in terms of the old one ; for Self-consciousness abstracted from Man is an abstraction from Reality. Man *is* Self-consciousness." The new philosophy, demanded by Feuerbach, was a negation of the old, scholastic philosophy, though it contained the latter's essence ; for it expressed Man as aware of being the conscious essence in Nature, and the substance of History, of State, of Religion. Hegel's concept of Nature posited by the idea was a mere rational expression of the theological dogma of Creation by an immaterial Being ; and while the sources of Theology lay in Anthropology, Theology itself was the source of speculative philosophy. Hegelian Logic was merely Theology transformed. For Feuerbach, Being is subject, Thought is mere predicate, though a predicate expressing the essence of its subject, just as with Spinoza Thought was a mode of Substance.

Marx's later statement that Hegelian philosophy was valuable if turned upside down was anticipated by Feuerbach's statement[21] that everything was to be found in that philosophy, yet accompanied by its contradiction (this seemed to Feuerbach less tolerable

---

[20] In his *Vorlaeufige Thesen zur Reform der Philosophie*, in Ruge's *Anekdota*, vol. II.

[21] Ibid., p. 67. Comp. also the concept of Space and Time as expressions of the actually Infinite (not as that Infinite itself), Ibid., pp. 72–3.

and necessary than it had been for Hegel). Feuerbach could hardly escape Marx's later reproach of having dropped, together with the irrational, idealist, element in Hegel the rational, dialectic element also : Man in general—not the men of a distinct period solving concrete problems under concrete conditions—is for Feuerbach the subject of History, of the State and of Religion. In the State —without any specification—the essence of Man is realised as a totality, for Feuerbach no less than for Hegel ; and in special estates the essential qualities and activities of Man are realised, and are reduced to Identity in the person of the Sovereign. In respect of him (but, obviously, not in relation to each other) all men have equal rights, because all of them are equally necessary.[23] Any oriental despot, provided he needed a State-ideology, would be prepared to subscribe to such a system of humanitarian sociology ; and Marx was rather polite in stating that the single individual in a " civic society " was the highest point accessible to the understanding of " contemplative materialism," Feuerbach's kind.[24]

What was the position of Marxism in the intellectual developments we have just described ? We do not need to dwell much on the personal attitude of its founders : two gifted youths, actively participating in the literary movements of the time but not leading in the philosophical field, accepted the Young Hegelian standpoint (Engels in the Straussean form, Marx in personal contact with Bruno Bauer), sided with Feuerbach immediately after the publication of the *Essence of Christianity* and expressed their further development, including their first statement of Communist principles, in the Deutsch-Franzoesische Jahrbuecher of 1843 and their criticism of Bauer's philosophy of " self-consciousness " in the *Holy Family*, in terms of Feuerbachian philosophies. Even in Marx's *Theses on Feuerbach*, of 1845, that signify his independent approach to philosophy, " the standpoint of the new materialism " is described as " human society, or socialised humanity" and this must not be taken as mere expression of a former stage in Marx's development. The concluding phrase of Feuerbach's *Essence of Christianity*—" Holy the Water, Holy the Bread, Holy the Wine,"—these being the essential conditions of human life and not some mystical sacraments—sounds somewhat strange, as the conclusion of a theoretical analysis of religion ; at the best it appears as an unlucky com-

[23] Ibid., p. 85.   [24] No. 9 of Marx's *Theses on Feuerbach*.

promise with the very ideologies criticised in the book. But in revolutionary Marxism they have been turned into the glorification of struggles honestly fought to create the conditions for Man's spiritual development by securing his material welfare.

With Marx as well as with his contemporaries[25] the transition from " self-consciousness " in Bauer's sense to humanism in Feuerbach's had been simple and hardly controversial, since the former was regarded as the latter inadequately expressed. Marx, Ruge, etc., had never been Hegelians in the abstract sense—for them, Bauer's, and, later, Feuerbach's approaches were progressive stages in explaining what reasonable beings could understand by the Hegelian formulas. But for Bauer, his struggle for the right to teach Young Hegelian philosophy in the theological faculties of Prussian universities was the essential link in the emancipation of Mind. The narrowness of the German conditions that had forced awakening middle-class thought into the limits of scholastic philosophy found a curious and rather ridiculous aftermath when Bauer and his circle accompanied the first attempts at creating a liberal political press by attacks on Marx's cautious editorial tactics intended to preserve the " Rheinische Zeitung " from the censor's grip. The disappointment of contributors whose " finest " verbal attacks were broken by the Editor's red pencil took the form of denunciations of the veiled forms behind which the editor disguised his opposition to the existing regime,[27] whilst the editor's growing consciousness that the unreasonable contributors failed to understand what was essential and what secondary, found modest expression in the demand that rather religion should be criticised by the indirect approach of criticising the political conditions, than vice versa. For " religion, which has no content of its own, does not live of Heaven, but of Earth, and will break down once the inverted reality is dissolved, the theory of which religion is."[28] One year later, in the first distinctly Communist writing of Marx, his Introduction to a Critique of Hegel's Philosophy of Law, the same idea was further elaborated in the statement, so frequently misquoted, that religion was the opium of the people but that it could not be rendered superfluous without previously removing the social

---

[25] Which becomes evident at a glance at Ruge's Anekdota.

[27] Comp. the criticism of the Rheinische Zeitung in Bauer's Vollstaendige Geschichte der Parteikaempfe in Deutschland, 1842-6, Charlottenburg, 1847, especially vol. I, pp. 77–8.

[28] Marx's letter to Ruge, of Nov. 30, 1842, M.E.G.A. I/1/II, p. 286.

disease that made the use of such opium desirable. Even here, the appeal is evidently made to people whose starting point was the desire to fight religious superstition ; the first appearance of the working-class in Marxist writings is as the social power needed in order to realise the German philosophy in its latest, Feuerbachian stage.[29] A year later, Marx and Engels, in *The Holy Family*, systematically attacked Bauer's philosophy of Self-consciousness, now grown into a revival of Fichte's idealism if not into solipsism ; but still they argued as followers of Feuerbach. Shortly after, in their famous *Theses on Feuerbach*, and more explicitly, 1846, in *German Ideology*, they criticised Feuerbach together with all the Young Hegelians for failure to get rid of religious ideology, though in the materialistically deformed shape of the " Essence of Man" or Anthropology. Feuerbach was actually unable to explain the differences and development of historical religions. Marx and Engels, in definitely dropping Feuerbach, completed his work, the analysis of religious ideologies ; and the literary and biographical evidence hitherto discussed seems to support the view widespread amongst Marxists since Plekhanov's days, namely, that Marxism, in its philosophical aspects, is Feuerbachianism[30] developed in order to understand historical development.

A quarter of a century after Feuerbach's main work was done, at the time when Marx's work was actually faced with the task of shaping human thought, religion had ceased to be an important issue, and a rather vulgar conception of materialism had become the predominant bourgeois world-outlook. There was no further need to interpret Hegelianism as admitting the belief in a personal God ; but there was an increased temptation to believe in Hegel's " reality of Moral Reason," the Prussian State. A man like Lassalle was a freethinker in religious matters but in political matters he worshipped the State ;[31] and at least the latter attitude was clearly and consciously connected with his

[29] *M.E.G.A.* I/1, pp. 617 ff.

[30] This is to say, ordinary materialism, differing from the earlier English and French kinds merely by its starting from the analysis of human thought, not from physics.

[31] It is hardly necessary to explain, in a scientific book, that by " state-worship " I do not understand his emphasis on the need for the application of political means, as opposed to the Manchester Liberals and the propagandists of their ideas amongst the working-classes, but the description of the struggle of the working-classes as the returning to its " eternal idea " of something supposedly estranged from it by Liberal misuse, in short, as Marxists would say, of the Prussian state.

Hegelian philosophy. Could Lassalle's attitude to " the eternal idea of the State " have been avoided if he had learned from Feuerbach to regard the most ancient of "eternal ideas," that of God, as a mere reflection of human needs ? To put the question in another way : is an explanation of ideas by " matter " sufficient in order to understand the historical limitations of ideas ?

Once the problem is thus formulated, it is obvious that mere verbal disputes on the essence of the World do not help to explain its various aspects by that essence. Hegelianism, Feuerbachianism, and Marxism are objectivist approaches to the World. Whether the objective substance of the World is described as Nature, or alternatively, as Mind, matters only as long as such a description facilitates the understanding of what has to be explained. The objectivist-idealistic interpretation of the substance of the world, if combined with a dialectical approach, is helpful in explaining the historical evolution of ideologies and their mutual influences ; for whatever the social forces behind the contesting ideological trends, it is indisputable that ideologies move by dispute and contest. But even in its own field it is incapable of explaining the reason why ideologies develop at certain times and places, and, once applied to Nature, it leads to mysticism of the most primitive sort. The materialist interpretation of the World, unless conceived dynamically so as to show the changing background of the ideologies undergoing change, provides the explanation only of those features of ideology which have a bearing on the rather long-term aspects of " human nature," such as lack of scientific explanation of natural phenomena during the primitive stages of human development. Even here the temptation to introduce ideological elements into the allegedly scientific explanation of the " superstructures " is great, as one can see from Feuerbach's interpretation of the idealised picture of the Holy Family of the early Middle Ages as family in general. Though Feuerbach did not intentionally drop the dialectical element in Hegelianism he undoubtedly neglected it ; indeed, it is difficult to see how it could have helped him with his concept of ideologies as mere reflections of a permanent " essence of Man." Now it is unquestionable that Marx and Engels retained the dialectical approach throughout the Feuerbachian stage in their development. In the *Holy Family* we find a recognition of the merits of Hegel's Dialectics as long as it is applied to the study of the development of ideologies[32] alongside the first and fundamental example of objective Dialectics in Society (as distinct from Thought) :

" Proletariat and Wealth are opposites. As such they form an entity. They are both formations of the world of private property. What concerns us here, is to define the practical position they take within the opposition. It is not enough to state that they are two aspects of an entity.

" Private property is forced to maintain its own existence and thereby the existence of its opposite, the proletariat . . . In the economic movement private property drives on to its own dissolution, but only by a development which is independent of, and opposite to, its will, unconscious, conditioned by the nature of the matter ; that is to say, by the production of the proletariat *as* proletariat, of poverty which is conscious of its intellectual and physical poverty, of loss of humanity, conscious of itself and therefore abolishing itself . . . If the proletariat is victorious this does not at all mean that it has become the absolute side of society, for it is victorious only by abolishing itself and its opposites."[33]

Here we have the basic approach of Marxism, the programme fulfilled by the whole of its further development. The object of criticism is still private (i.e., capitalist) property in general, not capitalism as a concrete stage in the evolution of human society. One year before writing his *Holy Family*, in the *Introduction to a Critique of Hegel's Philosophy of Law*, Marx had explained that the formation of a class " with radical chains " was the condition of radical, human emancipation ; and the Feuerbachian term " human " must be regarded not only as a clumsy expression for a social revolution, as distinct from a merely political, bourgeois-democratic one, but also as one of the channels by which the Utopian concepts of Christianity and its philosophical derivatives entered Marxism. If an equation between humanism and Utopianism is desired (as, possibly, by Masaryk) that element can be followed up ; but it should be noticed that it is the non-Marxist element in Marx's thought. But the statement that the German working-class was the only class capable of carrying through any revolution in Germany at all and that therefore not a social, but a " political " revolution in Germany was Utopian, was derived from quite an ordinary fact, namely, from the inability of the German middle-classes consistently to oppose the existing regime.

[32] *M.E.G.A.* I/3, p. 316.
[33] Ibid., pp. 205–6.

(c) ARE THERE ALTERNATIVE FOUNDATIONS FOR MARXISM?

The first Marxist writings—with the great exception of the *Theses on Feuerbach*—were neglected in later Marxist propaganda from Engels to Mehring, and re-discovered by modern Communism. With the distinctly left-wing Marxists such neglect may have been caused by the apparent obsolescence of the Young Hegelians (in opposition to whom original Marxism was shaped), rather than by influences from the vulgar materialism dominating contemporary bourgeois ideology. Marx and especially Engels even in their old days still " flirted " with Hegelian terminology, but merely in order to oppose the metaphysical materialism then predominant in bourgeois ideology. It is quite possible to explain the Marxism of the last quarter of a century of the founders' lives, not to mention that which is alive today,[34] without any reference to that terminology. Recent Communist theories and politics derive from later Marx and Engels at least as much as from the first formulations of the theory which may be tinged with Utopianism derived from classical idealist philosophy. But the very essence of Marxism demands that it be put into an historical connection : the theory of the socialist revolution cannot be properly explained except as a positive criticism of the theory of the bourgeois-democratic revolution.

Why should the German bourgeois-democratic revolution, which never passed the theoretical stage, have been singled out as the implied basis for the theory of socialist revolution ? The question was not asked as long as German Social Democracy was regarded as the model section of political Marxism ;[35] but quite apart from the national pride of the Great Russians it was bound to arise as soon as history had proved that the reactionary features of Hegelianism were not merely the infantile disorders of a democratic movement starting in a backward country like 19th Century Germany,[36] but that they were features in the German

[34] See above, p. 15.
[35] The tradition was continued even in the Comintern in the shape of descriptions of the German Communist party as the best bolshevised section, apart from the Russian. As regards its martyriology, under conditions when it had to fight against the current of nationalism, the statement appears not so obviously mistaken as if judged from results ; but the more the heroism of an elite is recognised the more hopeless appears the national milieu in which it had to fight.
[36] But it may be asserted that this very fact rendered Marxism a suitable tool in the development of the democratic movement in another backward country, Russia, as done in Rosenberg's *History of Bolshevism*.

national tradition which rendered her country the main representative of counter-revolutionary solutions of the issues of our
time. Whilst in 1813 York surrendered to the leader of the future
Holy Alliance, von Paulus at Stalingrad, 1943, did not surrender
to the revolutionary country of his day, although the situation of
his men was desperate and, as in the case of York, his nation's
future depended on his attitude; he fought to the last in the name
of a regime which embodied the tradition of Fichte and Hegel into
the ideology of the radical suppression of democracy. Had von
Paulus followed York's example, few people in Russia would have
bothered about exhuming all the outbreaks of Fichte's nationalist
pride, which were neither better nor worse than those of his
Russian contemporaries. But no one who really believes in the
social determination of ideologies can content himself with cheap
protests against the " misuse " of renowned intellectual leaders;
he must accept the political fruit of intellectual trees as at least
some contribution to their interpretation. In every ideology,
and especially in an idealist philosophy, there are diverse possible
trends and accessories ; and though the general intellectual
content of some achievement is likely to be common to the leading
nations of a certain period if they are confronted with similar
problems, its specific colour is conditioned by the circumstances
of the country where it is shaped. Once it becomes obvious that
a certain theory finds its main application in countries other than
that of its origin, the national colour of its background loses its
special value and the question arises whether the general
intellectual content could not as well be provided from elsewhere.

At this point the opinions of Westerners and Easterners will
divide. The fact that the founders of Marxism themselves found
the value of their German philosophic sources in their being
" intellectual reflections of the French revolution " suggests
turning to the sources, to the sociological lessons which the
French themselves learnt from their experience.[37] Those lessons
were most clearly drawn by the historians of the restoration
period (whose position in the whole historic process was very

[37] English sociological (as distinct, of course, from economic) theory is hardly a
competitor ; Marx's judgment on the Utilitarians as being mere vulgarised reflections
of pre-revolutionary French materialist thought, combined with the achievements
of a much earlier phase of English philosophic development, can hardly be disputed.
It finds an easy explanation by the position of England towards the French revolution
which could not encourage other than utopian thought amongst its sympathisers.
I personally think that as a source of Marxism Harrington is much more valuable than
Bentham.

similar to that of Hegel) together with the Utopian critics of the
Revolution, St. Simon and Fourier. These need little turning
" upside down " in order to serve as a starting point for sociological generalisations. Unhappily they also fail to provide more
material for such generalisations than is already contained in
their historical source, the experience of revolutionary France.
A glance at the works of Guizot and Thierry, and even more the
study of the writings of Lorenz von Stein who no less than
Marx brought a Hegelian propaedeutic to the study of French
Socialist literature (but, in contrast to Marx, was incapable of
using Dialectics for more than the systematisation of what he
found in his sources), is sufficient to circumscribe the extent of a
possible inheritance from Western thought at that stage. History
was conceived as the outcome of class-struggle, and the dominating
ideas of the French Revolution as the expression of class-interests.
But even with Lorenz von Stein the economic foundations of class
found a far less clear explanation than with the classical English
economists who had written a generation before. With the
historians of the restoration period the characteristic of classes
was confused by arguments about their non-economic origin
(e.g., by conquest) or about their first expressions in constitutional
life. With the more advanced of the Western writers, the mere
political revolution was an incomplete social movement—but it
should be added, that to them feudalism was merely incomplete
capitalism, and socialism, so far as they could conceive it, an
idealisation of capitalist industry. Anti-Marxists are likely to
be confirmed in the current doubts as regards the originality of
Marxist thought, but serious students of Marxism may learn
quite a lot about its real and distinct content when they read the
following statements of its most advanced non-Marxist fore-runner:

" The evolution of Society dominates that of Freedom ; and
every movement in the field of political freedom is conditioned by a
social movement, which can continuously prosper only if based
upon the acquisition of economic goods. Therefore the history
of Society, of Freedom and of the political order are essentially
based upon the distribution and development of the socio-
economic goods amongst the lower classes."[38]

" As the development of the revolution is based upon the
property already acquired by the members of Society, it cannot
proceed in its demands of State and Society beyond what is
demanded by the conditions of that property. Since it claims the

---

[38] L. Stein, *Geschichte der sozialen Bewegung in Frankreich* (ed. 1850), vol. I, pp.
LXXIX-X.

principle of equality as its ideal foundation, but is based upon actual, and therefore unequally distributed, property of the dependent classes, there is a deep contradiction in every revolutionary movement : it demands equal rights for all the dependent classes whilst it actually achieves the fruits of the revolution only for that section of them who actually own the social goods. Therefore, every revolution, by its inherent necessity, uses a class of society to help which it is neither willing nor capable. Therefore it is bound to be confronted, when accomplished, by the very masses who have carried it through."[39]

"French history from 1789 to our days is . . . merely a pure realisation of the laws which dominate the movements of political and social life."[40]

In his letter to Weydemeyer, of March 5, 1852, Marx wrote :

"Long before me bourgeois historians had described the historical development of the class struggle in modern society, and bourgeois economists the anatomy of the classes. What I did that was new was to prove (1) that the *existence* of classes is only bound up with *particular, historic phases in the development of production* ; (2) that the class-struggle necessarily leads to the *dictatorship of the proletariat* ; (3) that this dictatorship itself only constitutes the transition to the *abolition of all classes* and a *classless society.*"

In this formulation, which is older than the elaboration of the socio-economic interpretation of History in the Preface to the *Critique of Political Economy*, Marx's claim appears rather weak, because it is restricted to the statement of the historical character of class-division in general, without emphasising the succession of different class-divided social formations (which is already alluded to in the opening phrases of the Communist Manifesto) and the laws dominating their alternation. Only this discovery put Marx's expectation that the class-struggle in capitalist society would result in its abolition and the formation of a classless society on a level higher than that of the Utopians. The latter, too, had denied the eternal character of class-divisions, and some of them would not have rejected the accomplishment of the new society by an insurrection of the working-classes. Within that framework, Marx could still claim the combination of the law of progressive concentration of capital and progressive destitution of the working-classes, which was nothing novel for Ricardian economists, with an optimistic assessment of the chances of such an insurrection ; and German classic philosophy would have added the Utopian aroma of complete human freedom in a classless society being the outcome of the impending transformation. But

[39] Ibid., p. XCV.   [40] Ibid., p. CXXXVIII.

such a Marxism[41] would certainly not prove a sufficient basis for a serious sociology of pre-19th Century history. This is best proved by the spasmodic attempts of the post-revolutionary French historians to derive the origins of the classes of capitalist society from the German invasion of Gaul, or the attempts of the Russian advocates of the " Merchant capitalism " concept to establish the " capitalist " background of Monomach's crown.[42] Nor could such a Marxism be the grounds for revolutionary politics in other than completely industrialised countries. Lorenz von Stein was certainly a historical materialist in the sense that he derived ideological and political " superstructures " from socio-economic facts ; unhappily, he conceived those facts as mere distribution of " property " and " capital " in a very general sense. So they were incapable of other than merely quantitative evolution ; social progress consisted in ample opportunities for proletarians to become capitalists. As we have seen, every revolution was, with Stein, realisation of the interests of a property-owning class with the help of the property-less masses.

Pre-Marxist sociologists failed to see beyond the categories of the society in which they lived because such categories change very slowly : no scholar is likely to have any experience, even in books, that could not be somehow explained in terms of the society with which he is familiar. But apart from his contribution to sociology, which was neither very original, nor outstanding, Hegel analysed the movement of ideologies, i.e., things which change in much shorter periods. So a man like him (not to speak of his contemporary, Goethe, who experienced four or five fashions of thought, and proved a leader in at least three of them) could easily conceive that ideological contests turned about fundamentally changing issues ; and Hegel, by a stroke of genius, even though it was mistaken, discovered in that movement of ideology that motion of the absolute idea for which he and his fellow-idealists were looking. Although not every new school of writers is representative of a new social class, ideological struggles actually reflect social antagonisms ; therefore Hegel's Dialectics needed merely some turning upside down in order to produce the methodological tool of Marxist sociology. I fail to see elsewhere a possible alternative source of derivation. We

---

[41] Which certainly lingers about all the vulgarisations of Marxism that aim at " reflecting the proletarian class-struggle into past History " (Pokrovsky, *Istoricheskaya Nauka i Borba Klassov*, vol. I, pp. 18 and 94).

[42] Ibid., p. 28.

can, and should, drop the Hegelian terminology ; and we should assess the historical importance of Hegelian philosophy according to the part it played in the intellectual development of Hegel's nation, and the role it enabled that nation to play in World history. But we cannot construct a Marxism which has any value without the Hegelian[43] element of Dialectics.

It is quite another question whether within Soviet State ideology the Young Hegelian ancestry of Marxism may for domestic reasons be discarded in favour of progressive 19th Century Russian philosophy. (It is a significant question, as the major half of mankind may eventually receive Marxism *via* Soviet ideology). Leninism thus would appear as a synthesis of democratic Russian philosophy say of Chernishevsky with Marxism as conceived by Plekhanov and Lenin himself (who was very conscious of the connection, and gave his main tactical work the same title which Chernishevsky has used in order to explain to the revolutionary youths " What is to be Done "). The revolutionary character of the resulting ideology gains from the essential difference between 19th Century Russian intellectuals and their German contemporaries ; the counter-argument based on the non-proletarian character of such an ancestry loses importance once the problematic nature of the achievements of the German Labour movement, and the character of Bolshevism as closely *connected with* the working classes[44] is realised. If the comparative backwardness of 19th Century Germany is no argument against the reception of Marxism in the West, there is no reason why the ideological output of a country whose economics and government were some degrees more backward should not be accepted, especially when the intellectuals who produced the revolutionary ideology were certainly the most honest progressives the Century knew. It is completely legitimate for the Russians to regard their intellectual development in the 19th Century in its internal connections, with Hegel, the Young Hegelians and Feuerbach merely providing successive food which was absorbed according to the inherent logic of the Russian development ; it would be even legitimate for them to regard Marx himself as providing such material as made possible the progress from Chernishevsky to Plekhanov, and from Plekhanov to Lenin. The very fact that

[43] And the more we become conscious of the problematic of the application of Dialectics to Nature, as distinct from Society, the more Dialectics gets a Hegelian, as distinct from an Heraklitian, origin.
[44] See below, p.230.

Marxism has proved able to change Russia's outlook proves that it has an indigenous Russian ancestry which was more than a reflection of the current foreign fashions. All this being duly recognised, we cannot get rid of the fact that Byelinsky and Herzen would have been impossible without the Hegelian background, and that Marx got from Hegel just what enabled him to facilitate the progress from Chernishevsky to Plekhanov and Lenin. Marx minus Hegel, or, to put it differently, Ricardo plus Robert Owen and Bakunin, could never have done the job.

CHAPTER IV

THOUGHT AND SOCIETY

(a) MARX'S ATTITUDE TO THE FUNCTION OF THE REVOLUTIONARY IDEOLOGY

The most common misapprehension about Marxism is the assumption that it denies the power of ideas, as distinct from material forces, to influence the course of history. In order to refute this it is sufficient to reproduce the argument by which in Marxist sociology ideas are derived from material conditions. Men make their history themselves[1]; and their actions are immediately caused by the ideas prevailing in their minds. Material interests influence history only in that they give rise to certain ideas that inspire or prevent human action or, more frequently, cause re-interpretation of current concepts.[2] The popular interpretation of Marxism as laying down that a person's immediate material interests, as he understands them, prevail if confronted with " ideals," is completely alien to the spirit of actual Marxism. Marxism[3] does not assume that men normally behave in such a way ; but it declines any interpretation of " ideals " as fundamentally opposed to material interests. Ideals originated at some stage, present or past, from direct generalisations of material interests, or from generalisations from other ideas the origin of which can be ultimately derived from Man's desire to understand Nature and to improve his conditions of life. Ideas, however abstract, influence the course of history, including its most material and even technical aspects : there can be no doubt that America would have been " discovered " much earlier had not the ideology predominant in Christian Europe prevented a correct interpretation of the numerous partial discoveries. In the interaction of the various forms of social life

---

[1] See above, p. 18. [2] See below, p. 54.
[3] Not even in its popular propaganda, cf., the scorn poured by Berlin Radio on the American propaganda in the Western zones of Germany as " using the tin of condensed milk as its main argument."

economics are dominant only in so far as men must eat before
they can theorise, and in that the explanation of change in ideas
by economic change is the more fruitful scientific approach than
vice versa.   The relations between Man and Nature (science and
technique), which underlie the relations entered into by men with
each other in social production, are subject to an evolution
which can be understood by its own logic and therefore provides
that independent variable which is necessary for a dynamic
interpretation of Society.[4]   Very similar social structures have
proved compatible with ideologies so different as Shintoism in
Japan and Protestantism in Germany ; but it is impossible to
conceive similar social structures being compatible with the
handmill in some, and the combustion engine in other countries.
Thus the essential link in the causation of social events is formed
not by " economics " in general (a conception which is only
proper to our present society where one way of earning money
is just as good as any other) but by what Marx has called " the
relations of production," that is the socio-economic relations
which men enter in the production process where the impact of
changes in social technique is directly felt.[5]   In the social environment thus formed ideas originate and are moulded in such a way
that they become capable of influencing social developments.
The difference between the " materialist " and the " idealist "
interpretations of History does not lie in the recognition of the
existence and reality of ideological forces but in the explanation
of their origin.[6]

Such an interpretation of Marxism is supported by all the
explanations by the founders themselves, especially by the
famous Preface to the *Critique of Political Economy.*   But more
important than quotations is the support given by the very
existence of the Marxist ideology and of a Marxist party, which

[4] The derivation of " historical materialism " from its methodological advantages
rather than from any questionable hypotheses about the predominant motives in
human actions is implied in the whole classical Marxist argument, especially in its
recognition of ideologies as motive forces in history subject to some inherent development (see below, pp. 72–3), and its sharp rejection of the materialist fashions prevailing
in *bourgeois* literature, especially Utilitarianism.   But so far as I know its first explicit
statement is to be found in Stalin's chapter *On Dialectical and Historical Materialism,*
op. cit., 1940, pp. 607–8, where it forms the natural counterpart of the emphasis laid
on the importance of ideologies as motive forces.   See note 6 below.

[5] More than once (below, pp. 92–4 and 149) we shall have to return to the importance of a proper concept of the sense in which economics is regarded as conditioning
social life.

[6] Engels, *Ludwig Feuerbach,* etc., p. 59, and Stalin, l.c., p. 602.   For the Marxist
attempt at such an explanation, see the fourth section of this Chapter.

was regarded by the founders of Marxism as being of the greatest importance. At the cradle of Marxism stands the statement, in the *Introduction to a Critique of Hegel's Philosophy of Law* (1843), that the critique of existing society by armed force cannot be replaced by theoretical criticism, but that theory itself becomes power once it inspires the masses. In order to do so it must be radical, that is to say, it must appeal to the working classes.[7] It is worth noting that orthodox historians of Marxism explain this statement as a remnant of Young Hegelian idealism. But one year later Marx and Engels, in full cry against that idealism,[8] explained the failures of the French Revolution by the fact that the masses could only temporarily be inspired by an ideology that represented the interests merely of a much smaller mass, the bourgeoisie. In action for more radical aims the numbers of the masses who really act, instead of being mere ephemeral enthusiasts, would increase.

Do such statements merely represent the standpoint of a more or less idealist philosopher who is on the lookout for social forces prepared to realise his Utopia, only somewhat more realistic than Fourier who waited for many years at the appointed time and place for the millionaire who would supply the funds needed for the establishment of the first phalanx ? In the very document in which Marx breaks with the last stage of Young Hegelianism and of traditional German philosophy, in the *Theses on Feuerbach*, we read that " the question whether human thought can achieve objective truth is not a question of theory but a *practical* question. In practice Man must prove the truth, i.e., the reality, power, and this-sidedness of his thought. The dispute over the reality or unreality of thought which is isolated from practice is a purely *scholastic* question " (Thesis 2). The document, which started with the reproach that hitherto materialism had conceived reality only as an object of thought, not as subject, as human practice, concludes with the reproach that philosophers have only *interpreted* the World differently when " the point is, however, to change it." Obviously this is regarded as a possible function of an idea, which thereby proves its " correctness " as well as its foundation in the conditions of the period whose problems it attempts to solve. (For Marx, these are merely two aspects of the same relation). Against Robert Owen,

---

[7] See above, p.37.
[8] In *The Holy Family*, *M.E.G.A.* I/3, p. 253.

who regarded human action as merely dependent on circumstances, and especially on education, Marx states (in Thesis 3) that " the educators themselves must be educated " ; and in revolutionary practice he finds the " co-incidence of the transformation of circumstances and of human activity." An exposition of the same attitude is found, in September, 1850, in Marx's explanation of his position in the factional cleavage that split the League of Communists : " The standpoint of the majority (that is, of Marx's own group) is materialistic, that of the minority idealistic. We say to the workers : ' You have before you fifteen, twenty or fifty years of civil war and mass-struggles, not only in order to change circumstances, but also in order to fit yourselves for the assumption of power.' " The quotation seems to dispose of the interpretation of Marx's " materialism " as opposed to the recognition of ideas as motive powers in History : clearly, human ideas and attitudes are the only things that can be moulded by experiences in class-warfare. Marx calls for a certain kind of human activity as the " material " condition for making men fit for eventual success (" educating the educators," to use the language of the *Theses on Feuerbach*), as opposed to the minority whom he described as idealistic because of their thinking in terms of Utopia. Hegel's conception of a dialectical relation between subject and object, which remained abstract because of its author's limitations, thus found its rational interpretation ; but the object no less than the subject are now acting men, inspired by certain ideas which may be more or less in accord with reality. In his later writings Marx has emphasized more strongly that the priority in the interaction belongs to the object ; but this was his final attitude, and a year after his death Engels published the *Theses on Feuerbach*, without fundamental reservations, as an annex to his own main philosophical work.

In view of this array of documentary evidence the interpretation of Marxism as denying the historical effects of ideologies seems to be without foundation. However, it has dominated the current vulgarisations of Marxism and most of the polemics against it ; and Engels himself later [9] recognised that he and Marx shared responsibility for such misunderstanding by necessarily laying one-sided emphasis on the objective causation of ideologies rather than on their effects, which were sufficiently emphasized by current idealist philosophy. In such a position it seems

[9] Letter to Conrad Schmidt of Oct. 27, 1890.

necessary to discuss first the elements of truth contained in that current misinterpretation of Marxism.[10]

Fundamentally, as already implied in the term of "historical materialism," it is a reaction against the idealist conception according to which history, including the development of socio-economic conditions, has been shaped by certain ideas. This conception is refuted by the fact that rather similar social structures, say capitalist economics, in different times and countries have been brought into being with the help of ideologies so different as Calvinism, the concepts of the French materialists and Enlighteners, the semi-socialist concepts of Chinese and Indian nationalists, and the Meji-restoration. On the other side, an " identical " ideology such as Christianity has fulfilled very different functions at different times and places, or has even been a weapon in the hands of different parties contesting at the same time and place. The concept of social function, in this connection, should be associated not with any intentions or purposes (which an abstraction, such as an ideology, cannot have) nor is any teleological implication suggested ; social function should be associated with the objective effects of certain ideas or institutions upon the general functioning of a social organisation.[11]

It seems to follow that the function of the ideology, which is a certain type of socio-economic interaction between the members of a certain social formation, is the only real thing and the ideology, at best, a form in which they become conscious of what

[10] For a characteristic expression by a contemporary progressive sociologist see Gunnar Myrdal's book, *An American Dilemma, the Negro Problem and Modern Democracy*, New York and London, 1944, vol. II, p. 1033 : " It is the weakness, not only of the static and fatalist traditions in social science attached to the great names of Marx and Sumner, but of our common tendency to look for explanations in terms only of natural forces and material trends, that we blind ourselves for the dynamics of opinion as it develops from day to day ; or, in any case, we become inclined to deal with human opinions more as the result of social change than as part of the cause of it." The basic misunderstanding of Marxism contained in the just quoted statement is Myrdal's failure to realise that " opinion " and its dynamic trends may be conceived as an objective, " material " element of society just like any other one. The physical substratum of " opinion " namely, elaborate vibrations of the nervous substance of a plurality of individuals of the species *homo sapiens*, is no more, and no less a subject of sociology than is the physical substratum of an engine, namely iron crystallised in certain shapes. Sociology deals also with engines only as elements in certain relations, realised in the consciousness of men, amongst themselves.

[11] The first elaborate application of the concept of function (in a general Marxist framework), of which I am conscious, was made by Renner, 40 years ago, in *The social function of Legal Institutions* (English translation now in the International Library for Sociology and Social Reconstruction), notwithstanding the neo-Kantian paraphernalia of his personal philosophy.

they would be doing even were there no ideology at all.[12] A
Socialist ideology emphasizing class-solidarity is conducive to the
success of strikes ; but workers would strike (and do strike in
some countries) even without any specific class-ideology. Mere
consideration of their material position teaches them that strikes,
or threat of them, is the only means available to them to exercise
pressure upon their antagonists in the contract of employment.
Those who cannot conceive a socialist transformation of society
as fundamentally different from a strike, or its preparation through
the establishment of Trade Unions,[13] conclude from the comparatively small importance of the ideological element in strikes that
it is also unimportant as a means of more thorough social transformation.

But those who deny the efficiency of some ideology share the
limitations of those whose outlook is confined by the ideology.
A general idea may be accepted for various reasons. It may be a
traditional ideology, such as Christianity, and may perhaps have
won and preserved prestige for the very reason that its different
elements might be used to express the needs of very different
trends in society. The character of the appeal (e.g., the alleged
infallibility of Scripture) may prevent the dropping of certain
obsolete elements, and the dropping of other elements may be
unnecessary because of changed circumstances. It would be
mistaken to expect such elements of the Christian ideology which
formerly had revolutionary implications to be actually efficient
in conditions that have rendered Christianity a symbol for a
certain traditional way of life ; but it does not follow that
Christianity as such has ceased to be an efficient factor in the
decision of social issues.

The generality of an idea may also be due to its having
emanated from a revolutionary upheaval, long past, so that the
demand for generalisation has lost its stringent force, and the
accepted elements of the " general " idea correspond to that
non-utopian part of the once revolutionary ideology which is
related to reality. If that ideology has been established as the
State ideology of a society not coming up to the standards of all

[12] I intentionally use a formulation near to that in Marx's Preface to the *Critique
of Political Economy*, in order to illustrate the limits within which that famous formulation covers the allegedly Marxist denial of the efficiency of ideologies as motive powers.
The misunderstanding of Marx's thought lies in the assumption that men would act
even if there were no ideologies.

[13] See below, pp. 98 and 253-4.

the demands that inspired the revolution there will be a contradiction between the ideology (i.e., the verbal constructions by which it is expressed) and the actual actions of those who claim to be inspired by it. But only from the standpoint of the ideologist himself, to whom his own formulas are sacred, is the efficiency of the ideology questioned by such contradictions ; for the sociologist, the formulas are social facts like any others and thus have to be interpreted in the connection in which they arose. The concepts of human brotherhood, with the tacit rider that God has created some men as serfs, or of the equality of opportunity due to all American citizens, notwithstanding the natural implications of their colour, are no more irrational than, say, the statement that a majority of the British Parliament is omnipotent notwithstanding the fact that the minority is obliged to submit only if due consideration is given to the interests which it represents. An ideology, like a constitution, has to be interpreted along with all its tacit assumptions.

Our opponent may object that, by replacing the verbal meaning of an ideology by some " attitude " symbolised by it, we have already conceded his main point, namely, the inefficiency of the ideology as such. In further pursuing his line of argument he may state that the whole Hegelian interpretation of statements in the historical connection in which they have been made is merely a different way of denying the historical motive-power of ideologies as such.

Sociologists can hardly be expected to pay special reverence to the sovereignty of the King in Parliament, to the divinity of the Japanese Emperor, or to the assertion that " We, the people of the United States " (for example, the American workers) have actually established the existing powers of the Supreme Court (for example, to invalidate laws enacted in their favour) Marxists will state as the primary, fundamental fact that Britain, Japan and America are states with developed monopoly-capitalism, that the first two, as distinct from the third, have some aristocratic features whilst the first and third, as distinct from the second, share certain historical traditions, some important elements of civilisation, and especially certain fundamental concepts of the relations between State and Society. We may make fun of the assertion that these differences can be removed by an Imperial Rescript dropping the claim of the Japanese Emperor to divinity, because we are convinced that that claim was an expression of more deeply rooted social relations that cannot be removed by the mere dropping of one of their ideological expressions. The dropping of the claim to divinity by the Japanese Emperor means little to him, or to any educated Japanese Conservative, because a member of that class could not see in that claim more than a symbol for a basic attitude he continues to stand for ; nor does it mean very much for the Japanese peasant whose attitude toward his superiors will continue to be the result of the everyday relationship within which he moves. But it cannot be denied that that attitude itself forms a major defence of those relations. The very different patterns of behaviour that may correspond to social settings similar from the economic point of view are the basic aspects of what is called the " national character." As we are to see in a later chapter, they form the foundations for the element of variety in social systems (capitalist and socialist) which tend to propagate their basic economic characteristics in all the countries with which they have economic intercourse.

Engels has remarked[14] that whenever the political need for a certain type of personality (military dictators) arose, these personalities were available. This statement makes sense on the assumption that the personal qualities needed in a military dictator do not exceed what is likely to be found amongst the higher officer corps of a country heading towards such a political situation and that possible gaps may be filled by the right kind of propaganda build-up. This assertion would become much more questionable in cases where the qualities required—possibly from persons originating in a class hitherto oppressed and without opportunities to acquire political experience—should include creative leadership in complicated situations. Marx's statement, in the Preface to the *Critique of Political Economy*, that mankind takes up only such problems as it can solve, or the material conditions for the solution of which are at least in the process of formation, is relevant as a statement of the social conditioning even of abstract ideas. Nevertheless, it obviously allows plenty of scope for thought which remains Utopian, that is to say premature, for as long as, say, the period separating the birth-pangs of capitalism, which inspired More's Utopia, from the Russian revolution. Our interpretation of ideas according to their social function may imply that any society, once brought into existence, will shape any available ideology so that it may express

[14] Letter to H. Starkenburg, of Jan. 25, 1894. *Sel. Letters*, p. 516.

the attitudes necessary for its proper functioning ; but this statement does not imply an affirmative answer to the question whether
every conceivable ideological expression of functions of a certain
social formation is equally conducive to the development of the
attitudes and ideas necessary in order to bring a new social
formation into being. Some highly disputed historical arguments, such as the alleged propensity of Protestant countries to
develop modern capitalism, or of Catholic countries to have
social changes carried through by revolutionary methods, may
be suspected of having originated from a mere *post hoc propter hoc* ;
but it is hardly possible without reference to ideological elements
to explain some instances when a highly developed civilisation
broke down because of the inability of some social formation to
produce an alternative to stagnation and decay. The most
notorious instance is the breakdown of ancient civilisation.
Engels based his explanation[15] of it on the scorn of manual labour
on the part of the freemen, a clearly ideological motive, however
it was conditioned by the social conditions of chattel-slavery.
In this case it may be said that the very rapidity of the expansion
of a slave-owning society, by economically and ideologically
degrading the free craftsmen, wrought the destruction of the
potential source of further progress to free wage-labour. However, the immediate handicap was ideological ; and it lay on the
side of the ruling class, the slave-owners whose general attitude
preferred dignified leisure to the position of potential employers,
no less than on the side of the proletarians whose material corrup-
tion prevented them from becoming a working-class. The
vestiges of that ideological handicap were still felt fifteen hundred
years later, when the struggle for the establishment of capitalist
economics in another civilisation had to be waged within the
framework of ideologies originally shaped in the last stages of
ancient civilisation, and the merits of alms-giving and of a
contemplative life became contested issues on a new stage.

The preceding remarks concern ideologies whose social
function is the defence of the existing order—ideologies in
Mannheim's sense, which is narrower than the Marxist. Most
supporters of the vulgarised version of Marxism are prepared to
recognise the retarding influence exercised by conservative
ideologies, and what is actually challenged and thrown into
doubt is the efficiency of ideologies that promote social trans-

[15] *The Origins of the Family, etc.*, pp. 169–70.

c

formation (Utopias in Mannheim's sense). For it is true that the realisations of the ideologies that inspired all former revolutions were in marked contrast to those ideologies. But this very divergence demands an explanation which is impossible unless the efficiency of ideologies as historical agents is supposed. In order to overthrow the *ancien regime*, support of broader masses is needed than those likely to profit immediately from the reforms compatible with objective conditions, or demanded by the interests of the class leading a bourgeois-democratic revolution.[16] Restricted aims are generalised into a Utopia unobtainable at present and in the future having implications opposed to the interests of the new ruling group. Only when situations and social groups arise likely to encourage undesirable implications of " generally accepted " theories, does a tendency to add the necessary riders appear. In particular, the equalitarian principle that inspired the original revolutionary ideology may be reinterpreted by the adding of such qualifications as may transform their social function into that of an ideological cover for inequalities likely to form the object of the next wave of revolutionary opposition. Such re-interpretation does not prove that ideologies are not motive factors in history ; on the contrary, were they not efficient as motive powers, no trouble would be taken in order to enforce their re-interpretation.

(*b*) OBJECTIVE TRUTH AND THE TEST OF IDEOLOGIES BY
THEIR HISTORICAL EFFICIENCY

The existence of objective truth was not problematic as long as Man regarded his mind as a repository of the spiritual powers that created the Universe, and it remains a firm supposition (however difficult it may be to approach that truth) as long as the World is conceived as subject to objective laws independent of what men may think about it. But once ideologies, scientific interpretations of society amongst them, are conceived as motive powers in history, and their historical efficiency is even regarded as the decisive test of their " this-sidedness and reality "[17], the question arises how far a theory can exercise such power and nevertheless provide insight into the objective facts of social development. In times of rapid transformation involving important aspects of society generalisations may be made which are intended to cover the whole system of social relations,

---

[16] See above, p. 41.   [17] See above, p. 47.

including parts which are not yet subject to transformation.[18] Exceptions to the principle of civic equality of all inhabitants of the United States, and the reasons for which they were temporarily necessary, may have been very obvious for the contemporaries of Jefferson and do not necessarily impair their intellectual integrity ; but once the need for them has gone, an elaborate gamut of ideological assumptions from biased inability to see the truth to the intentional propaganda-lie is needed in order to defend the inferior status of the Negro in a state which has accepted the Jeffersonian ideology, however distorted, as its state-ideology.[19] During the ensuing contest no party is able to see the whole truth, though only one party is ideologically biased. At a certain stage in the development of the contest, those who honestly strive for the emancipation of the Negro may actually accept quite a lot of traditional falsehood about his inherent inferiority, and mainly object to his master's practice of torturing him ; and inability to see that the real problem of Negro emancipation starts at the point where torture, serfdom, disenfranchisement and lynching cease, may be accompanied by a biased over-estimation of the percentage of masters who torture their slaves. Thinking in the ideological terms of a certain social framework implies acceptance of quite a lot of the given assumptions, whether true or false, even on the part of the reformer, while the still partial character of his struggle will be reflected in over-emphasis on particulars suitable as objects of attack. In the example given, assessment of the typical attitude of masters versus serfs is likely to be coloured by an anti-master bias ; but criticism of the basic foundations of serfdom will be restricted by the intellectual limitations of a slave-holding society.

The existence of objective truth is not impaired by recognition of the inevitability of bias, that is, the interference of socially conditioned wishes with the theoretical explanation of burning issues. In a society divided by antagonisms, people are bound to pull in different directions and, correspondingly, to form different patterns of ideas. Objective facts may provide evidence in favour of one or another of those patterns, but the impact of those facts upon those who occupy different social positions is necessarily different. The employer-employee relation is given and characterised by certain facts that can be objectively established,

[18] See above, pp. 50-1
[19] For an excellent exposition see Gunnar Myrdal's above quoted book.

so that misrepresentation can be ascribed to lack of knowledge or bias. To some the employee is bound to appear as the seller of a certain commodity, labour, who should be measured by standards normal for all the sellers of other commodities. To others, he is a member of the exploited class, whose social subordination is preserved by the repetition of the sale-purchase operation for labour in a certain given set of social conditions. Those who regard him as a seller of labour tend to overlook those objective conditions that make the bargain unequal, while those who emphasize the fact of exploitation may overlook the way in which the interests of employers and employees in some industries or countries sometimes coincide. The question as to which of the contesting theories is substantially correct can be answered in the same way as the quest for the correctness of any other partial theory supported by a certain amount of individual facts : Does it fit into the framework of a broader and more general theory, correctly describing a larger part of reality ? We can explain why certain social groups are likely to cherish certain theoretical concepts, and even the directions in which the representatives of the respective concepts are likely to err ; but by taking up this attitude and by referring to errors, we are already supposing the existence of an objective standard by which their respective approachs to objective truth could be measured. The fundamental difficulty lies in the fact that this standard does not necessarily decide their chances of survival.

To the founders of Marxism, Communism was not a condition to be established nor an ideal to which reality must adjust itself, but " the actual movement which abolishes present conditions."[20] This seems the strongest possible rejection of utopianism and wishful thinking. But a Marxist as strictly opposed to utopianism as Stalin[21] describes as the merits of revolutionary theory its capacity to give the mass-movement " confidence, the power of orientation, and an understanding of the inherent connection between surrounding events " and to " help practice to discern not only how and in which direction classes are moving at the present time, but also how and in which direction they will move in the near future." Will the capacity to provide the maximum

---

[20] *M.E.G.A.* I/3, pp. XII–III, and I/6, pp. 294–5.

[21] Foundations of Leninism, in *Leninism*, ed. 1940, p. 15.

of confidence and strength necessarily reside in an ideology which passes the other tests mentioned, those appropriate to a scientific sociology in the Marxist sense?

Every theory is generalisation ; a radical theory is a generalisation which is broad as well as critical. The anti-theoretical attitude of many of the defenders of the past can be explained by the impossibility of leading a political attack, that is to say, mass-attack, against mere particulars which offend mere particular interests. Truth, said Lenin, is always concrete, that is to say, it presupposes perception of every particularity in all its general connections. So do efficient tactics. But a mass-movement simply presupposes perception of the evils to be fought in the context of a general explanation of the society that is ripe to be overthrown. The founders themselves desired to get inspiration from a defeat such as that of the Paris Commune which was obviously due to the lack of centralised and determined action, without regard to ideological niceties or utopian purposes. But this may result in the failure, including some of those traits which rendered it a failure, being described as a first attempted realisation of things to come.[22] Competition with representatives of current utopian outlooks[23] may further such an attitude. It may be said that Marxism, once properly put on its own feet, no longer had any need to join in a race for the realisation of anarchist ideals. But according to Marxist theory anarchist utopias do not derive from the minds of anarchist agitators, but from the decomposition of the lower-middle-classes ; and there is not the slightest reason to assume that Marxism, at least in our century, can approach realisation without having to compete with liberal and anarchist ideas for the support of broad masses. At present, it feels little need and shows little inclination to compete with such ideologies, but this fact may simply be explained by the temporary absence of a revolutionary situation. Quite apart from this, successful competition with more moderate parties is the general condition of the success of a revolutionary movement. The moderate reformers are those who attack mere particulars of the existing state of things, the revolutionaries are those who attack its framework as a whole. How can their ideology be prevented from attacking also those parts of it which are bound to be preserved at least during the next stage of the evolution of society?

[22] See below, p. 244.
[23] Engels' letter to Bebel, in *Critique of the Gotha Programme*, p. 41.

At first glance, this argument seems merely to prove that bias is not only inevitable, but at least in some situations conducive to the success of a revolutionary theory. But we should keep in mind that Marx regarded the dispute over the reality or unreality of thought which is isolated from practice as " a purely scholastic question."[17] Such an attitude, at least in some possible interpretations, may lead very near to pragmatism, which is an explanation of knowledge as a set of ideas that serve to systemize, to organise experience[24] from the point of view of the likely outcome of their application. The helpfulness of a system of ideas in obtaining certain practical results (its usefulness from the point of view of the person or the social group in the interest of which it is developed) is regarded as the only existing standard for ascertaining its truth. Obviously, there is more than one aim towards which human action may be directed. It follows from the very essence of pragmatism that there is no objective truth, though there are many fields of knowledge in which the aims to be pursued are hardly contested (such as medicine, or most, though not all, fields of applied physics). Clearly a concept of truth that allows for a dual or multiple truth in many important fields of knowledge cannot be regarded as objective even in those fields where alternatives play a very small part. Pragmatism is a subspecies of subjective idealism ; and Schopenhauer's concept of the world as will and imagination is its true philosophical basis.

Pragmatism is thus opposed to the basic tenet of Marxism and of Science in general that the World is an objective reality independently of human ideas.[25] Pragmatism contradicts itself : the differing usefulness of various ideas (say, conflicting physical theories) in fields where their usefulness does not depend on their respective ability to influence human minds cannot be explained except on the assumption that there is something objective in the World which can be more or less adequately expressed by human concepts, so that some of them collide with objective reality (and, therefore, fail to prove useful) whilst others coincide with that reality at least to an extent sufficient for the

[24] I intentionally introduce into this definition Mach's formula in order to illustrate the logical position of pragmatism as the activist sub-species of that outlook which regards the world as an ordered system only because the experiences of the individual human being (or all the individual human beings) need systemisation for reasons of ' thought economy.'

[25] Comp. Lenin in *Empiriocriticism, Sel. Works*, vol. XI, pp. 185 ff.

practical purposes of a certain stage of human development. The mere fact that in every intellectual process *some* part is played by the will-element does not prove anything in favour of pragmatism : for the latter's basic position implies that the fulfilment of wishes directed towards aims other than knowledge of an objective reality should form a suitable standard for the evaluation of ideas inspired by those wishes. For the scientist, science is not, as the formalist schools of modern logic assert, a game played according to certain rules which may be changed by a convention of sportsmen—but an objective approach to something which stands independent of human wishes and conventions. The pragmatist may answer that the concept just described presupposes a whole philosophy. So does his own.

Assuming that a correct political theory is bound to lead to action likely to be successful, the fact that a certain theory leads to policies refuted by political experience *is* a serious argument against it. But if an unsuccessful politician defended a theory it does not follow that the theory has led to his mistakes, even if he himself was convinced that he possessed a consistent scientific system from which all his actions followed. The tendency to project Marxism into a general " world-outlook " very indirectly connected with the concrete, and verifiable, applications of contesting general theories puts Marxism, as a State-ideology, at the mercy of the pragmatist—or simply the careerist. Things become extremely simple if the popularity or otherwise given to scientific statements and their authors are judged by their likely effects on the political struggle in a totalitarian state where political antagonisms are not unlikely to find some " unpolitical " expression. The Theory of Relativity might have been opposed in the U.S.S.R. on the ground that the public of the N.E.P. period (as did the general public in all countries) was likely to draw from it (or from what it could understand of it) the conclusion that " all things—including the State-ideology—are relative and devoid of objective truth," however such conclusions might contradict the actual physical meaning of the theory.[26] Such an approach is unscientific—and also detrimental to the interests of the State which it is alleged to serve. Outside the

[26] See my *Spirit of Post-War Russia*, London, 1947, p. 147, and my study in *Zeitschrift fuer Sozialforschung* (Paris), 1939, No. 1–2.

field of sociology, one may in due course get rid of it[26a]—(1) by keeping out of physics people whose political aspirations are more highly developed than their physical knowledge ; (2) by keeping in their proper place such generalisations of Dialectics (discussed in Chapter II of this book) as are bound to construct artificial links between physics and sociology and therefore to give physical theories artificial political implications, and (3) by preventing the propagation of the political theory of the State in the schools and adult education from being carried over as a " world-outlook " in the traditional German sense, i.e., as a counter-poise to religion. All this can be achieved once a revolutionary state, like the present U.S.S.R., is sufficiently stabilised to be able to rely on the loyalty of its intelligentsia. It can therefore, without regard for the party-ticket, appoint professors of physics who will take the State's existence (and also that of the class-struggle from which it originated) for granted and will thus be able to resist the temptation to prove them by Dialectics. The U.S.S.R. has also been able to put its disestablished Church in its proper place and no serious threat of counter-revolution now lurks behind statements from the pulpit that " modern scientists themselves are approaching concepts very different from those by which Man once hoped rationally to explain Nature," as priests in all countries continue to assert without great detriment to science.

But in addition to these more frivolous cases there remains the serious problem. Marx and Engels[27] wrote that the practice of Science is the experiment, i.e., the checking of theoretical speculations by experience produced under conditions intended to verify the speculation. No divergence between the scientific interest in the maximum approach to objective truth and the social interest is likely to arise in the purely scientific field ; on

[26a] The recent Soviet discussions on biology (the stenographical report has been published, in English, by the All-Union Academy of Agricultural Sciences, Moscow, 1948. See also my comment in *Soviet Studies*, vol. I, No. 2) and especially the fact that they resulted in the closing down of research institutes appear to refute such optimism (from the scientific point of view). But it should be kept in mind that the practical, agronomical usefulness of the contesting theories plays much more important a part in their estimation than their philosophical implications, however emphasised by the philosophical specialists. If the agronomical usefulness of Lysenko's theories should be based upon their psychological effect on farmers rather than on their biological correctness, what is below in the text said about political theories may be applied to them too. But if they are definitely wrong (not only indifferent) from the biological point of view, punishment will follow by experience refuting even their agronomical usefulness from the long-term point of view.

[27] Comp. *Ludwig Feuerbach*, pp. 32–3. For an only slightly different approach to the problem see Joan Robinson, *Essays in the Theory of Employment*, pp. 253 ff.

the contrary, the social interest in technical progress is likely to keep political theorists who attempt inference in the name of orthodoxy with scientific research in their proper place. But in sociology and history every scientific statement has obvious political implications. The demand that truth be verified in practical political action may have a double meaning, namely (a) that as in scientific experiments the application of the theoretical analysis in political tactics will prove its correctness, and (b) that all the ideological implications of the statement discussed will further that political activity which is regarded as corresponding to the general trend of historic progress. Even if we take the possibility of a scientific description of that trend for granted, as Marxists do, we have no guarantee that the second meaning of the " practical test " of sociological statements will always correspond to the demand for objective truth which is implied in the materialist approach to the World, as opposed to pragmatism. No Marxist has claimed that his approach is an infallible guarantee against error. What we have to ask, in discussing the issue of pragmatism, is whether the demand for a test in revolutionary practice is likely to override the demand for objective truth.

(c) MARXISM AND PRAGMATISM

In Marx's *Theses*, Feuerbach and other traditional materialists are reproached (a) for their purely descriptive attitude to the world. Marx regarded an active approach to changing the world as a moral duty of progressive people in our time, and he criticised Feuerbach and the other Young Hegelians for believing that they could fight religious delusions by mere theoretical analysis of the origins of those delusions. (b) Further, it is alleged that an essentially receptive approach cannot be successful in the search for truth. Part of this criticism belongs to the demand for a more correct description of the reality subject to investigation. " Contemplative materialism " is reproached for its incapacity to understand sensibility as a practical activity involving verification of scientific theories, and to understand historical reality as human practice, that is to say, not as a complex of stable factors but as social forces in motion. This involves the mere introduction of the most legitimate element of Dialectics into the materialist outlook. But further, we find (in Thesis IX) " contemplative materialism " reproached for its incapacity to see beyond[28] the limits of the bourgeois society, within which Feuerbach and Marx lived. If Marx had simply stated that a theory connected with the revolutionary movement within a bourgeois society, as distinct from one regarding that society as natural and permanent, knew the limitations of that society and, therefore, had a wider perspective, he would have been completely in his rights ; but in the next thesis he claims for " the new materialism " a standpoint in " socialised humanity " (a society which does not yet exist), simply because this new materialism is connected with the struggle for that society which is described as " human," i.e., it realises the Feuerbachian ideals. This statement gives a rational sense if interpreted as merely to mean (a) that Marxism (as distinct from Young-Hegelianism and all the merely critical theories) is conscious of the fact that society cannot be conceived as a mere sum of social atoms and that every sociological theory implies a certain mode of social integration, and (b) that classical Marxism (as distinct from the approaches of Feuerbach, Plekhanov, and even of those who have to realise of its concepts what is realisable in 20th Century Russia[28a]) wins a broader outlook because of its operating upon the historical trend of a social group fundamentally opposed to existing society ; but if verbally taken, it is an expression of utopianism which belongs to the transition of Marx from Hegelianism to Marxism.[29] Marxist sociology can easily be explained without its claiming a wider perspective than any scientific theory can have according to the Marxist theory of knowledge. Once we recognise its historical limitations, we have to ask what kind of truth it is able to supply in its practical application. Here we do not speak of bias,[30] which is certainly the least harmful where its inevitability is

[28] Characteristically Marx does not even utter at this point the reproach that Feuerbach has constructed his Man from the standpoint of *bourgeois* society and therefore had been incapable of understanding events in pre-bourgeois societies.

[28a] Notwithstanding the emphasis put by Zhdanov, in his speech in the philosophical discussion (*Bolshevik*, 1947, No. 16) on the qualitative change in philosophical thought implied in the rise of Marxism. The point is not whether the modern Bolshevists are conscious of the limitations of Plekhanov (see above, p. 35) and of all the others who tended to identify Marxism with its sources, but whether, while having to integrate quite a definite society in conditions not fundamentally different from those envisaged by Marx, they can develop so broadly critical an approach to issues such as the Family, the character of legal restrictions of any kind, etc., whether they can as clearly realise the limitations of the categories grown in *bourgeois* society as could Marx who simply would follow up the critical argument wherever it might lead (sometimes, it might be said, into utopianism).

[29] See above, p. 37.

[30] See above, p. 55, and below, pp. 66-7.

honestly recognised by a theory starting from social conflict,[30a] but of the guarantees for the objective truthfulness of statements that have satisfied the practical test suggested by the theory.

Marxism has three lines along which this question is answered.

(1) It demands of the revolutionary movement scientifically based tactics. It does not only submit itself to the test of rousing the mass-enthusiasm needed in order to carry through a revolutionary upheaval (as religious, legal, and other unscientific ideologies have frequently done in history). Whilst not claiming to be a substitute for knowledge of facts, commonsense, and even of political instinct, it claims to give a general setting, superior to any other, from the general premises of which, together with the facts known, correct estimates of actual conditions, and therefore correct tactics, can be derived. By conquering power and by being able to use it in the way foreseen by Marxist theory, a Marxist party proves not only the social usefulness, but also the truth of Marxism.

(2) The founders of Marxism at least have been extremely cautious in statements on the society to come. The popular demand for descriptions of it suitable to rouse revolutionary enthusiasm got its main satisfaction, so far as the founders are concerned, from generalisations not necessarily involving the truth of Marxism and partly even of non-Marxist origin (to this category belong the concessions made to anarchism in the hymn on the Paris Commune, some borrowings from Hegel and the Utopians, and also the quotation from Morgan at the end of the *Origin of Family, State and Society*), or from generalisations sufficiently broad to allow very different interpretations, as in those parts of the *Critique of the Gotha Programme* that deal with the second higher stage of Communism. Where Marx attempted a concrete analysis of the things to come, as in the *Critique*, his genius is at its highest in ruthless criticism of utopian concepts of what could be realised immediately during the next historical period. Two generations later, these predictions have stood

[30a] Evidently, a distinction should be made between the statement of the fact that philosophy has developed and is developing by controversy on the basis of social conflict (and, in that sense, is " partisan "), and the making of a virtue of the inevitability of bias, including the use of the term " objectivism " as a reproach against social scientists who fail not only to assess each source according to its bias (as scientists certainly should do) but also to develop themselves the desirable kind of bias. The latter reproach, which is widely used in recent Soviet polemics, is simply another way of reproaching them for being scientists instead of propagandists, or to proclaim pragmatism as the standard of truth.

the test of verification better than any other sociological theory. The principle " we are not out to build new utopias " and the sober criticism of the working-classes as they actually are[31] have proved extremely helpful in building a revolutionary party, though they would hardly have shaped a mass-party had they been followed by all its propagandists.

(3) The very foundations of the society to come are expected to prevent contradiction between what ideologies are socially useful, and what are objectively true. In a planned society there will be no risk of workers being dismissed in consequence of the effects of increased production on profits, and therefore no social interest in the spread of ideologies that hide from the workers the necessary results of increased efforts. In this sense Engels[32] spoke of the " leap from the realm of Necessity into the realm of Freedom "—Freedom as conceived by Spinoza and Hegel, in the sense of doing consciously what is necessary.[33]

Clearly there is a considerable truth in each of those lines of approach, but neither of the safeguards mentioned completely solves the problem.

(1) It is hardly possible to derive from the general principles of Marxism conclusions which can be used as the foundations for tactics with such an obvious necessity that the verification of the theory by its tactical consequences can be as exact as was, say, the verification of the Theory of Relativity when the rays of light, during a solar eclipse, were refracted in the degree predicted. For example, within Marxist and other sociological theories it is possible to find convincing arguments in favour of an interpretation of the Anglo-German war at least before spring, 1940, as an imperialist war, or as a war against an especially reactionary kind of imperialism (in opposing which Socialists and bourgeois democrats might have a common interest). There were elements in reality that allowed for either description ; the actual

[31] See Marx's statement, as early as 1850, quoted above, p. 48, and Lenin's very outspoken criticism of the actual Labour movement in *What is to be Done*.

[32] *Anti-Duehring*, p. 312.

[33] In 1922 an Hungarian Communist, George Lukacs, in his *Geschichte und Klassenbewusstsein*, made an atteapt to prove, in the Young Hegelian way, that already the formation of a party aiming at the realisation of socialism, and therefore capable of thoroughly criticising the existing fetishist ideologies, involved a leap of this nature. This might conceivably be construed as dispensing with the need for such a party to take account in its tactics of such awkward realities. The concept, which obviously contradicts the objectivist foundations of Marxism, had soon to be dropped by Lukacz ; but it is important as one of the stimulations for Mannheim's theory (see below, pp. 76-8).

question was which was predominant? It could not be answered *a priori* by Marxist theory pure and simple, and would not have been answered in a scientific sense even if Chamberlain had failed to obstruct collective security and if, in consequence, the political setting of the War had induced the Communists to apply the second interpretation from the very beginning. For, at least at the present stage of sociological theory, it is impossible to assess correctly, at the beginning of a war, all its results, e.g., the emancipation of India, the comparative chances of radical social transformations in Germany and Britain respectively, and even the respective importance of each of these factors for later history. If this were possible, there would be no war at all, because the powers concerned would employ sociological fortune-tellers to predict its outcome, and settle their dispute by a cheap compromise, whatever the sociologist's fee. Actually, the British Communists failed to convince the British workers, and Hess failed to convince the British Conservatives of their respective points of view. But even so, it may conceivably be asserted that the British Communists failed not because their approach was wrong, but because their audience was corrupted by colonial super-profits, because their propaganda was technically unsound, etc., etc., that Hess failed not because of some element in British democracy preventing an alliance with Hitler, but simply because the Tories were mistaken in assessing the strength of the U.S.S.R. and their own proper interests, and that happily (from the progressive viewpoint) these two mistakes compensated each other. In the last resort, it is possible to explain Britain's stand against Hitler (*prima facie* the weak side of the Marxist case) by Marxist arguments, and Hitler's *volte-face* against Russia, the enormous strength of the U.S.S.R., and the later rapprochement between Britain and some former supporters of Hitler's " new order " (the strong sides of the Marxist case) by non-Marxist arguments such as logics of mere geographical strategy.

In some instances Marxism is at an obvious advantage against its opponents, as in forewarning German Social Democrats of the fate of liberal democracy as long as the bourgeoisie remained in actual power. But in the case just mentioned we do not find the correct analysis crowned with political success for the German Communists. *Prima facie* this proves nothing against

Marxism ; outside the Roman Catholic Church[34] no one claims that a correct theory guarantees the achievement of the desired results. But the issue of pragmatism comes in when we consider that even independently of the theoretical truth of some statement, such as the description of the fascist tendencies invading German Social Democracy like all the other defences of the established regime, its tactical and propagandist application may have been bound to be exaggerated to such a point that it contributed to the political defeat of the German Labour movement, including the Communists themselves. No theorist is protected against being biased and getting one-sided results ; but once the outcome of the " practical test on the correctness of the theory " is decided not merely by the amount of objective truth contained in a theory but also by all distortions of the party's propaganda likely to occur and by the political consequences likely to arise from its opponents' reactions, there is no further practical test of the correctness of the theory as such : the relation of a sociological statement made in the course of the revolutionary struggle (i.e., under the very conditions regarded by Marx as essential for establishing the truth) to the maximum conceivable achievements of Marxist sociology is likely to resemble that between the description of diplomatic conflicts in blue-books and the later statements by historical research. The best that can be said is that favourable results are likely to reward the theorist who has a correct interpretation (a) of the facts and (b) of the practical outcome of that interpretation as expressed by him.

In some instances a correct statement of facts, made possible by Marxist theory and inconceivable from any other standpoint, has been the cause of the political success of the Marxist party. Lenin's correct assessment of Russia, in contradiction to the Narodniki, that she was undergoing transformation to capitalism, and of the political consequences to be drawn from that fact, is a foremost example. But in such clear-cut cases it is obvious that the correctness of the theoretical statement, though a necessary condition of the ultimate success, did not need the latter as its proof. And in less clear cases it could be asserted that the success was not due to the correctness of the definite theory submitted to the test of experience, but to other causes. In 1917 no reasonable being could have questioned the fact that

[34] And even it ascribes infallibility to the Pope only when teaching dogma and morals, not when appointing Cardinals, making election speeches or Concordates, supervising the Catholic press, etc.

Russia was a capitalist country—a glance at the statistics of production and occupation was sufficient. Certainly, if the Russian Marxists had not grasped the trend a generation before and waited till it became evident to every serious economist, the party prepared to draw its political conclusion would not have been available when the conditions were ripe. Further, had the majority of the Social Democrat Party drawn from their general concept not only the correct conclusion that Russia would go capitalist, but also the mistaken one that she would have to hold up a socialist revolution until she reached at least the German level as regards economics and labour organisation, there would have been no successful socialist revolution. This would not have proved that the Marxist prediction that Russia was going capitalist was wrong, but only that the Menshevik contention of the stage of capitalism to be attained for transition to socialism, the Trotskyist concept of World Revolution, etc., etc., were mistaken. In short, the result of the revolution could test the value of the tactics only of the revolutionary party, which is a truism ; but the analysis of Russian economics, necessary, but in itself not sufficient, for the success of the party, was verified in exactly the same way as, say, the Theory of Relativity, namely, by statistical facts that corresponded to what had been foretold by the theory.

(2) In the midst of a revolutionary struggle, no human being can retain two quite separate different compartments in his mind, one for analysing dry and disagreeable truth, and another to meet the demand for inspiring generalisations which go beyond what is scientifically predictable ; and no honest man can make such clear divisions between what ought to be said to the millions who make supreme efforts in order to realise what ideals are raised in their minds by the conditions of present society, and what can reasonably be expected to emerge for the next generation from their efforts, if properly directed. In order to keep utopian statements out of the further evolution of Marxist theory, we should have to assume either that the revolutionary state is a state of angels, without dissent amongst its leaders, or that the latter, especially those who are temporarily " out," are sufficiently angelic to refrain from appeals to utopian feelings and expectations of the masses in their arguments with the leading group.

(3) It is a truism that in a planned society all those divergencies

between the motives behind human action and the results likely to be achieved, which are due to the anarchic character of the present society, will disappear ; but it still remains for Marxists to prove that *all* the factors that prevent identity between purpose and outcome will thereby have gone, or at least failure to achieve the purpose will have become reducible to evident causes. For the next century at least, the national character of society will remain, and with it a certain anarchy in international relations. The world around such a planned society appears as an external force powerfully influencing its welfare, though not subject to technical direction as are the forces of Nature. In order to counter its influences, which may be consciously directed at creating internal difficulties for the socialist regime, appeals have to be made to civic loyalty in which the foreign sector of the social forces influencing the individual citizen's conditions no longer appears as individual social forces, but as a concentrated and anonymous power of evil. In order to be more effectively defended the Socialist Fatherland has to be described as something which it is not and cannot be at the present stage of development. It is especially obvious that social inequality, as foreseen already in the *Critique of the Gotha Programme* for the first stage of a communist society and conspicuous in the present U.S.S.R., can hardly be explained in all its implications by the State ideology of a state confronted with grave dangers and tasks. Once we agree with Marx, that the first stage of the Communist society—the only one about which there can be elaborate theoretical analysis and practical experience in our century—contains some internal contradictions in its social structure, some fetishism, too, is bound to prevail—though less than in a capitalist society where the most elementary economic processes had to be veiled from the eyes of those concerned in them. The new ideology may correspond to the interests of masses larger than in any previous revolution, and in the U.S.S.R. it may even co-incide with the whole of the urban and rural working-classes for the simple reason that the Revolution opened a new age of general expansion and formed its necessary condition. But so did the bourgeois democratic revolution in U.S.A., and to some extent even in France. The statement that a revolution has betrayed part of its supporters generally means merely that it did not solve all the contradictions involved in social life, that is to say it means that the revolution has not brought historical evolution to an end.

Trotskyism is the natural punishment for the utopian elements in Marxism ; but it is remarkable that scientific socialism has produced this as its punishment no less than did the English, French, and other revolutions with an " idealistic " platform. It is in any case logically inconsistent to say that Marxist ideology coincides with objective truth because it refrains from making forecasts about the future (argument (2) above) and because it overcomes the social contradictions within the society to be achieved (argument 3), an assertion which can hardly be made of that type of society the achievement of which is within the likely range of our experience.

Unhappily, these shortcomings of arguments (2) and (3) impair also the working of the strongest of them (1) : what is tested by the success of revolutionary policies is not only the scientific element in the prediction of their actual conditions but also the efficiency of the revolutionary ideology as a means of mass-mobilisation, which is by no means bound to coincide with its soberness and self-control. This capacity of revolutionary ideologies is held in check by its possibly detrimental effect on the realism of tactics (the expectations of a World Revolution delivering the U.S.S.R. from difficulties of reconstruction, or a quick " withering away of the State " are conspicuous examples). Even if such considerations eventually lead to the dropping of elements of the State ideology incompatible with reality, as in the description of the coming communist society, [34a] the process is bound to be prolonged, and can even hardly start before the new regime has achieved an advanced stage of consolidation.

In order to pass a just judgment, we must compare the position of Marxism as a new official ideology with that of any other State ideology. We must not ask from Marxists something which no reasonable being would grant, namely, that they risk defeat in a great experiment for the mere sake of preserving ideological purity, nor must we allow the issue to be veiled by the specific conditions of the U.S.S.R. and of its One-Party-system. The contradiction under discussion arises in Marxism not because Marxists had a lower degree of scientific integrity and certainly not because they are conscious of that bias in topical social research which only the blind can overlook. It arises because Marxism claims an immediate connection with social practice the absence of which is regarded by other schools of sociological

[34a] See below, p. 398.

thought as normal, or even as a desirable proof of detachment ; that is to say (if we take the dependence of social theories on social facts for granted) because Marxism puts the question on a higher level. Obviously the problem is not bound to the existence of a state capable of offering ample opportunities to schools of thought deemed helpful, and of oppressing others : however important the difference may be for the dissenting theorist, it is more likely that a state with large practical tasks and with an interest in using all its intellectual forces will be somewhat more broad-minded than a revolutionary opposition party whose main objects are propagandist. If, in the couse of the next centuries, Marxism should become some kind of new theology, our question would have no more sense than fundamentally heretical questions have in the framework of other theologies ; should there be free competition of ideas during the transition period, including original Marxism, its transformations in those countries where it enjoys a political monopoly, and also the lessons drawn from it by non-Marxist parties or by independent scholars—all these ideas would have the opportunity to undergo the test of practical experience.

I should be strongly inclined to accept that argument, and could refer to what Marx occasionally has said about the "party in the great historical sense " once I could clearly distinguish between the historic effects of Marxist theories and those of the activities of Marxist parties. Without the successes of the U.S.S.R.—which, obviously, are due not only to Marxism, but also to a One-Party-system inspired by it—there would be extremely little chance of elements of Marxist thought having the opportunity of being tested in competition with other ideas as to their ability to inspire actual transformations. There can be no question that the U.S.S.R. is the country where Marxism—apart from having become State-ideology—has also found its most thorough students. They may regard the " independent scholars " of whom I spoke as mere vulgarisors of Marxism whose successes merely prove how much more could be achieved with the original theory. Should we speak in private about the dangers threatening the development of the theory in their country, they would regard them as mere infantile disorders bound to be overcome in due course—unless they were in fact prepared to accept the pragmatist position, which would end our argument. But if we asked how infantile disorders involved in the very system by which the theory found realisation could be overcome, we could hardly get more concrete prospects than references to the second and higher stage of communist society, where the remaining contradictions will be solved. I think such reference is contrary to the spirit of Marxism, which prohibits prophecies going beyond the immediate results of the overcoming of a system the internal contradictions which can be observed here and now. Even presupposing the Marxist system we do not know whether the "second stage" is more than a certain trend of future developments[35]; and Lenin himself, though he regarded the " second stage " as not too remote a reality, accepted " absolute truth " as an asymptote. Should we add, that overcoming pragmatism is also an asymptotic process, that is to say, that absolute truth is inaccessible not only, as Lenin said, because the world is infinitely complex, so that no finite progress of knowledge can reproduce all its content, but also because Bacon's *idola fori* can never be overcome completely ?

Perhaps. But if it be so, let us accept the struggle against pragmatism as an infinite and permanent task, as a fundamental condition of human progress. Let us accept no armistice in that struggle, whichever direction human development may take. Let us call the people to fight for right causes, as well as they can grasp them, and let us explain those causes to them as well as we can. But let us never allow the statement that there *is* an objective truth to become the pedestal upon which we elevate some alleged truth because we regard it as useful. And if we, being human beings who fight for causes deemed right, cannot see and tell the whole truth at a certain moment, let us not claim that we have it. Some times the products of contemporary minds may become the subjects of hymns, as the products of the minds of the platonists and stoics have been for the last eighteen centuries ; but it is not the task of sociologists to aspire to saintliness. Every sociological theory serves as a link in the growth of the next social integration ; but history does not stop with the coming of any definite integration into being. We should write in such a way that coming generations should find in the writings of the ancients as much as possible help to proceed further on the endless way.

By interpreting the world as well as we can we shape the conditions for changing it without the outcome of action contra-

dicting the intentions of the agents ; and if we agree with Marx
that overcoming capitalism is an essential condition for such
coincidence of intentions and results, this will be a most powerful
argument in favour of socialism. Socialism will be achieved
through the world by social forces working in very different
ways, and many ideas will get their opportunity to undergo the
Marxian test, if we conceive of it in a sufficiently broad way.
There will be legends in many countries—including especially
those which describe themselves today as free; but History, not
Hagiology, will pass the definite judgment upon whether ideas
have proved their this-sidedness and reality.

(d) IDEOLOGIES IN GENERAL AS THE PRODUCT OF THE SOCIAL PROCESS

As long as ideologies were regarded as mere delusions, their
study could hardly proceed beyond stating the obvious connections between knowledge and practical intentions, and the no less
obvious discrimination exercised in the organisation of scientific
teaching, in the official encouragement of arts, etc., in favour of
those trends that happened to promote the interests of the ruling
class. Under those assumptions bourgeois " class-science " was
criticised on the basis of its belief that there was a " class-less "
science,[36] but with the rider that it was unattainable by the
bourgeoisie and that ultimate truth co-incided with the specific
Marxist bias,[33] in the utopian manner. Ideologies, as general
motive forces, have to be explained on the basis of the objective
conditions under which the different ideologies fighting for
supremacy in times of social crisis develop, even independent of
the will-element in human thought.

The answer to this problem should start from an analysis
of the general mechanisms of ideological development. The
nearest approach to such a theory has been given by Engels, in
the concluding section of *Ludwig Feuerbach* and in the letter to
Conrad Schmitt, of October 27, 1890. Ultimately all ideologies
originate from Man's desire to understand Nature and his social
surroundings. But in consequence of the social division of labour,
ideologies are developed by special bodies of men whose minds
work with the concept-material given in that specific sphere,
and who develop the standpoint of that sphere and preserve

[36] For the corresponding description of "class-justice" in terms that prove the
actual acceptance of the bourgeois concept of class-less Justice by its critics, see my
Soviet Legal Theory, p. 20.

its continuity and consistency.[37] Lawyers explain the legal needs
of the society in which they live in terms of *a priori* principles of
Law, derived from all its previous (and largely pre-capitalist)
development. Theologians work with a concept-material the
origins of which go back to the animist outlook of primitive man
and which has developed through the formation of national
religions, the religious syncreticism of the Roman Empire
modified by the achievements of philosophy, the establishment of
Christianity as the Roman State religion and all the subsequent
developments, culminating in the formation of the mediaeval
Church and its struggle with national states for supremacy, the
growth of a bourgeoisie and of Protestantism. Philosophers
develop the concept-material handed down to them by their
predecessors, and are influenced by the economic conditions of
society indirectly, in so far as these influence politics and political,
legal and other ideologies which enter the philosophers' synthesis.
" Here economy creates nothing absolutely new, but it determines
the way in which the existing material of thought is altered and
fully developed." This concept of Engels may also be expressed
as stating that changes in economic setting cause changes in the
social functions of existing ideas. But the latter do not cease to be
relevant : " Every ideology, once it has arisen, develops in
connection with the given concept-material, and develops this
material further, otherwise it would cease to be an ideology, that is
occupation with thoughts as with independent entities, developing independently, and subject only to its own laws. That the
material life conditions of the persons inside whose heads this
thought process goes on, in the last resort determines the course
of this process, remains of necessity unknown to these persons,
for otherwise there would be an end to all ideology."

Before discussing the last part of Engels' statement we should
notice some important implications of the first, which have been
strangely neglected in existing literature on the subject. If it is
recognised that ideological factors contribute to bringing about
transformations of society, and the Marxist interpretation of
ideologies as shaped by objective social conditions is accepted,
it follows that the ideas which help to bring a certain social
formation *a* into being, so far as their ideological form is concerned

[37] It should be added that self-assertion and even immediate material interests
induce any profession to cherish its specific tradition, to elaborate it in the slightest
details, and to make access to the profession dependent on expert knowledge of that
specific professional ideology.

have been shaped by the conditions prevailing in the earlier social
formation a-1, the overthrow of which was amongst the objective
functions of these ideas.[38] Objective changes in that framework
laid bare the points of contradiction (formerly merely potential)
between the framework and its ideological expression and rendered
some alternative to existing social structure feasible : so the idea
could be followed up in its implications. But these potential
implications must have originated somewhere : the idea has a
" revolutionary " quality because it is a generalisation of certain
aspects of the transition in which it originated (i.e., the transition
from a-2 to a-1),[39] and these very aspects come into conflict with
the further evolution of a-1 at a certain point. The current
ideological expression of such a state of things is the statement
that a-1 has " degenerated " from the point of view of the ideals
that brought it into being, thereby necessitating a return to the
original ideas (in terms of which a is interpreted). In an objective, sociological description we should prefer simply to state that
those ideological abstractions and generalisations from certain
aspects of the transition from a-2 to a-1, though they fitted the
needs of the establishment of the society a-1 did not sufficiently
describe the further stages of its development any more than a
tangent can describe the further evolutions of a curve. The
contradiction, and especially its regular appearance whenever a
social set-up is questioned, may be caused by some (be it even
merely formal) common factor existing between motive forces in
all the social transitions under discussion ; it may also be caused
by some common element in the social orders attacked in the
subsequent changes, so that all those transitions appear as
gradual realisations of some (negative or positive) progress.
Either explanation may be supported by certain interpretations

[38] For the concept of social function, see above, p. 49.

[39] In our schematic presentation we neglect the fact that many elements of the
revolutionary ideology have originated in stages much earlier than the immediately
preceding one (a–1). We can justify such procedure with the phenomenon of change
of social function of existing ideologies, and the implied assimilation of all concepts
originated in earlier stages (a–n) to the pattern prevailing in (a–1), from which the
transition to (a) has to start. In a very different direction point various attempts of
modern psycho-analysists to explain an allegedly permanent demand for freedom by
alleged fundamental experiences of primitive man, permanently repeated in the process of education (comp. E. Fromm, *The Fear of Freedom*, published 1942, in The
International Library for Sociology and Social Reconstruction). Apart from the
general shortcomings of all psychological approaches to sociology, this theory—like
the theological—is confronted with the difficulty that, if true, it proves too much,
and thus would have to introduce some Devil in order to explain all the non-compliance
of reality with the alleged trend.

of the historical process the discussion of which is not amongst
our tasks,[40] but the phenomenon itself stands beyond doubt ;
a proper appreciation of it should be sufficient to dispose of many
controversies in the application of Marxism to ideological developments.

There has been much argument between Max Weber, Prof.
Tawney and others about the respective priority of capitalist
development or Protestant ethics, with the implication that a
priority of the ideological factor, if established, would dispose
of the Marxist claim to explain the latter by objective, economic
conditions. But unless the mystical assumption is made that
ideologies are determined by their outcome ; or, no less meta-
physically, that they are a mechanical reflection of economic
facts, it is obvious that the transition to capitalism had to be
carried through under the ideological inspiration of a concept-
material evolved in, and fitting, feudal society. Only the
evolution of the feudal society turned the original fitness into a
contradiction and changed the social functions of the given
concepts. Protestantism has to be explained by feudal conditions,
just as Socialism—including Marxism—has to be explained by
the conditions prevailing in a capitalist society.

An important inversion of this theorem is the statement that
no social formation, in its original stages, can be distinguished
from its predecessor by ideological and similar " super-structures,"
for of necessity it grew in the spiritual world inherited from its
predecessor and was only gradually able to assimilate that world
to its own needs. This disposes of the frequent attempts to follow
the origins of a social formation into a past when its economic
characteristics were obviously lacking, for the mere reason that
the ideologies which helped to bring it into being, originated at
that time,[41] but it disposes also of the claims of Marxism to survive
the definite overthrow of the society in whose contradictions it
originated. As the founders themselves would have agreed, such
a claim is profoundly anti-Marxist ; it actually fits the Hegelian—
or even Aristotelean—demand that the historical process should
attain an end by establishing absolute truth.[42]

[40] In some occasional remarks (c.f. *Dialectics of Nature*, ed. cit., pp. 18 ff.) Engels
distinguished between an ascending and an eventual descending part in the course of
human development caused by the eventual cooling down of the solar system. The
argument is more characteristic of Engels' general outlook than convincing as a
scientific argument, as it takes the existence of mankind up to a very remote future,
technological forecasts on which are impossible, for granted.

[41] See below, pp. 89-90 and 121-3 [42] Engels, *Ludwig Feuerbach*, etc., pp. 23-4.

However, as an outspoken socio-economic analysis, Marxism claims a qualitative superiority over all previous explanations of social life that described the socio-economic antagonisms in terms of the religious, philosophical, legal and similar forms in which men become conscious of them and fight them out.[43] This "false consciousness" is bound to be replaced by outspoken recognition of social facts when it is recognised that all social consciousness is conditioned by the fundamental structure of society. In consequence, amongst ideologies in the broader sense of the word, that is, systems of thought which aim at inherent consistency, there is a fundamental distinction between scientific theories which more or less correctly represent reality (to which, of course, also the study of the history of religion, law, philosophy, etc., belong) on the one hand, and "ideologies" in the narrower sense, that is to say, distorted representation of class-antagonism on the other. This second concept of ideologies, as frequently applied by the founders of Marxism, is narrower than the identification of ideologies with "superstructures" (that is, thought as conditioned by the material facts of social life) to which they kept in other cases, and which is consistently applied in this book. On the other hand, it is broader than the current identification of ideologies (theoretically expressed by Mannheim, l. c.) with such concepts the social function of which is the defence of the existing social framework. Even the narrower ideology-concept of Marxism includes forms of "false consciousness" on the side of the revolutionaries, e.g., some Christian utopias.

In the statement above[44] quoted, Engels speaks of ideologies in the sense of "occupation with thoughts as with independent entities," and therefrom concludes that with the realisation of the material conditioning of those thoughts ideology would come to an end. This is a mere generalisation of Feuerbach's criticism of religion.[45] But people will not cease to be interested in Economics or Social Philosophy even though convinced that the thought material with which they operate is conditioned by the facts it sets out to explain. They may in spite of this be interested in such aspects of economics as Marxists would regard as leading away from those facts that show the basic structure and the decay of the capitalist world. Engels seems to have supposed that the mere knowledge of the economic

[43] Marx, Preface to the *Critique of Political Economy*.
[44] p. 73.   [45] See above, p. 32.

-conditioning of all social life was sufficient to destroy the ideological argument for the preservation of the existing social
framework ; but this holds true only if we assume that the foundations of a given economic system are in the process of breaking
down and that this process cannot be overlooked except by
specific, ideological, mechanisms of self-deception. Engels'
concept of ideology only fits those periods of rapid social transformation in which developments within the existing framework
may be regarded as secondary in comparison with the questioning
of its very existence. Certain types of ideologies fit Engels' or
Mannheim's definition, and in a social crisis some more assume an
"ideological" character, in the current sense of the word. But
there are many more that do not. Revolutionary periods are
measured in decades, whilst the "intermediary" periods of
organic development are measured by centuries and include
the most remarkable achievements of the human mind (true,
most of these seem to occur immediately after a revolutionary
period, when its main achievements are being digested, and
immediately before the next, when the growing tensions open the
ideologues' eyes to fundamental problems). Without the desire
to improve existing conditions there would be extremely little
progress, especially in social science. But there is little sense in
describing, say, the classical economics of Smith and Ricardo as
utopian in that it was inapplicable to the society which produced
it, though it might be realisable in the one to follow. Nor
should one describe it as a *bourgeois* ideology in the sense that it was
not only evolved in order to serve the needs of *bourgeois* society (as
it certainly was) but also failed to recognise those elements in the
existing social order that were bound to result in its eventual
overthrow.[46] Actually, classical economics were ambivalent
(as seen from our point of view) in that they contained those elements that eventually lead to a criticism of *bourgeois* society as well
as those upon which its theoretical defences were to be built.
But such an interpretation, starting from the issue of our time, is

---

[46] Either case could be made with reference to Mannheim, op. cit., pp. 175–6,
though Mannheim himself, who did not refrain from describing a liberal, and even a
conservative, utopia would certainly prefer the former point of view. Here, we are not
arguing against the difficulty of fitting certain ideologies (in our sense) in one of
Mannheim's patterns, which is recognised by himself (p. 177), but against his statement (p. 175) that " all those ideas which do not fit into the current order are ' situationally transcendent ' or unreal " and that only those ideas which correspond to the
concretely existing and *de facto* order are designated as "adequate" and "situationally
congruous."

unhistorical : the classics defended capitalism against policies and theories reflecting the needs of pre-capitalist society (which implied no utopianism, as feudalism had long been obsolete) and described it as well as they could—naturally with historical limitations, as every author has—without even thinking of the possibility that a mere half-century later their description of what they regarded as the natural order of things might become a weapon in the struggle between those who defended it and those who regarded it as obsolete, as feudalism had been in their own days.

In periods of social crisis when all the ruling interests are threatened by the consistent development of the established concepts, the " collective unconscious " of the ruling class and its ideological representatives is needed in order to obscure the real condition of society and thereby to prolong its existence. [47] Academic preference, the favour of Maecenas, etc., will look after the interest of the ruling class in granting officially recognised publicity to those trends that defend its interests ; and even successful attempts to break the official monopoly are more likely than not to result in the establishment of the new trend as an established sect.   The " outsider " position of Marxism forms the counterpart to the development of academic economics during the last century.   So far, Mannheim's narrower concept of ideology covers an important social phenomenon.   On the other hand, the concept of utopia is of real social importance. It covers not the mere truism that every fruitful idea transcends the immediate present, but also the fact that some ideas transcend not only the present stage of society but also that which follows it, and which is brought into existence by the help of those ideas. There is no necessary and permanent connection between the attainability of an idea and its moral influence inspiring actual progress.   So, the utopia of today may easily turn into the ideology (in Mannheim's narrower sense) of tomorrow. [48]

(e) IDEOLOGIES OF SOCIAL TRANSFORMATION

The " professional " ideologies (in the broadest sense of the word) like the people who develop them serve a certain social function.   Lawyers teach general principles which are supposed to form the foundations of society and according to

[47] Mannheim, op. cit., p. 36.
[48] See below, p. 90.

which cases should be decided. Historians draw the lessons of national history in a way suitable to educate the future servants of the State and to strengthen the feelings of civic loyalty. Priests teach a way of behaviour which, whilst compatible with the needs of this bad world, leads as surely to salvation. Philosophers generalise whatever trends are in the centre of the public interest. Thus ideas developed by the distinctly ideological professions may be generalised to such an extent that they influence the trend of thought even in purely scientific fields. But the connection of those realms of science with human practice is primarily represented by technical needs where too much "ideology" would spell backwardness and military defeat. Behind the ideologically distorted reflection of facts stand more or less hidden real laws of Nature, and even an obviously mistaken generalisation in economics, like the Malthusian, may prove the starting point for Darwinism, the most fruitful (though in itself partly mistaken) hypothesis in the history of biology. In the next stage of the socio-economic development Dialectical Materialism is raised from the status of an explanation of social change to that of a general world-outlook ; it too, is of assistance to scientists though, possibly, more in those countries where it is still a revolutionary, that is critical, ideology, than in that where it has been raised to the status of State ideology.

An ideology is of necessity a generalisation, reflecting the pattern of the society it serves. It is the professional function of lawyers to deal with the deplorable fact that the rights of their clients, though admirably granted by the legal order, are not automatically served. The professional function of historians consists of seeing that deplorable political mistakes of the past are not repeated by their students, while father-confessors deal professionally with the failure of men to live up to the standards of human behaviour established by the Church. But however incompletely realised, the pattern belongs to the society for which it stands : although the inevitable tension between ideals and reality occupies a central place amongst the dogmas of the Church, it has its Saints who succeeded in keeping original sin within reasonable limits and its Heaven in describing which the utopian elements reflecting its historical origin are overshadowed by an idealised feudal, if not modern, [49] society. The difficulty

[49] As characterised, for example, by the modern cult of St. Joseph in Catholic Trade Unionism which is strongly encouraged by the Church as an antidote against too much actual Trade Unionism.

with which the analysis of ideologies is faced concerns not their
failure to comply with all the details of existing society (only
inefficient ideologies would do that, for they would have no room
for partial reform), but the possibility of getting the ideological
instruments of thorough social change from the existing ideological system. We are here concerned with the derivation of
the concrete argument in favour of change from an ideology
dominated in all its aspects (including the outlook of its critics) [50]
by existing society, not with the general inspiration of change
which, as we have seen, [51] may be formulated in terms of the very
standards by which existing society has been brought into being.

To the Marxist, change in the social content of existing
thought material is explained by the priority of Man's relations
to Nature in comparison with the relations entered by men with
each other in the process of social production. The professional
ideology dealing with the first-mentioned field, science, is bound
to move forward with the access of new material. The main
resistence offered by the social structure to scientific progress takes
effect through other ideologists dealing with the " world-outlook,"
that is idealised society ; and, indeed, strong material interests
in scientific progress may form a main incentive to actual struggle
between social groups inspired by the different ideologies. But
there is no necessity for such conflict : the very professional
character of the various ideologies ensures that an Established
Church recognising Genesis as Holy Writ may happily co-exist
with the Copernican system and Darwinism in science. The
ideological professions—and, especially, the public to whom
they appeal—are not water-tight compartments, and in order
to be efficient, priests must be recruited from amongst people
who have enjoyed some general education. Therefore a gradual
re-interpretation of the meaning of Inspiration must proceed in
the midst of a Church needing honest ministers who are capable
of keeping in touch with their public. Similarly in the late
Middle Ages there was a gradual intrusion of non-Christian
elements of ancient civilisation into Roman Catholicism. There
is no actual conflict unless social antagonism intervenes : modern
Catholicism (as distinct from feudal Catholicism, which enforced
Galileo's recantation) has little objection to modern physics.
As it cannot change its concept of Inspiration (which is its very
raison d'être) it manages with the old device of the dual truth,

[50] See above, p. 55.   [51] Above, pp. 73-5.

with the more popular aspect of truth reduced to what other people would describe as a myth. But Roman Catholics are not the only people in the modern world who believe that it cannot be kept in due order without myths, duly enforced and accepted.

The present state of the social sciences still allows for the preservation of an enormous amount of mythological elements, the social demand for which is obviously strong in this field. Because the complicated character of social phenomena necessitates the use of simplified models in studying social problems, the mythological element can be introduced in an apparently scientific form by mere omission, in constructing the model, of what critics of the existing system would regard as its most interesting traits. " Say's Law " in economics and the treatment of employment problems in the persistent vein of accepted academic economics are impressive examples of that attitude. However, in critical situations such problems have to be tackled in some way and outsiders within the field of official science (though rather the more moderate amongst them) may attract a considerable amount of attention and even official recognition. Even if the crisis should be assumed to have passed in a society re-asserting itself and its basic myths, the temporary introduction of heretical thought material into respectable academic ideology can hardly be undone : it remains available for further attempts to adapt existing teaching to reality, and also as a lever for outside criticism which thus gets the backing of recognised authority.

A second path of ideological change is opened by the rise or intensified development of new professional groupings connected with new social interests. The rise of a group of non-clerical princes' servants educated in *humaniora* brought a new element into Western European ideology, even when an individual humanist such as Thomas More honestly opposed his prince and became a Catholic (and Communist) Saint. In England as well as in France the rise of the bourgeois connections of the legal profession resulted in opposition between their professional ideology, which became the ideology of the rising bourgeoisie, and the humanist-theological garment of absolutism. The process was repeated when economists rose against the lawyers. In order that the opposing sectional ideologies can meet and that intellectual battles can precede the parliamentary or military ones, there must be generalisation. This need is provided for by intercourse between the different professional groups of the intelligentsia and by the existence of a specific group of intellectuals, the philosophers, catering for it. Nowhere are the socio-political implications of generalisation[52] better realised than amongst the latter group and amongst the people who appoint them—if they are academic teachers—or decide upon the public and acclaim to be given to " independent gentlemen " writing on general problems. Some philosophers supplied essential elements of the synthesis of a revolutionary " world-outlook," but none of them has developed an ideology actually inspiring a revolution from below, whilst their place amongst the inspirers of " revolutions from above " is conspicuous.

As long as a social system can be preserved by gradual modifications, the re-interpretation of existing ideology and the shift of influence from some groups of ideologists (such as theologians) to others (such as lawyers) will satisfy its needs. But if fundamental changes in social structure, and therefore in social ideology, are needed, they can hardly be achieved by the mere gradual rise of new ideologies corresponding to mere sectional interests within the existing framework. Deep social fissures may, but need not, find expression in serious splits within the predominant ideology. The rise of Christianity, one of the most profound changes in social ideology which we know, can hardly be associated with a recent split in the scientific ideology of its time ; the utopian element, let loose by social changes, was quite sufficient to produce, out of the variations of Stoic and neo-Platonic philosophy, a new world religion.

---

[52] cf. Mannheim, op. cit., p. 132. On the other hand Mannheim (Ibid., pp. 136 ff.) assumes for the section of the intelligentsia that carries through generalisation an at least partially classless position. This is true only if by class not the great divisions on basic social issues, but the sectional groups within the ruling class are understood. Mannheim's assertion forms simply part of the professional ideology of that part of the intelligentsia. Such professional ideologies may influence their behaviour just to that amount as, for example, theologians cannot proclaim atheism, or legal theorists defend lettres de cachet. But it cannot render a philosophical system less class conditioned than, say, an honestly consistent legal system is bound to be. This argument also answers K. Popper's (op. cit., vol. II, pp. 205 ff.,) criticism of Mannheim, which is based upon the correct observation that in every science bias is supposed as present with the individual scientist, but rendered harmless by an institutional framework that ensures discussion and mutual control. At least in the field of social sciences with far-going political implications, institutional frameworks for scientific research are unable to check biases originating from the basic assumptions of that framework. Popper like Mannheim deals only with the problem how to check (sectional) attitudes that may appear as biased even when the basic characteristics of the system are taken for granted. They do not answer Marx.

True, in order to produce noteworthy social changes other non-ideological factors were needed, namely, decomposition of the economic system and the consequent external conquest. In the Reformation we find a well-prepared ideological fissure in scholastic theology combined with a mass-movement inspired merely by utopia and accordingly incapable of achieving anything beyond the negative effect of weakening the social powers that backed one of the contending trends in the theological camp. At the same time fear of its implications restricted the reforming spirit of the victorious trend. Marxism arose at a time when there were no longer serious splits in official bourgeois ideology, though preceding fissures had supplied the material for a very efficient synthesis achieved by Marxism. That synthesis, in combination with utopian inspiration, has produced an external effect comparable only with the rise of Christianity, and under its impact subsequent fissures in academic economics and history did not fail to appear. Notwithstanding this Marxism, like Christianity and Protestantism, originated from thought-material well-elaborated by contemporary official science.

In order to analyse the elements of thorough ideological change we start from the conditions under which an actual fissure in the central ideology of a society takes place. Being an ideology, the field where the fissure takes place is not identical with that where the social antagonisms standing behind the contesting parties have arisen : only a very narrow-minded trade-unionist or land-reformer may regard disputes amongst lawyers on the rights of trade-unions or tenants as potential starting-points for a renewal of the way in which a society thinks. On the other side, in order to concentrate in itself the intellectual energies of society, the field of the fissure must be not too remote from the general interest.[53] Therefore, the fissure arises in the generalising sector of ideology, religious or philosophical, according to the circumstances. For such a fissure to arise there must be, amongst the generalising ideologues, people under the influence of a variety of aspects of the predominant social issue of the day. Princes, with their satellite humanistically educated servants, merchants, landlords and burghers, were the people most likely

[53] Under extremely totalitarian regimes the most abstract issues, say formal logics with implications on the dogmas of the Church, or the strife between artistic schools with political implications, may prove just that kind of dispute which the average intellectual with moderate desire for stake or prison will join. But, in such cases, the issues only formally belong to the remote field.

to find expression in the decomposition of the mediaeval Church ; whilst spiritual and temporal servants of the " enlightened " absolutist State, landlords and capitalists were likely to have their say in the disputes of German classical philosophy.   This does not mean that the contestants were not honest theologians or philosophers (if they were not, their work would be quite in-effective and undeserving .of sociological analysis) ; but their work would be irrelevant from our point of view if they had not generalised from the conditions of human life.   They could generalise only from such fields of social life which were within their experience.   The fissure in the ruling ideology always reflects a fissure amongst the ruling classes.

It follows that fissures in one society can provide the ideology of the next only on condition that the latter's leading class has already formed part of the combination predominant in its predecessor, and therefore has been able to form a faction amongst the latter's ideologists.   The French Encyclopaedists, though not admitted to academic teaching and similar posts, were able to provide much of the ideology of coming bourgeois society because the bourgeoisie itself, in spite of all its complaints of " being nothing," already formed a recognised section in pre-revolutionary France.   In such cases the content of the new ideology is based upon thorough opposition to those metaphysical generalisations in which the coherence and class-character of the preceding State-ideology is expressed ; but the individual tenets of that ideology (which are likely already to have expressed much of the needs of the new ruling class) will be corrected no more than is needed in order to negate those institutions which the new regime is bound to overthrow, whilst leaving untouched all those that are to be preserved in its framework.   The meta-physical materialism of the Encyclopedists finds its explanation in the need of the French bourgeoisie to rid themselves thoroughly of feudal State-ideology based upon the Church, but not of the concepts of property allegedly based on Natural Law and of a State conceived as an agreement to protect property, as had been accepted with the rise of bourgeois attitudes in pre-revolutionary France.   Therefore some " eternal truths " had to be preserved. Hegel's dialectic idealism, including the inconsistency of its Dialectics, expressed the desire of the reforming wing of the Prussian bureaucracy to assert the need of reform in a backward state with very backward concepts of property and government without questioning the ideological continuity of the State (and its Established Church). No "ideological" attitude in the deprecatory sense of the term is needed in order to explain either way of thought, and it would be hard to establish [54] in view of the obvious lack of a working-class against whose claims capitalism should have needed defence in 18th Century France or in early 19th Century Germany. The Encyclopaedists as well as Hegel proceeded beyond the limits of knowledge and the level of generalisation which they found available, but they proceeded only in those paths along which they were driven by a strongly felt social need.

The position of the modern working-classes is different in that they were actually " nothing " before they were organised by their class-ideology and emancipated by the struggles which it inspired. Their ideology had to be supplied from outside existing *bourgeois* ideology, [55] typically by men who in consistently pursuing the bourgeois-democratic ideology went further than was compatible with their status in a country not ripe for bourgeois-democratic policies. This fact explains the German and Russian leadership in evolving Marxism as well as it explains the one really important utopian system, the socialism of Robert Owen who was a deserter of the early 19th Century British bourgeoisie. There are interesting contrasts with the origins of non-revolutionary panaceas—mainly in the field of monetary reform and frequently used by fascists—from lower-middle-class cranks.

A revolutionary system of thought, as represented by Marxism and to some extent by the Encyclopaedists, is backed by social forces the rise of which is sufficiently evident to attract the attention of serious and honest thinkers, and to provoke that minimum

[54] Apart from details in Hegel's *Philosophy of Law* as regards the structure of Constitutional Monarchy, which can be easily explained by the fact that Prussian state philosophers are usually not heroes and prefer an academic chair to telling the maximum of what their class would be able to understand.

[55] This fact, which is a mere implication of the fact that the working-classes were actually emancipated by Marxism, lies at the root of all the "psychological explanations" of the latter by "resentment" of its founders against their origins, or of the very current complaint, naïvely expressed by the fascist renegade, August Winnig (*From Proletariat zum Arbeitertam*, Hamburg, 1930, pp. 69–70,) that the German working-classes had been emancipated under the guidance of outsiders of the bourgeoisie, instead of its "enlightened" wing. The latter way, which, besides, was impossible in Germany in consequence of the lack of such an enlightened wing of the bourgeoisie, would simply have resulted in keeping the workers in their proper place, as a tail of the middle-classes. Comp. *The Federalist*, ed. 1867, pp. 218 ff.

D

backing by the public without which no literary production would be conceivable, yet not strong enough to grant them some representation in the official world and the opportunity to produce some fissure in the ruling ideology. The chance of a system like the Marxist forming the guiding ideology in a social transformation lies in the possibility and the need for such a transformation of a very thorough character arising somewhere before the new forces have had an opportunity to establish themselves as a sectional power within the system. If the sectional interest of the workers finds sufficient opportunity to develop its own sectional standpoint still within the framework of bourgeois society, the mechanism of ideological transition to its successor will be very similar to the preparation of the bourgeois-democratic revolutions by fissures within the official ideology of the pre-bourgeois world, even if the representatives of that standpoint should continuously be denied full academic and similar facilities. The representatives of official ideology themselves would be bound to take notice of, and to assimilate part of the opposition teaching.

But in that case not the essential part and certainly not the whole of the revolutionary ideology would find acceptance in the sectional world-outlook, even in those cases where the organisation of the sectional group and its rise to influence would have been inconceivable without the help of the revolutionary ideology. The sectional ideology of a group merely characterised by its occupying a certain position in the socio-economic system need not go beyond explaining the common interests uniting its members, in opposition to other groups characterised by different positions in the socio-economic system. The foundations of Marxist economics as explained in volume I of *Capital* are sufficient for this purpose, including even that of serving as a scientific foundation for the trade-unionist and similar representation of the sectional interest. If the most moderate reforms demanded in the sectional interest meet such strong resistance from all the powers that be as was to be found in 19th Century Central Europe, historical materialism may serve as an efficient agent in unmasking the State and its monarchical tradition, and those of the general philosophical tenets of Marxism which are needed in order to destroy the authority of established religion will meet with understanding. A rather vulgarised materialism may serve as the foundation of new habits, modes and traditions uniting those who without the new ideology would be an amorphous and

atomised mass. In such an environment, Marx's economic
analysis, which is at its best in explaining the contradictions
inherent in capitalist society will be less appreciated than his
rather questionable theory of value which, however, has the merit
at least of imbuing its holders with a belief in the justice of sectional claims ; and a thorough investigation of the origins of State
and Family will be needed no more than an elaborate system of
revolutionary tactics. Bourgeois society itself, at least in its more
progressive representatives, has produced the ideologies required
for the organisation of a Weimar Republic, or for the Labour
regime in Britain. A comparison of those of the elements of
Marxist theory most easily accepted by working-class sectional
interest with those which remain vital after a century of criticism
and historical experience, may explain why most people who
have been used to regard Marxism as represented by pre-1914
German or Austrian Social Democracy are bound to regard as
obsolete the one sociological theory that in our times has actually
proved capable of guiding transforming action. The vulgarisation of Marxism by those who tried to integrate it in the ideology
of the 19th century liberal bourgeoisie provides the background
for the standpoint of those who believe that the party-school of a
revolutionary party is the place where the most thorough analysis
possible in a given stage of social evolution can develop, in spite
of the dangers of dogmatism involved in the need for self-assertion. [56]
But theoreticians immediately serving the needs of the practical
struggle are likely to borrow even most important parts of the
theoretical system from suitable contemporary *bourgeois* production, not necessarily always with such genius as was shown by
Engels and Lenin in developing the ideas of Morgan and Hobson.
The new synthesis may be produced in a prolonged struggle for
the acceptance of ideas originating from the self-criticism of the
preceding society, and also partly in the reaction of the revolutionary movement to trends within its own ranks that aim at the
acceptance of some *bourgeois* philosophy fashionable at the time.
To a large extent, modern Marxist philosophy has been shaped in
rejecting the various attempts at introducing alien elements such
as Kant and Mach into the Marxist fold, and the results are not
necessarily superior to those achieved by Marx in his lonely study
in direct criticism of his Young Hegelian predecessors. However,
purity of an ideology is not a necessary condition for its serving

[56] cf. Mannheim, l.c., pp. 116-7.

D2

as a lever in the great transformations of human society. Where the final transition is achieved without revolutionary leaps, some derivatives of the less conservative among the ideologies characteristic of the old society are likely to be combined with vulgarisations of those elements of the new synthesis which proved helpful in sectional struggle, or perhaps even appealed to the commonsense of the least conservative members of the former ruling class (had such strata not been available, there would have been no " peaceful transition "). Where the revolutionary struggles have been fought out to the last, reaction against the vulgarisation of the revolutionary theory may combine with the acceptance of elements of the national tradition concerned suitable as a means of broadening the basis of the revolutionary state. In the resulting synthesis, acceptance of all elements of the national tradition that can be broadly interpreted as progressive in their times may fit strangely with sophisticated criticism of all those recent semi- and pseudo-revolutionary theories that happened to threaten the revolutionary party's internal coherence.

It is not necessary to give psychological explanations for the periodically reviving demand for more freedom[39] ; the very mechanics of social movements show the inevitability of certain characteristic features of utopian thought. When people go into action, they do so in order to get rid of certain restrictions that have become obsolete, they oppose certain social inequalities which can be rationally defended no longer, and they can succeed only if out of their isolation they unite in a fraternal group. Liberty and Equality, as conceived during a bourgeois-democratic revolution, must not necessarily include free access for all to the professions, nor must Fraternity apply to Negroes. But during the upheaval of a great social crisis Liberty, Equality and Fraternity are likely to involve the destruction of more features of society than those which have become intolerable and are likely to remain eliminated during the following period of stabilisation. The theorists of the revolutionary movement will go in advance of its minimum programme ; if they fail to do so, they fail in their most elementary function of leadership. Should there be an actual trend in human history towards the removal of restrictions and privilege the utopians of today will, for that period, be the prophets of tomorrow ; but nevertheless their ideology is utopian in that it does not correspond to other than ideological needs of today's movement, and cannot find immediate realisation. Its chances to prove prophetic are based not upon actual forecasts of observable trends and their further developments, but on the possibility that the same trend that brought some social formation into being will continue during the lifetime of its successor. For the origins of all utopias lies in the past : not, as some schools of utopians asserted, in past stages of society, but in the movements that brought the present social order into being and shaped its ideals.[57] In discussing utopias, the sociologist is not confronted with any difficulty in explaining their origin. They are available in every society, for they form abstract generalisations of its historical background. The genius of a Leonardo da Vinci or a Marx is needed in order to integrate and to develop existing knowledge into a system opposed to current generalisations ; and the contrasting results of the work of these two shows that mere genius is not a sufficient condition for the production of a theory relevant from the historian's point of view. But every monk who was sufficiently honest and brave could have developed the concept of Christian freedom into whatever utopia might bring inspiration to desperate peasants. Nor is it difficult for the anarchist with a lower-middle-class background to be " more radical " than Marxism ; for his roots are in those very currents of radical liberalism that brought into being *bourgeois* society, the overthrow of which Marxism tries to organise. His criticism may be inherent in so far as Marxism, for the reasons discussed, has itself absorbed much utopian thought ; obviously, much more of the liberal ideals can be realised in blueprints than in actual social life. But the test to which Marxism subjects itself is the test of practice, not of competing utopias.

Like the ideological trend in human thoughts, in Mannheim's[58] narrower sense, the utopian represents an intrusion of the element of will into the realm of knowledge. Thus it exceeds the limits of a rational explanation of the world which the observer can give within the conditions of his social surroundings. As distinct from an ideology, an utopia may prove right in the long run, but this is not due to its inherent merits. As distinct from the ideological outlook, not only the existence, but also the necessity of the utopian approach can be demonstrated by sociological analysis : to preserve a certain socio-economic

[57] See above, p. 74,   [58] l.c., pp. 36 and 84 ff.

framework, as long as it is viable, should be possible also without ideological falsifications ; but even the most obsolete society, if sufficiently entrenched in powerful interests, cannot be overthrown without the interference of the utopian element. From the pragmatist point of view the ideological, but not the utopian standpoint can be refuted. But this holds true only during the preparatory stage and up to the culmination of a revolutionary wave; from that moment onwards the utopia, because it transcends not only actual but also possible reality, is bound to serve as a mere pious hope, as an ideological explanation of the existing society, if not as a weapon of counter-revolutionary attack upon the actual results of the social transformation because they have failed to come up to the utopian standard. It is this mechanism that stood behind all the disputes between Stalinists and Trotskyists.

PART II

THE ANATOMY OF BOURGEOIS SOCIETY

CHAPTER V

THE MARXIST CONCEPT OF LAWS OF SOCIAL LIFE

(a) THE ROLE OF THE INDIVIDUAL AND THE CONCEPT OF SOCIOLOGICAL LAWS

Marx worked at a time when the concept of Laws of Nature appeared simple and uncontroversial. He regarded the social movement as " a natural process, guided by laws which are not merely independent of the will, the consciousness and the purposes of men but, conversely, determine their will, their consciousness and their purposes." [1] In our days, the concept of Laws of Nature has lost its simplicity ; some outstanding sociologists [2] are even inclined to describe the concept of causality as a residuum of theological thought. For our purposes, these general problems are irrelevant, whatever contribution the special analysis of sociological laws may make to their solution : for all practical purposes the existence of certain objective connections between natural events, accessible to scientific analysis, is obvious, and so also is the enormous progress which sociology would make if Marx's programme could be fulfilled. The only question relevant for us is whether it can be fulfilled, in view of the specific characteristics of Society as distinct from other parts of reality.

The concept of " blind laws of Nature, operating in Society " [3] appears contradicted by the way in which such laws can be realised by the actions of men who are conscious if not of what they are doing, then at least of what they intend to do. But the results of the actions of a multitude of agents impelled by a variety of motives seldom coinciding with those results, cannot be explained by their subjective intentions but only by objective

[1] Preface to the 2nd ed. of vol. I of *Capital*.

[2] Comp. H. Kelsen, *Society and Nature, A Sociological Inquiry*, International Library for Sociology and Social Reconstruction, London, 1947.

[3] Engels, *Anti-Duehring*, p. 307.

necessities which their actions realise, whilst they believe themselves to be acting freely.   In fact, they are only putting into
effect what they cannot prevent from being done.[4]   Engels'
argument appears atomistic, and somewhat obsolete as a result
of the fact that the society of Engels' day, composed of a multitude
of competing units of comparatively small size has been replaced
by what is called in terms of modern academic economics " imperfect competition," that is, by the interaction of units each of
which is important enough measurably to influence the result
by its actions.   In principle, however, the reactions of a powerful
trust to a price-cut by its only influential competitor need not
coincide with the latter's intentions any more than the outcome
of the action of a worker who undercuts his fellows' wages are
likely to coincide with his intentions.   The task of social science
is made more difficult because the law of large numbers cannot be
applied in the interaction of a restricted number of agents, and
differences of knowledge, skill and opportunity must be taken into
consideration.   But there is no reason to deny the existence of
objective causes, at odds with the subjective intentions of the
agents, in an " anarchic " as distinct from a planned society.   The
position would be different in a society which had accomplished
planning even on the international scale, to the extent that it had
succeeded in mastering Nature.

But to say that there are such things as laws of social life
does not imply that they can be found out.   In academic
economics[4a] the problem is usually avoided by accepting, as a
mere partial description of reality, a model in which men are
supposed to act exclusively according to economic motives
which are conceived in terms of an alleged typical and natural
order of society.   " Non-economic factors " such as tradition,
religious and moral attitudes, and even the State according to
orthodox Liberals, are described as interfering with the realisation
of the " laws " established by science.   This is simply another
way of stating that the coincidence of social reality with the laws
of Economics cannot safely be assumed.   Vulgarised Marxism
makes such an assumption by supposing that the majority of
men in their most important decisions are dominated by purely
economic motives, and that according to the laws of probability
the actions of the majority who conform with the model are

---

[4] *Ludwig Feuerbach*, etc., p. 58.

[4a] cf. V. Pareto, *Manuel d'Economie Politique*, chap. I, §§ 23–4.

bound to overwhelm those of the minority motivated by other factors, for instance by ideologies. The obvious shortcomings of such an attitude are mitigated by the fact that even vulgarised Marxism deals not with individual persons but with agglomerations of social power and with social institutions. It may be regarded as irrelevant whether heiresses actually marry to consolidate fortunes as long as we are merely interested in the fates of capitals, that is agglomerations of social power : capitals are more likely than not to be concentrated in the hands of people who behave in the " proper " way. But the value of first approximations arrived at in this way is greatly impaired by society's failure to comply, even in its " purely economic " structure, with the " pure models " of the academic as well as of the vulgar Marxist economists.[5] The behaviour of the peasantry in a typical continental European or Asiatic country, and all the " ideological superstructures " affecting the peasants' attitudes, cannot be explained as mere incomplete realisations of an alleged capitalist type of society ; in order to understand them, analysis must be made of the concrete society as a compound of various successive social formations the interaction of which, though dominated by the most important of them, must be studied as a whole in order to explain even as mass-phenomena the behaviour of its people. But the interpretation of a society as a compound of different social formations[6] presupposes the dynamic approach of Marxism to the social structure : only where the difference between successive types of structure is realised can their inter-connection and co-existence in national and international societies be analysed.

In orthodox, as distinct from vulgarised, Marxism a monist interpretation of social developments is sought not by questioning the efficiency of the " non-economic motives " but by investigating their origin and their ultimate dependence on Man's changing relations to Nature which involve changing relations between men.[7] Therefore, the objective determination of social events

---

[5] There is a difference in methodological approach between the former and the latter in that academic economists regard capitalist society as normal and "natural," whilst vulgar Marxists, while describing it merely as one of various successive types of society, confine themselves to the statement that all social relations are being assimilated to its typical structure.

[6] An impressive example of such an analysis of the different strata composing a certain national society has been given by Lenin in early 1918, in *Left-wing Childishness and Petty Bourgeois Mentality* (*Sel. Works*, vol. XII, p. 361), which was requoted by him in 1921-2 when introducing the N.E.P.

[7] See above, pp.45-6.

and their accessibility to scientific analysis do not depend upon
the extent to which the agents have been motivated by their
mutual relations in the socio-economic process either directly or
indirectly (say, through ideologies). But, however enormous
may be the difference from the standpoint of a philosophical
interpretation of the world, for the actual explanation of certain
social facts—say, in the law of inheritance—it matters little
whether some important factor is described as " inaccessible to
scientific investigation " or as " explicable as an ideological relic
of another social formation " which ceased to exist many centuries ago. The actual success of Marxist sociology in giving
more than a raw, statistical approximation to the explanation of a
given society thus depends on its ability to analyse the interaction
between the different historical strata by which the relations
existing in that society are conditioned. Failure of statistical
data to coincide with the forecasts of the analysis should always
be taken as a proof not of natural limitations of economics,
sociology, etc., but of the incompleteness of that analysis in
comparison with the theoretical demands of Marxist sociology.
Marxist sociology is thus far more ambitious than any other, and
the incentive to continuous research provided by the magnitude
of the task may compensate for the probable incompleteness of its
solutions.

(b) THE CHARACTERISTIC ABSTRACTIONS IN MARXIST SOCIOLOGY
    Every system of sociology, including the Marxist, presupposes
a certain model, a scheme of the social world as characterised
by certain typical relations between its members, so that certain
actions are bound to produce certain reactions. The task of
defining such relations, that is, of choosing those traits of complex
reality which should be neglected in constructing the model,
is most difficult for academic economists, apart from extremists
who regard even cartels and trade-unions as " disturbances of
the natural order."[8]   The Marxist model is more complicated :
amongst its economic elements it includes relations that belong

[8] The traditional liberal attitude of regarding State-influences as " extra-
economic " has been mitigated by the German " Katheder Socialists " who divided
Economics into a " purely economic " and a " policies of economics " part, without
evaluating discrimination. In the German Conservative concepts of " National
Economics " the State is regarded as the central agent whose purposes are realised by
free enterprise. Ultimately, such an approach leads to a fascist state-capitalism.
Apart from such extremes, neither approach is capable of providing a scientific
distinction which meets the characteristics as well as the common features of the
private and public agencies in the economic life of actual capitalist society.

not to the economic setting prevailing at the time but to assimilated relics of its predecessors, and conceivably also to growing elements of its successor. It is not restricted to "purely economic" relations,[8] but includes reactions in the political and ideological field : the enactment of a protective tariff or an imperialist war waged in order to open new fields of investments is just as legitimate an outcome of increased competition as, say, the formation of a monopolist cartel (which, in any case, could hardly operate unless supplemented by "non-economic" agencies such as political pressure exercised in order to establish protective tariffs and a state of *bourgeois* public opinion which reproaches the "spoiler of the markets" rather than extols him as a "champion of economic freedom"). Ultimately, the Marxist scheme of capitalism includes amongst the reactions to "purely economic" facts (such as reduction of wages, or permanent mass-unemployment) not only the formation of economic and political working-class organisations within its framework, but even revolutionary action aiming at its overthrow.

However broad, it is a scheme, a model based upon certain generalisations, and upon the omission of those elements of reality which are deemed as irrelevant for the purpose of the investigation. In Marx's classical analysis, as explained in his Preface to vol. I of *Capital*, in order to analyse capitalist society all local and national peculiarities of existing capitalist societies are neglected but the abstraction is carefully kept within such limits that the peculiarities of capitalist formations as distinct from others can be observed. Thus the pitfall of *bourgeois* economists who speak of "economics" in general can be avoided. For the more concrete purposes of historical analysis less far-going abstractions are needed ; and in the Marxist school of sociology as in any other the proper choice of abstractions[9] may form the starting point for fundamental cleavages.

Theoretical difficulties are met when generalisations valid at one level of abstraction are transferred to other levels characterised perhaps by the very fact that features of reality which were omitted when making those generalisations have been restored. The theory of value provides a most impressive example of this process. Its indisputable background has been

[9] For example, the preservation, or otherwise, of the assumption of a world-wide completely capitalist society. See Chapter XIII below, pp. 285-6 and 294 ff.

stated by Marx, in his letter to Kugelmann, of July 11, 1868 :

" Every child knows that a country which ceased to work, I will not say for a year but for a few weeks, would die. Every child knows, too, that the mass of products corresponding to the different needs require different and quantitatively determined masses of the total labour of society. That this necessity of distributing social labour in definite proportions cannot be done away with by the *particular form* of social production, but can only change the *form it assumes*, is self-evident . . . And the form in which this proportional division of labour operates, in a state of society where the interconnection of social labour is manifested in the *private exchange* of the individual products of labour is precisely the *exchange value*."

The " law of value " is thus (a) another expression of the materialist conception of History. It is " the economic expression for the facts of the social productive forces of labour as the basis of economic existence,"[10] and in this sense it is valid for all social formations. Happily it can be shown that (b) in a society composed of small producers of commodities who do not employ hired labour the prices of the different commodities tend to be proportionate to the labour needed for their production, so that " the law of value " (in another sense than that of (a)) governs average prices.[11]   From this it appears to follow that (c) the law, in the sense not only of (a), in which it is self-evident, but also at least in the sense of a modification of (b), " dominates economic events in a capitalist economic system " though even the average prices do not correspond any longer to the "values" of the exchanged commodities.   Marx was conscious of the difficulty of the task ; in the same letter to Kugelmann he wrote :

" The scientific task consists precisely in working out *how* the law of value operates.   So that if one wanted at the very beginning to explain all the phenomena which appararently contradict the law, one would have to give the science before the science.   It is precisely Ricardo's mistake that in his first chapter on value he takes as given all possible categories which have still to be developed, in order to prove their conformity with the law of value."

But Marx did not doubt that the task was solvable, and he believed he had actually solved it.[12]   Working from the fundamental importance of social labour as the factor dominating economic events Marx concluded that it must be possible to derive prices exclusively from this factor.   The fact that even

---

[10] Engels' Supplement to vol. III of *Capital* in *On Capital*, pp. 101 ff.

[11] Ibid., p. 99.

[12] See section (*f*) of the next Chapter.

great men occasionally make logical mistakes is not important
for us, but it is important that Marx derived laws valid for a
certain model from those valid in the model which was simpler
in structure and earlier in historical succession. Based upon an
original statement by Marx,[13] Engels[10] tried to demonstrate
how, with the growth of capitalist enterprise, values were
historically transformed into production prices. Transition
from one level of abstraction to another appears legitimate in so
far as it helps to analyse transition from one model of society
to another.

Within the Marxist system, " transformation of one model into
another " means something more than it would in an academic
conception of social evolution. Even those academic economists
who emancipated themselves from liberal metaphysics could
hardly interpret such a transformation more thoroughly than
by showing that the growth of monopolist elements in a system
originally based on free competition compelled the creation
of a new theoretical abstraction, that of imperfect competition,
which would provide a nearer approach to reality. As it seems
impossible to derive the growth of monopoly from the laws
governing the " free competition " model, that question would
have to be decided in an empirical-statistical way. Marxist
sociology is based upon the assumption of qualitative " leaps "
in the objective structure described by it, based upon the conception of each structure as an internally coherent system. For
example, in a society composed of feudal elements with an
admixture of small producers of commodities, the exploitation
of those producers by usury is conditioned by the prevailing,
feudal mode of production,[14] and conditions even those forms of
exploitation of dependent craftsmen, homeworkers, etc., which,
given a corresponding development of the whole social structure,
may eventually have capitalist implications. But as soon as the
capitalist mode of production can be said to predominate, its
pre-capitalist elements, such as land-rent,[15] have to be re-
interpreted as conditioned by its own inherent laws. This is no
mere theoretical scheme elaborated by the economist in order to
systematise the facts, but the reflection of an actual process
whereby one system of mutual conditioning of social relations is
replaced by another. Thus, to follow up our example, the law

[13] *Capital*, vol. III, pp. 206–7.
[14] Ibid., Chapter 36.   [15] Ibid., Chapter 47.

(a) prevailing in a feudal society that, in the long term, usurers and merchants cannot increase the exploitation of dependent craftsmen to such an extent that urban conditions cease to attract the average peasant who gets an opportunity to enter the lowest grades of town-life, is replaced by the law (b) that small craftsmen will not endure indirect exploitation beyond the point where their situation becomes worse than that of a skilled worker in a capitalist enterprise.[16]

(c) How far are scientific forecasts of social events possible?

The general sociological hypothesis of Marxism, and the laws governing social reactions within a given social model, do not differ fundamentally from the general hypotheses and the description of reactions within a certain model as applied in physics. It is true, that as soon as those reactions include organisational and political activities,[17] difficulties appear to originate from the fundamental difference between Nature and Society. However, experience has shown that the trend towards the formation of Trade Unions, the enactment of social legislation, tariffs, etc., is so strong in relation to the comparatively weak resistance to be overcome, that the initiative and personal qualities of the agents will hardly decide more than the pace at which the inherent needs of a capitalist society will be realised. But the position becomes very different as soon as we discuss transition from one model to another, especially the revolutionary mode of transition which in the view of Marxist sociology is fundamental. Analysis of a certain model of society may prove that conditions are bound to become intolerable for certain social strata and that events such as wars are likely to produce opportunities for overthrowing the existing pattern. Because of the close relation existing between radically democratic and revolutionary socialist movements,[18] it may even be possible, in some countries, to predict the existence of revolutionary organisations in sufficient strength to form a serious political factor. But in the present

[16] Under the theoretical assumption that economic decisions are motivated essentially by economic arguments, that is, in our case, that craftsmen would ascribe to their "independent" status no emotional value.

[17] Which is necessary for the understanding even of basic economic data. See below, pp. 115-6.

[18] See below, pp. 231 and 330-3.

stage of Marxist sociology it is simply impossible to predict the concrete shape which revolutionary opportunities will assume in different countries and the respective merits of the tactics of the defenders of the existing order and of the revolutionaries. In the event of the latters' defeat, it is again an open question whether such defeat will result in the establishment of a new model such as fascism. In such a case, additional investigation would be needed to consider whether the new model could be expected to overcome the existing contradictions and to survive for a longer period. On the other hand, total breakdown of the civilisation in question might result, as happened at the end of the Roman Empire, or else the existing order might linger on with revolutionary chances recurring at some later date. The last alternative is preferred by wishful-thinking Marxists, including the masters themselves. But there is no proof of its probability, even after the great transformation has already succeeded in part of the world and even if full allowance is made for the advantages accruing therefrom in the case of international conflicts: it is hardly possible to foretell the relationship of military power arising from such advantages and from some chance in the competition for the most efficient Atomic Bomb. As soon as we discuss not the broad issue of some kind of socialism in some part of the world but the prospects of concrete civilisations, it becomes impossible to give a scientific answer to the question, say, whether there will be a Western socialist civilisation, or conquest of the capitalist West by the socialist East, or a simple relapse into barbarism based on a fascist technique of social organisation which might conceivably be strong enough to discourage outside interference for some centuries to come.

However interesting this issue may be, it is not intended to try to answer it here, but it is discussed simply in order to illustrate the basic set of problems facing all " laws " governing social transformation when this transformation is no longer regarded as attainable by a multitude of individual actions following the laws of economics. It is possible to predict in the ordinary scientific way the transformation of a society of small producers of commodities into a capitalist one by the process of differentiation implied in commodity-exchange, and the rise of monopoly in consequence of the process of concentration of capital and of the increased competition implied in it ; but it is not possible to predict in the same way a socialist revolution, or even to answer the question whether after conquering power a socialist party will apply the necessary policies to transform the country's economy to enable it to withstand international conflicts.

Nor is the problem confined to large-scale social transformations involving the need for conscious political action. Marxism has grown as the development of the critical analysis of a society of competing private entrepreneurs, and involuntarily, some of the basic characteristics of that society have been included amongst the basic tenets of the theory. Within the general setting of such a society, the very mechanism of competition—notwithstanding delays imposed by the rise of partial monopolies—enforces continuous technical progress and a predominant tendency to apply new inventions. Unless the problem is seen within that general setting it would have been impossible to evolve the theoretical pattern of social relations and superstructures subject to permanent change in consequence of the changes in the independent variable, the productive forces of society. But every student of pre-history or ancient history is familiar with the phenomenon of civilisations stagnant for very long periods ; and most students of the subject would be inclined to regard the very phenomenon of a changing society and the underlying speed of changes in social technique as exceptional and demanding special explanation. Only a very primitive generalisation of conditions prevailing in a modern market-society allows for the simple explanation that some impulse to permanent improvement of technique may be taken for granted because Man's mastery of Nature is never—certainly not in primitive societies—sufficient to satisfy all his needs. The satisfaction of human needs may be attempted by irrational methods, such as magic, the predominance of which may be backed by the whole existing superstructure of society. The basic needs, whose satisfaction by technical progress might cause society to advance, may be experienced in those sections of the social structure where the material and moral conditions of technical improvement are absent, as in the case of the Egyptian fellahim ; in contrast, the ruling class, apart from being dominated by, and dominating by means of, the magical approach, can have their needs satisfied by raising the artistic level of existing handicrafts, a contrivance unlikely to result in any changes of social relations. Technical inventions may fail to coincide with social conditions that allow for their application. We know by historical chance a good deal about the outbreak of naturalist art in the reign of Ekhnaton, which was soon to be suppressed by the forces of ideological reaction. We are forced to conclude that it was impossible for an artistic tradition of that strength, in direct contradiction to the predominant trend hitherto encouraged by all the ruling forces of society, to develop within one or two decades. There must have been many attempts which were broken by external forces of which we know nothing except that we must assume their existence. What actually happened in the technical field during the three millenia of the existence of the most familiar example of a " stagnant " civilisation ? Supporters of " economic materialism " may assert that an " undesirable " artistic trend may be suppressed because of religious and similar prejudices, but that " ideology " ceases to be efficient when confronted with material needs. But the members of the Egyptian ruling classes did not need to compete for increasing profits, and it was not they who felt the material needs in their bellies. The much discussed influence of Protestantism on the evolution of capitalist society should not be exaggerated in the field of science with which we here are concerned (Galileo was a Catholic, and the Kopernican theory was opposed by Protestant as well as by Catholic fundamentalism) ; but it is indisputable that to a large extent the decision as to whether certain technical progress will be made, and especially whether it will be applied and create conditions for its further evolution, depends upon ideological struggles. Only in modern capitalist society, and in the transition to socialism the very survival of which would be threatened by backwardness in international technical competition, is it possible to assert that such ideological struggles are likely to be decided by an overwhelming social interest in technical progress. But even such likelihood is certainly no guarantee that, say, the reluctance of Trotskyists to burden the Russian working-class with the economic sacrifices needed to finance industrialisation would be overcome just in time to win the battle of Stalingrad.

The " laws " governing social transformations of a very critical character[19] whose success or failure is decided in a certain historical moment, cannot be expressed in a form more precise than " unless transformation A takes place at a certain

---

[19] Leontiev (l.c., pp. 516–7) speaks of a "law" of industrialisation and collectivisation governing Soviet policies in the late 'twenties and early 'thirties.

time, the event B (involving the destruction of a certain social system C) is bound to take place," or " transformation A is a condition for the survival of system C." This is the pattern say, of the Darwinist theory, or of cosmological theories analogous in their structure. Actually, it is the only pattern by which teleology in Nature can be explained in a scientific way ; and this very analogy of social events demanding maximum insight and activity of the agents with " blind " Nature should be sufficient to demonstrate that " laws " of such a structure are not irrelevant from the scientific point of view. But there is a difference caused by the comparative singularity and complexity of the event needed for survival, as distinct from simpler social actions the occurrence of which can be taken for granted, like the occurrence of mutations amongst which the law of Selection may operate in Darwinism. It is conceivable that from the point of view of a larger historical perspective the survival of distinct political regimes is irrelevant if we deem that only basic social structures matter : for a regime will only survive on condition it takes over, if necessary from its defeated foes, those attitudes that formed a necessary condition for survival. It is unlikely that regimes that cannot grant full employment will survive this century ; and Marxist economists may deem that, in the long run, the differences between regimes that can, in the long term, prevent unemployment are likely to be restricted to differences of State-ideology and such peculiarities as divide the bourgeois-democratic states at present. However, Marxists regard revolutions at least as the " locomotives of history " ; and it is difficult to say how they could exercise their impact if derailed a few years after their start, when the elemental mass-movements, which during those years considerably reduced the significance of skill and leadership, have receded.

CHAPTER VI

THE MARXIST THEORY OF VALUE

(a) The background and meaning of the theory

In order properly to assess the position of the labour theory of value within the Marxist system one must realise the connection in which it arose. Marxist sociology and the foundations of Marxist politics [1] were completed before Marx made any contribution to economic thought apart from his turning the accepted classical conception of value against the lower-middle-class utopians who complained of the workers being betrayed because they got only part of the value they created. [2] *The Poverty of Philosophy* written in 1847, is a Ricardian book, even including the derivation of surplus-value which is a mere consistent elaboration of Ricardian ideas. In the economics of the book, Marx differs from the master mainly in that he conceives as characteristic of a specific and transitory form of socio-economic organisation what Ricardo had regarded as inevitable though deplorable features of the only conceivable form of developed economic life. The original contributions made by Marx, in a later stage of his development, to classical economic theory should, in the analysis of his own sociological theory, be regarded as attempts at verification in a sense similar to that in which inventors of abstract physical theories look for implications which might be accessible to verification by the fact that they explain phenomena in a better way than previously accepted theories have done, or else they help to resolve contradictions in which the former theories had been involved. In some instances, such a quest for verification fulfils the purpose intended, while in others it leads into new difficulties which hint at the limitations of the new theory. But quite a number of attempts at verification simply fail in that it proves impossible to derive certain implications of

---

[1] With a few exceptions, amongst which further elaboration of the theory of the State (see below, pp. 393–4) may be of less permanent importance than the forecast of the " first stage of communist society " in the *Critique of the Gotha programme* (see below, p. 355) and the tentative approaches to a more general theory including revolutionary transformations of other than typical capitalist countries (see below, pp. 206–7). Neither of them can be regarded as dependent on the details of Marx's economic analysis as elaborated in *Capital*.

[2] See below, pp. 122–3.

the basic theory with such concreteness that confrontation with the facts would result in unequivocal confirmation or refutation. Marx's concept of value should be interpreted in the historical connection in which it was found by the authors of the Marxist theory and the new meaning which it assumed in their work.

Three basic, and very different, conceptions of value were available to Marx and played their part in the direction of his work, though his contribution was devoted to the elaboration of the third.

(1) Since the days of St. Thomas Aquinas the small producers of commodities, and the workers still dominated by a lower-middle-class outlook whom Marx found represented by Proudhon, had complained of not getting their due in commodity exchange, in that the labour applied in their work was not compensated for by the labour represented by the commodities they got in exchange. Marxists would conclude from the very existence of such a widespread complaint that (a) in a past stage of society there was actually a tendency of commodities to be exchanged in proportion to the respective amounts of labour needed for their production, and (b) that that stage of society definitely belonged to the past, though the complaints showed that there was still some reluctance to see its disintegration.

(2) Classical economics culminated in the attempt to explain actual fluctuations of prices by " the law of value," that is, by the amount of labour which was needed in order to reproduce those commodities, independently of the individual producer's skill and conceptions of Justice.

(3) Marx's own contribution, which found its clearest expression in *Capital*, vol. 1, Chapter I, section 4, centred round the dissolution of what he called " the fetishistic character of commodities," that is, the current delusion that the specific aspect assumed by the interconnection of the members of the society in a certain historical stage was in fact a natural condition of economic life.

In order properly to assess that contribution one must realise that the classical pre-Marxist economists (as distinct from their non-Marxist successors, who were reproached by Marx as " vulgar economists " on this count) when dealing with economics had always intended to deal with the life of *society*. For all of them " the wealth of nations " was the true subject of study. It had been described by the Physiocrats as natural riches appropriated by human toil, with emphasis shifting from the first to the second element of the definition in the development from Quesnay to Turgot, thus expressing at first the reaction against Colbert's mercantilist policies and the disappointment caused by Law's monetary experiments, and later expressing more of the issues of the coming revolution.[3] Adam Smith, the advocate of the incipient Industrial Revolution, had rather supplemented than refuted the Physiocrats by establishing that human labour, wherever applied, created wealth. Ricardo had carried the argument to its full implications when stating that natural riches, however necessary for the application of some special kinds of human labour, were important for the specific subject of economics only if their scarcity allowed those in control of them to appropriate parts of the product of labour. Thus the distribution of the product of social labour appears as the true subject of economics. This statement is essentially a definition. But in order to prove its relevance it is sufficient to show that in the economic life of modern humanity absolute scarcity of natural resources (as distinct from their different qualities which is taken into account by the theory of Differential Rent) plays a part subordinate[4] to that of labour as the basic cost element dominating the supply

[3] Comp. *Theories on Surplus Value*, vol. I, pp. 41 ff., where the theories of the Physiocrats, especially of Turgot, are interpreted as the ideology of capitalism penetrating feudal society. The physiocrats explained surplus value as appropriation of the product of other people's toil on the basis of the exchange of commodities; but, with them, value was mere useful matter, and surplus value a creation of Nature. As distinct from later economists the physiocrats clearly recognised the class origin of rent; but Marx, who could not know later bourgeois economists, described their derivation of surplus value, and thereby class, from Nature as "feudalist." Actually, the whole argument from section 82 of Turgot's main work onwards is based upon the assumption that accumulation of wealth takes place wherever human labour is applied under conditions that prevent the toiler from consuming his whole output, or from restricting his toil to what is needed in order to satisfy his personal needs. The priority of agriculture is simply based on the fact that the landlord's unearned income is the most conspicuous one. Turgot suggested taxing it merely in order to get the wealth at its source.

[4] As distinct from Ricardo, who was satisfied with stating the obvious predominance of the cost element of labour in comparison with such commodities (say works of art) whose supply is dominated by the element of scarcity, Marx (*Capital*, vol. 1 p. 7) actually attempted a monist interpretation in such difficult cases as those of diamonds. In such cases the element of hazard involved and the chance of winning a great price may actually induce the average worker—or searcher—to be satisfied with a rather under-average remuneration of his labour, whilst the hope of proving one of the few elect may induce the average artist (and even some over-average, whose success comes only after their death) to work for a remuneration much inferior to what could be earned in other fields with similar skill. Such "proofs" of the theory of value are mere truisms, implied in the very definition of the subject of economics, and even misleading because they extend to fields where the purely economic approach ceases to be relevant.

of goods in any social system ; and this basic statement, which is to be found in the first section of the first Chapter of Ricardo's *Principles*, has even been assimilated by Marshall to the modern system of academic economics. If consistently applied, it is incompatible with any " economic " theory that leaves out the fundamental subject of economics, i.e., society, by dealing with Robinson Crusoe's experiences. Strange as it might have sounded to Marshall's ears, it invites even Bukharin's description of the Viennese (" Marginal Utility ") school of economists as dealing with " the rentier's economics " because it starts from the consumer's choice between goods supposed to be characterised by scarcity, independently of their origin in production. Marx's definition of the basis of social life : " In the social process of producing their means of subsistence, men enter certain social relations, relations of production " is his definition of the subject of economics, and the Marxist theory of value is a mere implication of that definition.

If economics is defined as the material relations existing between men working for each other, the amount of work done for each other is the basic economic fact linking them, and any other economic fact has to be derived from it.

(b) EXPLOITATION OF LABOUR

Physiocrat thought had set out from the feudal system, but resulted in the description of the wealth of nations as the sum total of all capitals actually employed in order to appropriate rent, that is, unearned income, either directly on the land, or indirectly from the toil of industrial labourers whose employers made profits by selling their product to landlords who in their turn paid for the products from their rent income.[5] Adam Smith's main work opens with the statement that " the annual labour of a nation is the fund which originally supplies it with all the necessities and conveniences of life which it annually consumes." The father of classical economics, like Petty before, and Marx[6] after him, took it for granted that wealth, in its natural form, is as much the product of Nature as of Labour and that human labour creates no value unless applied for the production of useful things, the utility of which is a preliminary condition of

[5] cf. Turgot, op. cit., section 90.

[6] See the polemic in the introductory paragraph of the *Critique of the Gotha Programme* against the vulgarisation according to which labour is the sole source of all wealth. Marx there remarked that labour itself in that aspect in which it creates use-values " is merely the manifestation of a natural force, human labour power."

their being sold on the market.[7] Even for the most orthodox academic economist, when dealing with the actual transformations in the economic life of a nation, say, in war-time, there is no other way of analysing the economic life of *society* (as distinct from Robinson Crusoe's experiences, or Messrs. Woolworth & Co.'s struggle to win custom from Messrs. Marks & Spencer) than by starting from the study of the use made of its labour force. In social analysis it is impossible to refute the statement in Adam Smith's *Wealth of Nations*, Book 1, Chapter 6, that capitalist entrepreneurs make their profits by the sale of what the workers' labour adds to the value of the materials, and that the value which the workers add to the value of the materials resolves itself into two parts, of which the one pays their wages, the other the profits of their employer upon the whole stock of material and wages which he had advanced.[8] Once economics are defined as the study of the distribution of social labour and its product, it follows that unearned incomes are derived from other people's efforts.

We have just used Adam Smith's term " value," but only as a substitute for " element of the national wealth, created by the efforts of the working members of the society," that is, as a definition of the subject of economics. We have seen how it evolved from the Physiocrats' and Adam Smith's query as to the essence of the wealth of nations. It could be preserved when Ricardo[9] moved the emphasis to the distribution of that social product between the different classes of society, and when Marx turned to the analysis of the laws of motion dominating the changing relations between those classes. From the point of view of this fundamental analysis it is irrelevant whether the assumed substance of economic relations (that is to say, the chosen abstraction) is sufficient to explain the actual levels of prices, the circumstances of the individual entrepreneur, or even a branch of industry (as Ricardo and Marx believed). The derivation of exploitation in this way is implied in the choice of an approach to the study of a class-divided society where there are unearned incomes. It does not prove anything as regards the necessity

---

[7] This statement by Ricardo has been recognised by Marshall (*Principles of Economy*, 8th ed., Annex, p. 814) as a valuable restriction of the " one-sidedness " as allegedly developed by Marx. Marshall evidently failed to take notice of the first pages of *Capital*, where it is broadly elaborated, and of Marx's *Contribution to the Critique of Political Economy* (p. 21) where it is verbally re-stated.

[8] *Wealth of Nations*, ed. McCulloch, pp. 22–3.

[9] *Letters to Malthus*, ed. 1881, p. 175.

or otherwise of such a condition. No society can exist unless some provision is made for certain social needs beyond the maintenance of its working members. Concentration of what Marx called the surplus-product in the hands of a class of individual entrepreneurs (as, before, it had been concentrated in the hands of a class of feudal landlords and their merchant supporters) is, *prima facie*, one of the possible ways of making such provision. In the days of the classical economists it was obvious that the productivity of labour, and thus the wealth of nations, had made greater advances when controlled by a class of private entrepreneurs than at any time before. Exploitation of the human labour force had, with them, just the same meaning as the exploitation of any other national resources[10] ; it was rational, even from the point of view of the exploited, when it made for maximizing investment and thus the available productive resources. It was irrational, in the eyes of Ricardo and his consistent successors, when the exploitation was done by a merely parasitic landlord class. But the contested issue was that between landlords and capitalists, not the fact of exploitation itself, that is, the very existence of unearned incomes ; this latter fact seemed to have been given, ever since the days of the Physiocrats[11] because of the assumed tendency of wages to oscillate about the subsistence minimum which later, refined by Malthusian additions, has been called " the iron law of wages."

Only in the post-Ricardian period, when the very necessity of unearned incomes was questioned, could the statement of their existence in terms of " exploitation " be regarded as an argument in favour of their abolition. This was done by popular socialist propaganda[12] as well as by the bourgeois economists who believed they were defending the holy of holies when " refuting " the labour theory of value. But even if we should accept a definition of the subject of economics which includes scarcity of natural

[10] cf. Smith's equalisation of the productive activities of men with those of cattle, *Wealth of Nations*, Book II, Chapter 5 (p. 161 in the ed. by McCulloch, 1863). There is no reason to approach such equalisations from any moralist standpoint ; human labour, if not clearly analysed as a social as distinct from a physical fact, is certainly a force of Nature like any other one. It is simply inconsistent for people who complain of the " one-sidedness " of the labour theory of value, that is to say, who are incapable of understanding labour as something different from a natural agency which creates wealth alongside with others, to complain of its being regarded "as a mere commodity." There are also Societies for the Protection of our Dumb Friends ; but the moral aspect of the labour problem is precisely based upon a social, as distinct from a technological, concept of labour.   [11] Turgot, op. cit., section 6.
[12] Which, on its part, influenced the bulk of academic socialism in this country, including even G. D. H. Cole's *Introduction to Capital*, written in 1929.

MARXIST THEORY OF VALUE

resources, this would not be proof that the control of natural resources by a certain group in a given state of society is legitimate and socially useful.   Count de Mirabeau, that enthusiastic pupil of the Physiocrats, was to experience this to his great discomfort through the actions of other pupils of the Physiocrats.   So also Senior, Boehm-Bawerk and many other prophets of a not very original theory[13] spent much effort in vain when they tried to prove the legitimacy of interest by the obvious fact that a certain amount of labour, first spent on the production of labour-saving devices, results in a larger quantity of useful things than when spent on their immediate production.[14]   Unless this were true, there would be no labour-saving devices ; but it is impossible to prove by such a truism that certain individuals should control such devices and exact tribute through them.   In a capitalist society, as in any other, there must be some incentive to invest ; but only a sophist could argue that of necessity this incentive must be a recompense for those individuals who by virtue of their position in the established order of production[15] order others to " abstain " from satisfying their immediate needs ; and even less ingenious a critic than Marx might have answered this argument by the proposition that " the dictates of simple humanity obviously make it incumbent upon us to release the capitalist from his state of martyrdom and temptation."[16]   On the other hand, only the demagogue who asserts the worker's rights to " the undiminished proceeds of labour "[6] can conclude that capitalism should be overthrown from the mere fact that, in a society organised by capitalists, it is they who dispose of the surplus value.   Marx was well aware of the fact that a socialist society would be bound to fail unless it was prepared to invest and to defend itself, and that the main merits of socialism were likely to be found in its capacity to increase cultural expenditure

[13] Comp. Turgot, op. cit., sections 74 and 80/1.   It is true, the classics were not so naïve that they believed they had justified capitalism when they stated how it works.

[14] Besides, the argument presupposes the classical concept of " value," that is, of the subject of economics.   Otherwise it would be impossible to establish in a society based upon full division of labour the identity of the labour withheld from the production of means of consumption with that directed into the production of additional means of production.

[15] The decision whether and how to invest is in every society likely to lie with the individuals responsible for its management who are not likely to be the main sufferers under the austerity needed in order to make possible additional investments, as long as austerity and differentiation of income are needed at all.   But those who organise Five-Year Plans are not remunerated in inverse proportion to the austerity involved ; quite the other way, they are expected to conform with ideological standards shaped by the needs of austerity.

[16] *Capital*, vol. I, p. 609.   The point has been made as early as 1817 by John Craig.

and other kinds of social consumption. Consequently he directed the edge of his criticism of the Gotha programme against that very kind of " socialist " demagogy. The need for overthrowing capitalism can be derived only from the demerits of capitalist administration of economics—including the way in which the consumable part of the " surplus value " is distributed in comparison with other possible alternatives ; and the founders of Marxism were quite conscious of the need to direct the criticism of capitalist society against the anarchy and inadequacy of capitalist production rather than against the inherent " injustice " of the distribution of the social income.[17] Capitalism as a mode of production has to be abolished not because a few actual parasites consume goods which, if distributed differently, might raise mass-consumption by the—very small—percentage of the national income which, at present, is consumed by the capitalists, but because it results in waste of productive resources, wars, and unemployment. Its abolition is possible, because capitalism is bound to develop a method of management the quality of which is hardly improved by the profit incentive, because it is not the actual managers who receive those profits. The strength of the Marxist argument for socialism lay in its capacity to foretell such developments long before they took place. We may have strong suspicions that the founders, children of their time, took too many things for granted and burdened their argument with assumptions on the theory of prices which were current in their days but unnecessary for the argument itself. But we should not drop the argument as unnecessary because in our days non-Marxists, if not engaged in the apologetics of orthodox academic economics, can recognise many facts predicted by Marx and draw from them inferences as to the need for social change, although they do not accept the Marxist methodology which enabled those facts to be forecast. What appears essential to me in this methodology is the definition of the subject of economics contained in the so-called theory of value and the dynamic approach to it.[18]

(c) THE MARXIST THEORY OF CAPITALIST DEVELOPMENT.

The fundamental Marxist tenets about the trend of capitalist development are based on a few fairly safe assumptions : (1) The

---

[17] Engels' preface to *The Poverty of Philosophy*, ed. cit., p. 11.

[18] For this reason, I regard the concluding demand put forward in Joan Robinson's *Essay on Marxist Economics* for " using academic methods to solve the problems posed by Marx " as a contradiction in terms.

distribution of social labour between the various industries represents the basic relation existing between the members of a society based upon commodity exchange. (2) The various products of human labour are exchanged against each other at rates (prices) which tend to an equilibrium state which can be defined as a function of (though it is not necessarily proportionate to) the average productivity of labour applied in the different spheres of production. (3) Competition puts a premium upon application of above-average means of production, and threatens with destitution the producer who does not succeed in keeping pace. The first of those assumptions is identical with the definition of the subject of economics, and is backed by the consideration that changes in the technique and productivity of human labour are a much more promising subject for investigating the trends in history than alleged changes in the scarcity of diamonds or artistic qualifications.[19] It does *not* imply the assumption that this basic relation is the only one affecting prices. Nor is the second assumption dependent upon the derivation of the function in a way satisfactory from the economic and mathematical point of view[20]; no more need be assumed than the fact, admitted as much by Marshall as by Marxists, that the long-term trends of prices are dominated by costs, and that labour is by far the most important element of costs. The third assumption as to the functions of competition may be regarded as a truism to such an extent that even in those few cases where it does not hold true (delay of technical progress by established monopolies) the exceptions to it are an additional reproach to the working of monopoly-capitalism, and do not throw doubt upon the way in which monopoly-capitalism has grown.

Once we take those three assumptions for granted, it follows from elementary data :

(1) Because, in general, labour is more productive if applied on a larger scale of organisation, and even more so if expensive means of production are applied, every economic differentiation amongst the producers of commodities as well as any accumulation of wealth existing in pre-capitalist society[21] tends to be applied for the purpose of commanding the labour of others

[19] See above, p. 105.   [20] See below, pp. 136 ff.

[21] The transformation of such pre-capitalist positions of social rule into capitalist ones, namely, the transformation of feudal tenants into landless proletarians, is the essence of what Marx called the " primary accumulation."

in order to increase the amount of wealth applied in their employment by creating additional exchange-values. Wealth applied in this way is defined as capital, a distinct social relation. Capital is power to command wage labour : ownership of means of production (or titles to it) is the mere institutional form in which such command is exercised.

(2) Once capital has become a predominant factor in the economic life of society, because of the greater productivity of the labour applied by it, it tends to eliminate the pre-capitalist elements in such a society, or to integrate them as subordinate links into its machinery ; whilst amongst the competing units of capital the largest and therefore, as a rule, most efficient are bound to absorb and to eliminate the smaller ones. Hence the maximisation of profits (by reducing the costs of labour to the necessary minimum) and the re-investment of large parts of the profits made, are necessary conditions for the survival of economic units of capital as such. Marxism does not bother about issues such as remuneration for " waiting," as Marshall does, or " deferred enjoyment," as Boehm-Bawerk has called it, which the former requires as necessary in order to prevent capitalists from consuming their capital (which only individual capitalists can do, as edible railways and furnaces have still to be discovered). In a capitalist society, owning capital is synonymous with social power and social status. Capitalists will refrain from investments involving loss, or a rate of profit lower than that current ; but, apart from individuals who thereby leave the active capitalist class, they will continue to invest at any socially given rate of profits. The " tendential fall of the rate of profits," which was assumed by Marx as by his *bourgeois* contemporaries, may be relevant for the explanation of the industrial cycle, in so far as former expectations of profits are embodied in conditions of credit which involve bankruptcy of individual entrepreneurs if profits fall and in so far as, with a reduced rate of profits, small entrepreneurs for whom the smaller rate is not compensated for by the size of their capitals are thrown out of the running[22] ; but, from the Marxist point of view, it is completely mistaken to derive from that tendency forecasts as to a dying away of the capitalist system as long as it is capable of making and investing profits.[23]

(3) As, under modern conditions, technical progress means

[22] See below, pp. 167 and 189.   [23] But see below, pp. 189-90.

replacement of directly applied human labour by labour-saving devices, the demand for wage-labour per unit of the total capital applied is bound to decrease. There will be, in the long run, unemployment of workers " set free " by technical progress, apart from those " set free " by the replacement of labour-expensive pre-capitalist production by the output of capitalist industry. This "industrial reserve army" forms a very condition of the periodical quick expansion needed in order to assimilate new techniques ; it also enables wages to be kept down at a level allowing for profits, and it enforces the necessary discipline by the alternative of starvation. Thus the prosperity of a capitalist society is rendered compatible with that " freedom " which is theoretically granted to its members, including the wage-earners, namely, the absence of other than economic sanctions against behaviour incompatible with its basic needs.

These fundamental tenets are supported by the historical evidence available, though there is no lack of facts that allow for apparent escapes. The progress of social differentiation asserted by Marx may appear to be refuted by destitute peasants preferring to cling at any price to their glebe rather than to face the fate they anticipate in the towns,[24] by increase in the number of " independent " craftsmen doing " service " for the customers of some large-scale producer of wireless-sets or motorcars, by increase in the number of salaried employees, or even simply by increasing efforts of the ruling class to spread a lower-middle-class attitude amongst the workers. Wishful thinking may accept as a refutation of the predicted centralisation of capitals any success achieved by trust-magnates in mobilising the people's savings (and influencing the ideological attitude of their employees) by mass-holding of shares. The necessity of an " industrial reserve army " for capitalist prosperity may appear refuted in the leading capitalist countries by the " export of unemployment " and by the concentration elsewhere of much of the misery and destitution connected with the " setting free " of " superfluous " people. These modifications are not insignificant for they condition the replacement of the simple concept of class-struggle as being sufficiently characterized by the pattern employers versus wage-earners by the more complicated one we are to study in Part IV of this book ; but the more historical

---

[24] As Marx himself had envisaged in the 47th Chapter (section 5) of vol. III of *Capital.*

experience enables us to see the concrete forms in which Marx's basic prognoses are fulfilled, even though less simple in appearance than he foresaw, the more we are bound to see in his analysis more than a clever generalisation of the conditions prevailing during the first stage of capitalist development.

Marx's theses on the character and trend of capitalism were expressed in terms of the classical system of economics by developing the latter into an elaborate system of concepts and definitions. The interconnection existing between the members of a society of commodity-producers, which was assumed by the classics to be also the standard of long-term equilibrium-prices[25] is defined as *value* of the commodities produced. It is measured by the amount of human labour necessary to produce the respective commodities under average social conditions (so that producers with very advanced productivity of labour realise an extra profit, whilst the most backward ones are eliminated by continuous losses). The human labour creating values is defined as " productive expenditure of human brains, nerves and muscles."[26] Such a materialistic definition creates theoretical difficulties when productive labour of very varied kinds has to be compared : the labour of an engineer, whom Marx did not hesitate to regard as productive, in its physical aspects has little in common with that of the dock-worker, whatever yard-stick may be applied : what it has in common is the fact that it consumes the energies of one member of human society theoretically equalised with any other, as Marx himself has shown in his polemic against Aristotle.[27] But Marx deemed the definition necessary in order to account for the phenomena of lengthening and intensifying hours of work, which involve a larger expenditure of physical strength by the members of society concerned.

Profits in the broadest sense of the word, which includes interest, rent, and other deductions from the output exceeding the actual producers' requirements, such as the expenses of the State machine, etc., are conditioned by the fact that the productivity of labour exceeds what is necessary for the keep of the part of the population actually engaged in production. This basic condition is characteristic not only of capitalism, but of every society based upon exploitation of labour, and will continue also in a socialist society as the latter has to provide for various

[25] On the Marxist modification of that concept, see below, pp. 132 ff.
[26] *Capital*, vol. I, p. 11.   [27] Ibid., p. 29.

communal needs as well as for expansion of production.[28] But capitalist society is distinguished from its predecessors as well as from its successor by the fact that human labour power, (that is, " those mental and physical capacities existing in a human being which he exercises whenever he produces a use-value of any kind,"[29]) is purchased as a commodity on the market. Under equilibrium conditions, the price of this, like that of every other commodity, is supposed to cover its reproduction costs—in this case, the standard of life needed in the given social condition to preserve the workers' labour-power and to enable them to raise children who in due course will replace them on the labour market. The value, that is, equilibrium price, of labour power is not identical with the physical subsistence-costs, as in pre-Marxist classical (and later in Lassallean) economics,[30] but, in contra-distinction to the values of other commodities, contains a historical and moral element[31]; the results of the past class-struggle, that is, the conceptions of the workers as to what standard of life is adequate and what kind of life makes the raising of children worth while, are part of the setting from which every new wages dispute has to start. Only if Marxism is wrongly interpreted as a " purely economic " theory analogous to the academic system does it follow that such an interpretation would reduce Marx's argument to circularity, by deriving the value of labour power from the actually observed level of real wages.[32] But an interpretation of the data of Marxist sociology as purely economic is mistaken. The value of labour-power, the rate of exploitation, etc., cannot be defined as determined independently of the existence and efficiency of Trade Unions, etc.[33]; what can be demanded from Marxism, according to its own standards,[34] is the deduction of the basic conditions for

---

[28] Ibid., vol. III, p. 953.   [29] Ibid., vol. I, p. 145.

[30] See above, p. 108.

[31] *Capital*, vol. I, p. 150. See also *Value, Price, and Profit*, in *Sel. Works*, vol. I, p. 333.

[32] Joan Robinson, l.c., p. 30. It should be noted that Mrs. Robinson's argument can be made only as regards a long-term average of real wages; some time would have to pass before some improvement (or deterioration) of working-class standards of life would enter the conditions for the future supply of labour power. It is no mere circular argument to state that the conditions of reproduction to which the working-classes have been accustomed form the starting point for every new wages bargain.

[33] This recognition of the importance of Trade Unions formed one of the main dividing lines between Marxism and Lassalleanism, and one of the main reasons for the split in the German Labour movement in the late 'sixties and early 'seventies.

[34] See above, p. 95.

political, organisational, etc., action from economic developments. The "historical and moral element" in the definition of the value of labour-power, that is, the objective chances for improving the conditions under which labour power will be supplied, are derived from the general analysis of the historical trends of capitalism : on the one hand the concentration of enterprises involves favourable conditions for the organisation of labour, on the other the concept of the industrial reserve-army explains the difficulties to be overcome by Trade Unionism.

The surplus-product which exists in every society except the most primitive[28] assumes in capitalist society the shape of *surplus-value*, that is, excess of the *value* created by the application of the labour power over its own value. As only living labour creates values, only that part of the capital applied by entrepreneurs which is expended in wages, that is, in purchase of labour power, is immediately increased in value by its application : therefore it is called *variable capital*, as distinct from the *constant capital* (expended for machinery and other fixed capital as well as for raw-materials, etc.) which, however necessary as a condition for the exploitation of the labour power, merely transfers its own value to that of the finished product to the extent to which it had to be consumed in the production process. The distinction is inessential for the individual capitalist, because he expects the usual average profit on all the capital which he has expended ; but it is essential for the relations between capitalists and workers as social classes ; under equilibrium conditions, the outcome of the bargaining between capitalists and workers determines their respective share in the social product and thus the general rate of profits, whilst the purchase of elements of constant capital merely secures to the capitalists who have produced them the return of their expenditure plus the given rate of profits. The proportion between surplus-labour and necessary labour, that is, between that part of the labour effort creating surplus-value and that needed to reproduce the requirements of the workers, is called the *rate of exploitation* of labour (or *rate of surplus-value*). For society as a whole it is identical with the proportion existing between the sum totals of unearned incomes and of wages respectively. But in the individual enterprise, the rate of exploitation, in Marx's sense,[35] is a purely theoretical abstraction ; though in equilibrium conditions, the amount of wages expenditure tends to be proportionate to the " necessary labour " applied, only in exceptional cases are the profits realised by the enterprise proportionate to the " surplus-labour " (that is, the contribution to the national pool of profits from which all unearned incomes are derived) carried out in the respective enterprise.[25] What matters for equilibrium conditions of the individual enterprise, or industry, is the socially established average *rate of profit*, that is, the proportion between the total national surplus value and the total national capital (including constant capital) : for there will be no equilibrium unless capitalists make equal profits on equal capital expenditure, whether in wages or in elements of constant capital.

The amount of social labour available as a source of capitalist profits may increase either because, in consequence of a rise in the productivity of labour, a smaller part of the average working day is needed for the reproduction of the worker's requirements, or because the amount of labour-power, in the sense defined above, supplied by the individual worker for a given real wage has increased. Additional surplus-value, in comparison with the former level, achieved in the former way is described as *relative surplus-value* because, within the time of a given labour-day, its division between paid and unpaid labour has changed. In contrast, *absolute surplus-value* is created when for certain real wages longer hours or more intensive work are demanded— the latter being the normal procedure once prolongation of hours and demand for labour from additional members of the

[35] Of course, it is possible to define other "rates of exploitation," for example, the proportion between profits made, and wages expended in, an individual enterprise or industry. For the reasons explained below, pp. 133-4, it is likely not to correspond to Marx's "rate of exploitation" but to express, apart from it, a factor which is irrelevant at this stage of the argument, namely, the proportionate share of wages in the total capital outlay of the respective enterprises. Therefore there is no sense in comparison of such "rates of exploitation" between different industries ; they are bound to differ just when there is equilibrium as to the rate of profits realised by capitals with different proportions of constant to variable capital, and also as to the remuneration paid for comparable labour-efforts. The "rate of exploitation," in the sense discussed, may be better called a " rate of appropriation " in the sense of the basic Marxist tenet that profits made in the individual industries originate from the exploitation of the whole working-class by the whole bourgeoisie, but are appropriated by the individual capitalists in proportion to their share in the total capital (see below, pp. 135-6). Comparison of its evolution in a given industry may reveal, apart from these general factors affecting profits, also increased (or tightened) hours worked for a certain wage and differences of the wages actually paid from what was formerly regarded as normal ; in so far, they may illustrate " exploitation " in the sense usually complained of by the average worker, namely a rough deal from his respective masters in comparison with what is regarded as normal in industry.

E

worker's family is prevented by the Law or by Trade Union resistance.[36] Once longer, or tighter, hours have become general, no additional " absolute surplus-value " is appropriated as the new standard determines the amount of labour power normally brought by the current real wages ; but new " relative surplus-value " is created because the increased intensity of labour has resulted in lower prices of wages goods. " Absolute surplus-value " is thus being created in individual industries which happen to set the pace for increased exploitation of labour ; " relative surplus-value " whether originating from generalisation of their achievements or from mere technical progress in the industries producing wages-goods, is created for capitalist society as a whole.[37] From the point of view of the individual entrepreneur it makes no difference whether larger output per man-hour is achieved by quickening the pace of the conveyor belt or by some technical improvement which may perhaps even reduce the demands made upon the worker's strength ; nor does it make any difference to him (or to capitalist society as a whole) whether a reduction of the prices of *wages goods*, and the implied possibility of reducing money-wages, originated in either of the above ways ; but from the point of view of the relations existing between the main classes of capitalist society, and also of Trade Unionist struggle within the individual factory, the difference is enormous : the question how much human labour power has to be given for a certain reward is as much an issue of class-struggle as the other one—what reward can be exacted for a certain labour-effort. Marx's rate of exploitation, however abstract, is important because it expresses these issues, isolated from everything else.[35] It expresses the basic fact that capitalists cannot distribute amongst themselves any more profits than those they have exacted from the workers, while the rate of profits expresses such claims as capitalists may have to the common pool.

In the above sketch, we have attempted to define the main concepts of Marxist economic theory as set out in vol. I of *Capital*

---

[36] *Capital*, vol. I, Chapter 13, section 3, C., and Chapter 14, section 2.

[37] Failure to understand this caused the mistake of J. Wolf (criticised in Engels' Preface to vol. III of *Capital*) who tried to explain, by the creation of "relative surplus-value" the capacity of individual capitalists with advanced technique and a low share of wages capital in their total capital to appropriate the average rate of profits. Actually, Wolf's argument leads to the dynamics of the general rate of profits, the tendential fall of which is counteracted by the increase in relative surplus-value. See p. 147 below.

in such a way that they at least need no retrospective correction when applied to the concrete picture of capitalist reality as developed by Marx in vol. III. The purely hypothetical assumption that commodities were exchanged at their values was made in vol. I and published at a time when vol. III, with the explanation why this assumption could not correspond to capitalist reality, was already elaborated. In the letter to Kugelmann quoted above[38] Marx dealt with the theory of value in a way which hardly implies more than the conception of social labour as the basic relation existing between the members of a society founded upon commodity exchange ; and the basic tenets of vol. I of *Capital* can be derived from that conception. I do not think that the legitimacy of such an approach is impaired by the fact that at least in the *Theories on Surplus-Value*, vol. III of which was written in 1863, there are passages[39] hardly compatible with a conception of *Value* as a methodological approach which by mere incident coincides with the law of prices actually valid in a past stage of society.[40] In this book, we have to discuss the Marxist theory in the connection in which it is relevant for our days though we shall not neglect the historical connection in which it arose.

Following Petry, Dr. Sweezy[40a] has recently elaborated the distinction between the " qualitative " and the " quantitative " value problems. In my opinion, continued use of the term " value " for the first (which was simply the traditional form in which Marx defined the subject of economics) pays homage to the traditional application of the Marxist theory as a theory of prices ; but I cannot see any use for a theory of prices which is not quantitative, and the " quantitative value " problem stands and falls with the ability of the Marxist theory, however indirectly, to derive prices from *values*, which we shall discuss in section (*f*) of this Chapter. Even if such derivation should give no more than a first approximation, that is, the establishment of general trends, it would be a quantitative statement. Certainly the term " value"

---

[38] P. 96.

[39] cf. His polemic against Torrens in *Theories on Surplus Value*, vol. III, pp. 78 ff, and his stubborn attempts (Ibid., pp. 91 ff) to save for "value," in a stage when commodities are exchanged at production prices, a meaning which cannot be upheld except by tautologies. The *Theories on Surplus Value*, just as the bulk of *Capital*, were decisively edited in 1863, whilst Engels' explanation, which we mainly use, though based upon an original statement by Marx (*Capital*, vol. III, pp. 204-5) was written after his death.

[40] See above, p 96 and below, pp. 121-2.

[40a] l.c., pp. 25 ff.

owes its origin to Marx's belief that it formed a bridge between his historical theory and the theory of prices accepted in his days ; but this is no reason for us to use the term " value " merely in order to express our agreement with Marx's historico-dynamical approach to economics. The element of truth contained in Sweezy's distinction is the recognition that the correctness of Marx's characteristic of the entities with whose intercourse economics has to deal is independent of the correctness of his theory of prices.

In order to analyse the process of circulation, Marx divided capitalist industry into three spheres : one producing means of production, one producing means of mass-consumption (wages-goods), and a third producing luxury-goods for capitalist consumption. In the output of every group of industries one part represents the value of the means of production used (the *constant capital*), a second, that of the wages paid to the workers (the *variable capital*), and the third, the *surplus-value* appropriated by the capitalists (including their satellites, the landlords, money-lenders, etc.), which may be consumed, or partly re-invested in the shape of additional means of production and wages for additional workers. As in every industry all of these three parts of the total *value*-output are produced in a natural form corresponding to the character of that industry only some of the parts can be immediately consumed in the industry where they have been produced.[41] The capitalists in Group I (production of means of production) can immediately use that part of their total output that is destined to replace the used means of production and that part of the surplus-value that is to be invested in additional means of production. The capitalists of Group II (production of wages-goods) can immediately use that part of their product that replaces the applied wages capital and that part of the surplus-value that is destined to employ additional workers. The capitalists of Group III can consume immediately only that part of their output (of luxury-goods) that corresponds to that part of the surplus-value which they intend to consume themselves. All other parts of the national product have to be exchanged between the different spheres of production in order to fulfil their economic function. Group I exchanges that part of its product that represents its wages capital and that part of its surplus-product that is destined for wages for additional workers against that part of the output of Group II that is needed for replacement of means of production consumed in that industry, plus additional means of production to be puchased from part of the surplus-value. Both groups exchange that part of their surplus-value which is destined for capitalists' consumption against products of Group III ; the consumed part of the surplus-value appropriated by the capitalists of Group I replaces the constant capital (wear and tear plus new investment) of Group III, the corresponding part of the output of Group II replaces that part of the output of Group III that has to pay for wages (those paid in producing the exchanged goods as well as those intended to be paid to additional workers). In the most simple, but, as Marx frequently asserted, purely hypothetical case of " simple reproduction " there is no net investment in any of the groups, and all the surplus-value produced is consumed by the capitalists. Therefore, the rather complicated formula just explained is replaced by a simple exchange of the part of the output of Group I that has to pay for its wages against that part of the product of Group II that is needed in order to replace the used means of production. Either group exchanges the whole of the surplus-value *appropriated* against luxury-goods produced in Group III ; the machinery, etc., from Group I replacing the means of production used up in Group III, and the wages-goods from Group II sustaining the workers of Group III.

(*d*) THE HISTORICAL POSITION OF THE
LABOUR THEORY OF VALUE.

Marx's specific contribution to Economics started from a discussion of the concept of exploitation. Since the days of St. Thomas Aquinas the small producers of commodities who were characteristic of mediaeval society have complained of usurers, merchants, and, later, capitalist competitors who deprived them of the due remuneration of their labour by preventing them from getting the full value of their product. Such ideological terms have a certain significance ; they reflect a state of society in which the labour applied is the actual cost of a commodity not only to society as a whole, but also to its supplier on the market. Apart from regional differences (which form the opportunity for the interference of commerce complained of) that cost is nearly homogeneous within the individual guild or town. So the social labour cost, as analysed in the first Chapter of *Capital*, actually coincides with the number of hours which an average shoe-maker or tailor, duly acquainted with the trade and the customs of the guild, is likely to spend on the production of shoes or dresses. Failure to realise the due value of his product is generally regarded as misadventure due to external catastrophies, or to the natural process of purging the trade from completely incompetent crafts-men.

This position changes with the first intrusions of rising capitalism upon the craftsman's market. Differences between what Marx would call the " socially necessary labour costs " and the labour applied by the average craftsman of average skill (if measured by the standards of the craft) are no longer an occasional misfortune, but a permanent pressure upon the craftsman's status, till he is expropriated and reduced to the state of a proletarian who has to sell his labour-power to the successful competitor. But he carries his ideological standards with him into the rising labour movement. For a very long period the labour movement fails to make a clear differentiation between the craftsman's hopeless demand for restoration of his former position and the modern proletarian's claims for improving his lot as a proletarian, if possible, by the overthrow of existing society in favour of another where proletarians would fare better. In the theoretical protest against the worker's being overreached by having to sell his toil for less than its worth as well as in the demands of the French Socialists in the 'forties, and later Lassalle, for State-aided producers' associations, the future of the Labour movement was still overshadowed by its past. It was found in this state by Marx, and its ideological expression was Proudhonism.

Marx's answer to the problem is known. By reference to classical economics he shows that exploitation takes place not merely in those cases (the existence of which Marx would not deny) where the worker has to sell his labour-power below its true value, but also where he is actually realising the full value of the commodity, labour-power, which he is selling. For it is a basic condition of capitalist society that labour creates a higher amount of " value " than its own, i.e., that is necessary for the reproduc-tion of the labour-power under the socially usual conditions. It follows that the fact of " exploitation," complained of by the Socialists, cannot be overcome by any device intended to secure for the worker " the full proceeds of his labour " (which would be a contradiction in terms in capitalism, and, if applied to socialism, would prevent the progress of socialist society) but only by the overthrow of a social order where his labour-power appears as a commodity bought—even at its correct price—by others who use it in order to accumulate wealth.

The introduction of a basic constant derived from pre-capitalist society, and used by him in order to show the temporary character of capitalism, gave Marx a *locus standi* outside the different elements observable on the markets of capitalism. From this standpoint all those elements might be deduced without going into those vicious circles which catch anyone who restricts his analysis to the terms of the capitalist framework,[42] where labour is regarded merely as the cost element of wages. But even if the standpoint chosen is so deeply connected with the origins of capitalist society as is the labour-theory of value, the quantitative predictability of economic events in such a society cannot *a priori* be taken for granted. To justify such an assumption, the standard applied (a) must at least in principle be accessible to quantitative measurement, and (b) it must unambiguously determine the events subject to investigation. Assumption (a) holds true, for the labour theory of value, as a general approach to economics, in that, with some important restrictions,[43] the social labour expended in the different spheres of production can be measured. As to assumption (b), we have just[44] met a very important instance where the theory allows for establishing the basic trends in the development of essential data of the system but does not allow for forecasting it in quantitative terms. This happens because the Marxist theory is not restricted to the automatism of a purely economic model but shoulders the task of including the historical and political element in its analysis.

In using the achievements of classical economics as an answer to his opponents in the socialist fold, Marx subjected them to a change in emphasis which allowed for further progress of abstraction. The classical approach already implies definition of the subject of economics as relations between men ; and the first Chapter of *Capital*, which is devoted to the analysis of commodity exchange in general, starts from the historical fact of the division of labour, just as do the introductory chapters of the other classics. As early a writer as Thomas Hodskin had

[42] A point which has been well elaborated by Dobb, l.c., pp. 8-12.
[43] See below, pp. 128-9. [44] P. 115.

recognised capital, which to the classics had been a natural category, as a social relation between rulers and ruled.[45] But Marx was the first to derive the necessity of the growth of that relation from the very mechanism of commodity exchange at " values " idealised by the lower-middle-class utopia. The distinction between the individual and the average social labour cost (value) of a commodity enabled Marx to explain the troubles of the independent craftsman confronted with overweighty competitors, and also the reasons why capitalists are bound to accumulate lest they should fall out of the race. The implied growth of the industrial reserve army and the pressure which it is bound to exercise upon the conditions of the employed workers answers the lower-middle-class Socialists' demands for " a just wage of labour " as well as the academic economist's assertions that labour would get its full marginal product and that capitalist profits for the marginal investment would be reduced to nought if only technique were stable and labour permanently in demand. Marx answered the complaint of exploitation positively by forecasting the likely outcome of the further evolution of the capital relation, including its ultimate breakdown. By characterising as *relations between men* what even the classical economists had described as a *property of things*, he replaced the argument about the merits of the alleged thing by one about the appropriateness of a certain form of social organisation. In the first formulation (property of things) the institutional issue whether large-scale labour needs to be organised by individual owners of means of production is irretrievably mixed with the question of the obvious utility of improved means of production and with the other question of the possibility, at least in our time, of a workable society without any kind of property. In the second formulation the question of social organisation must be answered according to its merits, and Marx has shown why an increasing section of the population are bound to answer it in the negative. Thus he has succeeded in deriving the criticism of capitalism and the need for its replacement by another form of social organisation not from moral standards, which cannot be universally accepted in a class-divided society, but from an objective fact, the increasing productivity of social labour.

[45] *Theories on Surplus Value*, vol. III, pp. 352 ff.

(e) LIMITATIONS OF THE LABOUR STANDARD OF VALUE.

Up to this point we took the accessibility of Marx's standard to quantitative measurement for granted. To some extent we can do so, as a first approximation : even non-Marxist economists make comparisons, say, between the strength of the labour force in different countries, between the part of the national labour force devoted in different countries to industry and agriculture, or to war-industries, with only occasional remarks about the varying proportions of skilled workers in those different labour forces. The units compared are large enough for the difference to be regarded as negligible. Following Ricardo, Marx thought that the relations existing between large social units formed the most proper subject of economics, and his analysis of the relations between the main spheres of production[46] is probably the least disputed amongst his achievements.

However, as a scientific system exposed to certain—one might say, aesthetic—demands as to its homogeneity, Marxism is exposed to criticism. Even in its foundations, as laid out in the (fully elaborated) first volume of *Capital*, there are obvious gaps in the definition of the capacity of productive labour to create value, and they are complicated by Marx's attempts, in volumes II and III, to give a consistent answer to the question raised by the classical economists, which kinds of labour are productive.

In settling their disputes with Mercantilists and Physiocrats, the classics since Adam Smith[47] had established that only such labour is productive as is paid by capitalist producers and employed in order to make profits, as distinct, say, from domestics in a private household who are paid from revenue (not in a hotel, where " the same " kind of labour creates profits for a capitalist entrepreneur). In the development of economic thought this distinction marked progress towards the recognition of capitalism as a distinct mode of social production which should not be confused with the production of useful things in general ; but it conflicts with the obvious fact that not every activity which, in a capitalist society, yields profits to the entrepreneur who undertakes its organisation can be regarded as increasing the sum total of material wealth available for distribution amongst the members of society. Even non-Marxist economists, when

[46] See above, pp. 120-1.
[47] Op. cit., Book II, Chapter 3. See Marx's comment in *Theories on Surplus Value*, vol. I, pp. 258-9.

comparing the labour force of different countries, occasionally notice an unduly high proportion of clerks and other " non-productive " workers. Marx developed Smith's idea, and explained [48] the difference between productivity in the sense of abstract usefulness and in the sense of promoting the prosperity of a given social formation. In the Chapter 6 of vol. II, and 17 of vol. III, he made a further distinction in the category of those human activities that are " productive " in that they help some individual unit of capital to realise profits, and are even necessary for the smooth functioning of capitalist economics : he distinguished those activities that supply the market with goods and services (including transport, retailing, etc., which should not be confused with the commercial functions proper) from those that are needed merely in order to accelerate the turnover of productive capitals, that is, to enable the " productive " capitalists to use their capitals exclusively in production. Merchants bridge the gap between production and definite sale of the produced commodities to consumers, whilst bankers bridge the gap between individual savings of parts of the surplus product and actual investment. Both groups of capitals participate in the distribution of the surplus values that have been created only by the workers employed in production activities, and from the same source also their employees have to be paid. The distinction seems logical in connection with the historical derivation of " value " : immediate exchangers of commodities are " productive," in the sense of having created social values realisable on the markets, only on condition of having created actual use-values (including transport to the place of consumption) ; when capitalists are interpolated between them it is obvious, from the viewpoint of the social output, that the loss in output involved in the fixation of part of the social product during the process of circulation, etc., has to be deducted from such increases in social productivity as were made possible by the fact that the capitalists have organised the activities of the producers formerly isolated. Similar comparisons could be made, and have been made by Marx himself, [49] with a socialist society. But all these arguments impair an essential merit of Marx's analysis, its historical character in respect to a definite social formation : once we state clearly that an author is " productive " (in the capitalist meaning) not

[48] *Capital*, vol. I, Chapter 14.
[49] *Capital*, vol. II, pp. 152–3.

by his being creative, but by helping the publisher to make a profit[50]—why should not the sales-agent be productive also? In the concluding passage of vol. III, Chapter 17, Marx himself noticed the problem of his argument by stating that commercial employees, because their salaries entered the necessary expenditure upon which their employer was entitled to the average profit rate, were productive from his, though not from the industrial capitalist's, point of view. But what point is there in describing productivity of a certain group of wage-earners from the point of view of a certain section of the capitalist class, instead of from the point of view of capitalist society as a whole? Once the hypothetical identification of prices with *values* is replaced by the concept of production prices (costs plus average profits), as done already in the earlier Chapters of vol. III, the " productivity " of any group of workers can only mean (a) the contribution which they make to the total distributable profit pool, which depends upon their being necessary for the functioning of the given, capitalist, society, or (b) that they entitle their employer to a due share in that pool. Either question has been answered by Marx clearly in the affirmative. Thus the obvious phenomenon that certain capitalist societies are "over-clerked"[51] should be interpreted like redundancy of any other group of workers in relation to social needs, not by denial of the productivity of clerical labour in general.[52]

From Marx's definition of productivity follows a clear distinction between productive and unproductive labour. All members of society—including the capitalist himself, so far as he works as the chief engineer of his factory—who contribute to the actual production of commodities, sold with a profit, are productive workers and create value ; all those who merely carry on the

---

[50] *Theories on Surplus Value*, vol. I, p. 260.

[51] We are not speaking of the State machine proper whose members are clearly "unproductive" in the Marxist sense. In the most conspicuous examples of "being over-clerked" (Austria after 1918, perhaps also present Britain) the excessive development of banking and commerce may simply represent insufficient adaption to new conditions created by the dissolution of an Empire formerly served by the huge machinery.

[52] The question whether commercial, etc. workers are productive, or not, should certainly not be confused with the other, whether the objective conditions for their acquiring class-consciousness are so favourable as, say, with miners or engineers. (In this regard, besides, undoubtedly "productive" workers such as waiters, etc., are probably backward in comparison with the "un-productive" bank-clerks and shop-assistants). However, the problem was rather energetically discussed in the German Communist Party in 1931-2 under the unpleasant impact of the advances made by Hitlerism amongst the black-coated workers.

circulation process needed to keep the capitalist system functioning (including especially the non-technical supervision of labour)
are not. A socialist system may need more of the " unproductive " functions than the ideology from which it has originated
recognised as legitimate and productive in the preceding framework, and therefore if the argument is applied by its theoreticians
it may get them into political difficulties.[53] Here we are not
concerned with this aspect, but with another within the Marxist
system. It is undoubtedly a distortion of Marx to interpret
him as having reduced " productivity " to mere physical labour ;
and the more this is recognised as such the more important
becomes the question of finding a common denominator for the
value-creating activities of very different kinds of labour. Marx,
like most of his contemporaries, took the gradual destruction
of all privileges of skill within the working-class and the increasing
mobility of most of its members from one occupation to another
for granted ; but however this may be it can hardly be denied that,
in our days, the increased number of black-coated workers and
technical specialists makes for increased differentiation within the
wage-earning class according to different skills.

Marx[54] simply states that " skilled labour counts only as
intensified, or rather multiplied, simple labour, so that a smaller
quantity of skilled labour is equal to a larger quantity of simple
labour." He adds that " experience shows that skilled labour
can always be reduced in this way to the terms of simple labour,"
and he aims a warning foot-note at the current mistake of confusing the commodity value into which the worker's labour is
incorporated with the respective amount of his wages for work of
different qualities.[55] The last mentioned difference can be
explained comparatively easily by the different costs involved in
preparing a lad to do socially useful work as an unskilled worker
or alternatively as a doctor. But what, then, is the " experience "
to which Marx refers in discussing the *value-creating* capacities of
different kinds of labour ? The fact that commodities produced
by differently qualified labour are exchanged against each other ?
But, as already Boehm-Bawerk has noticed, this would be a

[53] Comp. the argument between Strumilin and Notkin-Zagolov in 1936-7,
reported in my article in *Zeitschrift fuer Sozialforschung*, 1938, No. 3, pp. 396-7.
    [54] *Capital*, vol. I, pp. 11-2.
    [55] Which did not prevent the mistake from being repeated by Ostrovitianov l.c.,
p. 248. This may be the one point where C. Landauer's (*American Review of Economics*,
1944, No. 2), otherwise unjustified reproach that some recent Soviet argument
implied a return " from Marx to Menger " may have some foundation.

petitio principii : in this stage of Marx's argument, *value*, that is, socially useful labour incorporated in the commodities exchanged, has still to be proved to give the correct explanation of the phenomenon of commodity exchange ; and a vicious circle is entered once an obvious difficulty in defining "value" is explained away by mere reference to the exchange of commodities.

This problem is certainly the most serious difficulty met by an inherent criticism of Marxist economics. A description of the value-creating activities of skilled labour as the outcome of the common efforts of all who have participated in giving that worker his specific qualifications [55a] would be the nearest to the spirit of the Marxist system, but would land us in new difficulties. The labour, say, of a public school master would create surplus value in a double sense : for his employer as well as for those of all his pupils into whose professional qualifications the master's teaching enters, and similar assertions could be made even as regards the producers of the pupils' food and clothes. A double *value*-creating effect of the same labour effort evidently contradicts the Marxist concept. Nor is it possible to drop the whole issue by asserting that the necessarily higher remuneration of skilled labour must be paid out of the surplus-value created by average labour in the same way as is done with the salaries of bank clerks, etc., [56] for such an assertion would lack even that element of truth as contained in Marx's description of banking and similar labour as "unproductive." From the social (though not from the banker's) point of view a society is obviously the more productive the lower the percentage of commercial, bankers' and similar employees in the national labour force ; but national wealth does not increase with an increased percentage of unskilled workers as compared with engineers, etc. Should no one succeed in solving the problem we should be left with no alternative other than describing Marx's continued use of the term "value" as an abstraction from the conditions of a disintegrating society of small craftsmen and peasants, simple producers of commodities with the corresponding ideology. This would not necessarily prevent it from remaining valuable as a first approximation to the realities of modern capitalism.

[55a] cf. Sweezy, l.c., p. 43. Dr. Sweezy's subsequent discussion of the issue of natural skill seems to me an admission of scarcity as a source of values.

[56] Besides, this would contradict Marx's own statement (*Capital*, vol. III, Chapter 8, p. 168) that skilled labour is not only supplied by workers whose labour power has a higher value, but also creates proportionally more surplus value.

(f) The Marxist Theory of Prices

If the subject of economics is defined in the Marxist way there is no inherent need for an economic theory to explain the actual development of prices ; but the general dynamic of prices, like any other phenomenon, should at least in principle be explainable by the theory. However, Marx inherited from his predecessors much more ambitious an approach to the price-problem, and up to our days his theory is questioned from the point of view of its capacity to explain what other schools of economists regard as their most important subject of investigation.

We have noticed that the class-struggles connected with the establishment of industrial capitalism as the ruling system enabled Turgot and Smith to proceed to the analysis of the social entities of which the modern nations were composed and amongst which their income is distributed, long before Marx analysed the historical character of those entities and of the capitalist mode of production. But, apart from general prospects, bourgeois economists from Smith onwards had to serve the needs of a society of competing individual entrepreneurs whose wealth was identical with their success in business, and of politicians who tried to render the conditions for the prosperity of individual businesses as favourable as possible. The more sensible of them wanted, and the classics tried to supply, forecasts as regards the general trends of events in an economic world the machinery of which worked behind the backs of its individual agents ; more superficially minded people and, some decades later, all those who regarded defence of the existing social system as the main task of academic science, demanded and received repetition of the arguments by which the individual business man rationalises his actions in a somewhat sophisticated form. In the last section of the *Theories on Surplus Value* Marx has given the analysis of the two trends, long before what Bukharin described as " the economics of the rentier " became nearly in all countries accepted academic theory and even appeared to get some justification from the growth of large-scale commercial enterprise with a need for scientific salesmanship. In analysing the demand side of the market, people accustomed to defend capitalism on the basis of the alleged freedom involved in competition attempt to escape the rather disagreeable aspects of capitalist monopoly in production.

ok3s

For the classics, capitalist society was something given and natural. Therefore they tried to solve their task[56a] by analysing the conditions of equilibrium under which supply would satisfy the demands of the market, that is to say, the average prices about which the actual prices tend to oscillate, those average prices themselves being bound to change with the development of the forces of production. Marshall's statement that supply tends to dominate the long-term evolution of prices but demand dominates their short-term movements would have satisfied them, and even Marx. True, Marx would not have failed to add the rider that the analysis of social production was concerned not with the short-term movement of prices but with the conditions of equilibrium in which short-term vaccillations are absent.[57] Smith and Ricardo, if questioned about the point,[58] could have answered that the basic branches of demand for consumers' goods, and the traditional ways of satisfying them, were actually given in their days; increased demand could be regarded as a mere function of cheaper supply in consequence of improved methods of production. Most of the new commodities appearing on the market were improved means of production. In our days such an explanation would not be quite sufficient, but it is still possible for a Marxist to explain the demand, say, for refrigerators by the development of modern technique plus the distribution of income given in a certain society on the basis of the distribution of the means of production, the organisation of labour, etc., etc. The need for a more elaborate Marxist theory of demand can hardly be denied,[59] but obviously there is a methodological approach from which it can start. At least so far as I can see, an approach from the other side, that is, an explanation of the dynamics of social production by the evolution of consumers' demands, is incapable of producing a consistent theory of social development.

The identification of social costs with part of the social labour effort is exposed to the misinterpretation that the costs incurred by the supplier of some commodity could ultimately be resolved into wages. Though the classics occasionally proved conscious

[56a] See above, p. 105.
[57] *Capital*, vol. I, p. 548, and vol. III, pp. 210–1 and 213–4.
[58] Marshall, op. cit., p. 503.
[59] The analysis in *Capital*, vol. III, pp. 214 ff, apart from being a mere sketch, presupposes certain types of demand curves. The task of Marxist students of the subject would be to derive concrete curves—which are highly important say in the study of monopoly—from the class-structure of society.

of the difference,[60] none of them before Marx stated it clearly, or attempted a solution. Even the definition of the subject of economics has occasionally[61] been impaired by confusion of the social labour whose distribution is to be investigated, with the labour power that costs its employer a certain amount of wages. This confusion was definitely removed only by Marx's distinction between abstract labour, that is, the share of the total social labour effort embodied in a certain product, and labour power, that is, wage labour as a commodity to be bought on the market. A certain commodity costs *society* as much social labour as has to be expended, under conditions of average productivity, on its production as well as on that of the means of production consumed in its production. But, even under the assumption that average prices are proportional to the social labour effort necessary for reproduction of the respective commodity (correspond to " values "), the commodity costs the industrial entrepreneur bringing it to market only the value of the means of production consumed in producing it, plus such part of the labour effort applied in the immediate production as has to be paid to the workers in the shape of wages.

The classics identified their general sociological statement that all commodities cost (society) labour with the individual entrepreneur's experience that equilibrium on the market will be achieved when the market price just covers this individual's costs of production (which the classics resolved in wages spent either by him or by someone else) plus the rate of profit customary at the time. At least in the more consistent of their statements which were followed up by Marxism, it was evident to the classics that the profits expected by the individual entrepreneur, as well as

---

[60] Comp. the utterance of Ricardo against Malthus quoted by Marshall, op. cit., Annex p. 816, amusingly as an anticipated argument against Marx. Actually, Marx (*Theories on Surplus Value*, vol. III, p. 89) in this point shared Ricardo's opinion. Consistently keeping within his mental blinkers and without devoting any thought to the question whether certain words must of necessity have had the same function in the Ricardian system as half a century later in his own, Marshall finds merits of Ricardo in the very points where the latter failed to complete his system, namely, in Ricardo's measuring the different amounts of value created by labour of different qualification by the paid amount of wages (see above, p. 128) and in his taking the amount of the rate of profit as given when the time-element is introduced.

[61] Especially in Smith's introduction of wages as the objective standard for measuring the value of commodities (*W.o.N.*, Book I, Chapter 5). In this point Marx has

those included in the costs of the means of production used by him, derived from a surplus of the total labour expended by the respective workers over that part of social labour which was needed to produce their means of subsistence. [61a] Rent, as a factor of production costs, had been disposed of by Ricardo's derivation of it from the very difference of the amounts of labour applied on different soils. Proportionality between the values created by different groups of workers and the wages paid to them was assured by the classical scheme—in which Marx shared—of regarding simple and unskilled labour as characteristic of the whole labour costs, and by the further assumption that some mechanism would in the long run equalise the rate of exploitation of labour in the different industries. According to Marx, [62] this mechanism was given by the interconnection of the class-struggle ; according to the older classics, it was bound to keep wages to the bare subsistence level. Accordingly, equal numbers of workers, wherever employed, would create equal amounts of surplus-value. But even under this simplifying assumption an evident difficulty arises from the fact that equal capitals, when invested in different industries according to the technical standards, employ very different numbers of workers whose labour, accordingly, is bound to create very different amounts of surplus-value, whilst application of these capitals is supposed (under equilibrium conditions) to yield equal profits.

There is no reason to suppose any special reason why the ratio of the share of the national labour effort contributed by equal numbers of workers in different industries to the share of the national labour effort needed to-produce the wages goods due to them should vary just in the way needed in order to equalise the profits made by equal capitals in spite of the fact

actually inverted the classic system : under the hypothetical assumption that the productive forces of labour remain stable during a certain period, there would have been complete equilibrium for Smith, and the modern school of marginal disutility, but with Marx still continuing class-struggle for the distribution of the social product. Once this fundamental difference is realised it is evident how completely Marx was misunderstood by those who associated him with what later was called by Lassalle " the iron law of wages " for the mere reason that he had no optimistic views on the likely development of wages in a capitalist society.

[61a] See above, p. 107.

[62] See above, pp. 115–6.

that they employ unequal numbers of workers.[63]   Within Marx's analysis of economic history, which is hardly controversial on this point, there is even some reason to start the analysis from the assumption of an equal " rate of surplus-value " in the diverse industries, because the age of machine-industries, with investments per employed worker greatly varying from industry to industry, was preceded by a period when capital controlled the labour of craftsmen turned into home-workers or started the co-operation of workers in manufactures without specially complicated means of production.[64]   Thus wages formed by far the most important component of the total capitals.   The competition of capitalists for the cheapest labour-power, which continues even in our days as an important factor in the imperialist struggle for colonies, might be regarded as an agent working to level out the rates of exploitation of labour which, in that stage, would largely determine the long-term rate of over-all profits.   However, with the development of modern technique, the numbers of workers employed by equal capitals applied in different industries are bound increasingly to differ. Hence, we remain confronted with an apparently insurmountable contradiction between the classical assumption that the average market prices were determined by the amount of labour needed for the production of the respective commodities and the notorious fact that equilibrium on a market supplied by capitalist producers supposes equality of the profits yielded by different capitals, whatever their " organic composition."

[63] The assertion that such a compensation takes place, i.e., that rates of exploitation differ between the different industries in such a way that rates of profit tend to be equal, has recently again been made by Joan Robinson (l.c., p. 16).   But the rate of exploitation, of which Marx spoke, expresses the contribution made by the individual capitals to the total capitalist pool of profits, not the share which they receive from it.   To define the rate of exploitation in Mrs. Robinson's way means simply to state that there could be no profits unless the net product of society exceeded the costs of reproducing its labour force, which is true, but holds equally true even of a slave, or serf-holding society.   Marx believed he had explained the amount of profits distributable by the interplay of competition by his analysis of capitalist production in vol. I of *Capital* : within the Marxist system there is no sense in a rate of exploitation (as distinct from the rate of profits) unless that rate reflects the actual processes going on in the exploitation of labour within the respective industry, though in the long run the fruits of that exploitation will be merged in the common pool.   If capitalists, for example, succeed in lengthening the labour day in all industries by an equal proportion, real wages remaining equal, the rate of exploitation will equally increase, and there will also be an increase in the rate of profits (which, by definition, is equal for all industries).   But because of the different part played by wages expenditure in the different industries and the equalisation of the rate of profits the proportion between the increased profits and the wages expenditure will greatly differ.

[64] *Capital*, vol. I, Chapters 11 and 12.

To the classics, a value completely divorced from the market prices had little meaning, and Ricardo was the only one amongst them who even noticed the contradiction, without solving it. Marx, whose mind centred on the alternation of social formations, continued the process of abstraction that had lead the classics from the surface-phenomenon of prices to that of an objective exchange-value, dominating the oscillations of prices, further to a concept of social value standing behind, but not necessarily identical with the exchange values. If value is the expression of a social relation, it is bound only to the existence of that relation, not to the rather accidental fact that in a certain phase of social development the prices of commodities actually tend to oscillate round a level determined by their respective values, nor to the fact that neither the classics nor Marx could have conceived of value as a social relation unless for a very long period[65] people had actually been used to conceive value as the "just price." However necessary that stage may have been for the development of the logical abstraction, it does not condition its validity, provided only that the fundamental social relation, division of labour, is preserved. In a developed capitalist society commodities cannot be exchanged in proportion to their values, for the simple reason that the labour socially necessary for the production of a commodity no longer determines its cost for the supplier. But value, that is, social labour, remains behind the scenes as the source and measure of the profits that by the mechanism of competition between investors can be distributed amongst the members of the capitalist class.

" The capitalist's costs consist of the capital applied by him, not in the labour which someone other than he has done and which has cost him no more than he has paid for it. This is an excellent reason for the capitalists to distribute the surplus-value produced in society amongst themselves according to the size of their capitals, not according to the amount of labour applied by the individual capitals ; but it gives no reason to explain

---

[65] Upon which Engels (*On Capital*, p. 106) laid rather strong emphasis. I do no think that pre-historic, and even ancient conditions mattered very much. According to Marx himself (vol. I, pp. 29 and 43 ff) the relevant conditions are those of a society which has already developed the ideological concept of the equality of its members. It may be added that they will develop concepts of "value" mainly during the time when "independent" producers of commodities are still predominant, but already threatened by the progress of the new capitalist order, as they were in the Italy of St. Thomas Aquinas, and in the Germany of Marx's days.

the origin of the surplus-value distributed in this way."[66]

Marx's derivation of " production-prices " from values, in Chapter IX of the 3rd volume of *Capital*, is actually no more than an elaboration of the statement just quoted in a long deduction with arithmetical illustrations. Capitals applied in the different spheres of production have a very different " organic composition," which means that the wages expended form different percentages of the total capitals applied. If it is assumed, that equal amounts of wages expended in different industries buy about equal amounts of social labour[67] and that the rates of surplus-value are similar in all industries, then different amounts of surplus-value will be created in the application of equal capitals with different " organic composition." But in order that capitalists may find all fields of investment equally attractive (ceteris paribus), equal amounts of surplus-value (profits) must be appropriated by the appliers of equal capitals, whatever the sphere of application : commodities must be sold at what Marx called their *production prices*, namely, their cost-price plus the average rate of profit on the *total* capital applied. If this condition is to be fulfilled, the capitalists selling commodities in the production of which a high proportion of *constant capital* is required (whose capitals have " a high organic composition ") will appropriate a share of the national funds of surplus-value exceeding the share of their enterprises in the national labour force (in Marxist terminology, the production prices of the output of their factories will exceed their *values*). Accordingly, the appliers of capitals with an " organic composition " below the average will appropriate a lower amount of surplus-value than would be proportionate to their labour force (to their *variable capital*) ; the production-prices of the commodities sold by them will be " below their values." Yet still, as social labour is the only source of social income, the total of all the commodities produced would still be sold at their value. Boehm-Bawerk's oft repeated criticism that " a total is bound to equal a total " is unjustified : a total has no meaning apart from the way of abstraction by which it has been arrived at, and this way of approach may, or may not, express a relevant approach to the subject under investigation. In its connection, Marx's

[66] *Theories on Surplus Value*, vol. III, p. 81. See also *Capital*, vol. III, pp. 232–3.

[67] A statement which should not be confused with the assertion that they hire equal numbers of productive workers, whose qualifications and *value*-creating capacities may greatly differ. See above, p. 128-2.

equation of total prices with total *values* implies the restatement, in a very important and original form, of the basic classical teaching that profits are derived from the difference between the amount of social labour applied minus the amount of social labour needed in order to reproduce the labour force.

The Marxist method of deriving production-prices can be explained without any resort to specific Marxist terminology, and indeed with avoidance of that confusion which is bound to result from the fact that in the analysis of the annual value-output the constant capital (that is, depreciation of the fixed capital plus consumed raw-materials) denotes something different from its meaning in the calculation of the average profit (and therefore the production prices) which is calculated on the total capital applied, not merely that part of it which has to be regarded as consumed in annual production. Continuing the analysis by Engels in the 4th Chapter of the 3rd volume of *Capital*, we may define " production-prices " (that is, the equilibrium-level at which equal capitals, wherever invested, yield equal profits) in the following terms :

If f is the fixed capital of a given enterprise, d the number of years needed for its replacement (on the average), r the cost of raw materials and w the wages expended during a single circulation period, and e the number of circulation periods in a year (in which the circulating capital returns)[68], and if $\int f$, $\int r$, etc., denote the sums of the respective expenditure in the whole national economy, the production price of the whole annual output of that enterprise, like any other, must equal :

$$\left(\frac{f}{d} + (r+w)\,e \right) + (f+r+w)\,\frac{\text{national net income} - \int w}{\int f + \int r + \int w}$$

It should be kept in mind that we speak of an equilibrium-condition to be realised in the course of the cycle, not of more or less legitimate profit-expectations of entrepreneurs during the individual stages of the cycle. Therefore, d has to be defined

[68] The apparently clumsy factors d and e are applied (instead of taking the return-periods of the circulating capital as unit) because those return-periods are different in the different industries, the total value-output of which has to be considered in calculating the average profits. Otherwise enormous " rates of surplus-value " (as with Engels, l.c.) are bound to result in industries where there are many returns of the wages capital during the year, that is, where there is a quick turnover. Actually the relation annual profits/applied wages capital has no sense whatever in the Marxist system ; it is neither an expression of the rate of surplus value (annual profits/annual wage-expenditure) nor of the rate of profits (annual profits/total capital applied).

in dependence on the actual consumption of the fixed capital and the average rate of technical progress bound to result in obsolescence of existing fixed capital, and e has to be defined in terms of the average technical conditions of the circulation period and the given organisation of commerce. Any definition of e in terms of the circulation period likely at the given state of business, and of d in terms of the period during which invested capital has to be amortized in view of conditions at the stock-exchange, would invite legitimate accusation of using a circular argument : so conceived, the derivation of production prices would actually say no more than that profits depend on the state of trade.[69]   But from the Marxist point of view production prices (or values) in another sense but as an equilibrium-level to be realised during the cycle, and helpful in its explanation, would be quite uninteresting. The formula in the form expressed above is, at least in principle, accessible to statistical check and verification ; therefore it should not be regarded as merely formal or scholastic. But it may be asked how far its derivation differs from that of some of the formula of the orthodox economists, say, Marshall's " long period normal price," and thus could be regarded as a specific merit of the Marxist theory. Indeed, the surplus-value created by the workers of the individual enterprise, or by any individual worker, does no more appear in the formula explaining the production prices ; nor does the wages-capital (w) of the individual enterprise appear in a position different from that of the circulating part of the constant capital (r). So it may be asked why it should be regarded as privileged in creating surplus-value.

I do not think that the answer to this criticism from the Marxist point of view can be sought in the formal structure of the formula for prices. If Marx's criticism of Ricardo[70] is taken seriously, the characteristics of Marx's theory cannot be found in the resulting formula for the description of observable phenomena but in the way in which what otherwise would appear as a purely empirical observation has been derived from basic insights into the essence of capitalist production. It is quite true that the surplus-value created by the individual worker—or group of workers—no longer appears in the formula of equilibrium prices ; but this does not mean that it is irrelevant for its content. The

[69] Joan Robinson, l.c., pp. 41-2.
[70] See above, p. 96.

national pool of "surplus-value," from which profits can be derived, is partly affected by factors working on a national scale by decreasing the costs of living, so that a larger part of the applied labour power is available as a source of unearned incomes. To that extent, it may be regarded as an ideological (or rather political) question whether the application of advanced technique, or the labour employed with that technique is regarded as the source of profits. But profits are also affected by the sectional conflict going on in the sum of individual enterprises for the amount of labour demanded for certain wages and for the share of wages in the total receipts of the enterprise. According to Marxist theory, every shift in the balance of those conflicts affects the average rate of profits ; according to the critics of the concept of surplus-value, the employer who was successful in reducing wages-costs merely gains some initial advantage comparable with that achieved by the man who first discovered a source of cheap raw materials without directly affecting the long-term distribution of the national income. According to those who deem that capital as well as labour creates value no problem is involved in equal capitals, whatever their organic composition, yielding equal profits. According to Marxism, some struggle is bound to go on within the capitalist class in order that the owners of capitals with quickly increasing organic composition may receive their due share in the profits created by the workers in other industries, and such needs may back monopoly in the former group.[71] Such questions are certainly relevant and should be accessible to factual verification.

Unhappily, the incorrectness of Marx's derivation of production prices from values is already implied in the basic assumption (of the incompleteness of which he was conscious)[72] that the transition from cost-accounting in terms of *value* (that is, from a society of small craftsmen and peasants) to cost-accounting in terms of capital-costs plus the average rate of profits (that is, to a well-developed capitalist society) could even *in abstracto* be conceived as carried through during a single circulation-period, at the beginning of which characteristic traits of capitalism were already present such as the varying percentages of the total capital applied in the different industries formed by wages capital. Only

---

[71] Comp. Hilferding, l.c., Chapter XI.

[72] *Capital*, vol. III, p. 194, *Theories on Surplus Value*, vol. III, pp. 209-10.

under that assumption is it possible in a scheme of social reproduction to start from expenditure in terms of values, in order to arrive at production prices, by distribution of the surplus-value produced in all spheres of production in proportion to the total capitals applied. As soon as we drop that assumption and suppose that capitalist production was given even before the start of the cycle, means of production as well as wages-goods have to be bought not at their values, but at production prices. Generally, it may be assumed that means of production themselves are produced with an advanced social technique (large-scale application of machinery, etc.), and therefore tend to be sold at production-prices exceeding their values, whilst wages-goods, and means of consumption in general, amongst which agriculture with its comparatively backward technique plays a conspicuous part, [73] tend to be sold at production prices lower than their values (that is, the proportionate share of the social labour effort embodied in them). In consequence, only a part of that part of the new social labour effort which is needed in order to enable the workers to continue production (" necessary labour " as distinct from the " surplus-labour " which forms the source of profits) will be spent on wages-goods, whilst another part will be spent in order to raise the prices of means of production (without the application of which the wages could not be paid) above their values. Thus, in our scheme based upon production prices, the proportion of unearned incomes to the expenditure on wages-goods will be higher than the rate of surplus-value was in the scheme based upon exchange of commodities at their values.

As long as we assume that the transition from *values* to prices has been effected as late as in the preceding cycle, the rate of profits, that is, the proportion between the newly created surplus-value and the total capital expenditure, remains unaltered (because only the distribution of that expenditure between wages-

[73] Amongst Marxist authors it has become current to make further assumptions as to the different "organic composition" of that part of the industries producing consumers' goods that work for working-class customers (and thus reproduce the wages-capital) and those producing luxury-goods into which unearned incomes are expended (see below, p. 144). It remains an open question whether the likelihood that higher proportions of more highly skilled labour are used in the production of motor-cars and wireless-sets for bourgeois consumers than in that for working-class consumers is likely to compensate for the fact that most workers have no motor-cars at all and that agricultural products form a higher proportion in their total outlay. With further artificial assumptions as to the character of "luxury-goods" (for example, description of a commodity such as gold which is mined with a highly advanced technique as typical of them) one can prove nearly everything—on paper.

goods and means of production has changed). But that assumption is no more realistic than Marx's scheme of a direct transition from *values* to *production prices*. Already in producing the means of production used in the analysed period, use was made of means of production bought at production prices, as distinct from values. It follows that the rate of profits will be lower than in the simpler schemes discussed above (because the newly produced surplus-value is now compared with a higher capital outlay). All these observations are based upon the unrealistic supposition of stable technique and prices (apart from the re-distribution of surplus-value amongst capitalists proportionate to the size of their capitals). Actually, means of production produced in earlier production periods enter the present reproduction scheme at lower values and at lower production prices than would correspond to the social labour expended on their actual production, because social technique has meanwhile advanced and less labour is needed to reproduce them. But there is not the slightest reason why this tendency, which according to Marx is characteristic of capitalism, should just compensate for the fact that, if his simplifying assumptions as to the transformation of *values* into *production prices* are corrected, production prices of means of production produced with an advanced technique are bound to be higher than they would be if directly derived from *values* (on the assumption of stable productivity of labour). There is no direct relation between *values* and *production prices* accessible to mathematic demonstration.

Now this result is not so horrifying to Marxists as it may appear in view of the emphasis laid by friend and foe on the alleged identity between the two sum totals (which is, actually, no more than one of different possible expressions for a certain methodological approach). It may be extremely difficult concretely to derive the average market prices of the different commodities from their *values*, for it would be necessary to trace back the actual composition of the capitals applied in producing the means of production used, as far back as that period when market-prices became divorced from *value*, but it should be conceivable, at least in principle; and failure to develop a practicable mathematical method of derivation would not prevent the deduction from the theory of value of verifiable statements on the dynamics of prices under the influence of technical progress as well as of social struggles on the outcome of which the amount of the rate of profits depends.[74] This logical aspects of the problem should be kept in mind in order that the actual results, whether positive or negative, of all the attempts[75] at finding a suitable formula for the transformation of *values* into prices may be seen in their proper perspective.

If his attention had been drawn to the point, Marx[72] might himself have noticed that his scheme of deriving production prices from *values* is of no value whatever except as expression of a methodological approach. If this approach be directly followed up, it leads into insurmountable practical difficulties, if for no other reasons, than because of the complete absence of the necessary statistical data for earlier periods. But an outlet from the difficulty appeared to have been found when Bortkiewicz discovered that an apparent contradiction within the Marxist system, which since Tugan-Baranowsky's days had been used as a criticism of the theory of production prices, might be used as a means to correct its shortcomings.

In Marx's scheme of "simple reproduction" described above,[76] that part of the product of the industries producing means of production and luxury-goods respectively that represents the wages-expenditure in those industries, has to be exchanged against those parts of the product of the industries producing articles for mass-consumption that respectively correspond to the latter industries' need for replacement of the used means of production and the profits made by the capitalists selling commodities for mass-consumption. (According to the basic assumption of the scheme of "simple reproduction" there is no net investment, and all profits are turned into luxury-goods by the capitalists themselves or their creditors, landlords, etc.). Similarly, those parts of the output of the industries producing means of production or wages-goods that represent the respective capitalists' profits have to be exchanged against those parts of the output of the luxury-industries that are destined to cover the need

---

[74] See below, p. 145.

[75] The English reader will find a summary, though not quite complete and with a rather unjustified preference for the Bortkiewicz solution, in Sweezy, l.c., pp.115 ff. Apart from Bortkiewicz's works also Moszkovska, l. c., should be kept in mind. All of them appear to have ignored the historical conditions for the transformation of values into prices (of which at least Sweezy and Moszkovska were certainly conscious) and, possibly like Marx himself, prejudiced by the assumption that everything could be proved by a mathematical example.   See now also I. Winternitz in *The Economic Journal*, June, 1948.

[76] p. 121.

of those industries for new means of production and the real wages
of their workers. In general, the industries producing means of
production have a higher " organic composition of capital " than
the average and those producing consumer goods a lower one.
Therefore the prices of their output are affected in an opposite
sense by the transition from values to production prices. It
obviously follows that that relation between the main branches
of production which would be proper if commodities were
exchanged on the basis of their values cannot fit the needs of
exchange on the basis of production prices. There is no problem
—logical[77] or historical—in this point : in his scheme of social
reproduction, which originated when Marx had already found
what he believed to be the solution of the price-problem, he
operated, for simplicity's sake, with *values* ; but he knew very
well[72] that in all stages of developed capitalist production com-
modity-prices were regulated by production-prices, as distinct
from values. *Value* is a theoretical abstraction necessary for
the understanding of the changes in production prices[78] ; but,
clearly the proportions between the different branches of national
production must correspond to the price-relations at which their
output has to be exchanged, not to the theoretical abstraction
needed for the explanation of those relations. Changes in the
productivity in social labour (that is, in *value*) condition changes in
production prices and thereby in the proper relation between the
different spheres of production, and may cause disequilibrium
until a crisis restores proper relations, but there has been never
such a thing as sudden change from exchange according to values
to exchange according to production prices.

But there seems to be another difficulty. With very few
exceptions[79] Marxists think it essential—not only as a simplifying
example, but as a test of the correctness of the theory of value—
that the total of values should equal the total of production-
prices, and the total of surplus-value the total of profits (including
that part of them transferred to rentiers, landlords, and other
satellites of the capitalist class). In isolation, the equations may be
meaningless—but taken together, they assert that the proportion
of surplus-labour in the total social labour effort embodied in the

[77] As even Sweezy, op. cit., p. 115, seems to think.
[78] Comp. the letter to Kugelmann quoted above, p. 96, and Marx's Preface to
the 2nd edition of vol. I of *Capital*.
[79] Moszkovska, l.c., 1929, pp. 30–1.

annual output equals the proportion of unearned incomes in the sum total of the prices of that output. Under conditions of " simple reproduction " the total surplus-product of society is exchanged against luxury-goods ; it follows that only if the organic composition of the capitals applied in the production of luxury goods should just correspond to the social average, do capitalists consume just the same proportion of the national product as the labour needed to produce it has formed of the total national labour effort. Quite apart from the fact that Marx regarded " simple reproduction " as a purely theoretical abstraction contradicting the inherent needs of capitalist expansion, I cannot see what horrible consequences for capitalist society would arise if capitalists should actually consume (in terms of prices) more or less than their due share (in terms of labour effort exceeding the amount needed to reproduce the means of production and the real wages) in the total *value* of the annual output. But in the unhappy scholastic atmosphere in which the schemes intended by Marx as illustrations of economic arguments assumed some theoretical importance of their own, extensive argument[75] has centred round Bortkiewicz's discovery that the hypothetical purity of the scheme presupposes average organic composition of the capitals applied in the luxury industries, which seems to contradict everyday experience as to the actual composition of those capitals. Many authors attempted to derive from the equilibrium-conditions between the different branches of production formulas for the transformation of *values* into production prices. Evidently it is assumed by those who indulge in the construction of such schemes that they may thereby by-pass the probably insurmountable difficulties involved in a direct derivation of production prices from values. However, even their method can never produce more than arithmetical illustrations. But whilst Marx, whatever his mistakes, illustrated his own theory, the derivation of all economic phenomena from the conditions *of production*, the Marxist followers of Bortkiewicz, if successful, would illustrate a theory which they abhor, namely, the derivation of prices from the conditions *of exchange*.

(*g*) THE PROBLEM OF VERIFICATION OF THE MARXIST
THEORY OF PRICES

Of all the applications of the theory the most accessible to verification is probably that suggested by Marx in *Capital*, vol. III, Chapter 11. If profits are derived from a general addition to capital outlay, there is no reason why a general increase of wages should result in a fall of prices of any commodities ; but if the derivation of profits from surplus-labour holds true and a general wages-increase thus implies a reduction of the rate of profits, the average market prices of those commodities in the production of which an under-average percentage of the applied capital had to be expended in wages, are bound to fall, whilst the obviously inevitable rise of the prices of commodities for the production of which a very high percentage of wages-capital is needed will be smaller than it would have to be if the former rate of profits prevailed. Defenders of the current price-theories may explain the first-mentioned phenomenon by reduced demand for investment goods (in the production of which, in general, a lower percentage of wages capital is applied) because of the reduction in short-term profits (and, a fortiori, of the part of profits available for investment) ; but it should be possible to afford examples of consumers' goods produced with a rather high organic composition of capital (say, motor-cars in countries where they are bought by the average skilled worker even in periods of average earnings[80]) or, better still, instances where the changes described took place without any absolute decrease of the demand for investment goods and without very remarkable changes in technique that could explain their becoming less expensive. It is not our task to dwell on the enormous difficulties which any attempt at unequivocal verification of the Marxist theory of prices is bound to meet, especially in view of the need to combine long observation periods with the assumption of the stable value of money (or clear corrections for changes in that value). For us, it is sufficient to have shown that the task is not insoluble in principle. But the difficulties to be encountered would suggest that verification should be attempted in the way applied by the most difficult hypotheses in Science, namely, by the use of a hypothesis developed to explain one phenomenon for the explanation of other completely independent ones.

Marx indeed believed he had found such a test. In classical theory, a tendency of the rate of profits to fall had been assumed as a given fact demanding an explanation. The Marxist explana-

---

[80] In conditions where purchase of a motor-car is a symptom of working-class prosperity the immediate effects of the increased wages rate on the demand-curve could not fail to over-compensate any conceivable change in production prices.

tion appears extremely simple : With technical progress, the amount of wages capitals, even if rising in absolute terms, is bound to decrease in comparison with the sum total of capitals. Therefore, the rate of profit, namely, the relation of the surplus value created by the employed workers to the sum total of all capitals applied, is bound to fall, unless very substantial changes in the relation between the part of the social labour needed to pay the wages and that available as a source of profits, etc., should have taken place. Unhappily, the argument seems to prove more than there was to explain, and Marx had to open Chapter 14 of *Capital*, vol. III, with the question : Why did not the rate of profits fall to the degree one would expect from the increased proportion of constant in relation to wages capital in consequence of technical progress ?

Quite a number of those reasons could be enumerated : the very progress in the productivity of labour that was made possible by the increase of the natural elements of the constant capital implies their depreciation ; and the rate of profit is assessed in relation to the value of the capital applied, not to the physical size of the machinery, etc., used. It also implies an increase in the degree of exploitation of labour (and therefore an increase in the rate of profits calculated on a total capital the *value* of which has not increased in the same proportion as the number of the workers employed) because a smaller amount of labour is needed in order to satisfy the usual, and even somewhat increased, demands of working-class consumption, and because the replacement of living labour by machinery may increase the " Industrial Reserve Army " and thus the pressure upon the working-classes even to accept reductions of their real wages.[81] Lastly, exceptionally high rates of profit enter the process of its equalisation[82] whilst capitalists in those very spheres where the increase of fixed capital is largest, and therefore a comparatively small amount of living labour is applied, may be justified with a lower rate of profit : their enterprises are organised as Joint Stock Companies and, if sufficiently solid, they can issue new stock even at the

[81] Modern Marxists may be inclined to emphasize in this connection export of capitals to undeveloped countries with a large peasantry expropriated by "original accumulation" and with a pressure upon the conditions of the working-class similar to that experienced during the Industrial Revolution in the old industrial countries.

[82] Marx refers in his sketch mainly to external trade with backward countries, but the phenomenon mentioned in the last note may play an even more important rôle in the same direction.

current rate of interest, which is lower than the rate of profits which has to cover interest for creditors as well as entrepreneurial profits. These last factors should be left out in the analysis of a closed capitalist system without the possibility of exploiting non-capitalist countries and with all industries already dominated by Joint Stock Companies ; but even after this correction in Marx's enumeration has been made, considerable intellectual effort is needed in order to imagine a sufficiently realistic model where *any* fall of the rate of profits would take place.

Increase of the constant capital applied for the exploitation of a certain amount of labour makes sense only on condition that the output in use-values will increase in a higher degree than the applied capital, so that the first appliers of the new improved techniques, when selling at the hitherto current production prices, will be able to realise an extra profit. It follows that the depreciation of the existing constant capital, and the creation of additional " relative surplus-value " because of the fall in prices of wages goods, are bound not only, as Marx thought, to delay the fall of the rate of profits, but even to question its possibility ; but it does *not* follow that such a tendential fall is impossible, as some critics of Marxist economics[83] believe. Rises as well as falls of the rate of profits are hypothetically possible,[84] but there is very small likelihood of such movements assuming dimensions unequivocally observable by statistical methods. It may be conceded, say, to Mrs. Robinson's criticism[83], that a tendential fall of the rate of profits is conceivable only if real wages tend to rise (which would contradict the alleged revolutionary consequences of that fall) ; but it should also be noted that the one very important conclusion drawn by Marx from the " law " can be based upon the mere fact of the existence of antagonistic tendencies realised during the industrial cycle, whatever the ultimate balance. From the point of view of explaining capitalist reality Marxism does not get into difficulties if the tendential fall of the rate of profits is questioned ;[85] it appears that

[83] Bortkiewicz, op. cit., 1907, Joan Robinson, op. cit., pp. 36 ff. For extensive discussions of the mathematical aspects of the problem see Moszkovska, op. cit., pp. 72 ff, and the sources mentioned in the note to Sweezy, op. cit., p. 105.

[84] Bortkiewicz's assertion to the contrary is answered partly by Sweezy's note, op. cit., p. 104, partly (also so far as Sweezy is concerned) by the argument made above, pp. 142-3

[85] The same attitude is taken by Dobb, op. cit., p. 110, as opposed to Sweezy, op. cit., p. 106.

the classics, including Marx himself,[86] when bothering about the fall of profits in a capitalist society actually dealt with facts relating to the origins of that society. Profits were higher when they were derived from the commercial exploitation, mostly in monopolist forms, of backward countries or of pre-capitalist elements such as peasants and craftsmen, than when they had to be produced by capitalist society itself. But the hope of checking the Marxist theory of prices by the movement of the rate of profits is lost once we have realised that a specific direction of these movements can be deduced neither from the Marxist theory, nor can it be presumed in social reality.

Our generalisations become even more abstract once we attempt the analysis of the monopoly stage of capitalism, which had not sufficiently developed in the lifetime of Marx and Engels to be described by them. Marxism gives a favourable start for such an analysis in its explanation for the need of progressive centralisation of capitals and the rise of such specific forms of enterprise as Joint Stock Companies. At the end of his life Engels[87] noticed the connection of those organisational forms with the growth of monopolies, and also the possibility that the organs controlling investment might play a decisive rôle in shaping monopolist organisations as well as the external policies of capitalism. Hilferding's *Finanzkapital*, in spite of many shortcomings in details, offers easy reading to the Marxist who may accept it as a continuation of the 5th division of *Capital*, vol. III. Marxism helps us to understand why monopoly, and all the connected forms of State interference, were bound to develop ; but beyond the general statement, not restricted to Marxists,[88] that whatever extra profits are gained by monopolies must derive from a reduction either of real wages and/or of the profits of the non-organised entrepreneurs, Marxism does not give us any quantitative laws governing economic events in the new formation even

---

[86] Comp. *Capital*, vol. III, p. 178, where Marx does not refrain from arguing quite in the Ricardian way about the respective rates of profit in developed European and in Asiatic pre-capitalist countries. Comp. also Ibid., p. 930, but also Ibid., pp. 251-2, where the difference is realised.

[87] In his remark on pp. 574-5 of *Capital*, vol. III, and in his sketched postscript " On the Stock Exchange," in *On Capital*, pp. 115 ff. The difference with Hilferding, as expressed already in the title, may be partly explained by the difference between English and Central European banking.

[88] Though Marxists will be inclined to claim such statements by non-Marxists as an involuntarily recognition of the basic Marxist tenet that there is some objective substance of wealth which could hardly be explained in terms other than of social labour.

in such an abstract and in many parts questionable way as does the law of equalisation of production prices for the period of fully developed industrial capitalism. The quantitative laws governing the intercourse of "independent" producers of commodities, or capitalist entrepreneurs, to be found in Marxist and academic economics up to our own days, are based upon the intercourse of molecules each of which is assumedly unconscious of the consequences of his actions[89] and only recent academic theory[90] has envisaged the possibility that the actions of such a molecule by itself (not only by the influence of its example upon other molecules) may influence the general position to a noticeable extent. Marxism, including modern Leninism, clings to the description of every stage of capitalist development as governed by the laws of competition, and without *some* kind of competition those mutual antagonisms within the capitalist world from which the Marxist expectation of its eventual breakdown is derived would, indeed, be inconceivable. But these antagonisms, or " competition " do not necessarily explain the working of any model in which quantitative laws governing the movements of prices, etc., would be predictable. Once we take the interweaving of "economic" and "political" aspects of competition for granted—and Marxists should regard it as a main advantage of their outlook that it allows for such a synthesis as a matter of course—the predictability of economic events in the stage of modern monopoly capitalism is reduced to that of political ones : economics can be no more an exact science than politics.

(g) VALUE IN A SOCIALIST SOCIETY

Marx asserted the validity of the law of value for a capitalist society as a background necessary for the understanding of economic events. In such a society, commodities tend to be exchanged at prices different from their values. Accordingly, it seems in no way essential for the relevance of value for the analysis of events in a socialist society whether prices should be fixed proportionate to the social labour efforts needed for the produc-

[89] See above, pp. 91-2.

[90] cf. Joan Robinson, *The Economics of Imperfect Competition.* London, 1933.

F

tion of different goods[91] or in some other way. On the other hand, the law would be reduced to a truism if intended simply to mean that socialist society, like any other, depends on its labour effort ; as a specific form in which that general natural law is realised,[92] *value* remains relevant only as long as that society needs book-keeping in terms of some common denominator distinct from the labour time actually applied in the production of that product.[93] Every attempt to balance the production costs of some commodity (however subsidised, or taxed) has to be based on the assumption of a certain normal productivity of labour.[94]

At two places in *Capital*,[95] Marx has explained the two-fold function of the social labour time as the accountancy factor in a society of the type of the present U.S.S.R. : due allotment of social labour in accordance with a definite social plan enables the various kinds of labour to be duly proportioned to the various social needs ; and the labour supplied by the individual member of such a society forms the standard according to which his share in the consumable part of the social product is measured. In the second place Marx used the term " value " and emphasised that book-keeping in respect of the labour-time

[91] Marx has never asserted that something of that kind would be necessary or likely. Of the three quotations interpreted by Joan Robinson (l.c., p. 23) in the opposite sense, the first says no more than that a socialist society, in establishing ratios of exchange, will consciously start from the basic fact of the social labour effort needed for their production, and deviate from that standard only for sound reasons ; the second says no more than that rent is a tribute levied from all consumers of the commodities the prices of which are regulated by marginal production costs because of the capitalist structure of society, whilst in a socialist society it would be sufficient to subsidize the marginal producers without demanding excessive prices for the whole product. The third quotation says no more than that payment of the members of a socialist society would be proportionate to the work done. This has nothing to do with the question at what prices the State should reasonably sell the products produced by their efforts, as long as products are best distributed by being sold.

[92] See above, p. 96.

[93] See *The Poverty of Philosophy*, espec. pp. 64–6, and Annex. p. 113 (quotation from the *Critique of Political Economy*).

[94] Therefore, the most fruitful applications of the value concept in recent Soviet economics seem to concern issues such as the theory of rent (see E. Salertinskaya, *Differential Rent in Socialist Agriculture*, in *Planovoye Khozaistvo*, 1946, No. 5) where the output of equal amounts of social labour applied under different conditions is compared. But it is a pure matter of politics how much of the differential rent, resulting from higher productivity of successive investments and improved efforts, is left to the kollkhozes as an incentive and a mere matter of economic technique how to get the other part of the differential rent from the kollkhozes into the treasury. Here, different labour efforts applied in producing the same commodity are compared ; the real difficulties of the value-concept, in socialist as well as in capitalist society, arise just when social labour realised in different commodities is compared. See below, pp. 154–5.

[95] Vol. I, p. 50, and vol. III, p. 992.

spent becomes in a socialist society more essential than at any previous stage. The first argument is interwoven with a general criticism of the fetishlike delusions bound to arise in a society based upon the exchange of commodities, in the sense that the social labour done by the producers of the commodity appears as some " value " inherent in the product. There is no necessary contradiction between these two approaches, though it was inevitable that they were quoted alternatively in the Soviet discussions to which I shall be referring. Immediately before the argument that might be put forward in favour of regarding value as a mere ideology, bound to wither away with a society that needs such delusions, Marx[96] states that the scientific discovery of the essence of value by the classical economists could not alter the average commodity-dealer's behaviour towards his goods ; it may be added that even a State-ideology and popular education that describes the price of commodities as the expression of the social labour spent upon their production cannot prevent the Soviet housewife from regarding some dress as " expensive " and another as " cheap." What truth there is behind the ultimate determination of the distribution of goods by the productivity of the labour applied in producing them, is shown as soon as a discrepancy arises not because of some intentional correction of the " natural " price-level for political reasons, but simply because of the non-fulfilment of the plans either for producing consumer goods or for " decreasing the costs of production "—that is to say, for keeping the rise of consumers' purchasing power within such limits as can be satisfied by the supply of consumers' goods. In such a case there will be queues for the shops and the Soviet state, like any other which does not indulge in laissez-faire ideologies, will face the alternative of rationing goods or raising their prices according to the productivity of the labour applied in producing consumers' goods.

The validity of the " law of value " in developed Soviet society[97] was recognised as late as 1944, and this fact demands ideological rather than economic interpretations. Certainly there is a strong tendency in Marx's and Engels' writings to

[96] *Capital*, vol. I, p. 46.

[97] We do not speak here of the private sector which was highly important before the collectivisation of agriculture, nor even of the non-socialist elements in the kollhkoz-compromise (free marketing of part of the output by the kollkhozes and their members), though the latter elements play an important part in the argument of Leontiev as well as Ostrovitianov, l.c. The complete assimilation of kollkhoz-economics to the general pattern of Soviet society is only a question of years.

emphasize the elementary, automatic character of the determination of prices by value, and thus to encourage juxtapositions of value and planning as alternatives incompatible with each other as are capitalism and socialism.[98] The natural tendency to overemphasize the revolutionary change was bound to strengthen such tendencies amongst Soviet even more than amongst Western Marxists. Further, the determination of economic processes by the laws of market economics, which, in itself, was not contested by Soviet economists during the N.E.P. period, was employed by the scientific supporters of the right-wing opposition in the C.P. of the U.S.S.R. as an argument against the revolutionary transformation of Soviet economics by the forced industrialisation of the country and collectivisation of agriculture, and such an argument provoked general reluctance to operate on " value " on behalf of the victorious trend. In itself this was a logical mistake : the ability of the planning State to deviate from the " natural " price-levels, wherever this seems to be in the common interest, forms no stronger an argument against reasonable conception of the Marxist theory of value than does the existence of capitalist monopolies : any conscious correction presupposes some subject of the transformation. But the limits of such transformations were not emphasised in Soviet ideology during the years of enthusiastic offensive : Ostrovitianov's[99] and Voznesensky's[100] explanation of the statements that "the sum of prices in a socialist society must coincide with the sum of values," in that society cannot distribute and invest more than it has produced, would not have been popular in 1929. For it is bound to mean : if the sum total of the prices of the output is increased in a higher degree than the social labour applied in producing that output, there will be monetary inflation and the over-investment will be paid for from reduced incomes, which was true, and necessary for the survival of the U.S.S.R., but not the sort of thing you would say in public. Further, the recognition of the existence of value in the U.S.S.R. involves the recognition of the existence of surplus-value ; and this contradicts popular concepts of the aims of the Labour movement. Ostrovitianov's explanation of the preliminary condition of socialist accumulation : The growth of the productivity of Labour must outstrip the growth of wages,

[98] Sweezy, op. cit., quoted by P. A. Baran in *American Review of Economics*, Dec., 1944.   [99] Op. cit., p. 250.
[100] l. c., p. 147.

however true, just would not fit the early stages of Soviet propaganda at home and abroad ; and even in 1944 the official recognition of the validity of the concept of value for Soviet society did not fail to serve as an argument for Trotskyites abroad.[101] From the end of the N.E.P. up to 1944, the application of the term value to Soviet economics was avoided with a care corresponding to the eagerness with which Soviet economists applied it on any occasion in their analysis of capitalist economics. The actual use of the concept as well as the comparative uselessness of the specific terminology can be assessed by the extent to which the Marxist concept of value was used without mentioning it by its familiar name. In the earliest textbooks, the publication of which soon followed the definite shaping of the foundations of fully nationalised economics in 1931,[102] it was recognised that in applying the system of Economic Accountancy (under which Soviet enterprises are individualised units the efficiency of which is checked by their Bank account) "we make use of the forms of money and commodity exchange in order to strengthen our planned economics."[103] Amortisation of the fixed capital " as a form of accounting the expenditure of labour for the means of production used in producing the commodity in question " was said to remain a relevant concept for the study of Soviet industrial economics.[104] On the other hand an interpretation of the relations existing between the Soviet state and its employees as being the purchase of the latters' labour power, which would imply the conception of surplus-value as a category surviving under the Soviet system, was emphatically rejected as a counter-revolutionary deviation threatening the identification of the Soviet workers with their State and their industry.[105] Soviet

[101] cf. R. Dunayevskaya's comments to Leontiev, op. cit., and her rejoinder in *American Review of Economics*, 1945, No. 4.

[102] The "Six guiding principles" for the organisation of socialist industry, developed by Stalin in his speech in June, 1931, before the leaders of industry (op. cit., pp. 368 ff), may be regarded as the starting point for all further developments.

[103] *Economics of Socialist Industry*, ed. E. L. Khmelnitskaya, Institute of Economics of the Communist Academy (Russian), vol. I, Moscow, 1931, p. XXIV. The remark is connected with a description of Economic Accountancy as characteristic of "the last stage of the N.E.P." This statement is clearly refuted by the further development of Soviet economics towards complete removal of private entrepreneurs and stricter application of the principle of Economic Accountancy, and thus should be regarded as a residium not of the N.E.P. but of the Utopia of " abolition of money."

[104] Ibid., pp. 472-3.

[105] *Economics of Labour*, Institute of Economics of the Communist Academy, ed. M. M. Krivitsky (Russian), Moscow, 1933, vol. I, pp. 29-30 and 36 ff.

economists have not failed to realise that in the balances of Soviet economics prices represent expenditure of social labour[104] [106] ; such recognition does not yet imply a direct connection between labour expenditure and prices. In a society based upon commodity exchange, equilibrium as regards the distribution of social labour and means of production between the different industries is supposed to exist when commodities are exchanged at their equivalent : in a society of small producers of commodities equivalent expenditure of labour, in developed capitalist society equivalent capital expenditure (including means of production as well as wages costs). In a socialist society the desired distribution of labour and means of production is being realised by direct adjustment of the plans, without interference of an equilibrium concept[107] : in the U.S.S.R. (as well as in a capitalist country driven by needs inherent in its external position towards autarchy) an investment of an additional rouble in metallurgic industries is not necessarily characterised as " unproductive " by its resulting in an additional production priced at half a rouble as against two roubles which might be achieved by an alternative investment in the textile industries.[108] Planned economics may overcome disequilibrium in the resources needed for the desired direction of economic development by re-distribution of reserves (including exchange of gold or other commodities regarded as less necessary against the deficit resources on the world market) and diversion of materials and current production processes from alternative courses.[109]

But such diversion has its limits. In Soviet planning practice, they are established by a system of natural balances (i.e., in physical units as distinct from terms of money) attached to each of the alternative plan variants between which political factors have to decide, and provision is made in such balances for alternative uses to which natural resources as well as human labour power can be put. In deciding between the variants, the Party and the Government thus are conscious that some of them will yield not only more factories or armaments, though less consumers' goods, but also that the desired effect will have to be paid for by bottlenecks, say, in railway transport, or in special

[106] Voznesensky, l. c., pp. 146–7.
[107] Notkin-Tsagolov, l. c., pp. 134–5.
[108] *Economics of Socialist Industry*, as quoted above, note 103, pp. 545–6.
[109] Notkin-Tsagolov, l. c., p. 137–8. See also Voznesensky, l. c.

types of skilled labour, which will have to be resolved by special efforts which may have implications of their own. Some of the natural balances are of a very broad character, because natural elements entering nearly every aspect of production can be allowed for in the same terms : power resources of different kinds may be expressed in horse power, freight in weight units or railway waggons to be loaded and unloaded, production and consumption of fuels in calorific units, etc. But these very examples make it clear how fundamentally the position differs from that in a capitalist system where, at least in principle, one of the possible variants is characterised by minimised costs in money and maximised profits : apart from economic policy, based upon assessment of the situation and the needs of the country, which may be controversial, there is no common denominator according to which access of additional calorific power of fuel can be compared with the increased number of loaded and unloaded railway waggons needed in order to bring fuel to the place of consumption.

Money balances play some part, but only as corollaries of the different plan variants. Pricing in money is applied in order to test the efficiency of production units and to ration scarce commodities in a way which gives the individual consumer some freedom of choice ; so there must be equilibrium between the purchasing power transferred to consumers as wages and the supply of commodities brought on the market, unless the value of money, and the incentive to earn high wages, is to collapse. Profits made by State enterprises plus the proceeds of taxation, internal loans, etc., must equal the prices of that part of the national product which is invested or devoted by the State to public purposes. But within certain limits imposed by the desire to let every production unit earn its costs and to allow for some profits to check its efficiency and to encourage its initiative, prices themselves are determined by the needs of the plan : Mrs. Khmelnitskaya's hypothetical comparison between alternative yields is quite meaningless if the high yield in textiles results from the very fact that the State has to ration them because it prefers investments in metallurgy and wishes to let the consumers of textiles contribute to the overall costs of metallurgic production. In so far as a socialist state, in making its decisions, has regard for consumers' demands, the fact that consumers' demand for some commodity is so strong that high sur-taxes have to be charged in order to keep it in equilibrium with planned supplies may be an indicator as to the directions in which consumers would like new investments to be made. But, quite apart from the fact that an actual socialist state (as distinct from some co-operative socialist Utopia) cannot merely cater for short-term consumers' interests, a State with a policy as regards the desirable forms of national life will not be indifferent whether extra-profits are made on the sales of books, textiles, cosmetics or entertainments of various kinds.

In spite of the long-standing reluctance to apply concepts of *value* to a socialist society, there has been no hesitation to apply the Marxist division of the national product as well as of the product of each industry into three parts, of which one has to replace the consumed means of production, one represents wages, and one the surplus-product available (in a socialist society) for investment and communal needs.[110] As Lenin[111] noticed, this implies recognition of the continued validity of the Marxist scheme of the circulation of the social product.[112] In a socialist no less than in a capitalist society, that part of the product of the industries producing means of production which has to pay for the wages expended as well as that part of the surplus product which is destined for wages of additional or unproductive workers, has to be exchanged against that part of the product of the industries producing means of consumption which has to pay for the means of production used, or needed for expansion of production. And for Soviet economists it was obvious that social labour applied in the different spheres of production is the actual object of such exchange. But in the very application to a socialist society, where no alternative interpretation would make sense, these statements are purely tautological, and the sterility of the " qualitative value problem," to use Dr. Sweezy's term, becomes obvious. As soon as a Soviet economist attempted to derive from the characteristics of the social circulation process conclusions as to the balance of Soviet economics, he was reproached with perpetuating the conditions

[110] cf. Marx's statement (*Capital*, vol. III, p. 953) that even in a socialist society surplus labour, that is labour performed above the normal requirement of the producers, is bound to persist, and to be materialised in a surplus product. The additional characteristic of surplus labour in a capitalist as well as in a slave system is merely that it assumes an antagonistic form and is supplemented by the complete idleness of a portion of society.
[111] In his critical glosses to Bukharin's statements (in Bukharin's *Economics of the Transformation Period*) that " the end of capitalist society implied the end of Political Economy."
[112] See above, pp. 120-1.

of capitalist commodity exchange and denying the ability of socialist planning to re-adapt the given relations according to social needs. " In every instance, the relations between . . . . the elements of the socialist reproduction process are determined by the dictatorship of the working class according to the needs of socialist reconstruction, not to the law of value."[113] I am not aware of fundamental changes in Soviet economics, or in their interpretation by Soviet economists, since the later 'thirties when such statements were made : the present emphasis on the fact that deviations are made from relations of value rather than on the deviations as such seems merely to prove (a) that the enthusiasm of early planning has given way to a sober appreciation of its conditions and limitations (b) that the need for a theoretical system for the teaching of Soviet political economy, as distinct from mere ideological statements, is now fully realised, and (c) that the rulers of the U.S.S.R. are convinced, by now, that unpopular statements of economic facts like the above quoted by Ostrovitianov will be accepted by the broad masses of the people not as acknowledgments of a restoration of exploitation but as explanations of common social needs.

For our purpose of assessing the value of the theory of value Soviet economists' subjective convictions are not sufficient. We may accept O. Lange's[114] distinction between " value theory as a tool of analysis of the automatic processes of the market and value theory as a basis for the normative principles of welfare economics " ; but the value of that basis depends on the use that can be made of it. According to Ostrovitianov,[115] " the Soviet state applies the law of value in accounting for labour in money form, in planning prices, in realising the socialist principle of payment according to labour ; it utilises this law as a tool of economic book-keeping and as one of the laws affecting the kollkhoz market." The last-mentioned use is connected with the incompleteness of present Soviet socialism, and therefore outside our theoretical interest ; book-keeping in the U.S.S.R. is carried through in terms of money ; and in planning prices the Soviet state, " guided by the interests of socialist construction, can set prices on some goods below their value, and on other goods above their value."[115] Value, here, comes in only in the very general sense that subsidies in one sector must come out of production elsewhere.

[113] Notkin and Tsagolov, l.c., p. 84.
[114] *American Journal of Economics*, 1945, No. 3.
[115] Op. cit., p. 250.

158 THE ANATOMY OF BOURGEOIS SOCIETY

Those who are stating the theory of value for present Soviet conditions have recognized its importance just because it is *not* possible to reduce economic transactions in the U.S.S.R. directly to terms of social labour. This would be possible as long as the problem were restricted to the reduction of labour of different intensity and productivity to a common denominator, but money as a standard independent of labour spent under average social conditions comes in for the very reason that workers and peasants, workers and intellectuals cannot be equal under present Soviet conditions, that the hour or day of the one cannot be equal to the hour or day of another.[116] The way in which their average output is compared and remunerated depends on the public demand for the different kinds of labour ; and even as to the wages offered to workers of comparable skill, a policy differentiating in favour of the most necessary industries is regarded as desirable (as is done also in present-day Britain). In support of the differentiations within individual industries Ostrovitianov states that " skilled and mental workers create a higher value per unit of time than unskilled workers, and should therefore receive higher pay." *What* " value " do they create—marginal utility or social labour ? The first interpretation implies dropping the Marxist foundations, the second is a purely circular argument. In a free market economy all this is veiled by the fetishism of commodity exchange : *because* in the general exchange of commodities one kind of social labour is exchanged against another, it appears that in the exchange of the commodity " skilled labour " against those commodities representing its real wages, the former is also a mere agglomeration of labour expended in its production. But in a socialist society nothing remains of this appearance but the fact that, for very good reasons, a larger part of the social product is spent in remuneration of the working-day of a skilled worker than of that of an unskilled one. Possibly[117] the issue of the different value-creating capacity of different labour is the pitfall of the Marxist theory of value in general, because here we meet the element of scarcity in a role more important for social economics than the current arguments about diamonds, etc. In the general analysis of capitalism, the Marxist theory could still be regarded as a very important approximation because of the origins of capitalism in a society of approximately equally skilled

Leontiev, op. cit., p. 522, Ostrovitianov, l. c., 1948.
See above, p. 129.

producers of commodities and because of the persistence of their standards during the whole existence of capitalism, on account of the large part played by unskilled labour and because of the importance of the equalitarian element in modern Labour aspirations. But the abstraction approaches irrelevance once it is regarded as a main purpose of the theory to explain that element of social reality from which the abstraction is made, namely, the differences between different kinds of labour. And the qualitative laws describing the general outcome of the progress of labour productivity as regards the ownership of the means of production on which we[118] could rely quite independently of the helpfulness of the Marxist theory of prices, cease to say anything once their working has resulted in the nationalisation of all the means of production.

So we are left with some very general statements as regards the distribution of the national income. As distinct from a capitalist society, where confusion as regards the different "factors of production" could intervene, under socialism it is obvious that the prices of all goods are composed of wages-costs, profits of the state-enterprises, and costs of replacing the consumed means of production, which are to be resolved in the same way. Production costs in every unit are composed of costs of the means of production, and wages. The sum total of all the profits, minus that part of them which may be distributed as premia amongst the employees, plus what can be deducted from wages-incomes by taxation, saving-campaigns, etc., must equalise that part of the national output that is represented by additional investment and accumulation of reserve stocks. Hypothetically, it is conceivable that profits might be made by an equal surtax of the wages-expenditure of every industry[119] : in this, but *only* in this case standard prices from which all deviations for political reasons had to start, would equal *values*. The rate of the surtax would represent the rate of exploitation which should be accounted on the total labour expenditure as, in a socialist society, distinctions between "productive" and "non-productive" categories of workers are meaningless. But if the socialist State were to apply such methods, the amount of surplus-labour embodied in the commodities directly consumed by the State (as all investment goods, armaments, etc., are) would have to be recovered by

---

[118] See above, pp. 111-3.
[119] As tentatively suggested by Joan Robinson, l. c., p. 25.

traditional devices of finance ; but excessive demands on income tax, or on internal loans placed under a certain amount of social pressure, would reduce the incentive to work. In the U.S.S.R. especially, direct taxation of the peasant majority of the population has been felt undesirable : it was preferred to transfer the Land Tax, which under the N.E.P. had formed a mainstay of the national budget, to the peasants' own local self-government and even to keep the fees demanded for the services of the State-owned Machine Tractor Stations at a minimum. The peasants make their contribution to the national pool of surplus-value in the shape of the enormous profits made by the State in trading their output to urban consumers ; but it is difficult to say why the State should plan those profits just in proportion to the share of peasant labour in the national labour expenditure without regard for the fact that the urban consumers of agricultural products are virtually the only people who contribute to national expenditure by direct taxation.

Even more important than this difficulty is the inadequacy of a surtax on wages expenditure as a means to achieve the ends for which profits are planned for Soviet enterprises. Profits have (a) to check the efficiency of the production unit and, by a suitable way of distribution, to interest both workers and managements in maximum output, and (b) to grant the production unit a certain amount of autonomy, so that routine investments and small-scale application of suggestions for expanding production which have originated within the industrial unit can be carried out without troubling the central planning authorities and increasing the danger of red tape. The first aim could be partially achieved by suitable disposition of extra-profits made by reducing production costs under the planned level : however, in order that encouragement should be given not merely to a few outstanding enterprises it is necessary that even quite ordinary achievement should find expression in some visible improvements of the conditions of those to whom it is due. Actually, the so-called Director's Fund in Soviet enterprises, which serves to finance extraordinary expenditure in the interest of the enterprise and its employees, is fed by the larger part of its profits made in excess of the Plan, but also by a certain percentage of the planned profits. In no case could the purpose be achieved by making profits proportionate to wages expenditure, the very restriction of which (in relation to output) is intended to be encouraged. Nor is there any reason why wages expenditure should be singled out as the basis of the profits planned for the individual enterprise in order to give it a certain amount of autonomy in matters of smaller investments. In actual Soviet practice profits are calculated on the fixed as well as the circulating capital. Once it is realised that, in a socialist state of the type of the U.S.S.R., profits are planned in proportion not merely to wages but to total capital applied, and in as many production units as the State deems fit to grant such a degree of autonomy, it follows that even the standard level of prices can correspond to values in no more definite a sense than that, if the value of money is to be kept stable, the sum total of profits plus taxes, etc., must correspond to the surplus value created in society. It depends not only on political considerations, but actually on mere administrative expediency how many times, in the process from the original raw-material to the final product, transfer from one economic unit to another should take place, and profits for that unit should be planned. Changes in the degree of autonomy granted to the various production units and the larger organisations embracing them belong to the most current decisions in Soviet administration ; it is clearly senseless to speak of a " value " which can be affected by such events conditioned by, but happening outside, the production sphere. Certainly there will be some general connection : effective demand being supposed as constant, increased productivity of labour, that is, reduction of the amount of socially necessary labour embodied in the individual product, is likely to find expression in a reduction of prices. But exact quantitative relations between the productivity of labour achieved and the interrelations between the distinct spheres of national economy are bound to be even less accessible to generalised investigation than under private monopolies which, in any case, might be expected to direct their new investments to those spheres where the rate of profits might be maximized. In short, what happens is just the opposite of what Marx [95] expected : we have no direct accounting in labour-time, but a system of money prices which, though no longer a fetish-like mask of value (for their connection with social labour is ideologically recognised) are inaccessible to exact quantitative analysis. To state the validity of the " law of value " under such conditions, beyond the inter-relations between the socialist and the non-socialist, or semi-socialist, sector of economics, has no meaning beyond emphasizing the need for distribution according to quality as well as quantity of the work done, and to proclaim continued adherence to the derivation of social developments from the evolution of the productive forces.

CHAPTER VII

THE THEORY OF THE INDUSTRIAL CYCLE

What today is called the industrial cycle emerged in the aftermath of the Napoleonic wars in the country leading in the Industrial Revolution, and with the cycle emerged the three approaches to its explanation current until our own day. To the businessman's commonsense, a glut meant overproduction, and the liberal economists were at pains to show him that such a thing was impossible. Omitting in his abstraction the very mechanism by which equilibrium-conditions in capitalist society are preserved, Ricardo stated that, in the typical model of a capitalist society, commodities were ultimately exchanged against commodities[1] : if the production of all commodities were equally raised, society would be richer in use-values, and no change in the proportions of exchanges would result. Economic depressions thus were explained only by disproportionate development of *some* industries. This fitted the needs of the critical liberal looking for mistakes made by individual entrepreneurs, avoidance of which would have enabled avoidance of the depression within the cherished framework.[2] Say carried the argument *ad absurdum*, by omitting in the abstraction the process in which equilibrium is restored and simply asserting that every supply implicitly creates the

[1] Ricardo's *Principles*, Chapter 21, starts with a simple assertion that obstacles in adapting production to equilibrium conditions were likely soon to be overcome. The ancestry of the statement that commodities are exchanged against commodities has not been pursued by its opponent Malthus (*Principles of Political Economy*, p. 354) beyond his contemporaries. Marx (in a note, *Capital,* vol. I, p. 15) went further back to the Physiocrats ; indeed, the *Tableau Economique* (or any other scheme of the reproduction process) was inconceivable without such a (methodological) assumption.

[2] " What I wish to impress on the readers' mind is that it is at all times the bad adaption of the commodities produced to the wants of mankind which is the specific evil, and not the abundance of commodities." Ricardo, *Notes on Malthus*, ed. Hollander-Gregory, Baltimore-London, 1928, p. 161. Such statements compare very favourably with Say's (e.g., in the introductory pages of his *Letters to Malthus*) enjoyment of the paradox and his reasoning away of the fact of depression. Ricardo's famous exception to the alleged impossibility of a general glut (overproduction of food for labourers, exceeding the natural rise of the population), though not taken very seriously by himself, points to a disproportionality theory, with emphasis on " underconsumption."

demand needed to absorb it ; and this masterpiece of apologetics has survived up to our days as the academic explanation of unemployment as merely frictional.

The conservative-romantic opposition to the Industrial Revolution and classical economy found its expression in the assertion that depressions were caused by insufficiency of consumers' demands ; its dual aspects were respectively expressed by Malthus' defence of " third persons " other than capitalists and workers with a high propensity to consume, and Sismondi's demand for an increasing share of the working-classes in the national income. In either concept a high rate of investment is resented because of its propensity to result in " overproduction " in proportion to effective demand.[3]

All these arguments were brought forward as explanations of the cycle, but actually dealt with long-term tendencies of capitalist production. This was quite natural in view of the very general abstractions current at the time. Marx paid his tribute to this tendency by connecting his explanation of the cycle very closely to the axiom of the long-term falling rate of profits, which he had inherited from the classics[4] ; but, as distinct from many of his followers, he realised that the cycle is the agency by which the equilibrium of capitalist production is periodically restored.[5] He could never accept a denial of the necessity of the cycle, which had originated at a certain stage of social development, by reference to commonplaces valid for all societies based upon division of labour, and he would not accept an argument directed against what he cherished in Ricardo, namely, his advocacy of maximum development of the productive resources.

[3] cf. Dobb, op. cit., p. 89. There is a difference in the methodological approach, in that the Malthusian school of "underconsumptionists" is bound to keep the rate of surplus-value high (in order that it can support both capitalists and rentiers, etc.), whilst social reformers tend to keep it low. Malthus found the justification of his approach (and of the existence of the class he stood for) in the "iron law of wages" (see above, p. 108), which would (at least short of fundamental changes in the birth-rate) prevent increased working-class consumption ; but Marx regarded progressive investment as the only, however temporary, justification of capitalism, and, besides, as the most favourable condition for the workers, because the pressure of the Industrial Reserve Army would be at its lowest (Wage Labour and Capital, in *Selected Works*, vol. I, p. 213).

[4] See above, pp. 145-8.

[5] Comp. *Theories on Surplus Value*, vol. II/2, p. 301, and *Capital*, vol. III, pp. 297 and 299. So far as I know, Rosa Luxemburg, in her polemic against Bernstein, written in 1899, was the first who, whilst emphasising with Marx the role of the cyclical depressions as regulators of capitalist economics (*Sozialreform oder Revolution*, pp. 24-5 in the 2nd ed. of 1908), distinguished between their analysis and that of the eventual breakdown of capitalism.

From the human point of view, "the parson Malthus" who defended the claims of the Established Church to consume as large as possible a part of the national income might be less sympathetic than the reformer Sismondi who wanted to delay progress by increased mass-consumption[3]; but both of them opposed that historical trend without which the conditions for the establishment of a higher social order could not come into being.

Apart from numerous and often important isolated remarks, Marx has left two compact studies on the subject : One, neglect of which is responsible for most of the current misunderstandings, is contained in *Theories on Surplus Value* (vol. II/2). It centres round an attack on the assertion that effective demand is implied in sales and that some inherent automatisms are bound to preserve, or immediately to restore, when disturbed, equilibrium on the market and continuous flow of capitalist production. The basic characteristics of capitalism are "potential causes of crises"[6] : in every society regulated merely by the mechanism of the market purchases are divorced from sales. Production is divorced from consumption and is "anarchic" in that its regulating mechanisms work behind the back of the producers. This equilibrium may have to be restored by the very rise of disequilibrium leading to a crisis in which "unsound" enterprises are destroyed and prices adapted to new conditions. Additionally, in capitalist society savings are divorced from investments. If the bulk of investments has been made at a certain time (usually after the last depression) the sums of money reserved for their amortisation do not represent immediately effective demand, though they are expected to be realised by sales on the market. Thus there are sales to which no immediate purchases correspond. Marx, with the experience of the cotton-famine in the 'sixties, would not deny that crises of capitalist production could arise for various other reasons ; but crises arising from occasional disproportionality are accidental, and enumeration of their causes cannot be accepted as a sufficient explanation of the cycle.[7] It is incorrect to describe disproportion, which is the general form of crisis, or factors that are mere potential causes of crises, as their actual causes, that is, as the reasons why the mere possibility is realised. The general

---

[6] L. c., vol. II/2, pp. 274 ff.
[7] Ibid., pp. 263 and 290-1.

conditions of crises have to be derived from the general conditions of capitalist production. [8]

This task has been tackled in the second of Marx's elaborate studies on the cycle, which has been preserved as the 15th Chapter of the 3rd volume of *Capital*. The whole argument centres round the demonstration that overproduction of commodities (as distinct from overproduction of use-values, which is certainly absent in present society), while *possible* in every society based upon exchange of commodities, is periodically *necessary* in a capitalist society where commodities cannot be produced unless they are sold at a profit. Overproduction of capital signifies overproduction of means of production and of consumers' goods for the working population in relation to what could be applied in order to exploit labour at a certain, socially given, minimum rate of profits. Expansion of the production of capital goods implies reduction of their value, including the value of the old capital equipment, which thus cannot be returned with a profit. Technical progress implies reduced equilibrium-prices of the output as well as of the capital-goods used in its production. In the long run, the fall of prices of means of production restores profitableness threatened by the reduced prices of output, but this is no short-term help, when capitalists compare the prices to be had for the increased output with the money capital which they have originally invested or, even worse, borrowed, and upon which they expect the usual rate of profits. [9] Thus they will not be prepared for major capital-outlay. The fall in the costs of materials, which otherwise might compensate for the necessary reduction of prices of output, may be delayed by speculative purchases by capitalists who seek short-term investment, or who are thrown out of their functions as active entrepreneurs because their capitals have become too small for such functions on account

---

[8] Ibid., p. 289. The statement seems to contradict the attempt recently made by Sweezy, op. cit., to reconcile the different current interpretations of the Marxist theory of crises by a pluralist approach in which different causations of economic depression are regarded as equivalent. Different interpretations of the cycle may be valid for different stages of the development of capitalist society. I should see no contradiction in terms if someone would accept, for the ascending phase of capitalism, Marx's tentative explanation of the cycle by periodical absorption of the industrial reserve army (see below, p. 170), and for the descending phase the interpretation suggested below (pp. 182–5) of Sweezy's interplay of underconsumption with "counteracting tendencies." Theoretical difficulties arise once for a certain period two or more mechanisms, which may compensate as well as support each other, are supposed to produce the cycle.

[9] *Capital*, vol. III, p. 293.

of technical progress demanding larger enterprises.[10] On the other hand, the part of the national income purchased by the workers, though likely to increase, in absolute terms, in times of comparatively good employment, is likely to be proportionally smaller because of the increased application of machinery. "The true barrier to capitalist production is *capital itself*, is the fact that capital and its self-expansion appear as the starting and closing point, as the motive and aim of production."[9]

Instead of simply delaying the process of capitalist expansion the reluctance of capitalists to invest appears periodically because of the need for periodical replacement of the fixed capital.[11] Depression occurred for the first time in the modern period in the aftermath of the disturbance caused by a major war. As soon as a major number of investments has been made after the depression, it takes a certain number of years (which depends on the state of social technique), before reluctance to make further investments, increased by the speculative movements mentioned above, will produce disturbances on the market of capital goods sufficient to bring the whole artificial edifice of prices into motion and thus to destroy the delusion of profitableness, in relation to the prices at which the fixed capital has been invested. The strongest of the competitors will try to override the threatening crisis by making use of the accumulated stock of inventions, and thus promoting obsolescence even of those invested fixed capitals which are not yet physically used up.[12] Thus a need to replace a very large part of the national fixed capital will coincide with a situation where this cannot be profitably done before raw material prices as well as wages have been brought down, and values of existing investments which no longer correspond to social reproduction costs have been written off, which implies clearing industry of the smallest and least efficient entrepreneurs.. Once this has been achieved by the very process of depression, large-scale

[10] Ibid., vol. II, p. 362, and vol. III, p. 294.

[11] Ibid., vol. II, p. 211.

[12] This exposition differs somewhat from that given by Marx who regarded obsolescence because of quicker technical progress as compensating for the increased share of fixed capital with very long (physical) expectation of life. From the point of view of Marxism, consistently interpreted, technical progress should be regarded as a function of socio-economic developments. Some important machinery becomes obsolete not because someone has made some invention, but because some competitor of the owner has found it profitable to use the new invention.

investments by the surviving capitalists, and the next cycle, can start again.

The argument just developed may be characterised as an interpretation of crises as the periodical destruction of the incentive to invest. So far, it should sound quite acceptable to modern Keynesians unless they are inclined to emphasize " underconsumption " as the basic cause of that destruction as opposed to Marx[13] who certainly regarded it as not more than one important factor affecting one of the possible fields of investment. In the development of Marx's thought, but not in logical connection, his explanation of the cycle is bound to the axiom of the falling rate of profits, and the contention that his argument stands and falls with the correctness of the assumption that the forces tending to lower the rate of profits overbalance the " counteracting forces " has dominated nearly all the critics as well as the defenders of his theory.[14] However important or otherwise the answer to this question[15] may be for the assessment of the general prospects of capitalism[16] it has nothing to do with the explanation of the cycle. The incentive to invest depends on comparisons of the realisable profits with those to which entrepreneurs have become accustomed during the immediately preceding period, not with those current during a comparable stage of the preceding cycle. But the general trend of the rate of profits, that is, the question whether profits tend to form a decreasing or increasing proportion of the sum total of all production prices, cannot be decided in the short-term period ; for production prices themselves are realised only in the average of oscillations extending over the whole cycle.

Marx's argument merely supposes the struggle between counteracting tendencies influencing short-term profit-expectations by entrepreneurs, and some mechanism that explains why those tendencies alternatively predominate, instead of a mere delayed action of the predominant tendency. The argument might well have been placed in the first volume of *Capital* (where the concept of the rate of profits is not yet developed) as soon as it was proved (1) that average prices (whether of individual commodities, as assumed in volume I, or merely of the total

[13] See below, p. 173.
[14] With the exception of Dobb, l. c., pp. 108 ff.
[15] See above, p. 147.
[16] Which I would deny, in agreement, I think, with the majority of modern Marxists. But see below, pp. 189-90, on Grossmann's theory.

output of capitalist society, as shown in vol. III, is irrelevant for the argument) are determined by the labour effort needed under the given social conditions for the reproduction of those commodities ; (2) that capital is invested in money form at a certain price level in order to be returned with a profit ; (3) that the development of capitalism and the accompanying technical progress imply investment of additional and depreciation of the existing capitals, and (4) that the cycle has started at some time with sufficient strength to cause a large number of investments to coincide. It seems to me impossible to dispose of the logic of the argument unless (a) the present circulation process of capitals could be modified by a continuous depreciation of money (which would change the otherwise periodical destruction of capital into a less visible, but continuous process[17]) and (b) such a policy could be carried out without danger that the country making such an experiment would be called to order by the guardian of international investors' interest and thus be forced either to honour the Dollar and to import depression, or completely to turn away from traditional market economics. As the Marxist argument supposes the alternative predominance of the conflicting tendencies, it should not be applied to a model in which depreciation of existing capitals is organised as a continuous process : the relevant question is whether capitalism in any traditional sense could work without the delusions of investors as to the solidity of their new investments, and hopes of individual capitalists that their investment will escape depreciation during the next depression. This question is identical with the question whether Keynesian economics, in a sense more ambitious than that of filling the gaps left by the failure of " private enterprise ", are a practical proposition.[18]

The comparative simplicity of Marx's theory of the cycle has been impaired partly because he died before it could reach more than a fragmentary stage of elaboration, and partly by its author's inability to exclude arguments apparently clear enough in his days[4] though not necessarily involved in the issue in question.

[17] This hypothetical assumption should not be confused with the monetary explanations of the cycle repeatedly refuted by Marx as dealing with mere symptoms. In those explanations it is supposed that a different monetary policy might keep prices at a stable level corresponding to "normal" profits from the invested capitals ; in the Marxist explanation (including our hypothetical modification, in which depreciation of capitals would be continuous, instead of being intermittent) destruction of capital values is supposed as a necessary implication of capitalist progress.

[18] See below, pp. 367-9.

To the latter fault we owe not only the title of the 15th Chapter of *Capital*, vol. III, " Unravelling of the internal Contradic-tions of the Law " (of the tendential fall of the rate of profits), which invited misunderstandings by most of Marx's followers, but also Engels' combination of the second section of that chapter (which contains the general argument) with the next, where changes in the rate of surplus-value during the industrial cycle are analysed under the simplifying assumption that expansion would temporarily proceed to its theoretical limit, that is, to absorption of the whole industrial reserve army so that additional capitals could yield no additional profits. Obviously,[15] the increase in the rate of surplus-value involved in the very technical progress that tends to lower the rate of profits is one of the main forces counter-acting the latter tendency (in so far, Engels was right in inserting the fragment into the chapter with the mentioned title) ; but absorption of the industrial reserve army within the limits of the general framework of Marxist theory [19] can hardly bring about crisis in the sense described in the section, namely, general competition between increased capitals for appropriation of a mass of profits which can increase no more. By chance, this section is the best-elaborated of all statements on the cycle left by Marx, and its failure to be balanced by corresponding sections deriving the mechanism of the crisis from other " counteracting forces " was bound to result in misunderstandings.[20] Lastly,

[19] At least to me, *Capital*, vol. I, Chapter 23, section 3, seems to exclude the possibility of Marx's considering complete absorption of the industrial reserve army as an actual possibility relevant for the explanation of the regular events of the cycle. In vol. III, Chapter 15, Marx made a purely hypothetical assumption in order to illustrate overproduction of capital, the very possibility of which had been denied by orthodox economists.

[20] Sweezy has gone to the length of concluding from this well-elaborated fragment, in connection with what Marx said in the first volume of *Capital* on the effects of the cycle on the industrial reserve army, the statement (op. cit., p. 154) that in Marxist theory "the chain of causation runs from the rate of accumulation to the volume of employment, from the volume of employment to the level of wages, and from the level of wages to the rate of profits." A similar argument has been developed by Mosz-kovska (op. cit., p. 179) who shares with Sweezy the preference for the explanation of the cycle by underconsumption, and also the failure to distinguish between the ultimate tendencies of the rate of profits and those short-term vaccillations in which it is realised, and which form the only available explanation of the cycle. According to Moszkovska, it depends on the struggle of the working-classes whether increased productivity of labour will result in increased real wages, which would mean that the rate of exploitation of labour would remain constant, and the rate of profits therefore fall ; or the counter-acting tendency of creating additional "relative surplus-value" would have its way and the rate of profits remain constant. In the second case the underconsumption, which is regarded as the primary cause of all crises, would have to work also as the immediate cause of depression ; whilst in the first case Marx's explan-ation of the cycle by the fall in the rate of profits would work. Moszkovska then

Marx[21] made his basic argument that crises were the outcome of overproduction of capitals, as distinct from use-values, in the form of a juxtaposition of a capitalist society to a hypothetical socialist society serving the producers' needs. In another Chapter of vol. III which deals with the functions of credit in the process of crises, he inserted a remark which should illustrate the importance of the subject of discussion by hypothetically stating what would happen if it were omitted : supposing, that the whole society were composed merely of capitalists and industrial workers, and supposing that those changes in price relations during the cycle which prevent the replacement of large parts of the national capital in average relations[22] and the additional tension by speculations promoted by the credit system were absent, crises could not originate except from disproportions between the various branches of production, and between those parts of the surplus product as are respectively being invested and consumed by the capitalists.[23] But in actual capitalist society the replacement of the capitals invested in production depends largely upon the consumption of (Malthus') non-productive classes, as the workers' propensity to consume is restricted by the economic laws governing their wages and employment. " The last cause of all real crises always remains the poverty and restricted consumption of the masses as compared to the tendency of capitalist production to develop the production forces in such a way, that only the absolute power of consumption of the entire society would be their limit."[24]

For reasons soon to be discussed this argument has got more popularity than all the original work of Marx on crises. But it is not conclusive. It bears the traces of a tendency to take from the opponent's argument more for granted than is actually

directly faces the problem of having two different and alternative explanations (so far as the " immediate cause", the only one accessible to verification, is concerned) for one apparently homogeneous phenomenon. In Moszkovska's formulation what is only implied in that of Sweezy, is explicitly stated, namely that any development of Trade Unionism (and, on the other side, a state of things like that existing since the conclusion of World War No. 1 when the industrial reserve army is not absorbed even at the culmination points of the cycle) impairs the essential chain of causation.

[21] *Capital*, vol. III, pp. 286-7. In the following section, pp. 292-3, the same basic idea is expressed in a much more balanced statement which could be quoted in favour of an " underinvestment " just as well as of an " underconsumption " theory.

[22] Which provided the basis for Marx's own explanation of the cycle discussed above.

[23] Which would mean that in such an abstraction Ricardo, if not Say, were right.

[24] *Capital*, vol. III, p. 568.

172 THE ANATOMY OF BOURGEOIS SOCIETY

accepted, in order to make what is deemed the main argument more impressive. It juxtaposes the alleged " underconsumption " in capitalist society to some hypothetical alternative society serving the needs of the consumer. But consumers' needs in the two societies are quite different things. " Underconsumption " with capitalism, that is, lack of effective demand for consumers' goods, has a definite meaning only as an alternative to other conditions conceivable within capitalist society (for example, reform policies increasing mass purchasing power). But the assertion that a communist society serves the needs of consumers (or of defence, etc.) is irrelevant for the market, which would exist no longer. At the best, " underconsumption," in the sense of Marx's statement, is a certain aspect of capitalism, just as " disproportionality " is another. There could be no crises if capitalism consisted of production for satisfaction of actual needs, instead of the return of the invested capitals with maximised profits ; and there is, in an unplanned society based upon mass-production, an additional risk of crises because its equilibrium may be disturbed by the investments being wrongly apportioned to the different industries. Both statements are of a conditional character and actually deal with the " potential causes of crises", but the concrete Marxist explanation of the cycle is based upon another characteristic of capitalism, namely, its need for reproduction on an increasing scale implying investment of part of the surplus-value and depreciation of part of the existing investments. Only from this point of view is the cycle accessible to explanation, because of the periodicity of large-scale investments. It may be added that economic depressions generally start in those branches of industry where recent investments have been largest, which in our days (as distinct from those of Marx, when textile manufactures were most important) means industries producing means of production. Nor is there a tendency for economic depressions to start from colonies where a much larger part is played by industries producing consumers' goods.

Marx has not failed to criticise the main theories of crises current already in his days. He described the explanation of crises by " overproduction ", unless concretely defined as overproduction of capitals, as an obvious tautology[25] ; he reproached the " disproportionality " theory with its inability to explain the

[25] *Capital*, vol. II, pp. 475-6.

regularity of the cycle ; and he argued against the explanation of the cycle by " underconsumption " that the periodical depressions are immediately preceded by a phase in which mass-consumption is at its highest.[25] But the social forces that had brought Ricardo's and Sismondi's approaches into being continued to work in countries and conditions where nearly all progressives described themselves as Marxists, and ascribed their own theories of the cycle to Marx even where it should not have been too difficult for an unbiased observer to notice that Marx had explicitly rejected those theories. Ambiguities in Marx's own expression, such as we have noticed, were bound to give such tendencies ample encouragement.

The struggle of the various trends of those who ascribed their theory of the cycle to Marx provides a most interesting illustration of the influence exercised by political interests on theoretical thought. Trade Unionists and social reformers tried to establish, to well-meaning capitalists, that the success of their endeavours to increase mass-consumption would prolong the life of that social order the abolition of which had been regarded by Marx as a condition of human progress, whilst the idealisation of sectional activities within existing society permeated the Utopian aspects of the revolutionary ideology itself. Once the " anarchy " of the market ceased to be regarded as an essential element of capitalism and the possibility of monopolist regulation arose, the concept of disproportionality which to Marx and his contemporaries had been an additional reproach to capitalism, turned into a potential weapon of those who made allowance for its ability to become " organised."[26] The struggle against such tendencies encouraged a certain revival of the original Marxist theory in the West, while in Russia[27] the position is still influenced by the tribute once paid by Lenin to the more

[26] cf. Sweezy, op. cit., pp. 159 ff.

[27] In his Introduction (pp. 6-7) to vol. I of the collective work of the Section for World Economics of the Academy of Science on World Economic Crises, 1848-1935 published (in Russian), Moscow, 1937, Varga distinguishes three strata in the genesis of the crisis, excessive emphasis on each of which results in a mistaken theory : (a) the potential cause (which he identifies with disproportionality, evidently in order to find a parallel to his criticism of existing theories ; but Marx's concept was much broader) ; (b) the fundamental cause (underconsumption) and (c) the concrete cause of the cycle, periodical need for replacing the fixed capital. For a critical review (in German) see my report in Zeitschrift fuer Sozialforschung, 1938, No. 1-2. In his work on Changes in the Economics of Capitalism in the result of the Second World War (in Russian, Moscow, 1946) Varga even stronger emphasised his derivation of the cycle from " underconsumption " but was strongly criticized in the following discussion.

propagandist aspects of underconsumption[28] after he had for a time joined hands with Tugan-Baranovsky, Struve, and similar advocates of the capitalist industrialisation of Russia against the Narodniki who rejected the possibility.[29] Whatever the merits of the explanation of crises by under-consumption within the framework of the Marxist theory, in the next discussion of the cycle, which is bound to accompany the next economic depression, its traditional hold within the Marxist fold is unlikely to be impaired by the fact that meanwhile a theory hardly distinguishable from it [30] has won academic recognition.

The roots of the theory of " underconsumption " are in A. Smith's description of investment as the mere employment of a different kind of workers. This description was historically important as a stage in the development of the monist approach to all the factors applied in production, but it is an obvious implication of the dynamic approach characteristic of Marxism that progress in modern society implies increasing demand for means of production. Therefore, the " underconsumption " theory makes no sense unless it means to say that proceeding investment is bound to result in the output of consumers' goods outrunning effective demand. This, if applied to the industrial cycle, would put it formally in the position of a subspecies of the explanation of crises by disproportionality. Combinations of both concepts are accepted by the majority of authors who regard themselves as orthodox Marxists.

Whilst Marx's reluctance to accept disproportionality as a sufficient explanation of the cycle is evident, there is in the part

[28] To describe Lenin as an advocate of the theory of " underconsumption " as frequently done with references to the statements in the Annex to the German edition of the 2nd volume of *Capital* (for a summary in English see Sweezy, op. cit., pp. 184 ff) would be clearly mistaken. In *The Development of Capitalism in Russia* (*Collected Works*, Russian ed., vol. 3, p. 36) he explicitly rejected the current derivation of such a theory from Marx's statement quoted above ([24]) and stated that in the formation of the internal market means of production were more important than consumers' goods.

[29] See below, pp. 190-1.

[30] Lord Keynes' own point of view cannot so easily be described as "underconsumptionist." His basic assertions as to the ultimate direction of economic activities towards consumption (*General Theory*, pp. 104-5, 166, and even 211, where he is polemizing against Say's Law) obviously contradict Marx's analysis of capitalist production as directed toward increased social power of those controlling the means of production, and thus form the logical basis of an explanation of crises by "underconsumption." But his declaration of sympathy with such explanations (l.c., p. 325) is balanced by the preceding pages, and his analysis of the American situation of 1929 (p. 323) would be even compatible with Marx's theory of the cycle, as explained above, pp. 166-8. But most of the Keynesians may be regarded as " underconsumptionists," the more as even in their pleading for public investments they prefer those directly serving mass-consumption (see below, p. 366).

of his argument dealing with the " potential causes of crises "
no lack of material upon which the advocates of such an explanation could build. Tugan-Baranovsky, the first modern representative of that tendency, believed, indeed, that mere demonstration of the complicated conditions which capitalism had to fulfil
in order to preserve equilibrium, conjointly with Marx's hint at
the importance of the periodical need for replacing the fixed
capital for the formation of the cycle, [11] was a sufficient explanation of the latter. So he could combine his advocacy of the
explanation of the cycle by disproportionality with a direct attack
on Marx's explanation, which he deemed dependent on an actual
prevalence of the factors tending to reduce the rates of profit.
Hilferding [31] shared this common mistake, but, as the first post-
Marxian author, he recognised that Marx's theory was connected
with the tendential fall in the rate of profits. But he did not
accept Marx's argument, made in *Capital*, vol. III, Chapter
15, as an explanation of the reasons which prevented the stronger
of the counteracting forces from being expressed in a continuous, though delayed, movement of the rate of profits. He
believed he had found the explanation of the cycle in the fact that
large-scale industries with a huge amount of fixed capital are
slower in adapting their output to changed conditions of profit-
ability. To express the idea in terms of academic economics,
disproportionalities are bound to arise because of the comparative
failure of large-scale industries with a low elasticity of supply to
comply with Say's law. Hilferding's argument does not make
sense if the general validity of that law is questioned, as is done by
both orthodox Marxists and Keynesians. Hilferding's theory
regards fail-investments as the true cause of the depression, and is
general only in stating reasons for which they are likely to be
made in certain industries.

The only advantage of Hilferding's analysis is that it produces
the hypothetical centre of the crises where it is found in actual
investigation of a modern depression, namely, in large-scale
industries producing means of production, as distinct from the
" underconsumption " variety of the explanation of the cycle by
disproportionality which at this very point comes to grips with
reality. Unhappily, the very development of monopoly, to
the study of which Hilferding's work is devoted, results in the

[31] Op. cit., pp. 318 ff.

comparatively low elasticity of supply implied in the technical structure of the large-scale industries being compensated for by their larger propensity to monopolist organisation. Hilferding may have reproduced one of the subjective reasons that cause the owners of large-scale industries with high amounts of fixed capital to combine, but his basic theoretical approach is refuted by the fact that, in spite of their combinations and also in opposition to his expectations [32] economic depressions, with a tendency to become deeper from cycle to cycle, continued to follow each other at decreasing intervals (apart from the wars which, however, would be explained by Marxists as alternative expressions of the same forces that produce the cycle).

As regards its political implications, the explanation of crises by disproportionality demands regulation of supply and investments according to the likely developments of demand. This could conceivably be done by private monopolies. But the fact that some industries are comparatively easily accessible, and others nearly inaccessible, to monopolist organisation, is bound to result in new disproportionalities, this time in the opposite sphere to that in which Hilferding's primary theory had to envisage over-investment. [33] General State control of investments should be sufficient to meet that difficulty and, according to Hilferding's initial assumption, to produce that "organised capitalism" where prices and rates of profit would be adapted to changes in the objective conditions of production without a cyclical rise and fall. No more than partial realisations of that Utopia are available. The defenders of the disproportionality theory get into some difficulties when asked for an explanation for the continuance and increasing strength of the cycle in spite of a

[32] Especially in later years Hilferding became a main advocate of the conception of "organised capitalism." In *Finance Capital* his forecasts on the development of crises under monopoly-capitalism are rather careful. However, he questioned (l. c., pp. 365 ff) the likeliness of further breakdowns of large-scale banking, which played such an important role in the 1929-32 crisis, and even envisaged the possibility that in the monopolised industries—as distinct from those on whose shoulders the former could transfer the main burdens of the depression—the cycle might take the shape of a mere continuous up and down in production and profits.

[33] Thus the explanation of the cycle by disproportionality comes apparently near to that by underconsumption which would also expect depression to start in the same spheres (though for a different reason, namely, because of their producing consumers' goods). In such formulations of the "underconsumption" theory like that of Hobson (op. cit., p. 85) where the basis of "over-saving" is found mainly in rents and monopoly profits instead of the general characteristics of capitalism, the difference to the last-mentioned form of the disproportionality theory is rather formal.

fundamental change in its alleged cause.   But they may still resort to the dialectical argument that only as long as monopoly dominates mere parts of industry and therefore only shifts the burden of depression to other parts (with ultimate repercussions upon the monopolised industries themselves) does it increase the general depression, whilst its complete control of all industries would end disproportionality, apart from occasional mistakes, as unavoidable even in a planned society.

CHAPTER VIII

STAGNATION AND BREAKDOWN OF CAPITALIST SOCIETY

(a) MARX'S GENERAL THEORY OF THE COLLAPSE OF CAPITALISM

Marx's famous forecast of the expropriation of the expropriators, at the end of *Capital*, volume I, Chapter 24, is based upon a limited number of statements derived from his basic analysis of capitalist society. While (1) there is a progressive diminution in the number of capitalist magnates which creates the necessary condition for the management of nationalised economics (a statement which could be further elaborated in the stage of monopoly capitalism), there is (2) a corresponding increase in the mass of poverty, oppression, enslavement, degeneration, and exploitation ; but at the same time there is (3) a steady intensification of the wrath of the working class—a class which (4) grows ever more numerous, and is disciplined, unified, and organised by the very mechanism of capitalist production. In consequence, the contradiction between capitalist monopoly and the forces of production developed under its rule will be solved by the abolition of capitalist private property, by the expropriation of a·few usurpers by the mass of the people. On other occasions Marx explained that this expropriation is to be carried through by nationalisation of all the essential means of production by a state originating from a working-class revolution and prepared to break capitalist resistance with dictatorial means.

This argument is sufficiently clear to allow for critical analysis. The truth of the statements (1) and (4) is hardly questionable. Most polemics concentrate on statement (2), increasing exploitation and oppression of the workers. Conventional Marxist propaganda simplifies the problem, and especially its implications upon statement (3), by repeating statements that were true when Engels' *Conditions of the Working Classes in England*, and even when *Capital* was written, but contradict the actual conditions of the employed section of the working-class in the leading capitalist countries in our days, when conditions have improved because of economic and political action of the sectional organisation of the workers (at least on the Continent to a large extent under the impact of Marxism itself which provided the ideological tool for shaping that organisation). The basic Marxist concepts do not imply stability of real wages but only an increasing rate of exploitation, as a condition of the increased investments.[1] It may be argued that such increases in real wages as are actually observable hardly exceed the increased expenditure of human energies implied in the general intensification of labour ; but such an argument, however helpful in an ideological criticism of capitalist society, does not answer the question of the incentives to revolution, with which we here are concerned : workers who enjoy improving standards of life will not face the risks of revolution merely on the ground that these improvements are conditioned by the interest of the capitalists in keeping them fit for increasing toil.[1a] Increased fatigue, as implied in the modern conveyor-belt methods of work and compensated for by recreation of the standardized type as provided by capitalist enterprise, may render the average employed worker less prone to serious thought about the merits of capitalism amongst other things. A very large part of the increase of the industrial reserve army (within the capitalist system as a whole) may be concentrated in colonial and semi-colonial countries where peasants and craftsmen are expropriated under the impact of invading capitalism without being offered a corresponding amount of industrial employment.

As early as 1847, in *The Poverty of Philosophy*[2] Marx observed that short periods of prosperity for the English workers might be purchased by permanent starvation in India ; however, as he

[1] See above, pp. 117–8 and 177.

[1a] Pareto (*Manuel d'Economie Politique*, Paris, 1829, Chapter VII, pp. 401 ff.) tries to prove that economic prosperity promotes " democracy," in an extremely vague conception which embraces democratic constitutions and revolutionary mass-movements as well as economic prosperity of the masses, and extends from ancient Greece over the Reformation period to modern times. It is obviously true that prospering communities—especially those prospering from exploitation of other parts of the World—allow for a comparatively high share of the non-property-owning masses in the national consumption fund, and it is also true that the *bourgeoisie* could not aspire at political power before it was consolidated as an economic group which, by definition, presupposes its economic prosperity (though it is not less true that even *bourgeois* revolutions presuppose activity of non-bourgeois masses which will not move unless there was at least temporary deterioration of their conditions of life). But it does not follow that a new society based upon the organisational efforts of a class hitherto excluded from the direction of economic life is impossible, and certainly the extreme efforts necessary to bring it into being would not come forward except under the alternative of starvation, loss of national independence, etc.

[2] Ed. cit. p. 85.

granted even the English workers only three years of comparative prosperity out of the industrial cycle of ten years, their own propensity to revolt appeared unquestionable. Whatever the general trend of the conditions of the " average worker " in the capitalist world as a whole, the chances of revolution look different as soon as the bulk of continuous mass-misery is localized mainly in colonies and the employed part of the working-class in the leading capitalist countries enjoys a fairly tolerable standard of life even in times of general depression. This does not affect the basic truth of the Marxist analysis : a national revolution in a semi-colonial country can produce socialism in any reasonable sense just as well as could the realisation of the expectations expressed in the *Communist Manifesto* that bourgeois-democratic revolutions in the leading capitalist countries might lead to socialist consequences. However, the concrete course of the great transformation is bound to be affected by such modifications. As soon as the Marxist abstraction of a homogeneous capitalist compound is dropped, the concrete incentive to revolution loses the simplicity assumed by Marx. We shall return, in section (a) of Chapter XIII, to this issue.

Statement (3), in the general sense that the growth of capitalism involves rising mass-protest against capitalism, and even rising mass-conviction of the necessity to abolish it, corresponds to an obvious reality. It is not difficult to prove that the growth of capitalism is bound to be accompanied by a growing opposition, which is not bound to its mere birth-pangs, as the apologetics of young capitalism asserted, but is sure to get ample and increasing food by its " normal " functioning. Such a proof is sufficient as a foundation for sectional mass-organisation of the workers which, for this reason, found in *Capital*, vol. I, its Bible[2a]. But criticism of capitalism is by no means revolutionary action, about the difficulties of which Marx cherished rather realistic views, and certainly it involves no guarantee that such action would be successful.

Marx has not approached that problem clearly. In the *Poverty of Philosophy* it is not even realised : the statement that the working-class is bound to organise itself and to acquire class-consciousness[3] is directly followed by another statement that an

---

[2a] Besides, Engels' reference, in his preface to the English edition of 1886, to such current descriptions of the impact of the book on the Continent does not necessarily imply identification. See above, pp. 86-7.

[3] Which we shall discuss below, pp. 225 ff.

oppressed class cannot emancipate itself as long as the existing productive powers could co-exist with the existing social relations. But, " of all the instruments of production, the greatest productive power is the revolutionary class itself." The statement makes easy reading in our days, and seems to cover both the reasons for the slight resistance met by the nationalisation of coal-mines in Britain as well as the difficulties confronting the French bourgeois parties in their desire to purge the political stage of the party commanding the support of the bulk of the working-class. But, evidently, such developments are secondary to developments which have questioned not only the continued preparedness of the masses to comply with capitalism but also the ability of countries like Britain and France to survive without maximum efforts of their working-classes. Even so, it is impossible to decide in advance whether incapacity of a capitalist ruling class to keep " the greatest productive power " somewhat satisfied will result in social transformation or simply in the loss of national independence in favour of a stronger capitalist power.

(b) TENDENTIAL DESTRUCTION OF EFFECTIVE DEMAND

Capitalism is directed not towards satisfying human needs but towards reproducing value, increased by appropriated surplus-value ; but profits cannot be realised unless commodities are sold. Ultimately, increased output even of investment goods results in increased output of consumers' goods, the sale of which at prices enabling the realisation of the surplus-value is prevented by that very lack of real wages behind the increase of the social productivity of labour which is needed in order to keep profits at their proper rate. If we overlook armaments and other direct purchases of investment-goods by the State,[4] and if the whole capitalist world is regarded as a unit (so that exports of capital goods imply mere geographical dislocation of the conflict) contradictions between the quick expansion of capitalist production and the limitations of the markets for consumers' goods implied in the capitalist mode of production are bound to lead to economic or political crises (the latter implied in State purchases of investment goods for public services and armaments, and the

[4] Public investments for Welfare purposes come in only in so far as, by the nature of things, they do not compete with private enterprise, for example, schools as distinct from housing.

G

likely use of the latter). Thus it may be regarded as a first generalisation about the causes of the general crisis of capitalist society.[5]

As we have seen in the last chapter, this general statement does not lead to a satisfactory explanation of the industrial cycle. But more relevant applications of a theory of " under-consumption " are possible in the analysis of the long-term trend of capitalist prosperity. As the contradiction between potential output and effective demand results in increasing difficulties in selling the output, not depression but prosperity is the part of the industrial cycle which needs explanation. That explanation has to be provided by the enumeration of counteracting forces which prevent " underconsumption " from producing permanent depression just as Marx has enumerated the forces counteracting the tendential fall of the rate of profits. (The apparent formal difference disappears when the term " underconsumption " is translated into exact economic language such as " fall of effective demand for consumers' goods in relation to output ".) Dr. Sweezy to whom belongs the merit of having first elaborated a theory on those lines,[6] has only failed to notice that, in this framework, the theory of the " counteracting forces " *is* the theory of the cycle. Movements of the rate of profits as well as disproportionality have their place in the system not as separate causes of depression, as Dr. Sweezy deems, but as limiting the factors counteracting underconsumption, mainly the investment of part of the surplus-value in new industries. (State activities[7] would be influenced indirectly by the movements of the rate of

[5] Only by complete confusion on this point which, however, is implied in the reformist approach to fundamental problems and therefore popular, is it possible to conclude from the part played by "underconsumption" in the mechanism leading to economic depression within capitalist society that crises could be prevented by the establishment of a society directed towards maximised mass-consumption. The only socialist society which we know directs its economic activities not towards maximised mass-consumption, but towards increased investments (see below, p.356). It has no realisation problems because it is not directed towards the achievement of maximised profits, not because of any specific merits of the commodities which it happens to produce.

[6] His assertion (l. c., pp. 177–8) of having elaborated a theory indicated by Marx himself should be regarded as a continuation of the above-mentioned tendency of Marxist writers to generalise some of the different facets in the master's fragmentary elaboration of his theory into the theory preferred by themselves. By this procedure Sweezy has impaired the elaboration of his own theory : the obvious existence of different facets of the Marxist explanation forced him to recognise the existence of various types of crises, underconsumption being only species.

[7] About the inclusion of which amongst the "counteracting forces" we shall speak below (p. 185).

profits mainly in so far as business interests and orthodox academic economics may prevent " offset-spending " in favour of deflationary policies). With these improvements, Sweezy's theory clearly appears as the counterpart of the Keynesian theory in the Marxist camp : either theory introduces new factors, " extra-economic " from the point of view of classical economics, as necessary " offsets " against tendencies bound to bring the classical liberal model to a standstill The different description of those tendencies (" excess of savings," or " under-consumption ") reflects no more than the different ideological milieu in which each writer works. Both theories may be regarded as interesting attempts at replacing the Ricardian-Marxist pattern which starts from investment by a new concept based upon the entanglement of invested capitals in the process of realisation.

Marxism does not necessarily exclude any tendency of real wages to rise, and the apparent evidence of the underconsumption theory is based upon the increasing output of *use-values*, consumers' goods. But a discussion of the conditions under which, in the Marxist system, a chronic contradiction between output of, and effective demand for, goods for mass-consumption is bound to arise, has to start in terms of *value*, that is, distribution of *social labour*. We may illustrate the " underconsumption " theory by assuming that of a workers employed in a society in producing wages goods, with a certain technique of production, b workers are diverted to the production of additional means of production ultimately destined to produce other wages goods.[8] With the improved means of production $(a-b)$ workers will produce more wage-goods than was formerly done by a workers (otherwise there would have been no incentive to introduce the new, improved means of production which

---

[8] In the construction of our model we have assumed, for simplicity's sake, that the total labour force remains constant. The argument can be made also for an extensively or intensively (creation of absolute surplus value) increasing total labour force, the increase being totally directed towards the production of means of production, an assumption which is not unreasonable for a period of stagnation. A further simplifying assumption made by us is constant manpower and technique applied in the luxury industries, so that their output remains stable (which is conceivable if the rise of the bourgeoisie is accompanied, say, by the decay of an old aristocracy with a high propensity to consume luxury-goods) ; the whole increase in surplus-value is invested in the industries producing means of production ultimately for the use of industries producing wage-goods. Thus our model forms the counterpart to Tugan-Baranovsky's single worker producing infinite amounts of means of production and luxury-goods.

are more expensive because of the addition of b workers to the former staff of the industries producing them). But the total *value* of the increased supply of wages goods will be not larger than the value of those formerly produced by a workers. There will be no lack of effective demand as long as the total real wages of all the workers—those employed in direct production of wages goods as well as those producing additional means of production—increase to the same extent to which the productivity of labour in the industries producing consumers' goods has increased, in short, as long as no *relative surplus-value* is created. Not every decrease in the share of the working-classes in the national outcome is bound to produce the specific problems of " underconsumption " [9]: in general, the productivity of labour makes less progress in the industries producing wages goods than in the industries producing means of production, which form the bulk of modern industry. Scientific methods of increasing the human energy appropriated by employers are most efficiently applied in the large-scale industries producing means of production, and thus " absolute surplus-value " may be created in a shape which does not necessarily imply increased output of consumers' goods. Further, not only in the markets for consumers' goods but even in the statistics of the total earnings of the wage-earning and salaried classes, a certain lagging of the increase in real wages behind the increased productivity of the industries producing wages goods may be compensated for by increased consumption of unproductive workers (mainly in the distribution of goods), civil servants, etc., who are paid by the comparative raising of the prices of consumers' goods by increased distribution margins, indirect taxation, etc. (though it is theoretically correct to mention this factor, as Dr. Sweezy does, amongst the forces counteracting underconsumption). Only what remains after these restrictions have been taken into consideration represents *prima facie* " underconsumption " which is bound to produce chronic depression unless compensated for by counteracting forces.

From a purely theoretical point of view, all factors that delay the replacement of human labour by additional means of production might be enumerated amongst the forces counteracting

[9] Those theorists who, like Joan Robinson (op. cit., p. 80) deny the existence of such a decrease should, *a fortiori*, reject any concept of " underconsumption," or at least take its compensation by the consumption of unproductive workers (see below in the text) for granted.

underconsumption, but this would not carry us very far.[10] If there is no creation of "relative surplus-value," that is, if capitalism is somewhat stationary, there will be no "underconsumption "—this was the utopia put forward by Sismondi, Hobson, and many lesser spirits. Its refutation lies in the inherent need for capitalism to accumulate and to expand. Importance can be ascribed only to such factors " counteracting underconsumption " which preserve at least the appearances of such expansion. The two most important of Sweezy's " counteracting forces "[11] imply investments in the industries producing means of production which, over a long period, do not result in increased output of consumer goods. In the ascending phase of capitalist development huge investments are needed for the establishment of new industries and especially for the capitalist industrialisation of new countries (which, it is true, will later reproduce the dilemma on an enlarged scale) ; in the period of stagnation and decay of capitalism investment goods are diverted from the supply of marketed consumers' goods by unproductive consumption by the State, mainly for armaments. In the replacement of the first by the second factor we find the key to the replacement of classical economics (and those trends in later academic economics as preserved classic assumptions when they had become mere apologetic ideologies) by Keynesian economics.

[10] Sweezy (l. c., pp. 222 ff) mentions, for example, population growth, because it results in pressure upon the wages and thereby reduces the incentive to replace workers by machinery. But that "counteracting force" is itself counteracted by the fall of the birth-rate and by the rise of Trade Unionism. The question whether some factor increasing working-class consumption reduces or (by increasing the incentive to replace workers by machinery) increases the discrepancy between supply of, and efficient demand for, wages goods cannot be answered *a priori* by theoretical assumptions.

[11] The others are of less importance. It is a matter of presentation whether the support of unproductive consumers (civil servants, etc.) by the State who pays them from the proceeds of taxation of productive workers is arranged together with the consumption of unproductive distribution workers, the unemployed, etc., or under a special heading " the State." I can find no justification for the latter procedure outside liberal ideology which regards State interference as something abnormal, or in discussing that ideology. I should agree that separation of the costs of the support of soldiers from those of material armaments is somewhat artificial ; but this is involved in the very concept of underconsumption which puts demand for consumer goods, and diversion of output of industries normally producing means of production into unproductive channels under different headings. Subsidies to working-class consumption paid from taxation of capitalists form part of the real wages and belong to the conditions preceding the very rise of the issue of "underconsumption," whilst payment of unproductive civil servants, soldiers, etc., from the same source means a mere diversion of capitalist consumption. Evidently the whole consumption of the capitalist class plays a rather subordinate role for the issue in our days, as distinct from when Malthus defended the usefulness of landlord and rentier consumption.

The " underconsumption " argument is thus relevant as a refutation of the apologist's assertion that capitalism automatically creates the demand for the commodities supplied by its development. It does not : the deficiency of effective demand for consumers' goods compared with their output must be compensated for either by continuous expansion of capitalist production which creates a proportionally increasing demand for investment goods, or by public " offset-spending " which is most efficient if it diverts part of the " overproduced " investment-goods into channels where they cannot ultimately result in increased supply of consumers' goods, (though they may well result in the destruction of prospective consumers, if not of the whole system). The second stage, measured by the standards of the first, may be described as " stagnation " : but it should be kept in mind that this does not imply any fundamental difficulty within the famework of the system. Capitalism, in itself, can be stable with any amount of " underconsumption " compensated for by " offset-spending," provided that the stagnation affects equally all the more developed capitalist states. Capitalism may break down in a military collision between those states which have built pyramids and made atomic bombs, and others which, being non-capitalist, could put the latter activity on sounder foundations by continuing to expand their productive resources to a degree surpassing that allowed to capitalism even in the heyday of its expansion ; but this is not the question here under discussion. Within the capitalist system, there will be differences between countries where the stagnation of the system is expressed in periodical deep depressions and others where it is expressed in " full employment " in partially unproductive activities ; but such differences, however important from the political point of view, would not necessarily imply inability of either type of solution to hold its own in competition with the alternative on the international stage. Sensible differentiations are likely to arise in the relations between highly developed capitalist countries, undergoing " stagnation," " offset-spending," and younger ones, mainly emancipated colonies, still with ample opportunities for expansive investment ; and these differentiations may form a new and important aspect of what Lenin has called the law of uneven development of capitalism. That element of truth which we have found in the " underconsumption " argument leads to important features of the new stage of the capitalist system which increase its propensity to war-catastrophes, and thus may imply opportunities for revolutionary transformation. But " underconsumption " itself involves no threat to the existence of the system ; in this regard, after having discussed it as a long-term trend, we stand exactly where we stood after our discussion of the industrial cycle.

Now this conclusion contains no promise for capitalism ; it rather consistently follows from our general approach which rejects any separation of the " political " from the " economic " aspects of Marxist theory. If the process leading to a new social formation is taken as a whole, it follows that isolated parts of it, even if generalised into a special model, the subject of a special science, cannot produce the result—for the simple reason that various conceivable " political " reactions may result in various outlets from the economic " blind alley." This conclusion could be avoided if it were assumed that the two sole alternatives were capitalism of the " free-competition " brand (hitherto, unhappily, not completely realised) and socialism ; and even under that assumption there would still remain the possibility of simple decay. If one looks to Marxist theory for the promise of a better future for mankind, then one has to look for its analysis of the conditions of political action. True, such analysis spares nobody the hazards involved in actual political struggle.

(c) THE BREAKDOWN-THEORIES PROPER

The search for " natural laws " forecasting the inevitability of the socialist triumph was easy enough as long as the analysis was restricted to the economic field, and especially to the discussion of the classical model of the free market-economy from which Marx had started. Within such a model, the laws governing the general trend work behind the back of the immediate agents, just as the law of gravitation governs the movements of a falling stone, or a mountaineer, whatever the latter may think about. The automatism of the " economic laws " works, within the model, only under certain assumptions ; and if the model could really be shown to come to a standstill " automatically," like a piece of bad clockwork, political action to remove some of the basic assumptions might emerge even within a capitalist society the other characteristics of which would be preserved. But 19th and early 20th Century Socialists had become accustomed to regard their argument with the bourgeois opponents of " State-interference in the natural play of economic laws " as the most essential thing in the world, and the mere proof that the automatism would suddenly stop and need political help appeared to them no mean triumph for their principles. With some wishful thinking as regards the political strength of the labour movement and the degree of resistance to be expected from its opponents they could easily take the socialist outcome of such interference for granted.

Those Socialists who before and after World War I tried to elaborate theories of the " automatic breakdown " of capitalism paid a more generous tribute than Marx himself had done to the spirit of the 19th Century ; and Rosa Luxemburg's desire to avoid the implications of Leninism with its purely political concept of capitalist breakdown for the internal structure of the Labour movement[12] played an important part in her forecasts of the automatisms of the breakdown. So far as she and her Narodnik predecessors are concerned, it is unjust to reproach the advocates of the breakdown-theory with a desire to delay revolutionary action till the time when objective forces independent of working-class action should create the inevitable need for a socialist transformation : in the final paragraph of her *Anticritique* she rejected such implications of her theory in the most emphatic terms ; long before capitalism should come to its " natural " end, the horrors and destitution involved in imperialist wars and colonial conquest would force revolution as the only alternative upon the peoples. Rosa Luxemburg's successors in evolving the theory of " breakdown " have carried on her opposition to Leninism rather than her struggle against reformism ; but German Communism, too, originated amongst her pupils. Thus I should be inclined to regard the whole breakdown-argument, at least before World War I, as the historic form in which doubts as regards the further viability of capitalism were uttered in an intellectual climate which had been accustomed by Marxism itself, or at least by its current economic interpretations, to identify " laws of social development " with " economic automatisms working in the classical model."

In the various attempts made to establish a theory of " breakdown ", the tendential fall in the rate of profit up till very recently only in popularisations (or in writings of opponents who failed to understand Marx's meaning) was regarded as important for the

12 See below, pp. 229–30, and 258.

forecast of the ultimate fall of capitalist society. It is obvious that capitalist production can go on, whatever the rate of profits to which capitalists are accustomed, and that a fall in the rate does not matter if it corresponds to a rise in the absolute mass of profits according to the assumptions under which Marx had derived the law.[13] Apart from the horror caused by the tendential fall of the rate of profits to bourgeois economists, Marx deemed that law important mainly because it denoted the progressive centralisation of capitals, the inability of the small capitalist to hold his own, and the progress of the objective conditions for eventual nationalisation of production.[14] He had no illusions that the law might result in an automatic stoppage of capitalist production, or even in its stagnation.

But in the intellectual climate created in the late 'twenties by the " breakdown "-controversies starting from the " underconsumption " angle (which we are soon to discuss), by the approach of the Great Depression (which was foreseen by some of the German left-wingers), and by a tendency to restore the Marxist theory *of the industrial cycle* against the current " underconsumptionist " and " disproportionist " distortions, Henryk Grossmann made an attempt to derive from the law underlying the theory of the cycle conclusions as regards the inevitable breakdown of capitalism as well.[15] Freed from all his schemes, his theory may be summarized in the statement that, in order to employ and to exploit the natural increase of the population, capitalism must every year increase proportionally the constant capital applied,[16] which (because of technical progress) must be higher than the annual increase of the population, whilst profits are bound to fall in relation to the constant capital.[17] At some point profits, after deduction of the necessary consumption of capitalists, will be insufficient to allow for continued investment on the supposed scale.

[13] *Capital*, vol. III, pp. 255 ff.

[14] *Theories on Surplus Value*, vol. III, p. 517.

[15] *Das Akkumulations und Zusammenbruchs-gesetz des Kapitalismus*, 1929. A short summary in English—which, perhaps, makes more of Grossmann's schematism than justified when his fundamental concept is kept in mind—is given by Sweezy, op. cit., pp. 209 ff.

[16] The variable capital is not bound to increase with increasing numbers of employed population, if the latter's growth does not exceed the rate at which "relative surplus-value" is created.

[17] This statement is not identical with the tendential fall of the rate of profits, which are calculated in relation to the *total* capital applied.

Marxists would simply reply that full employment is not an inherent condition of capitalism and that, besides, the rate of the growth of population must be regarded as a function of economic structure, in a capitalist society as a function of the rate of investment, not *vice versa*.[18]   Quite apart from this Grossmann's theory, though formally not an application of the law of the tendential fall of the *rate of profits*,[19] is exposed to all the difficulties inherent in it as soon as it is regarded as denoting a distinct tendency of the resultant of the struggling forces. This rather recent episode apart, the " breakdown "-controversy can be identified with one aspect of the " underconsumption " theory.

Russia, a country whose pre-revolutionary intellectual development has been strangely neglected by Western thought, was the scene of the first appearance of the " breakdown "-argument behind what was at least a Marxist facade. The similarity to the conditions of pre-1848 Germany had resulted in Marxism finding almost general acceptance amongst the progressive intelligentsia as the last word of progressive Western thought, as since has happened in China, Japan and India : All conceivable trends in the public opinion of a country faced with the task of a revolution against feudalism—from Liberalism and revolutionary socialism to the protests of the destitute peasantry—found their expression in Marxist terms. Such terms were also used by the *Narodniki* in order to prove the alleged impossibility of capitalist development in Russia, and the need to find a direct transition to socialism from the basis of the traditional village community. Their argument was essentially that of Sismondi ; capitalism is bound to increase the rate of exploitation and to invest an increasing part of the profits, but to make only a decreasing part of those investments in wages for additional workers ; therefore it can never provide the markets for its own output. The Western countries, being the first in capitalist development, had solved this problem, for the time

[18] *Capital*, vol. I, p. 645.
[19] Being a long-term theory, Grossmann's concept is obviously impaired by th effect of all the forces counteracting the fall of the rate of profits ; fall in the prices o investment-goods reduces the increase of constant capital necessary in order to employ a certain additional population, whilst creation of additional (relative or absolute) surplus-value increases the amount of profits available for investment. As Grossmann envisages an extremely far-going consequence (breakdown of the whole social order, presumably by mass-unemployment with resulting revolutionary action) his conclusions from the questionable assumption of (in the long term) tendential fall in the rate of profits are even less impressive than those of those theorists who regarded the existence of such a decreasing tendency as essential for the theory of the cycle.

being, by monopolising colonial empires upon which they forced their excessive goods ; but Russia, being late, could not develop on such lines : her alternatives were to become a capitalist colony, or to evolve a socialism of her own upon foundations fortunately preserved since pre-capitalist times.

Two different trends of the progressive intelligentsia rallied against such a conception : those who opposed it in general, that is to say, who envisaged for their country a capitalist future— Liberals in spite of their Marxist phraseology,[20] and those who desired a socialist revolution, but did not believe that it could be achieved without the creation, by capitalism, of its most essential conditions, namely, at least some elements of large-scale industry and a revolutionary class of industrial workers. When Lenin and even more his successors, found themselves confronted with the alternative which the Narodniks had envisaged, the Bolsheviks relied on surviving traditions of the old village community and on the revolutionary anti-Tsarist intelligentsia. But they could never have done it unless the village-community had been split by the development of capitalist elements, the *kulaks*, within it, a split which resulted in a rapprochement of its other members to the industrial workers, and unless capitalism had brought to Russia a Marxist working-class party which could assimilate whatever it found valuable in the traditions of the Narodnik revolutionaries.

In arguing, in Chapter VIII of the *Development of Capitalism in Russia*, against the Narodnik conception, Lenin developed the Marxist argument against Sismondi and all the subsequent theorists of " underconsumption " who had repeated Adam Smith's mistake of neglecting the constant capital as an element in the analysis of costs and, consequently, also as a market in which part of the surplus product could be realised. But apart from this he reproached the Narodniks for their misuse of the foreign market for evading problems which have to be solved within the framework of capitalist society : in order to sell goods abroad (or to non-capitalist elements in their own country) capitalists have to buy others ; thus only difficulties arising from the specific form of the output of the industries of a certain capitalist country, not the problem of realising any part of its

---

[20] Not by mere chance Tugan-Baranovsky, a main representative of this trend, has also been the main representative of the explanation of the industrial cycle by mere disproportionalities of investments.

value, can be solved by exchanging one sort of commodity against another. Lenin recognised the existence and importance of the colonial elements of the Tsarist Empire, if only for marketing the output of capitalist industries which developed quicker than was compatible with the general development of capitalism, delayed as it was by Russia's backward regime. This was nearer to a theory of underconsumption than is suggested by the sharp tones of Lenin's polemic. But " underconsumption " is derived only from the actual backwardness of the regime in Tsarist Russia, not from the general traits of capitalism : the main commodities exported to the colonial parts of the Tsarist empire were textiles, etc., which were produced on a larger scale than Russian workers and peasants could buy. In Lenin's presentation of the Marxist theory of crises [21] there was a distinct shift towards greater emphasis on the element of underconsumption as soon as polemic against the Narodniks ceased to overshadow his differences with the Liberals whom Lenin had formerly supported in that common struggle for the recognition of the need for a capitalist industrialisation of Russia. The historical conditions under which most of Lenin's utterances on the problem of crises were shaped should be clearly kept in mind in order to assess their relevance for an analysis of capitalism in general. In his revolutionary politics he made ample use of the forces of resistance raised by capitalist expansion in Russia's colonial border-regions, and his first economic work of importance, *The Development of Capitalism in Russia*, had been largely devoted to the study of the decomposition of pre-capitalist economics under the impact of capitalism. But he did not stop there. The colonial border-regions of Russia were not important to him as mere outlets for Russian capitalism and as the scene of the suffering of ex-propriated peasants without other outlets than the prospect of becoming in due course proletarians (this would have been the important point for Rosa Luxemburg), he saw new national bourgeoisies rising and striving for national independence against the Great Russian bourgeoisie, and his approval of Stalin's study of the national question seems not to have been qualified by the latter's tendency to describe every national issue in *bourgeois*

---

[21] The relevant parts of *The Development of Capitalism in Russia* (*Collected Works*, Russian and German, eds., vol. III) are partly reproduced as Annex to the German ed. (Marx-Engels Institute) of vol. II of *Capital*. See espec. pp. 550 ff and 581 ff.

terms.[22] Thus Lenin's argument leads not to economic break-down but to the explanation of the necessary rise of political conflicts with revolutionary implications.

Rosa Luxemburg evolved a more developed version of the break-down theory in attempting to make modern imperialism understood to German Social Democracy. Whilst avoiding the primitive pitfalls of the Narodnik theory,[23] Rosa Luxemburg based her argument on a real difficulty in the Marxist scheme of reproduction which Marx had failed to solve in the un-completed vol. II of *Capital*, though she did not deny that he appeared likely to solve it without recourse to the assumption that a breakdown of the capitalist system was here necessary. Marx regarded "reproduction on an enlarged scale," that is, investment of part of the profits, as the normal condition of capitalist society, notwithstanding the likelihood that some years of the industrial cycle might even show reproduction on a reduced scale [24]; he started from "simple reproduction" merely as the simplest starting point for the concrete analysis. In "simple reproduction" the necessary exchange of that part of the output of the industries producing means of pro-duction that represents variable capital and surplus value (that is, revenues) against that part of the consumption goods indus-tries that is needed for replacing their constant capital, can be carried out without difficulty once we assume that marketing is in progress and every capitalist is in possession of the capital needed for carrying through the necessary transactions.[25] In the normal case of "reproduction on an enlarged scale" further conditions of equilibrium which we have already noticed,[26] hold true. A better mathematician than Marx could easily have produced fitting numerical examples ; and Rosa

[22] See below, p. 344.

[23] Rosa Luxemburg was completely conscious of the historical connection and discussed the Narodnik argument as the "third tournament" (after those of Sismondi and Malthus versus Ricardo) in her dispute. She may thus be described as the first Marxist who was prepared to some extent to accept Malthus' argument.

[24] *Capital*, vol. II, p. 456.

[25] Already the necessary exchanges within the main spheres of production (mutual exchange of the produced means of production within the first, advance of money wages enabling the workers to buy consumers' goods in the second sphere) presuppose that every capitalist is in control of money capital appropriate to his operations. This assumption—and not the theoretical division of industry into two or three spheres—is the starting point of the analysis ; without it, the exchange of addi-tional coal against additional machinery would cause difficulties identical with those involved in exchange of additional coal against additional bread.

[26] Above, pp. 120-1.

Luxemburg's problem begins just behind the point of numerical exemplification : how, so she asks, can the goods representing the part of the profits destined for additional investment be realised and turned into money capital, which is the preliminary condition for their value being invested ? In the " simple reproduction " there was no difficulty because, by definition, the completion of the exchanges needed in order to realise one year's output put in the proper places the purchasing power needed in order to carry through the transactions of the next year. But in reproduction on an enlarged scale, the markets must increase ; who can carry out the additional purchases that are needed in order that additional investment may create additional markets ? The producers of the additional means of production cannot employ additional workers, and thus realise the invested profits of the industries producing consumers' goods, before the latter have purchased additional machinery, and *vice versa*. Thus we seem confronted with a vicious circle. Rosa Luxemburg deemed it was inescapable : capitalism was able to carry through reproduction on an enlarged scale, that is to say (for a Marxist) to exist, just because not all the world was capitalist. That part of the surplus-product which is destined for re-investment has first to be sold to non-capitalist elements ; not, as in Malthus, to parasites dependent on capitalist profits (which was simply a way of replacing reproduction on an enlarged scale by the utopia of simple reproduction), but to non-capitalist producers, mainly peasants in the less developed parts of the capitalist countries and in the colonial world. But by opening these markets, by replacing the primitive peasants' domestic industries by the output of the capitalist industries of the motherland, capitalism, like a cancer, destroys the tissues on which it lives : when all pre-capitalist peasants have been absorbed as expropriated proletarians into capitalist society (or rather before, during the struggle of the imperialist powers for the right to plunder the colonial peasants), capitalism will break down.

Rosa Luxemburg was far from thinking that the end would come without the working-class inheritors shouldering their historical task and destroying by revolutionary action what was doomed by History. But the absoluteness with which it was doomed, in her concept, made the task appear easier than it was—and might also tend to encourage waiting till it was simplified to the pure alternative of dying by starvation, or facing death in fighting for the only possible way out. We shall return in the 13th Chapter to the fact that her analysis, like that of Marx himself, starts from an abstract capitalist world theoretically assumed to be an international unit, not from the likelihood that individual nations may be confronted with the need for a socialist revolution as the only means of independent survival long before, and even independent of whether the death knell of capitalism has already sounded in leading countries. Whoever has read the second part of the *Accumulation of Capital* knows where her heart would have been during the struggles of Riff Cabyles, Abyssinians and Indonesian " extremists " ; but if the first part of her argument was consistently followed up, she was bound to see in all the horrors of capitalist " civilisation " progress, and the only means of progress, to a better social order for humanity. Lenin who, as distinct from Rosa Luxemburg, believed in the possibilities of socialist revolutions in backward countries, could consistently side with colonial insurgents, not only from the point of view of preventing the capitalists of the motherland from finding an outlet for their difficulties but also from the point of view of the prospects of the revolutionary colony or semi-colony, proper leadership and international support being supposed.

Being historically connected with the Narodnik argument, that of Rosa Luxemburg was only able to avoid some of its pitfalls.[27] She reduced her generalisation *ad absurdum*, and actually obscured the element of truth in her analysis by omitting from her abstraction that very link in the chain which temporarily counteracts " underconsumption," namely, the investment of means of production in the territories newly opened to capitalist expansion. But even when the decisive crisis takes the shape of a conflict of the new national bourgeoisie of the colonial countries with the investors of the imperialist countries, the first contested

[27] Mainly the primitive identification of the *whole* market ultimately needed for the capitalist output with the market for consumers' goods. Lenin's argument against reliance on the foreign markets in general as a device of solving the problem of effective demand (see above, pp. 191-2) hits her less, first because she did not believe that the problem was soluble in the long run for any country (as distinct from the Narodniki, who asserted the impossibility of capitalism *in Russia*, as distinct from the West) and secondly, because she allowed ample space for direct robbery from pre-capitalist producers, with or without supplying them with commodities as useful as opium. It may be said—and R. Luxemburg herself would have recognised—that such an argument is "non-economic," but this is not quite true: opium wars are waged, and find support even in comparatively civilised countries, because they are supposed ultimately to open channels suitable for the export of cotton and bibles.

issue is the market for consumers' goods, though the conflict becomes insoluble by compromise only when the development of the new colonial industry has proceeded sufficiently to render control of the imports of investment goods desirable. Rosa Luxemburg was also the first clearly to see the importance of armaments as an agency not only for opening new fields for capitalist expansion (or deciding conflicts amongst the capitalist competitors for such markets), but also for diverting part of the " over-investment " into channels where it is not bound ultimately to result in increased production of consumers' goods. But, as we are soon to notice, her very concept prevented her from seeing the main purpose of those armaments and the reasons why international free trade is such a complete utopia, long before the hypothetical period when non-capitalist markets for consumers' goods should acquire a scarcity value.

In the abstract form in which it has been made, Rosa Luxemburg's argument is not conclusive. Once we assume equilibrium on a progressive scale (and there is no sense in elaborating any schemata without that assumption) there is no inherent difficulty in expanding the credit system in such a way that the capitalists can sell each other their output without entering a vicious circle ; and a safety limit may be covered by the invested part of the profits of the gold-mining industries which need no preliminary realisation because they are already produced in the money form. If we drop that assumption we get an additional reason for the breakdown of the credit system in times of depression which is an obvious fact and open to more general explanations, but this is not Rosa Luxemburg's problem. True, this answer, like that once given by Lenin to the *Narodniki*, is subject to serious limitations, and therefore involves a partial justification of the theory it attacks ; only a difference in emphasis distinguishes the statement (a) that the part of the surplus-product destined for re-investment can be realised within the limits of the possible expansion of the credit system, from the statement (b) that that part of the surplus-product must be sold on non-capitalist markets, apart from such margins as may be absorbed by expansion of the credit-system and additional gold production. In either case the alternative theory may be somewhat integrated in the concept upon which the analysis is based ; it is just as possible to describe export of capitals as part of the sale of the surplus-product of the industries producing means of production to non-capitalist countries as it is possible to enumerate new markets, along with cheap labour and raw materials, as agents attracting exported capitals to colonial countries, as was done in the 1928 programme of the Comintern. But it would be mistaken to neglect the difference in emphasis in its political implications : the flag (in whatever disguise) follows the investor with even greater certainty than it follows trade, and the rise of a national revolutionary bourgeoisie and working-class (with its implications as regards the prospects of the struggle for national independence) can much more easily be explained on the basis of a theory of imperialism that centres round the phenomenon of capital export, with the positive industrialisation of the colonial countries involved, and not merely destruction of the pre-capitalist self-sufficiency.

(d) THE HOBSON-LENIN THEORY OF IMPERIALISM

The current Marxist explanation of the economic roots of imperialism has been elaborated by the non-Marxist Hobson, independently of the studies of his contemporary Hilferding, and probably without being aware of certain hints thrown out by Marx and Engels.[28] This fact may be regarded as an indication of the superiority of the general Marxist approach as well as of the non-essentiality of all those complicated Marxist schemata that render, say, Rosa Luxemburg's theory unacceptable to anyone who does not share all the Marxist tenets. Increased competition (which, as Marxists would say, is itself a mere expression of the reduced value of commodities and rates of profit in consequence of technical progress) forces the capitalists to restrict domestic markets by monopolist organisation, and these restrictions as well as the increase of the profits of monopolists press towards export of capital for investment abroad. There is ample scope for elaboration of details, and Marxists will strictly reject the utopia of a non-imperialist capitalism as introduced by Hobson with the help of that old reformist device, the theory of " under-consumption " : a capitalism that would cease to invest at home or abroad would cease to be efficient. The very fact that competition continues in the monopolist stage of capitalism makes of imperialism, in Hobson's sense, a necessity. Hobson's suggestion, like that of the average advocate of " full

[28] See above, p. 148.

employment in a free society," that the surplus-product be consumed by the workers instead of by the expansion of the investment-industries demanding export of capitals with all its implications, bears no more relation to capitalist reality than Malthus' suggestion of having it consumed by "third persons" in order to avoid gluts of the markets as well as restriction of the incentive to work : the scheme of "simple reproduction" is utopian, a mere synonym for economic and political suicide. As introduced by Lenin into the Marxist system, Hobson's theory changes its function : it is no longer the description of a powerful but avoidable alternative to something else, but simply an explanation of what happens today.

Lenin elaborated his theory of imperialism in the early stages of World War I when his main interest centred on the explanation of what to him, as to all sincere Socialists, appeared as the betrayal of international obligations by most Socialist leaders in nearly all the belligerent countries. As early as October 7, 1858, Engels had observed in a letter, that Britain's vast colonial possessions and her monopolist position on the world markets created a privileged position even for the British working-class, and in the Preface to the 1892 edition of his *Conditions of the Working-classes in England* he stated that the benefits accruing to the English working-class from the country's industrial mono-poly were shared amongst its members in a very unequal way, with a privileged minority pocketing most, but even the broad masses having at least a temporary share now and then. To Engels, the concept of Britain's monopolist extra-profits evidently served as an explanation for the failure of British industrial conditions to develop in such a way as envisaged by himself and others in 1844, when *The Conditions of the Working-classes* was first published. The concept also helped him to refute the expectations of at least the upper strata of the German working-class for achievements similar to those of British Trade Unionists. These were emphasized at that time by the right-wing of German Social Democracy. For Lenin, the "corrup-tion," and the corresponding policies, of at least a "workers' aristocracy" in Germany, France, etc., as well as in Britain were established facts, and were to be explained by the extra-profits accruing to monopoly-capital from imperialism, that is, from colonial investments.

Such an explanation is not quite so easy as usually assumed

in Communist writings. The kind of workers' aristocracy likely to be produced by imperialism in a group of advanced industrial nations, whose upper classes draw large tributes from Asia and Africa, has been described by Hobson[29] as " great tame masses of retainers, no longer engaged in the staple industries of agriculture and manufacture, but kept in the performance of personal or minor industrial services under the control of a new financial aristocracy." Clearly, the conservative tendencies in British Trade Unionism cannot be explained by reference to the butcher interested in his lordship's custom and in favourable domestic jobs for his relatives, or even to the skilled engineering worker employed in service by some wireless-set producer on the distribution side. The actual forces backing "social imperialism" should not be interpreted in an over-simplified way as perhaps encouraged by clumsy utterances of the leaders of steel-makers' and shipwrights' Trade Unions prone to appreciate the merits of armaments and of continued deliveries of iron-ore from Franco-Spain. The immediate motives for the support of the national war effort are emotional. However, Marxists cannot accept such an explanation as definitive : they have to ask on what foundations the support of a war even of the type of World War I, the constellation of which was not aligned with the aspirations of the Labour movement by the bulk of nearly all Labour movements, could rest. Mere emotional nationalism leads to the dropping of the ideological foundations for sectional organisation of labour in favour of some organisation of the type of the German *Arbeitsfront*, controlled by the " leaders of the enterprise." In all those cases where such a development was avoided, continued support of the imperialist policies of a capitalist ruling class by the bulk of the Labour movement can only be explained on the assumption that the leaders of the existing organisations of Labour were able to point out to the masses of the organised workers that success in sectional struggle depends on the size of the cake to be divided, that is, on the successes achieved by the imperialism of their own country.

There are certain distinct ways in which successful imperialist expansion enables the ruling class of a monopoly-capitalist country to make larger concessions to its own working-class than would otherwise be possible. Mere export of capitals will

[29] *Imperialism*, 3rd ed., 1938, p. 364.

not do; investments in countries with a cheap and unorganised labour-force may even be described as a way to evade, or even to break the strength of domestic Trade Unionism. But if the actual owners of domestic enterprises are identical with the beneficiaries of high profits from investments abroad,[30] such a position may enable them to meet demands for higher wages in their factories at home ; such compromises may be necessary for political reasons as well as because of the impossibility, and even undesirability, of producing in still backward colonial countries the means of production necessary to exploit them. The whole bourgeoisie of the imperialist country, independent of whether the individual entrepreneur at home directly participates in " colonial extra-profits," may be capable of making greater concessions to the demands of labour at home because of the reduced costs of raw-material which result from successful investments abroad. The best organised strata of the working-class are likely to benefit most from " imperialist extra-profits " distributed in the way just described, whilst the least skilled, and especially strata such as women who are most exposed to competition from cheap colonial labour, will receive less, or may even suffer an actual deterioration of their position, because of the imperialist expansion of their country. For a country with a distinctly monopolist position Engels' scheme of profits unequally distributed, but to some extent enjoyed by the whole population may fit the facts better than Lenin's concept of a mere " workers' aristocracy " benefitting from imperialism, however conducive the latter may be to the self-assertion of the Communist parties in the leading capitalist countries. At the end of his life, Lenin envisaged the possibility that the great struggle would have to be fought out between the imperialist and the " underdog " nations,[31] taking the support of at least the bulk of the formers' working-classes for their own bourgeoisie as likely. Should the crisis of capitalism be very protracted, so that colonial emancipation movements, including the rise of the South American republics to actual independence from U.S.A. Big Business, have time fully to develop, even in U.S.A. material conditions may arise in which

---

[30] Lenin's study on Imperialism starts from the continental forms of monopoly-capitalism, where control of the decisive industries is concentrated in the hands of a few big banks, all of which are likely to have also a large interest in foreign investments. Under British or American conditions the argument would have to be made at least in a different form.

[31] See below, p. 318.

a majority even of the employed workers may have an interest in the revolutionary overthrow of existing society. It goes without saying that the case for socialist transformations in the leading capitalist countries does not depend on such developments : it mainly rests upon the question whether security against periodical mass-unemployment, and even more against war, can be achieved within capitalist society.

CHAPTER IX

SOME PROBLEMS OF THE ECONOMIC INTERPRETATION OF PAST SOCIAL FORMATIONS

Marxism, as a suggestion more or less digested by non-Marxist scholars, contributed more than any other general concept to the progress of modern historians beyond the mere elucidation of isolated facts which half a century ago was regarded as the characteristic of true and sober scholarship ; but the problem interesting us in this book is implied in the words " more or less." The recognition of the great importance of economic developments as a basic factor in historical changes, to some extent due to the Marxist influence, contradicts the ideological terms in which ancient as well as mediæval sources are presented. In consequence, any historian who is not a mere ideologist—and an ideologist in terms of religions and philosophies whose days have long passed—is bound to proceed beyond his sources in the direction of an economic interpretation of an increasing number of facts. No serious historian, unless politically biased, will deny the great suggestive influence of Marxism ; but such general recognition still does not justify the claim of Marxism to give a monist interpretation of History. On the other hand, the position of orthodox Marxism—outside the U.S.S.R.—as an outsider to official academic research could not fail to restrict the amount of actually Marxist contributions to fundamental research. The orthodox Marxist, with his general propensity to specialize on more " topical " problems, is unlikely to make contributions to ancient and mediæval history other than occasional excursions based upon other people's specialist research ; and apart from his conclusions being dependent upon the acceptance of his source's views as correct from the specialist point of view,[1] he will always be exposed to the reproach of not having sufficiently digested the philological and other forms in which the full impact of the ideology of the period under investigation is felt by the professional historian. Even when the divorce between Marxist sociology and specialist historiography

[1] Engels' study on the *Origin of the Family*, etc., based upon Morgan—in his time certainly a most impressive source—forms a conspicuous example.

has been overcome, the cleavage may still be perceptible in the different terminologies and backgrounds of scholars.

In the study of the most primitive social formations the impact of technico-economic developments is so enormous (and even recognised in the traditional description of the various pre-historic periods) that there is a great temptation, for Marxists, to apply their outlook in the most primitive form,[2] with the result that it cannot suffice as a monist explanation. Even Engels, in his study of ancient forms of the Family, could not avoid that pitfall, and paid for it by " correcting " the materialist derivation of historical developments from the evolution of the productive forces. Thus he introduced the evolution of the forms of the Family—the " production of men "—as a parallel cause additional to that of ordinary production, instead of deriving it from changes in the latter and in the general relations between Man and Nature. The fact that this was possible[3] seems to suggest that the derivation of historical materialism from the unique position of the productive forces as an independent variable in the historical process[4] was not realised by Engels in all its implications, and it also demonstrates the pitfalls in the 19th Century concept of " materialism." Imagine what Engels would have said if some of his friends had tried to " supplement " the monism of socio-economic explanation by another motive power not so expressly " material " as sex !

In studying more recent periods the opposite mistake of inter-preting the driving socio-economic forces in too broad and general a sense has frequently been made by Marxists. For Marxism, the relations entered into by men in the social process of *producing* their means of livelihood are the basic factor in social development. Usury and Commerce exploit a given mode of production, but cannot create it.[5] From this standpoint it seems obvious that capitalism could not be a relevant factor before, say, the 16th Century—to a full extent only since the Industrial Revolution in North-Western Europe, with some prelude in late mediæval North Italy. Accordingly, it is impossible to ascertain any bourgeois phenomenon in economics, state and ideology

[2] See above, pp. 92-3.
[3] The mistake, though noticed, of course, by many Marxists, was corrected in official Soviet curricula as late as by Leontiev, l. c., p. 505 ; and this fact provides another illustration of the conservative character of accepted Party-creeds.
[4] See above, p. 46.
[5] *Capital*, vol. III, Chapter 36, pp. 700 and 716.

before, say, the later stages of the Renaissance, the Dutch, English and French Revolutions, and the emancipation of the serfs in Russia. Such a clear approach would save us many apparently insoluble problems, such as the priority of Calvinist religion and capitalism respectively[6] ; but it contradicts the tendency of any society to think of the social forces that have helped to shape its own pattern and ideology in terms of the latter. Even the opponents of a social system are prepared to interpret the past " in terms of the proletarian class-struggle," " to reflect the great issues of our times into the interpretation of history," etc.[7] Their standpoint will receive the appearance of support from the fact that, to a very large extent, the modern bourgeoisie has grown up from merchants trading within a predominantly feudal society, and the modern state from the absolutist state power established by the strongest of the feudal lords, not without support from the merchants. Modern bourgeois ideology has grown from the Reformation, the origins of which (quite apart from its own delusions as regards primitive Christianity) have to be derived from the mediæval struggles between Nominalists and Realists, from the peasants' revolts in the late Middle Ages which, on their part, were provoked by the increasing rôle of the merchants in a feudal society, etc. If someone indulging in retrospective projections of modern society tries to find the " capitalist " foundations for the Protestant " superstructure " (which, in our days, undoubtedly corresponds to capitalism), he has no other choice than to start from the commercial sphere of mediæval economics, the only one which may be described in capitalist terms though it did not dominate production and though, therefore, it is possible to derive from it " superstructures " only by means of a vulgar concept of " Economic Materialism " in the sense that men's actions are determined by their immediate economic interests.[8] But the superficial analogies to later bourgeois development, and also the impact of the natural tendencies of modern bourgeois ideology to follow up its ancestors to the sources, are so strong that most Marxists—including the founders[9]

---

[6] See above, p. 75.

[7] As proclaimed by Soviet representatives of "Economic Materialism." See Part III of my article in *Zeitschrift fuer Sozialforschung*, 1938, No. 1–2.

[8] See above, pp. 923.

[9] cf. Marx's description of the Tudor monarchy as "itself a product of bourgeois development" (*Capital*, vol. I, p. 741). But, on the other hand, see above, p. 203, and Marx's polemic against Mommsen in *Capital*, vol. III, p. 914.

—have occasionally tended to interpret pre-capitalist periods in
terms of capitalism.   The whole set of problems only became an
issue when the Soviet state found itself confronted with historical
teachings that described the society against which all the bourgeois
revolutionaries of Russia had revolted as capitalist, so that there
had apparently been no sense in revolution at all except to establish
a socialist utopia.   The bourgeoisie, and especially its earliest
predecessors, has never proved capable of making any revolution
itself ; every revolution since the later feudal period contained a
strong plebian element which developed the utopian aspirations
of the revolutionary ideology.[10]   Identification of that element
with the modern proletarian class-struggle forms the natural
counterpart of the identification of merchants and absolutist kings
with modern capitalism and the modern bourgeois state ; and in
view of the strong emotional (though hardly Marxist) appeal
made by the genealogy of every movement, such identification
served as an argument in favour of the " merchant capitalist "
interpretation of the late Middle Ages.   On the other hand, it is
bound to carry on the liberal and egalitarian elements of the
pre-capitalist revolutionary ideology into the ideology of the
proletarian opposition to capitalism which may become State-
ideology after the latter's overthrow.   The implied collisions
between utopia and reality explain the restatement of consistent
Marxism by recent Soviet ideology.

We are confronted with a deeper problem when approaching
the division of history into periods.   Every civilisation is built
upon foundations derived from others, some of which represented
previous stages in the socio-economic development of the same
nation, and some of which were built by other nations.   No
serious historian in our days is narrow-minded enough to believe
that the historical chains linking ancient Egypt and Babylon
though Judea, Hellas and Rome with our days are the only
relevant, or even of necessity the most eminent, elements of
human history.   However, they are the antecedents of *our* history,
and they are emphasized especially in ideology, where the
appearance of gradual progress can be preserved, in spite of some
" set-backs " in the " Dark Ages."   Thus did Hegel conceive
them ; and Marx's explanation of " oriental, ancient, mediæval
and modern " society as the subsequent stages in the development
of the relations of production should not be taken too seriously :

[10] See above, pp. 41 and 89.

they indicate no more than the natural limitations of the pupil who has not acquired specialist knowledge in these fields.[11] At the end of his life Marx, whilst he insisted that in principle every instance of a certain socio-economic formation being succeeded, or not succeeded, by another one could be explained causally,[12] rejected generalisations of his sketch of the genesis of capitalism in Western Europe as bound to result in " a general historico-philosophical theory the supreme virtue of which consists in its being super-historical."[13] The special occasion at which this statement[14] was made should be kept in mind : Marx, supporting the Narodniks, directed it against that trend of Marxist orthodoxy from which, later, Russian Social Democracy[15] arose and which asserted that Russia could not achieve socialism without previously passing through a capitalist stage. Siding with those who appeared prepared to tackle the task of the anti-Tsarist revolution in Russia immediately, and probably influenced by wishful thinking as to the imminence of a socialist revolution in Western Europe, Marx [13] stated that, if Russia should go capitalist, as appeared likely in consequence of the splitting of the village community after the 1861 reforms, she would miss " the finest chance that history ever offered to a nation," namely, that of direct transition to socialism without previously having to undergo all the sufferings

[11] *Critique of Political Economy*, Preface, p. 13. In the unhappy atmosphere of Marx-philology, the obviously occasional character of the remark, and the no less obviously lacking qualifications of its author (and, probably, of any of his contemporaries) to make authoritative observations on the economics of the ancient oriental societies, has not prevented its being used as an argument in the controversy between Wittfogel (*Wirtschaft und Gesellschaft China's* Berlin, 1930) and Radek and others on the correct description of the pre-capitalist stage of modern Chinese economics.

[12] In this connection ([13]) Marx referred to the ancient world where events "strikingly analogous" (to the formation of the modern proletariat by expropriation of the small peasants and craftsmen) "but taking place in different historical surroundings lead to completely different results" namely, to the formation of a (parasitic) proletariat in the ancient sense, as distinct from a modern working-class. The argument is not strong, as the analogy between the formation of "capitalism" in the ancient and the modern world loses much of its "striking" character if "commercial capitalism" is returned to its proper place (see above, p. 203). Engels' explanation of the failure of ancient society to produce a modern working-class (see above, p. 53) is strictly endogene, "different historical surroundings" come in only in so far as without them (that is, without the possibility of developing an economy based upon successful slave-hunting) commercial capital would not have come into being (nor the ideological obstacle that prevented the ancient craftsmen from becoming, in due course, a working-class).

[13] Letter to the Editor of the *Otechestvennye Zapisky*, reproduced in Marx-Engels, *Selected Letters* (Marxist-Leninist Library), No. 96.

[14] As well as the other important source on the issue, Marx's letter to Vera Zassulich, reproduced in original (with Marx's preparatory drafts) in Marx-Engels Archiv., vol. I.

[15] See above, p. 191.

implied in the growth of capitalism.   If this basic issue of the letter
under discussion[13] is kept in mind, even in isolation it says no
more than that in a world where the experience of large-scale
capitalist industry and the Marxist theory of socialism were
available, Russia could conceivably turn directly from the village-
community to socialism.[16]   And this is remarkably near to the
truth of the actual events although factional self-assertion of the
Bolsheviks has restricted the tribute due to Marx for this prediction.   However sharply Marx criticised the liberal tendency
with which original Russian Marxism was allied,[17] the issue
whether the village community was to grow into capitalism
or socialism was made dependent on the historical milieu in
which it would be placed at the decisive stage, and in the Preface
to the Russian edition of the *Communist Manifesto*, of 1882, it was
clearly stated that direct transition from the village community to
socialism was possible on condition that the Russian democratic
revolution would coincide with a socialist revolution in the West.
In the latter formulation the possibility of avoiding the capitalist
stage in Russia is reduced to what, from the point of view of
consistent Marxism, should be regarded as a truism, namely,
that just because capitalism (and socialism) by their very nature
tend to dominate world-economics, adaption to the most progressive of the social formations found in the world is a condition for
the survival of nations entering the international community
from a more backward stage.   But even the former statements
take it for granted that progressive changes in social structure,
no matter where they have originated, presuppose that the necessary techniques and ideologies developed by the preceding
structure are at hand, even if (in modern conditions of international communication) that structure should not yet have fully
developed in the country actually initiating the transformation.
In such a conception, there are certain successive socio-economic

[16] In the drafts of the letter to Zassulich (esp. l. c., pp. 320 and 322) Marx strongly
emphasized the comparative stability of primitive social communities (which might
be an argument in favour of the Russian *mir*'s ability to survive even a prolonged
transition period before socialist surroundings were available) as well as the struggle
between the stabilizing and the (disrupting) individualist trends within the community, in terms that are interesting for the student of modern kollkhoz problems.
The whole argument, starting (because of its *Narodnik* origin) from the village community does not touch the issue whether the industrial conditions of Russian agriculture's turning socialist were available inside or outside the country, which would
make a large difference from the point of view of modern Bolshevism.   See below,
pp. 294-5.
[17] Comp. Stalin in the *History of the C.P.S.U.*, pp. 124-5 in *Leninism*, ed. 1940.

formations, and one forms the preliminary condition for the development of the next though this may not necessarily take place in the same country. This does not imply recognition of the Hegelian scheme of successive social structures, nor even the assertion that any distinct scheme of successive stages is necessarily typical for all times and countries in which a certain result is achieved.

But the attempt to establish such a scheme is made even today, in spite of the enormous theoretical difficulties arising already with the definition of the stages whose succession to Marx's industrial capitalism is supposed. As long as we study different stages of the development of identical national civilisations this may be a mere matter of terminology, but the assumption of a gradualist progressive development itself is questioned as soon as we are confronted with a change in the national stratum, say with the downfall of the Roman Empire. Were its last stages already feudal (this would involve gradual progress from slavery to feudalism), and were the economics of the Germanic conquerors already feudal in consequence of progressive differentiation of their primitive society? And if so, were the germs of slavery observable in their own development important enough to justify the recognition of a slave-holding society as a necessary intermediate stage between primeval tribal community and feudalism, even if it should emerge that the estate of a feudal Roman Empire though devastated by an age of wars, was taken over by another feudal system? The questions are far too complicated to be answered by a historian who has not specialised in those fields, but the sociologist may note that, for Western Europe, even the traditional progression "slave, serf, proletarian" appears rather questionable as a scale of subsequent social formations bound to change into one another with increasing productivity of labour. We can interpret the end of the civilisation of the ancient world either in the sense that a slave-holding civilisation simply broke down after the failure of attempts to reach a capitalist stage without intervention of feudalism,[18]

[18] It is remarkable that very close approaches to the manufacture stage of capitalism have been made not only in ancient, but also in various stages of Chinese society, where all those personal conditions absent in a slave-holding society (interest of the worker as well as of the controller of the means of production in efficient work) were present, though those intellectual conditions favoured by quickly expanding economics (for example a development of mathematics comparable with that at the culmination point of the ancient world, and at the eve of the industrial revolution in modern Western society) may have been absent.

and was replaced by a new, technically lower, civilisation in the development of which slavery played but a subordinate part ; or we shall find, in a world already grown feudal, a change of leadership from a group of nations where feudalism had grown from unsuccessful experiments in slavery, to other nations where it grew directly from differentiation in the tribal community. In the latter case, large elements of the ideology of the new society and lesser elements of its technique had originated from the formerly leading group of nations during the slave-owning period of its life ; but even on this basis the Marxist is confronted with the question whether the slave-owning antecedents of one element of the synthesis deserve description as a necessary stage in the evolution of society towards feudalism and beyond. The assimilation of the ideologies of the superseded society, especially if their authority is backed by the latter's apparently higher level of civilisation, is the most common phenomenon in the transition of political leadership from one nation to another. It forms the background of the current assumption that all the national civilisations some parts of which have entered and been recognised in a later synthesis, form necessary preliminary stages to its formation. But it does not prove anything in favour of or against that assumption in the one sense in which it would be relevant for the Marxist, namely, that these civilisations actually and of necessity represent successive stages in the development of the relations of production.

Chattel-slavery, by its very nature, is possible only in a few parasitic civilisations during the period of their expansion, and has broken down in the two instances in which we know it, the classical mediterranean civilisations, and the modern exploitation of colonies. In 'the second instance failure in competition with a higher form of social organisation, capitalism, is obvious ; but the first can be explained by the mere exhaustion of the opportunities for parasitic expansion which, for some centuries, had veiled the inefficiency of slave-labour in comparison with the alternative of serf-labour in a feudal setting. In important instances the evidence for a slave-owning stage in the existence of some national civilisation appears questionable to Marxist historians who may not be expected to diverge from Stalin's scheme unless moved by strong factual evidence.[19] Generally it may be said

[19] Comp. the discussion of recent Soviet investigations on ancient Georgian history in *Bolshevik*, 1946, No. 7–8, pp. 68–9.

that the introduction of large-scale slave-owning as a necessary element in historical progress contradicts the Marxist principle of preferring indigenous explanations of social developments, leaving external conquest as a mere accessory. This principle is applied especially by the Russian Marxists in opposition to the " Norse " explanations of their country's history. In the economic, as distinct from the ideological, foundations of present civilisation there is no element of first-class importance[20] which could not be explained as having evolved directly through feudalism from primitive tribal communities, with capitalism emerging in some civilisations from a certain stage of feudal development and dominating the further evolution of the other civilisations by virtue of its superior productive forces. In such a concept, societies with economics based on slave-owning, along with certain " oriental " and other earlier civilisations, would appear as different branches in the tree of evolution, just as do all the non-human living *hominidae*, and most of the fossils in the evolution of man as conceived by modern evolutionists. Economic structures conditioned to continuous external expansion would appear as abnormal phenomena demanding special explanation and unsuitable as links in the typical evolutionary chain. It should be noticed that Marx's treatment of pre-capitalist structures, in *Capital*, vol. III, Chapter 47, as well as Engels' explanation of the origins of the State[21] do not include in the typical chain of evolution a system of economics based on slavery (which, along with the plantations, is regarded by Marx as a special phenomenon). True, if the conception of social evolution under discussion is applied to the future, the eventual achievement of socialism ceases to be a necessary implication of modern social conditions. It may happen in some of the civilisations existing today and they may be confronted, on the international stage, not only with capitalism (which is supposed to represent an earlier stage of evolution) but also with other possible

---

[20] For modern capitalism would hardly have been prevented from developing by the absence of chattel-slavery in some colonies, including the Southern States of U.S.A.   Apart from this, Russia is the only leading nation in whose historical records slavery (as distinct from serfdom) may have played a certain part (in the early Kiev period).   But her further evolution, and present importance, started from regions which were hardly affected by that episode.

[21] The part dealing with the formation of the Germanic states could completely stand on its own ; and the former existence of economics based on slave-labour in the Roman Empire (the conquest of which is regarded by Engels as the occasion for the formation of the Germanic states) is irrelevant, as preceding transformation of those economics into feudal ones is assumed by him.

attempts at overcoming the difficulties inherent in present society ; and the outcome of the conflict alone would decide which of them had been a side-track. But such an interpretation merely confirms us in dropping the ideological Hegelian approach, in which all preceding societies known to the philosopher and likely to have made some contribution to the ideology he stands for, are interpreted as steps towards the achievement of that supposedly highest integration—just as other theologians have interpreted Nature as a series of preparatory steps to the Creation of Man.

PART III
CLASS AND STATE

CHAPTER X
THE CONCEPT OF CLASS

(a) CLASS, ESTATE AND CASTE

Few sociological statements have made a greater impact on the further evolution of human thought than the opening phrase of the *Communist Manifesto* : The History of Mankind is a history of class-struggles. But only at the time when it was made, could the impressive force of that statement obscure the fact that theoretical elaboration of its content was then absent. In its primitive form, it opposes to the concept current at the time of history made by " great men " and by the ideas produced by them, the concept of history shaped by social entities based upon the economic structure of society. But some of the illustrations following the introductory phrase of the Manifesto are distinctly unfortunate, even in the light of such historical evidence as was available in those days. Patricians and Plebians, as well as Guildmasters and Journeymen, were distinguished by legal status rather than by their respective relation to the means of production[1] ; and at no time did other than legal obstacles prevent a journeyman from setting up as a master. Thus Marx's examples hint at an explanation of history by the struggle of estates, that is, socio-economic groups based upon legal characteristics, and fighting for the preservation or abolition of those characteristics. In a reformist conception of socialism the emancipation of the working-class may be conceived in a similar way by the assumption that within capitalist society Trade Unions would grow to the position of recognised partners not only in bargaining for conditions of labour, but also in management of industry and government of the State, so that the eventual removal of capitalist interests would involve no more than an abolition of obsolete fetters of development. Indeed, if we

---

[1] In the first-mentioned instance, at least at the historical period of which Marx speaks, Plebs versus Optimates would have been much more fitting an example of typical class-struggle, though less promising in its outcome. For Marx's contemporaries the analogy between the struggle of the Plebeians, who successfully strove for the removal of obsolete legal barriers, and the recent bourgeois revolutions against an obsolete feudalism was impressive, and accepted into the vocabulary of the French revolution.

conceive the transition to the new social order as a protracted
process on an international scale, it may easily contain such
developments in some countries. However, this transition has
already started, and is likely to make further progress in countries
where, before shouldering the responsibilities for national reconstruction, the working-class was actually " nothing " not
merely in that it was not satisfied with its legal status (the complaint of the revolutionary *bourgeoisie* in France as regards the
Third Estate) but also in the sense that it lacked the economic
predominance which the Third Estate had already achieved. In
any case Marx regarded the rise of the working-class from a
position of oppression to that of control of economic life as
typical; and the difference between the position of the class
emancipated by the bourgeois revolution, and that to be emancipated by the proletarian revolution has been noted in all Marxist
literature as essential for a proper assessment of the difficulties
and tasks of a proletarian revolution. But, so far I know, the
implications of the definition of a class which cannot be
characterised by the contrast between its economic power and its
legal status have never been elaborated.

   Class, as a socio-economic category, is logically prior to any
legal, or moral,[2] division of society which it is intended to
explain. Historically, the concept of class arose from the
realisation that the mere abolition of legal discriminations did
not establish social equality, which had been demanded by the
ideology of the bourgeois-democratic revolutions : the first explanations of the course of the French revolution in terms of class
coincide with the realisation that the expectations of the urban
poor, who had borne the main burden of the struggle, were
disappointed by the result, the access of the *bourgeoisie* to power.[2a]
It is essential for the concept of class (unless it be reduced to a mere
synonym of social organisation) that the social group under consideration should be fairly stable : there seems to be no cause for
speaking of class in a society where the positions of influence and
increased responsibility (even if associated with higher income)
are equally accessible to all members of society not only in
law but also in social practice. From this point of view the

---

[2] The presence or absence of established legal rules is not decisive for the treatment
of our problem. Besides, they can hardly be clearly discerned from mere generally
recognised social prejudices. Marxism seeks for socio-economic explanations of the
position of the American Negro just as for that of the peasant's son who had received
Holy Orders in the mediaeval Church. [2a] See above, pp. 40-1.

H

phenomenon of class is contrary to what Gunnar Myrdal, in his study of the Negro Problem, has described as the American Creed, according to which the status of news-boy is described as a step on the ladder which leads to the status of millionaire, and where it may be helpful for presidential candidates if their parents' home can be somehow described as a cabin. In this formal approach, the essential element in class is stability of the social group, that is, the absence of equality of opportunity ; and caste, that is, social status to which the holder is bound by birth, should appear as the most complete consummation of class. There seems to be no sense in a definition of class which does not suppose its comparative stability ; but it does not follow that class is most obvious in such cases where the formal characteristic of stability is best developed. The names of the most ancient castes in India and elsewhere seem to prove that they originally corresponded to groups holding a definite socio-economic status and thus deserving the description of classes ; and certainly the American Negro slaves held a definite class status in Southern society. But at present, neither of the groups most obviously deserving the description of caste is exclusively made up of people holding a certain characteristic status in the socio-economic structure ; divisions and prejudices surviving from the past are used by the ruling class (which, in itself, is not a caste) in order to keep the under-dog, be it a worker, a smallholder, or even a Negro businessman or intellectual, at a disadvantage in comparison with his white competitors and in " his proper place." The very origin of the concept of class shows that it does not start from the formal fact of inequality of opportunity, but that it explains why such inequality arises and persists even where it is not embodied in legal privileges or caste prejudices.

In recent time, the formalist interpretation of class as mere absence of equality of opportunity has made great strides because of (a) the expansion of Marxism, and the modern Labour movement, to parts of the globe where the caste-problem in its most visible forms, including colour discrimination, is present, and (b) the far-going replacement, in the leading capitalist countries, of the owner-entrepreneur on the middle scales of the social ladder by the salaried employee, which has resulted in increased social mobility in the sphere between the skilled workers and the holders of appointments carrying considerable responsibilities. The intelligentsia and the representatives of the reformist Labour movement, while bothering little about the very high barriers which still prevent the rise of members of the lowest strata of society into that middle sphere of comparative social mobility, find themselves confronted with the fact that the very process of capitalist concentration which has given them access to positions formerly held by the lower-ranking members of the *bourgeoisie* has concentrated actual power in the hands of an oligarchy of " sixty," " two hundred," etc., families holding private property on so enormous a scale that newsboys, whatever myths they have to sell to the public, can hardly aspire to enter its ranks. The members of that oligarchy appear to belong to a caste. The issue relevant for the average newsboy is not whether he has a lottery chance to become a millionaire, but whether he and his like, independent of the colour of their skin, of the legitimacy of their birth, or of their adherence to this or that Church, etc., have, if they so desire, reasonable prospects of becoming members of the editorial staff or of obtaining any other job which is more satisfactory in itself and also substantially remunerated. The position of the small oligarchy is not relevant in itself, but because it stands for a whole system of social controls which prevent the free development of human personality. From the tactical point of view it may be sensible to emphasize that no one except a very small caste stands to lose from the abolition of capitalism ; but the problem of modern socialism consists not in merely cutting off the apex of the existing social hierarchy, but in replacing the fundamental principles upon which that hierarchy is now based by new ones. The demand that, whatever stratifications may arise in the new hierarchy, the new society should be socially fluid is, in itself, no solution. Every social structure, in the future as well as in the past, is based upon certain relations between men who have to fulfil different functions in social life ; and in a somewhat complex society relations of subordination cannot be avoided. The presence, and the characteristics of classes depends on the socio-economic relations upon which the mutual position of the members of society is based.

(b) Characteristics of Class

In Marxist sociology, class is regarded as the link between the objective relations of production (discussed in Part II of this book) and the human action by which the existing mode of production is preserved as well as transformed ; and this concept is regarded as valid through the whole process of human history[3] though the modern working-class is regarded as the singular instance of a class becoming conscious of its historical function. The concept of class is not necessarily dynamic : also the ruling class, with its obvious interest in preserving the established order, is a class. From the mere fact that a class is oppressed it is impossible to derive its propensity to transformatory action, even in those cases where it forms the main existent productive force[5] : neither the ancient slaves, nor the revolting serfs of the late Middle Ages could produce more than negative results of their class-struggles. In a realistic scientific, as distinct from a propagandist, approach to the phenomenon of class, it is impossible to exclude those actual characteristics which are conducive to its continued acceptance of rule exercised over it. The Church's predominance over the minds of the mediæval serfs as well as the influence exercised by respectable ways of life, Hollywood pictures, the popular press, etc., upon the minds of the Western working-classes, are elements essential to a description of the position of the respective class ; though Marxists may add that, ultimately, no more is likely to emerge from such elements than the theological character of the reforming ideology, or a possible vulgarisation of mass-tastes during the transition to socialism respectively.

There is no definition of class in classical Marxist writings. The last Chapter of vol. III of *Capital* was interrupted by death just at the point where Marx was attempting his solution of the problem, and the only argument preserved in the fragment is a criticism of the derivation of class from a common source of income : such a characteristic, Marx deemed, would result in recognition as social classes not only of the main groups such as

[3] The later restrictions of the validity of the concept to the period from the decomposition of the tribal community to the eventual achievement of a class-less society (Engels' Preface to the engl. ed. of the *Communist Manifesto*, 1888) are purely tautological. Class presupposes a polar structure of the relations of production : before those relations assumed a polar character, and after the latter's eventual withering away, the determination of human actions by the relations of production could not and cannot assume the character of a conflict between polarised forces. But the question whether the removal of that polarisation of the social structure as existing today outside the U.S.S.R. will imply the removal of any social polarisation is purely factual.

[4] In a book supposing some acquaintance with the elements of sociology, this remark may be sufficient to dispose of the childish ideology that the workers could be "deproletarisized" by Catholic, fascist or similar propaganda inducing them to drop the concept of class. Marxists would simply have to analyse for what objective reasons such attempts might have temporary success.

[5] Lower classes degenerated to a parasitic rôle, such as the poor freemen in Athens and Rome, would not matter for this issue.

capitalists, landowners, and wage-earners, but of every sectional group within the main classes which happens to be held together by some common interests. Amongst the examples mentioned by Marx in order to show the absurdity of such a conception are not only workers of different skill, or groups of landowners owning different types of land, but also " doctors and officials " who are thus supposed to belong to one class. Neither of them enjoyed definite ownership of means of production, but the former had—at least in Marx's time—a status assimilated to that of independent entrepreneurs, while the latter, of course, were salaried employees. Not too much should be made of this hint at a definition of class by common social background and status rather than by the legal forms in which income is received, because nothing in the fragment—or, indeed, in any classical Marxist writing—contradicts a description of both doctors and officials as forming an annex of the *bourgeoisie* which, itself, is defined by a certain characteristic type of ownership of means of production. So it remains a matter of speculation whether Marx, if allowed to complete his work, would have stopped at describing property-relations to the means of production as the characteristic of the social structure, or would have proceeded in his analysis further towards regarding them as mere symptoms of fixed relations of production. In Marx's days, when the private entrepreneur—as distinct from the manager employed by some big anonymous corporation—was still the characteristic representative of capitalism, the point seemed less important ; in our days it is decisive because mere dwelling on property-relations would result in placing in the same class as the workers the social group whose members immediately direct the production process and represent the interests of capital against the workers. This argument refutes Kautsky's[6] attempt to derive

---

[6] *Die materialistische Geschichtsauffassung*, vol. II, pp. 9–12. The examples of class-antagonisms not based upon different positions in the production hierarchy which are mentioned by Kautsky (money-lender versus mediaeval craftsman, absentee landlord versus tenant, parasitic rentier versus proletarian) concern classes whose position has become obsolete or (in the first mentioned case) has not yet grown into a clear production relation, and this corresponds well to the tendency to describe the proletarian revolution as a mere removal of obsolete legal privileges, analogous to the bourgeois, (see above, p. 2:2). Bukharin, against whom Kautsky polemiced, certainly simplified the issue by omitting legal forms of expression ; but he regarded the socialist revolution as an actual process of social reconstruction, as distinct from mere abolition of obsolete property relations. Actually, Kautsky's classes are no factors shaping human history ; they are mere realisations that printers and dockworkers, grain-growers and owners of vineyards respectively, have some common interests, and should act accordingly.

class, in the Marxist sense, from property in means of production as a source of income creating specific interests of all those who derive their income from that source. If the abstraction should stop at property-relations, the abolition of classes in a socialist society would, indeed, be reduced to a mere tautology.[7] I do not intend to reduce the argument against the now fashionable concept of a "managerial society" to such a cheap commonplace; it should be made dependent upon whether in any society there is an actual stable group, characterised by its exercise of managerial functions and distinct, in origins as well as in social status, from other groups existing within that society.[8]

Ownership in means of production may be important in the characteristic of certain classes as the form in which the underlying social relation is stabilised. By the institution of inheritance, social status is comparatively stabilised within the property-owning group even if legal privileges barring the rise of members of the lower classes to positions of social responsibility are absent. Even the positions of those strata who enjoy high social status without being directly concerned with the direction of production is likely to be assimilated to the predominant type of a property-holding society by institutions such as expensive schooling, purchase and sale of doctors' practices, etc., etc. Thus the institution of private property in means of production carries the element of stability and of actual, even if not formal, privilege into all relations of subordination existing in the society under discussion; and by granting control over holders of responsible positions in all other fields of social life to the holders of property, it justifies the characteristic of the ruling class by the predominant type of property in means of production. In a feudal society, Lords spiritual enjoyed at least as much social prestige and power as Lords temporal, and at least occasionally the ranks of the former—as distinct from those of the latter—could be entered by gifted sons of the lower classes. But the Church was a social power because, and insofar as, it administered large estates in the typical feudal way. In modern U.S.A., the chances of a

---

[7] Kautsky (l. c., p. 14) was very proud of this consequence; he deemed that according to Bukharin's position classes were bound to survive as long as big enterprises needed managers. (This hint at an argument brought 20 years ago amongst Marxists may be helpful in view of recent claims for originality made in this field).

[8] Comp. my *Spirit of Post-War Russia*, p. 44. If not only the existence of a managerial class, but its character as the modern ruling class is asserted, the demand for ability of that class to control the planners should be added to the above-mentioned characteristics.

University Professor becoming President may be greater than those of a big businessman ; but it is the latter and his fellows who, by means of a press organised on capitalist lines, control public opinion, and in their capacity as patrons, even University appointments. Thus ownership of means of production works as the agency by which controlling social power is exercised by, and stabilised amongst, the group controlling social production, whilst the absence of such control (or of privileges and status assimilated to it) may be regarded as characteristic of the lower classes. Mere existence of relations of subordination, even if combined with inequality of incomes as between individuals, does not constitute the phenomenon of class; and the concrete institutional forms in which class is constituted need investigation. But it does not follow that ownership of means of production, however important as the institutional form from which the class-concept was abstracted, necessarily provides the only conceivable formalisation of class.

Once the function of the concept of class in Marxist sociology is realised, definitions of class other than that implied in that function need not be sought. Classes are comparatively stable groups of members of a certain social formation united in occupying certain places in polarised relations of production, or other relations assimilated to them, which include non-economic activities in administration, the professions, etc., as well as mere rentier-functions.⁶ The persons occupying certain characteristic positions in social life are thereby influenced in all their social contacts, interests, attitudes and behaviour. The Marxist approach to sociology is firmly upheld by the failure of the alternative, more popular definitions of class, except if interpreted as mere partial elements in a broader characteristic. Interpretations of social stratification by size of income or typical leisure-time-contacts raise questions as to why the members of a certain group do command higher income,and why they should identify themselves socially with certain other people. Besides, they are one-sided and cover only a restricted part of the experience to be explained. This is illustrated by the familiar type of the official's widow who nearly starves herself in order to preserve conventional standards of housing and clothing (while complaining of the " extravagances" of a working-class neighbour who, with an income lower than her pension, can afford holiday travel), and by the extension of class-solidarity to foreigners (perhaps in Russia

or China) with whom common membership in a Church or base-
ball-club can hardly be imagined even as a projection of familiar
local experience. Community of the source of income explains
community of sectional interest (which may be subject to
numerous sub-divisions) but not class ; and for this reason it has
been explicitly rejected by Marx. If taken seriously, it would
ascribe every grocer to the bourgeoisie, and every manager to the
working-class. Class-consciousness as a characteristic of class is
incompatible with the Marxist system, which to a large extent is
based upon the tension between such consciousness and objective
class-existence (in terms of the modern working-class struggle
"class in itself" versus "class for itself.")[9] To the opponents
of Marxism it may denote a cheap way of conjuring up actual
class-antagonisms[4]; but opponents as well as prophets of the
allegedly world-changing activities of the well-organised " class-
conscious " worker (that is to say, of the Trade Unionist with a
creed to be recited solemnly at Union celebrations) should notice
that this consciousness need not be revolutionary at all. An
estate, that is, a class well-established in its position by the legal
order and possibly distinguished by special dress, etc., forms, in
a sense, a peak of class-consciousness, though restricted to knowledge of one's " proper place in society " and one's rights and
duties towards the ordained masters.

All the above elements of class have some bearing on the
actual process whereby people holding a certain objective position
in the socio-economic process form distinct social groups,
evolve ideologies and attitudes determining their impact on
society ; but none of them is able to stand on its own feet, while
each of them can be easily derived from the fundamental relations
of production. Class-consciousness can be conceived as resulting
from class-position, and may form one of the most important
agencies through which the latter may influence the course of
events. From class-position results the opportunity of frequent
contacts with class-fellows, and this certainly forms a most
important agency creating a common outlook ; and in the framework even of a loosely developed class-ideology[10] it may serve

[9] *The Poverty of Philosophy*, p. 144, see also below, p. 227.

[10] A completely developed class-ideology like Marxism enables the establishment
of class-solidarity according to purely objective criteria, independently of any potential
direct associations, and even across apparently high ideological barriers (such as
divide the believing from the rationalist workers). But it should be kept in mind
that the average worker is not a Marxist sociologist.

its purpose by representing people in other regions or countries, personal contact with whom is impossible, as potential fellows of that narrower circle surrounding the individual, presumably sharing the same views about what is right and wrong, and presumably worthy of support. Class-position carries a certain standard of income, and the implied ability to share the class-standard of life, for its holder. For the members of the ruling class, it implies ample opportunity even outside the directly economic occupations to promote those who conform with the " right " pattern of thoughts, to positions of influence in the public service, in the professions, etc., where they will enjoy the income associated with the class, keep the right type of personal contacts, and be strengthened in their desirable views.[11]

(c) THE CLASSES OF CAPITALIST SOCIETY

Marx was conscious of the fact that every existing national society contains strata representing its pre-capitalist past. Especially in the continental countries such strata as the peasants may play a highly important part in social and political life and may even develop a remarkable degree of class-consciousness. But he expected all such groupments to be assimilated to the predominant, capitalist structure, and in any case he looked for a model of the latter as pure and classical as possible. He thought he had found it realised in England ; and in the last chapter of *Capital* workers, capitalists and landlords are enumerated as the three main classes of modern capitalist society. Such procedure was conditioned by his regarding the British system of landownership as characteristic of modern capitalism, and is exposed to the criticism that he was over-impressed by the struggle fought by the Freetraders against such feudal relics as might still be embodied in the landed interest. Even supposing he was right in his days, as opposed to economists like Rodbertus who regarded landowning entrepreneurs as the normal representatives of capitalism in the countryside, it might be questioned whether his approach should still be regarded as topical, in view of the present structure of the British aristocracy, with the landed

---

[11] There is no necessary implication of "buying consciences" in the primitive sense ; once we assume that people's views upon what is right and what is wrong depend upon their objective position in social life and the surroundings in which their thought is being shaped, the mere desire to put the right people in the most influential places is bound to result in "the ideas of the ruling class being the ruling ideas."

interest evidently assimilated to the Big Business and financial one. Once we regard the class-concept as a bridge between economics and politics, there is no reason to derive a class—and especially a " main class "—of existing society from an economic category which originated in past political and social conflicts, unless socio-political facts of first-rank importance suggest the introduction of that category as their underlying explanation.

These are details, which conceivably may invite different answers for different countries. A more important difficulty is implied in the character of the basic relations of production in terms of ownership of means of production, as clearly intended by Marx when he attempted his answer to the problem. In our days command of wage-labour, in a typical case, is divested of juridical ownership of the means of production, not because it is transferred to an alleged managerial class, as suggested by a fashionable theory which shows an unmistakable interest in sidestepping the issue of ownership, but because the economic functions of ownership are actually exercised by an oligarchy distinct from, or only partially identical with, the legal owners, some of whom may even fail to belong to the capitalist class at all.[12] This oligarchy of controllers of the great monopolies, to which the holders of the political key-positions and the survivals of the feudal aristocracy are assimilated, forms the apex of the social pyramid. They are immediately followed by the more important of the still surviving individual entrepreneurs, the holders of the most important managerial, professional, etc., positions, and further by the bulk of those who are still regarded as belonging to the *bourgeoisie* (medium entrepreneurs, managers of large enterprises with a considerable freedom of disposition, and most of the professions). As opposed to them, we find the working-class, with noticeable differentiations between the skilled workers (to whom the bulk of the black-coat workers are assimilated, even if they need only moderate skill for their jobs) and the great mass holding jobs demanding neither special and expensive preparation nor extraordinary gifts, followed by a lower stratum which at least in times of depression is exposed to the risk of completely losing any place in social economics and the social status connected with it. Between bourgeoisie and working-class we

[12] That is to say, are not decisively conditioned in their social and political attitude by share-holdership or by savings the proceeds from which form only a moderate addition to an essentially earned income. Otherwise, the ascription of all shareholders, etc., to the bourgeoisie would be a pleonasm, however unrealistic.

generally find a middle stratum, for historical reasons[13] known as the lower-middle-class. It is composed of the smallest industrial, commercial and agricultural entrepreneurs, most of them with responsibilities for directing productive activities far inferior to those of the average foreman, blackcoat worker, or Civil Servant in a fairly responsible post, who usually are assimilated to them.

The borderlines between the classes are naturally vague, and all along those borderlines the ideological influence of the upper upon the lower stratum is predominant, at least in normal times when society is integrated to a greater extent.[14] Even in the purely economic sphere clear definitions are excluded by the social importance still ascribed to ownership, along with statistically measurable characteristics such as the amount of labour commanded and the question whether such command is exercised in a comparatively[15] independent position or as a medium link of an established hierarchy. In non-economic fields, such as the professions, the Civil Service, etc., there are parallel stratifications roughly (by means of comparable income and corresponding social contacts) assimilated to the predominant economic one. However difficult the decision in individual cases may be, no considerable difficulties are met in ascribing the typical representatives of larger social groups to one or the other class.

(d) SECTIONAL AND CLASS CONFLICTS

Class, as a sociological concept, can be defined in an unequivocal way and corresponds to evident traits of social reality to be seen in most nations over very long historical periods. But the explanation of history as a history of class-struggles appeared obvious only within an intellectual environment where the predominant importance of events such as the French revolution, and the interpretation of its course by class-conflicts[16]

[13] Because of the traditional inclusion of the now obsolete anti-feudal issue in the class-scheme, so that the bourgeoisie appears as the "middle class."

[14] In times of social crisis there is a strong desire of the average bourgeois to be regarded as a mere "middle-class" man as distinct from the ruling oligarchy, and strong sympathies of, for example, the lower-middle class intellectual with the working-classes, though his external ways of life are likely to continue being assimilated to those of the lower middle-classes.

[15] Even the "independent" entrepreneur's actual relations to his bank are frequently nearer to those of a manager to the main shareholders than to his ideologically supposed independence.

[16] See above, p. 41.

could be taken for granted. Once it is supposed that the important decisions in human history deal with changes in social structure, no difficulty is implied in defining class as a group having an interest in a certain change in social structure,[17] or else its preservation, and to derive that class-interest from the position of the members of the group within the given social structure. And as major revolutions are characterized by an overwhelming increase of the political interest even of groups which remained comparatively apathetic in " normal " times, there is no difficulty in explaining how the members of a certain class defined in that way are actually brought into action according to their class-interest : the smallest incident may be sufficient to group all members of society according to their relation to the fundamental cleavage of the time.

But the great revolutionary decisions form comparatively short episodes in the history of mankind, and even their explanation in terms of class would be impossible unless class could be described as the predominant factor during the preceding non-revolutionary period. Obviously, the characterisation of the members of a given society by their class-position, however important, is not the only factor affecting their stand in all the contested issues of the time, and in discussing class we have met quite a considerable number of " border-phenomena " where the stand of the members of society concerned is even likely to differ from that implied in their theoretical class-position.[18] Nor is there any self-evident mechanism which induces members of a certain class to act in a certain homogeneous way : but without the demonstration of such a mechanism the assertion that " the bourgeoisie " or " the working-class " take a certain stand in issues other than those implied in the definition of their class-position is sheer mysticism. Few Marxist authors have devoted much thought to the problem because it is silently assumed that political parties, having certain planks in their platform and appealing to certain groups, actually work as the political representatives of certain social classes, and can rely upon their support. But that assumption can be proved in no general way, and in many cases is disputed by the Marxists themselves.

[17] Such definitions are applied by the large majority of Marxists, without all the problems involved being realised. See, for a recent example, M. Dobb, *Studies in the Development of Capitalism*, London, 1946, p. 15.
[18] See above. pp. 219-20.

Marxism attempts to bridge the gap demonstrating the contradictory character of the relations of production in general, that is, the need for continuous sectional struggle.[19] In this field its case, as against those who assert the inherent harmonies of any existing social order because of its mere existence and survival, is extremely strong : the real problem lies in deriving from the obviously unharmonious character say of capitalist society the likelihood of that ultimate general upheaval that would bring it to an end. There are many degrees between, say, a jurisdictional conflict between two Trade Unions only formally directed against the employer, and a general strike such as Britain experienced in 1926 which itself might be regarded as forming rather the lower end in a scale of events leading to a thorough transformation of society.

In the Marxist system—and in the general opinion of the Labour Movement, including those countries where Marxism has not become its official ideology—progress from local and isolated sectional struggles to those involving the working-class as a whole is taken for granted by the interconnection of analogous tensions within the model. Long before, and even independent of whether, improvements achieved by some group of workers or, *vice versa*, reduction of wages forced upon them by their employer, could influence the position of others by the mechanism of the labour market as envisaged by classical economics, the very knowledge of such changes would influence the relation of strength between the main social groups opposing each other on analogous issues. Anticipation of such implications of any strike or lock-out even of moderate importance would cause either side in the conflict to be supported by the whole Labour, or employers' interest respectively. Even local sectional conflict appears as part of a large-scale battle continuously fought out between the main camps opposing each other[19] and contributing towards establishing the general relation of strength upon which the division of the social product between capital and labour depends.[20] Consciousness of such interconnections is bound gradually to bridge all conflicts of interest existing within either camp and to

[19] This statement does not necessarily exclude community of interest in both camps, say against feudal survivals, or in the international sphere. It should be clearly kept in mind that our argument, here, is of an essentially sectional character, and does not involve any assertion that the conflicts whose inevitability is established are ultimately the most important ones.

[20] See above p. 133.

render phenomena such as conflicts on jurisdiction merely transitory.

This division of capitalist society along sectional lines is raised to a higher level by its political implications.[21] Individual social reforms intended to generalise partial achievements of Trade Union struggle by legal enactment, though they encourage the unions to enter the political stage, do not necessarily imply actual divisions on class-lines : on the contrary, expectations of likely support from bourgeois philanthropists and even from those employers who have already had to grant the concession and naturally desire to see it enforced upon their competitors, may encourage such Labour activities on the political scene at a time when any proposal sure to meet opposition on closed class-lines was thereby ensured of being defeated. But some political conflicts on such lines, especially for the achievement and defence of the right of combination, are not of the Labour movement's own choice. Their impact on its cohesion and general attitude may have encouraged Marx's statement[22] that every class-struggle is a political struggle. This statement should not be inverted unless it is desired to reduce the concept of class so as to cover any sectional conflict between, say, the oil-interest and the coal-interest, which certainly was not Marx's intention. But when the Labour movement is involved in political conflicts which force even the average citizen not directly interested to take sides, these conflicts become a rallying point for all tensions existing in society round the central point upon which its economic structure hinges. Once this process has gone so far, all fundamental constitutional issues, such as suffrage, and many issues of foreign policies tend to be interpreted by all those concerned in terms of class (whether they use the term of class or not), that is, of their likely effects upon the relation of strength between the two main camps into which the body politic is divided. Politics[21] are important because they raise the class-issue above the sectional level : a foreman whose general attitude is so thoroughly influenced by having in the shop to defend the employer's interest that he usually sides with his betters, may be in general sympathy with rises in wages (especially

[21] It should again be kept in mind that we are arguing about politics on the most elementary level and speak of recourse to legislation and administration as distinct from the "free play" of sectional forces, not of the analysis of political machinery to be discussed in the next Chapter.

[22] *The Poverty of Philosophy*, p. 145, repeated in the *Communist Manifesto*.

of black-coated workers) ; but should a *bourgeois* government attempt to enact prohibitive legislation against general strikes, he will know where to stand. On the other side, a poor peasant, if sufficiently enlightened about basic social issues and the parties likely to defend his interests against landlord, banker and merchant, will also know where to stand. Politics act as a catalyst upon the formation of class as distinct from sectional fronts not merely by correcting the few deviations of class from sectional stratification (such as employees in a position where their interest is largely linked up with that of their masters, or bourgeois members of Consumers' Co-operatives) but mainly by enabling the grouping of the manifold sectional divisions, and of those large parts of society which have no direct sectional ties with the main classes of society, into camps dominated by the major class interests in the given social structure. This does not necessarily imply a restriction of the number of relevant classes to two : this depends simply on the issue whether social cleavages other than those dividing *bourgeois* society are still relevant.

In the *Poverty of Philosophy*[9] the turning of " class in itself " into the " class for itself " is directly described as a necessary implication of trade unionist organisation forced upon the workers by modern industry, but attacked by the employers so that the workers are forced to defend their class-organisation in what is bound to be a political struggle. Without a very simple conception of that turning point, the description of the 1848 revolution in Germany, on its eve, as a bourgeois-democratic revolution bound to form the immediate preface to a proletarian one, would have been sheer nonsense ; but it should be noted that after the defeat of the revolution the authors of the *Manifesto* envisaged a very prolonged period of social conflict during which the working-class would grow fit for the conquest of political power.[23] After a succession of failures, attempts at reforms as well as revolts in which the necessary political experience would be achieved,[24] the class, rallied in sectional and political struggle

[23] See above, p. 48.

[24] " Proletarian revolutions, like those of the Nineteenth Century, are very self-critical ; again and again they stop short in their progress, retrace in order to make a fresh start . . .Again and again, they shrink back appalled by the vague immensity of their own aims. But, at long last, a situation is reached whence retreat is impossible, and where the circumstances clamour in chorus : *Hic Rhodus, hic salta !* Here is the Rose, dance here ! ". *The Eighteenth Brumaire*, ed. cit., pp. 27-8.

within existing society, would ultimately conquer power and fulfil
its historical task.

We shall later[25] deal with the problems of the last-mentioned
identification of class, as a subject of sectional struggle, with
class as an agency of social change. Evidently the whole concept
stands and falls with the forecast of a tendential and obvious[26]
destitution of the working-class in those countries where they
(plus those lower-middle-class elements who by the mere everyday experience of capitalist economics are assimilated to them)[27]
have become the decisive majority of the people in consequence
of the very capitalist evolution. It does not answer the problems
raised for revolutionary Socialists by the prosperity of the working-
classes in the leading imperialist countries however temporary
and conditional,[28] nor the socialist aspirations of the workers
in countries where—perhaps in consequence of the very prosperity of the imperialist countries—destitution may be present,
but any approach to a working-class majority absent.[27] Sectional ideology may claim that a socialist transformation can
grow out of sectional struggles even without organised activities
of a revolutionary party, but if this were the only path to a
socialist transformation it might be delusory even supposing
that Marx's analysis, conceived as it was for the capitalist world
as a whole, was correct : the increasing mass-destitution may not
be concentrated where the obvious working-class majority exists
along with the implied opportunity of a comparatively easy
reorganisation of the economic system.

At this point the issue is joined by Lenin's distinction between
Trade Unionist and revolutionary class-consciousness.[29] The
first is accessible to the working-classes by their own efforts.
They may be assisted in this by some familiarity with popularised
Marxist theory, which was current in the non-Bolshevist Continental labour movements, and take political action to forward
their sectional interest against employers.[30] And after long

[25] See below, note 34, and pp. 253-4.
[26] "Relative destitution" derived by Marxist theorists from a comparison between
the rising standard of life of the working-classes and the even quicker rise of capitalist
profits would not help.
[27] At this stage the Leninist concept of skilful tactics by which an alliance of the
working-class with other potentially anti-capitalist, but fully self-conscious forces is
achieved (see below, Chapter XV) does not enter our investigation.
[28] Use of the opportunity for a socialist transformation caused by a defeat in
imperialist war would, again, presuppose the Bolshevist party-concept. See below,
p. 279.
[29] What is to be Done? Sel. Works. vol. II, pp. 52-3.
[30] Ibid., pp. 65 and 81-2.

painful experiences, a socialist transformation may arise even from this type of class-consciousness ; indeed, it forms a preliminary condition for Bolshevists envisaging a comparatively early socialist transformation in countries where the conditions for the formation of a powerful Bolshevist party are conspicuously absent.[31] But, in the typical case, the long-term interest of the working-class in a socialist transformation of society is assumed to be not realisable without revolutionary class-consciousness, that is, knowledge of the general conditions that demand a thorough transformation of society and of the tasks therefrom arising for themselves. Such consciousness has to be inculcated in the workers by an elite of professional revolutionaries whose outlook starts from the inter-relations of all the classes of society as a whole. So they need not be of working-class origin, provided only they have realised the necessarily predominant rôle of the working-classes in the impending revolution. Even if themselves of working-class origin, they need to rise above the level of the " Trade Unionist class-consciousness," that is, the experiences of the everyday sectional struggle (including its immediate political implications)[32] because the problems of the impending revolution cannot be correctly answered from that narrow starting point.[29] Long before Lenin's days, the distinction between sectional and revolutionary class-struggle was a common-place amongst the *bourgeois*, especially the " armchair-Socialist " critics of the Labour movement who aimed at a distinction between the former, which ought to be integrated into a system of reasonable social reform, and the latter, which should be dropped as a Utopia. Correspondingly, the Revisionist Bernstein in the concluding paragraph of *Evolutionary Socialism* proclaimed that Social Democracy should dare to appear as what it actually was, as a party of social reform ; and we may accept that he was right if we analyse the actual social content of the revolutionary phraseology of pre-1914 Social Democracy, which merely emphasised the need to bridge the differences between the different branches (trades, localities, etc.) of the sectional interest. Within the current Marxist ideology, such arguments were answered by the assertion that the logic of class-struggle was bound to force the

[31] Evidently for this reason, quite recently Bolshevist writers who, by overstating Lenin's criticism of Trade Unionist " class-consciousness," neglected that theoretical possibility, have been called to order. Cf. also Lenin's *State and Revolution*, pp. 64–5, in *Sel. Works*, vol. VII.
[32] L.c., pp. 138–9.

labour movement, whatever its subjective intentions, into revolutionary channels ;[33] but envisaging the necessity of such a transition did not necessarily imply its conception as a distinct step. Such distinction was made in 1906 by the left-wing of German Social Democracy, under the obvious impact of Lenin's writings as well as of the (first) Russian revolution, and its immediate purpose was just that which Lenin's distinction between " Trade Unionist " and " revolutionary " class-consciousness implied.[34] But at least Rosa Luxemburg[35] rejected Lenin's main conclusion that there was a necessary and fruitful tension between the higher stage of class-consciousness (as represented by the revolutionary party) and the lower one (as represented by working-class mass-organisation) : in her opinion, there was no clear distinction between the nucleus of class-conscious proletarians already organised in the working-class party and the adjacent strata already involved in class-struggle and proceeding towards class-consciousness. For Rosa Luxemburg the Party was not, as for Lenin,[36] a disciplined organisation of " jacobins, closely *connected with* working-class organisation," it was the movement (and the implied organisation) of the working-

[33] *The Holy Family*, *M.E.G.A.* I/3, p. 207.

[34] It was made in Rosa Luxemburg's pamphlet *Massenstreik, Partei und Gewerkschaft*. Immediately after its publication, and in close co-operation with Luxemburg, Kautsky when moving, at the Mannheim Party Congress, his amendment to the official resolution argued that the Party, though in its capacity as representative of the workers' need for political reforms it had merely equal rights with the Trade Unions, could claim to lead them in its alternative capacity as promoter of the struggle for the ultimate replacement of capitalist by socialist society. Both knew, and at least Rosa Luxemburg (see below in the text) rejected the Leninist concept of Party, developed four years before. The obvious implication of their description of the relations between Party and Trade Unions was the obligation of Party-members, in their capacity as Trade Union members, to work according to the directives issued by the Party congresses (against such distinctly reformist currents in the Trade Unions the outbreak of which at the Cologne Trade Union congress had caused the whole dispute). It was embodied in an amendment, which was withdrawn, allegedly because the more sensible Trade Union leaders regarded it as a commonplace, but possibly hurtful to Trade Unionist feelings. It is impossible now to establish how far such tactical reasons actually dominated the attitude of Kautsky (without whose support Rosa Luxemburg might actually have been put into an insignificant minority) the only thing evident at least in our days is the obligation of any Socialist who realised the importance of the issue to register his dissent by a vote, large or small. But it should be noted that the first phrase of Kautsky's amendment, which established the theoretical superiority of the Party, was carried without a division—even the right-wing Trade Unionist being evidently prepared to pay lip-service to it.

[35] In her article on *Organisational Problems of Russian Social Democracy*, reprinted from the Menshevist " *Iskra* " in *Neue Zeit*, vol. XXII/2 (1904).

[36] *One Step forward, two Steps back*, in *Sel. Works*, vol. II, p. 432. In its essence, Lenin's attitude was already implied in the statement in *What is to be Done ?* (Ibid., p. 98) " that class political consciousness can be brought to the workers only from without."

class itself; for, apart from general principles, there was no established tactique of class-struggle which the working-class could be taught by a central committee. In spite of her attempts to establish a principial superiority of the Party in relation to the Trade Unions[34] (which, thus, were doomed to defeat) Rosa Luxemburg failed to realise that the differences existing between the two levels of " class-consciousness " were differences not in tactics of " the working-class-struggle " but in basic approach to the existing society; and Leninists would not fail to reproach her with having, at least in her teachings on Party, reduced to a mere tactical error what she herself during World War I was to describe as a betrayal of socialist principles.

It is not difficult to recognise in Lenin's theory the impact of the conditions of pre-1905 Russia, where a bourgeois-democratic revolution against Tsarism was obviously impending (Russian Socialists differed only on the exact definition of the part to be played by the young working-class in that revolution) and where the traditions of " professional revolutionaries " from the ranks of the revolutionary intelligentsia were available. Nor is it difficult to notice the analogy of those conditions with those in which the *Communist Manifesto* was born, and also the fact that up to our days the Bolshevist concept has been crowned with success, or seems near to success, only in countries where conditions are somewhat comparable. This would provide no counter-argument as long as there has appeared no example of a consistently socialist transformation of society resulting from political intensification of the sectional struggle of the working-classes. Even if this should happen after the impact of successful realisations of the Leninist concept has been felt to the full, it would provide no counter-argument against the latter which left some loopholes for the alternative course and, besides, was not so narrowminded as to exclude even gradualist transition to socialism in individual countries once the decisive battles in the international sphere were won.

Since Rosa Luxemburg's[35] days, many critics have concluded from the obvious origins of the Bolshevist concept, that it leads to no working-class, socialist revolution at all, but, at the best, to the working-classes successfully exercising the temporary dictatorship necessary for the success of a bourgeois-democratic revolution in backward countries. But this criticism merely re-asserts the sectional Utopia derived from " Trade Unionist class-consciousness," plus (as in Trotskyism) some disappointment that the revolutionary realisation does not come up to the standards of Utopia.

CHAPTER XI

STATE AS AN INSTRUMENT OF CLASS RULE

(a) DEFINITION OF THE CLASS-CHARACTER OF STATES

When dealing in Marxist theory with the concept of State, we are not concerned with commonplaces such as the fact that in any modern society some social organisation enforcing some discipline is needed, and that there must be rules (" laws "[1]) which prescribe such behaviour as is necessary in the interest of the continuation and prosperity of the existing social order. Were this the whole story, there would be—outside the anarchist Utopia—no sense in a discussion of the continued existence of the State after the abolition of class-divisions. Nor can the economic and welfare functions of any state—including the U.S.S.R.— be regarded as a sufficient characterisation, unless it is interpreted in connection with its main function as a machinery of compulsion. Further, the State as a historical phenomenon has to be defined as a separate body designed for the enforcement of the rules of social behaviour, as distinct from mere informal meetings (and, if necessary, the collectively exercised violence) of the members of society. In his letter to Bebel, accompanying Marx's *Critique of the Gotha Programme*, Engels defines the State as " the government machinery . . . or the State in so far as it forms a special organism separated from society through division of labour." Hence all the problems involved in the sociological analysis, from the Marxist point of view, of the State : it is an institution composed of functionaries whose professional self-assertion demands emphasis on their enhanced standpoint above social antagonisms, and whose activities would meet continuous resistance without the assertion of such a standard and at least occasional attempts to live up to it. And because of the very social division of labour their social status defies simple attempts

[1] I use inverted commas in order to denote the problems implied in the necessity of such rules obvious for any non-Utopian, whilst their description as "laws," in Marxist sociology, is made dependent upon the character of the machinery by which they are enforced. I have dealt with this issue in *Soviet Legal Theory* (International Library for Sociology and Social Reconstruction, London, 1945)

at definition in terms of the basic social division between owners of the means of production and proletarians employed by them.

According to Engels, the State originated when rising class-differentiations could no longer be handled by the primitive self-government of tribal society and made necessary a power, *apparently* standing above society, in order to moderate the conflict and to keep it within the bounds of " order."[2] There is no need to discuss the extent to which this indigenous explanation of the origins of the State should be accepted, and how much historical data backs the exogenous explanation of the State by external conquest : even if there were only isolated examples of the former, they would be methodologically important by demonstrating the necessary rise of the State in connection with that of class-differentiations, quite apart from historical chances such as external conquest (which, too, was likely to result in a class-differentiation of the new society, according to the Spartan and perhaps also Roman pattern). However it originated, the State is conceived by Marxism as an instrument for preserving the power of the ruling class ; but unless the question is begged by introducing this characteristic in the general definition of the State,[3] there is a *non sequitur* in the Marxist statement that the State, having originated with class-struggle, was bound " to wither away " with the abolition of class-conflicts. Conceivably the very differentiation of civilised society, which appeared first in the shape of class-conflict, but is bound to continue in some form as long as civilisation continues, necessitates the preservation of a special machinery of compulsion. The necessary amount of compulsion may be restricted when, because of the abolition of class-divisions, the justice and necessity of the existing law will not be questioned any more by a large part of the population and when social education will have made clear to individuals the implications of their actions to society with such clarity as could be taken for granted in a primitive tribal community. However, a repressive machinery of whatever kind, even if called on to function comparatively rarely, is a State in any reasonable sense of the word. It gives all rules of behaviour established in such a society a legal character, and this is still more the case when the functioning of that machinery is " objective "

---

[2] *The Origins of the Family*, etc., ed. cit., pp. 193-4.

[3] As in the *Communist Manifesto* : " Political power, properly so called, is merely the organised power of one class of oppressing the other."

and independent of the relations of subordination necessarily existing in the production process.[4]

In the primitive concept of the proletarian who feels himself to be discriminated against by the working of a machinery dominated by his " betters," the class-character of the State is realised in a sum of experiences proving that the (economically) ruling class dominates the State machinery, distorts State legality whenever the workers' legal claims confront the interests of a member of that class,[5] and applies the laws merely when and in so far as this fits its interests. Engels approached this view when stating that the State, because it arose in the thick of the fight between the classes, is *normally* the state of the most powerful, the economically ruling class, which, by using the State, becomes also the politically ruling class and so acquires new means of holding down and exploiting the oppressed class.[6] Such explanations seem quite appropriate when applied to the reading of ancient history, the records of which are full of group-struggles the political element of which is sometimes more conspicuous than the clearly class-character of the contending groups, and generally the record of societies in which politics are regarded as a gentlemanly leisure-time activity ; but in approaching the realities of our time we are confronted with the difficulty that only in exceptional cases can the upper links of the State machinery (not to speak of their subordinates, who are usually assimilated to the lower-middle-classes) be verbally described, in the words of the *Communist Manifesto*, as " a committee for managing the common affairs of the whole bourgeoisie." Such a description would to some extent fit the case of the Third Republic in France, the Weimar Republic, or parts of recent British history. But even the American bourgeoisie has shown readiness to despise and dissociate itself from its political agents. The founders of Marxism themselves were not firm on the formula

[4] For a discussion of this problem, see my *Soviet Legal Theory*, pp. 161–4.

[5] Usually such experiences—conceivably excesses which could be remedied without impairing the essential class-character of the state in question—are described as "class-Justice," an interesting symptom of the influence exercised by the ideology of an allegedly class-less legal system upon its very critics.

[6] *The Origin of the Family*, etc., p. 196. The word " normally " would make no sense if the political rule of the economically ruling class is assumed by implication (see below, pp. 237–8), but there is a possible explanation by reference to the conquest of power by the working-class which uses it as a means of transition to a new economic structure. The whole connection in which Engels' remark was made gives little support to such an interpretation.

of the *Manifesto* : impressed by the failure of the 1848 bourgeois revolutions in France and Germany, and again by the obvious failure of the Prussian Liberals to stand up against Bismarck, Engels, in a letter to Marx of April 13, 1866, expressed his growing conviction that the bourgeoisie was unable to exercise direct rule. " Unless, as in England, an oligarchy is ready to lead State and Society for good remuneration in the interest of the bourgeoisie, a bonapartist semi-dictatorship is the normal instrument of government : it defends the essential material interests of the bourgeoisie, if necessary even against the latter's resistance, but it does not admit the bourgeoisie to a share in government itself." In spite of the above-mentioned instances of direct government by Big Business, and the hypothetical exclusion of modern Britain from the examples used by Marx, such an analysis does not appear unrealistic in view of recent fascist experiences.

But how then can the modern state be consistently described as the State of the (economically) ruling class ? In cases where social structure is fairly static in its essential characteristics, the argument can be made even without any reference to specific Marxist terminology on the basis of the very assertion that it is the State's function to carry out the Law. But in order to argue from this assertion, we must accept a realistic sociological interpretation of Law. We may assume that concepts of social morality " are always the product of a dominant group which identifies itself with the community, and which possesses facilities denied to subordinate groups or individuals for imposing its view of life on the community,"[7] Law being " a meeting place for (socially prevalent) ethics and power."[8] It follows therefrom that Law is a meeting place where an ideological elaboration of the interests of the ruling group as a whole, established by its " power over opinion," and such direct pressure as the individual vested interests may exercise, are synthesized. The State enforcing the Law of such a community would realise a compromise between the actual short-term interests of powerful groups and the rationalisation of the long-term interests of the ruling class as a whole.

The issue becomes more complicated if, as in all Marxist arguments, the very concept of class is conditioned by the assumption that the basic social structure is questioned. If, as is obvious

[7] E. H. Carr, *The 20 years crisis*, 1919-39, London, 1940, p. 101.
[8] Ibid., p. 218.

in our days, government by direct representatives of the *bourgeoisie* is no longer the rule, assertions by the actual holders of State power that they are prepared to carry through fundamental social reform can no longer be rejected by mere reference to their social origin and interest. What are the current prospects of states with essentially bourgeois economics, but with a government recruited partly or mainly from the ranks of parties of labour and perhaps holding a non-bourgeois ideology? As Marx observed, in a country where actual social power lies with the bourgeoisie the latter may well remove its place-holders whenever they should cease properly to represent its interests, and it may be added that in the present state of international interdependence such pressure may be exercised by the bourgeoisie of a more powerful capitalist country on which the country in question happens to depend. Only an answer to the problem which is consistent throughout, can render a fundamental statement of Marxism independent of changes in local circumstances and of the impact of possible changes in U.S.A. foreign policies, and remove it from any dispute about the extent to which abuses recognised as such by every liberal reformer can be overcome without basic changes in social structure. Such an answer, which is widely accepted amongst Marxist theorists, is given by the socio-economic functions of the State.

Every state has to protect the existing economic system and to ensure its proper functioning, and this implies care for the prosperity of the class responsible for social production. Laws are bound to be interpreted and administered in accordance with this supreme function of the State, and civil servants are bound to be educated, selected, and promoted according to the corresponding standards. Quite apart from any individual or group bias due to social origin, education, and method of appointment, judges are simply doing their duty in preserving the existing order of society and its functioning, and by interpreting all ambiguous formulations of laws in conformity with their conception of the ultimate purpose of Law; and parties and witnesses appearing in court are bound to be appreciated according to the degree in which they have proved successful and respectable members of society according to its own recognised standards. Thus quite a lot even of those phenomena that may invite the liberal reformers' critical attitude find an explanation implied in the very roots of State and Society. But the class-character

of a state does not depend on such details : it is another expression
of its function, namely, of the fact that no state, whatever the
composition of its government, can protect more than one social
structure. And it does this even in protecting its labour-force
against the short-sighted interests of the ruling class. [9]

However strong this argument may be, when confronted with
the concept of gradualist transition to socialism without revolutionary changes in State machinery it fails to provide such a
simple answer as the popular explanation of the " bourgeois "
character of existing states outside the U.S.S.R. by the class-
structure of their leading personnel. Allowance must be made
for the traditional element inherent in State-machinery and
likely to lag behind changes in the social order thus protected,
unless it has originated recently from a revolutionary upheaval.
But, even so, it remains an undeniable fact that if the social
character of the British state is derived from the character of the
social relations which it protects, since January 1, 1947, nationalisation of the mines must be included in its social character as
private ownership of mines was before. Within the framework
of the functional derivation of the class-character of the State, the
only test of an actual change in the class-character of a new
government is its ability to carry out social changes. There
remains no fundamental argument against the gradualist concept
of transition to a new social order, provided that concept can
hold its own in the economic field and avoid international and
other complications that would prevent its realisation. True, as
soon as the " nationalised " industries cease to be administered
as subsidiary organs of the predominant capitalist sector of
economics, compact resistance by all supporters of the traditional
order is likely, and it may get considerable encouragement
by the natural reluctance of a government pledged to the concept
of gradual reform to apply energetic measures which may gain
the support of all those wavering elements who are out to back
the winning side. On the other side, a new State machinery

[9] Occasionally, such care may have to be enforced even by the workers' sectional
interest—forming, in this case, part of the interest of existing society—if within the
ruling class no groups are forthcoming who are willing and able to enforce the general
interest of capitalist society (say, in preventing mine-owners from employing children)
against the individual capitalists concerned. In such a case, the differentiation of
actual interest existing within the ruling class is unlikely to find more explicit expression than lack of homogeneity and firmness in the front resisting the miners' demands.
Conceivably, the latter may be left with the feeling of having scored against capitalism
as such, whilst questioning the bourgeois character of a state which gave them the
opportunity of such successes.

which has originated from a revolutionary upheaval, even if it starts with a moderate programme of social change, is likely to be driven on the way of nationalisation further than it desired. Even if it should succeed in stopping after comparatively moderate initial reforms in order to consolidate them, the impact upon the total social structure of a certain degree of nationalisation, if carried through by new State machinery and by a new type of administration in the nationalised industries, is bound to be greater than that of an analogous percentage of nationalised industries administered according to an already familiar pattern, and subordinated to a State which appears to differ from preceding regimes merely by the party-allegiance of its ministers. A case can thus be made for the Marxist assertion that even in cases of gradual transformation of economics a show-down of the conflicting class-forces is inevitable, and that the class-character of " mixed economics " should be interpreted according to the outcome of that decision. However, if we agree that in the international process of transition to a new social order gradual transformations are likely to occur in some countries, and if we decline acceptance of the Truman-doctrine and of the Soviet counter-measures as characteristic features of the whole transition period, it is hardly possible to prove the inevitability, in every country, of events distinct enough to allow for a definite statement of the time and mode in which mixed economies, including their nationalised elements and the State protecting them, cease to be *bourgeois* and become socialist, including again the N.E.P. elements of the mixed economies. Every instance of seriously attempted social transformation without previous destruction of existing State machinery (including that of Czechoslovakia where initiative and leadership were in Communist hands), provides an argument against the idea that the class-character of a state is simply derived from the social origin of its personnel.

In a very important remark[10] Lenin has gone the length of denying the possibility of an exact definition of the class character of a revolution except in relation to the element of dictatorship, that is, mass-initiative destroying and replacing the existing State machinery. This statement might be inverted to say that the class-character of a state is indefinite except

---

[10] *Contribution to the History of Dictatorship, Sel. Works*, vol. VII, p. 245.

during, and in the immediate aftermath of, a revolution, when its origin from the mass-initiative of a certain class is obvious. In order to define the class-character of the eventually established new state-machinery recourse to the functional analysis of that character would still be unavoidable. Thus we would have to work from two different derivations of the class-character of State ; one for periods of comparative stability, when that character would have to be derived from that of the economic system protected by the State, and one for periods of transition, when the State operates as a factor transforming economics, and therefore has to be explained as the organ of the class from the revolutionary actions of which it emanated. This result seems sensible enough from the point of view of the socialist revolution, the economic outcome of which, nationalisation of the means of production, is inconceivable except as the outcome of political action ; but it clearly contradicts the concept of the bourgeois-democratic revolutions as current not only amongst their contemporary supporters but also amongst Marxists, according to which such revolutions merely remove political obstacles in the development of an economic structure already predominant. In that case the whole explanation of the class-character of the State would have to be functional, independent of whether the pre-revolutionary structure of the State machinery was actually feudal (as to the social origin of its officials), whether the post-revolutionary machinery was actually bourgeois or otherwise,[11] and whether in a certain stage of the revolutionary process the government originated from class-movements of the lower-middle classes, and in some modern colonial countries perhaps even from the working-class. Lenin's " democratic dictatorship of the workers and peasants," as envisaged in 1905, should, in the sense discussed, be described as a bourgeois government. Actually Lenin occasionally has gone the length of describing even the proletarian dictatorship after the complete nationalisation of production as " a *bourgeois* state without the bourgeoisie," in so far as it enforces (in the interest of the stimulation of production) unequal distribution of the means of consumption.[12] This was a clear exaggeration, resulting from simple identification of inequality with a " bourgeois " regime, but it

[11] See above, p. 236.
[12] *State and Revolution*, ed. cit., vol. VII, p. 90. For a criticism see my *Soviet Legal Theory*, pp. 32–3.

illustrates the confusion bound to arise from alternative use of the
definition of the class-character of the State by its origin and by
its socio-economic function respectively.

The record of the new regimes in East Central and South
Eastern Europe has recently induced Soviet theorists to elaborate
the concept of " Democracy of a new Type."   It is described as
" a constellation, in which the remainders of feudalism, large-
estate-ownership, is liquidated, where there is private property
in means of production, but the large-scale enterprises in industry,
transport and credit are nationalised, and where the State itself,
the machinery of repression, serves not the interest of the monopolist bourgeoisie but of the urban and rural toilers."[13]   As
even in the " new democracies " the State machinery has
occasionally to oppose the workers' short-term interests, this
statement can only be interpreted in the sense of gradualist
transition to socialism.   This is described as possible because,
as distinct from normal capitalist countries even with a considerable extent of industries nationalised, the State is supposed to
support the socialist elements in the mixed economics of those
countries, and to promote the subordination of the remaining
private capitalist, and small-scale commodity-producing industries to the plan.   As distinct from states of the proletarian
dictatorship (which may have a mixed economic structure,
as did Russia under the N.E.P.) the " democracies of the new
type " do not completely dissolve and replace the old State
machinery, but merely transform it by continuous introduction
of supporters of the new regime.   Such procedure is made
possible by the historical conditions above mentioned which
grant the new regime a support broader than merely that coming
from the revolutionary working-class and the strata nearest to it,
and by the external support of the U.S.S.R. which prevents
external support for the counter-revolutionary elements.   As
the less radical political transformation leaves even the economically expropriated part of the former ruling class with an ample
amount of political support which might form the basis of
operation for outside capitalist intervention, the new type of
democracy can only develop on the fringes of the U.S.S.R.,
which is obviously interested in its strengthening for security
reasons and can afford it sufficient protection ; but Varga took
occasion to point out, with back-reference to a book published

[13] E. Varga in *Mirovoye Khozaistvo, Mirovaya Politika*, 1947, No. 3.

by him in 1920, that, quite apart from these special circumstances, the external form of state (Soviets, government by a T.U.C., or by a parliamentary Labour majority) is irrelevant by contrast with the fundamental issue of socialist reconstruction, and that Lenin, when making critical annotations to that book [13a], did not object to this particular statement. In more recent Communist statements there is even greater emphasis upon the capacity of " People's Democracies " to proceed to a socialist society, though their affinity with the classical Marxist Leninist pattern is asserted by increased emphasis laid upon the complete destruction of the former State machinery (in these cases, the German occupation authorities, or Quislings) which preceded the establishment of " People's Democracies " not less than that of Soviet republics.[13b]

(b) The State of the Proletarian Dictatorship

The very description of the political conditions necessary for the case just discussed prevents its being regarded as typical of the great transformation. In the classical Leninist concept of the political revolution, a change in the social structure of the State, in the most elementary sense of the word, is produced by destruction of existing State machinery and its replacement by a new one (not necessarily in the sense of removal of all the existing members of the State machine, but certainly signifying the creation of completely new connections between its links and between them and society as a whole). The policies of a state attempting a socialist transformation of society do not necessarily coincide with the sectional interest of the working-classes as formed in the capitalist past ; but the working-class is the only class capable of consistently supporting the pattern of the new social formation,[14] and without its continued action the overthrow of the *ancien regime* would be impossible. Its capacity to develop that mass-initiative and activity needed in order to create a new State machinery fitting the new purposes is the real reason for the description of the socialist revolution as " proletarian." In the event of a working-class revolution, the well-known stage in all major revolutions when existing State machinery was at least temporarily replaced by a new one originating from the most consistent representatives of the

---

[13a] *Leninsky Sbornik*, vol. VII, p. 371.
[13b] cf. B. Bierut's report on the foundation congress of the United Workers' Party of Poland, in *For a Lasting Peace, for a People's Democracy*, 1949, No. 1.
[14] See below, pp. 332-3.

revolutionary class, can be realised in so far as the members of
the new State apparatus are elected in the actual centres of
production ; and the position of representatives of allied classes
whose standing in the process of social production does not allow
for such a method of appointment (Village Soviets, peasants' and
housewives' representatives in Committees of National Liberation, etc.) may be assimilated to that of the representatives of this
nucleus. Distrust of lower-middle-class people offering their
services to the victorious revolution, and experiences of the
sectional bureaucracy of the workers themselves during the
preceding complications of their own sectional struggle, may
induce the working-classes to safeguard the continuously working-
class character of their representatives by restrictions of income
imposed upon the latter[15] as well as by provision for speedy
recall if they do not comply with their electors' intentions. The
procedure is helpful to the revolutionary party because it gives
institutional expression to the transfer of leadership from the more
moderate to the consistently revolutionary parties, as implied in
the ascending phase of all revolutions, and also as a means by
which the party's influence on the masses can be used in order
to check the individual party-members promoted to positions
of responsibility. When a successful revolution experiences the
stage where the Jacobins defeat the Dantons, or the Stalinists the
Trotskys, even in the latter case where the authority of the mass
organs over their individual representatives is enhanced by
State ideology, the actual contest may be between an organisational bureaucracy embodying the permanent trends of the
revolution and some popular individuals with bonapartist
pretensions. However, in the earlier stages of a revolution where
the new institutional machinery is weak, but mass-initiative at
its highest, it is actually the latter which prevents individual
leaders, who, originating from the only class which enjoyed
privileges of education, may be linked with the past by a
thousand connections, from betraying the Revolution.

   The new State machinery has to be surrounded by a larger
circle of activists who link it with the broader masses of the
revolutionary class, help in the execution of the decisions arrived
at, and thereby acquire the experience needed in order to enable

---

[15] Which are supplemented, as guarantees against a "degeneration" of workers'
representatives, by the enforcement of puritan standards upon society as a whole.
See my *Spirit of Post-war Russia*, pp. 36–8.

their promotion to more responsible posts. From the long-term
point of view, this is merely the process in which a new institutional machinery emerges, more efficient and progressive than its
predecessor. But if the long-term perspective is hidden by early
defeat the elements of primitive democracy implied in such
conditions might provoke not only Marx's enthusiastic remark,
strongly tinged with wishful thinking, about the Paris Commune
as an attempted socialist revolution but also Engels' description of
the experiment as " no more State proper in the current sense "[16]
and Lenin's[17] repetition of the phrase when facing the growing
Soviet revolution. At their face-value, these statements belong to
the most conspicuous examples of Utopian thought available in
classic Marxist writing, whatever allowance may be made for the
fact that the Paris Commune, the Russian revolution, and Engels'
critique of the Lassalleans were directed against the most
conspicuous examples of bureaucratic State machinery.

With the actual abolition of the economic foundations of the
former ruling class, in the typical case repression is exercised
not against that class (or its former members), but against
individual citizens who fail to come up to the standards demanded.
With this process of stabilisation, and with the transfer of its
group-ideology from the realm of hopes and from the struggle
necessary in order to uphold it against a world of foes into
sober reality, the working-class ceases to be the immediate
and predominant wielder of State power. Some of its members
use the opportunities opened to them by the victorious revolution,
some within the State machinery, more in the professions, etc. ;
but the average working-class man or woman's interests turn
away from the predominant concern in politics excited by the
preceding crisis to a more balanced outlook, and if the revolution
is successful in achieving its cultural aims, an outlook wider than
before. Democratic achievements may be consolidated by
increasing participation of interested citizens in Administration
and Justice and increased opportunities for successful activists
to be promoted to responsible posts in the State machinery ;
but the efficiency of that machinery is safeguarded by established
rules as regards professional qualification and promotion in the

[16] Engels' letter to Bebel of March 18-25, 1875, accompanying Marx's *Critique of
the Gotha Programme.*
[17] In *State and Revolution, Sel. Works,* vol. VI, pp. 60-2.

hierarchy, and integration of the defeated former ruling class into the body politic is sought by its children being granted equal access to positions of responsibility.[18] At this stage, the class-character of the new state, though it may be still asserted in order to emphasize in State-ideology the continuity with the revolution, conveys no other meaning than it would have done in the event of a gradual transformation without revolutionary replacement of existing State machinery by a new one : namely, that it protects a certain social order and, therefore, is the state of the class (or classes) interested in the functioning of that order. This meaning is even less distinct than it would be sometime after the successful initiation of a gradual transformation : in the latter case, there might still be considerable elements belonging, according to their economic position, to the class formerly dominating social production, and accordingly feeling themselves threatened by the progress of nationalisation, however conciliatory its execution might be. Conceivably, they might still form the hard core of resistance to the policy of nationalisation, rallying round them all the lower-middle-class elements disappointed by short-comings in nationalised industries, and might speculate on changes in the international situation. In such conditions they, as a class, would form most legitimate objects of repression by the state defending its economic foundations even if, in consequence of favourable conditions and remarkable initial successes, that state should be able to preserve through the whole period its gradualist ideology and therefore carry out that repression by due process of law. In spite of avoiding, for ideological reasons, a description of its system in terms of class-rule, which our first-mentioned state preserved for the opposite ideological reasons, the gradualist state holding its own against a still dangerous minority would better fit such a description than the meanwhile consolidated revolutionary one whose former ruling class has become assimilated. Its internal opponents would certainly describe it as a " dictatorship " because it takes no notice of their legitimate interests. There would be just as much or little truth in such descriptions as in the general application of the term

---

[18] See my *Spirit of Post-War Russia*, pp. 38–40.

I

in Marxist literature as a synonym of class-rule in the most general sense described in this chapter.[19]

(c) MODIFICATION OF THE CONCEPT OF CLASS BY ITS APPLICATION TO REVOLUTION

Above[20] the concept of class has been derived from a typical model economic structure, with those not directly participating in economic production, Civil Servants, soldiers, etc., amongst them, being assimilated into the one or the other of the main classes by their upbringing and conditions of living. This concept is of a distinctly static character : that is, the interests round which the main classes are rallied are interests within, and formulated in terms of, the existing social structure ; but it served quite well to explain the likelihood that resistance of the *bourgeoisie* against thorough transformation, if it arose, would be supported by the existing State machinery, thus forcing upon the revolutionaries its replacement by an essentially new one. It is reduced to a commonplace when the class-character of a state (and its machinery) is simply derived from the social order protected by it : in this dynamic conception every sectional interest, even if enforcing the needs of the existing social structure in the face of the vested interests, is part of the interest of the ruling class ; and the only interest with which an abstract-interest of the ruled class can be associated, is that in a thorough change of the social structure. This interest cannot hold the minds of the members of the ruled class—nor of non-working-class people ideologically assimilated into it—for more than comparatively short periods of transition : if interpreted as meaning " the history of mankind is the history of the struggle of groups interested in the preservation or abolition of the existing social order respectively," the introductory phrase of the *Communist Manifesto* would be a considerable overstatement.

If a pessimistic interpretation of likely international developments is accepted, or if the importance of fascism as the modern form of capitalist rule is highly estimated, there would be little

---

[19] See above, p. 238. The ideological purpose of this general application of the term is the legitimation—against a background of alleged "objective Justice"—of ruthless defence of the interests of the new social order by states representing it, especially in the narrower case when they are clearly based upon a new machinery originating from the revolutionary class (see above, p. 239), and thus may be described as dictatorships in a more distinct sense. Even this would not imply such a state's necessarily violating its own legality. See my *Soviet Legal Theory*, pp. 34-5.

[20] Pp. 222-3.

chance of change in the basic contents of socio-economic systems in other than very obvious catastrophic forms,[21] and the functional derivation of the class-character of the State would have to be resorted to only in a moderate number of exceptional cases the possibility of which few Marxists would deny. On the other side, from the purely economic point of view it is hardly possible to define socialism otherwise than as nationalised economics conducted on a planned basis, especially if the Marxist distinction between socialism and the higher stage of communism, to which the application of egalitarian standards is referred, is clearly kept in mind and one is realistic about the possibilities of realising present sectional demands of the working-classes after the establishment of socialism. If every state establishing and protecting such a structure is described as socialist—or, if a class-terminology is preferred, as defending the interest of the working-class in the achievement of socialism—there seems to be no more sense in the introduction of the political characteristic of working-class rule into the definition of socialism than, say, in Mr. Attlee's postulate that a regime deserving to be called socialist should safeguard all those civic freedoms current in present-day Britain.[22] A variety of socialist regimes of non-working class origin is conceivable. One has been described in Kautsky's[23] post-1919 statement, typical of reformist concepts (independent of local constitutional differences[24]) that between the period of bourgeois and that of working-class rule in a democracy lay an inter-

---

[21] Even a very large part played in those catastrophes by military conquest and establishment of regimes based upon a considerable part of the existing State machinery and introducing a moderate amount of new elements (because no internal upheaval had brought such elements forward) would not prevent Marxists from explaining the change in terms of class : without the assumption that political (class-) fronts in every country cut across the international divisions the triumph of either party in armed international conflict to an extent sufficient to alter the trends in international society would be unexplainable.

[22] Speech of May 5, 1946.

[23] *Die proletarische Revolution und ihre Programm* (2nd ed., 1922). The statement was made in explicit opposition to that of Marx (*Critique of the Gotha Programme*, p. 28) that to the period of revolutionary transformation of the capitalist into communist society corresponds a political transition period in which the state can be nothing but *the revolutionary dictatorship of the proletariat.*

[24] Under the British suffrage a "majority-government" of the Labour party, supported by no safe majority in the electorate and depending upon any shift in the lower-middle-class vote which might be easily provoked by bourgeois or traditional resistance, could play no part distinct from that of a coalition-government as envisaged by Kautsky for countries with proportional representation and political camps fairly stabilised by the basing of all important political parties upon individual membership and sectional mass organisation.

12

mediate period of coalition government supposed to carry through transitory measures. Such an attitude should be clearly distinguished from mere gradualism which may pre-suppose working-class activities as its main foundation. Another would be the wholesale nationalisation of the economy by a fascist system or some other realisation of Burnham's concept of the " managerial revolution," divorced as it is from the class-struggle of the working-classes. Lastly, there is the theoretical possibility that the *bourgeoisie*—in some country, where its domestic rule was very stable and could withstand the impact of an international evolution which would have rendered preservation of capitalism in an isolated country hopeless—may vote itself out of existence because this was the safest way to preserve a privileged position for its members at least during the next stages of social development, and as many as possible of the traditional legal, moral and cultural standards.

This final possibility can hardly be excluded if socialism is regarded as an internationally valid prospect for economic development and if one is realistic about the likelihood of revolutionary mass-movements ,in all the capitalist countries. Its realisation in particular cases would not affect the historical estimate of our period any more than local experiences of a similar character do as regards the assessment of the socio-political character of the U.S.S.R., or even the existence of the Meji-regime, adapted in a similar way to modern needs. Real issues are joined as regards the two first-mentioned varieties of socialist transformation without the working-classes playing a leading part ; for their realisation could conceivably reduce the alternative Marxist pattern to the importance of a local variety of the general transformation (though the importance of its impact for the realisation of the other varieties could hardly be denied). I do not think that historical alternatives can be excluded by any theoretical generalisation. A relevant criticism of the possibilities of transition to socialism by coalition government—open or veiled—has to be based upon the latter's ability or otherwise to proceed along the road of nationalisation to what Lenin has called the " commanding heights," that is, those mainsprings of economic power the character of which is bound to determine the general connection in which the lesser elements of the economic system work, and to pursue a foreign policy compatible with such domestic progress. Relevant criticism of the managerial utopia has to be based upon the continuing control of monopolist economics by the financial oligarchy and the implications of such control for the characteristics of any system, whatever its formal organisation, which is not prepared to remove it.   And to look for theoretical short-cuts to a concrete analysis in such issues contradicts the scientific claims of Marxism.

CHAPTER XII

THE SOCIALIST CONQUEST OF POWER

(a) THE CONCEPT OF REVOLUTION

Because of Marx's work, the term " revolution " for us is full of problems. But when he started his work, " revolution " was an established technique of carrying through even minor tranfers of political power, such as the shift from the remains of the pre-revolutionary nobility to the leaders of the financial oligarchy in July, 1830, or from the latter to the industrial entrepreneurs in February, 1848, in France, the country at the time accepted as leading in political progress ; and there could be no reasonable doubt that a liberal transformation of Germany presupposed a revolution in an even more serious sense. The impact of English domestic politics—as distinct from economics—upon early Marxism was small ; but even if it had been larger, in the days of Chartism it would not have contradicted the assumption from which all continental progressives started. Marx and Engels did find themselves confronted with the task of explaining not what was the true meaning of revolution, or why it was necessary (these were commonplaces, at least in the surroundings in which they moved), but what was bound to happen during the next revolution, the approach of which was obvious to anyone approaching German realities without the wishful thinking typical of the established authorities.

Nor was theoretical genius needed in order to demonstrate the part played by the working-class in the preceding bourgeois revolutions in terms of their immediate purposes and outcome. It had been noticed by serious pre-Marxist students.[1] Marx himself[2] claimed no merit other than that of having stated, in opposition to these historians, that the ultimate tendencies of the

---

[1] See above, p. 41.   [2] ibid.

working-class struggle lead beyond the framework of bourgeois society. With the statement of this tendency he took the proletarian character of the " revolutions of the 19th century,"[3] as opposed to the " bourgeois " revolutions of the 18th, to be proved. As his concept of the need for a completely new State machinery developed only later, in connection with the struggle of the Paris Communards directed against the extremely centralised State machinery of the Bonapartist dictatorship,[4] a large amount of generally accepted revolutionary teaching could be taken for granted. Marx's early conceptions of the alternative government formed during the revolutionary period in order to conquer in the decisive crisis the power of the established one[5], and of the need of the revolutionary party to choose the right moment for decisive action[6], are easily acceptable to minds familiar with Lenin, as long as we are prepared to overlook the fact that in *The Class-Struggles in France*, which was nearly contemporary with the just mentioned statements, the traditional attitude of the revolutionaries who deemed that conquest of the Paris Hotel de Ville and establishment of a new revolutionary government would grant them control of the State machinery, was accepted without criticism.[7] If we take the utterances of Marx and Engels simply at their face-value, conceding to the defenders of the established order that the issue that really matters is that of violent revolution (which was no problem at all for the founders of Marxism) we get the strange impression that the latters' minds moved from revolutionary optimism to a belief in the slow working of economic mechanisms, and then suddenly reverted to revolutionary Utopianism caused by the fact that the Paris Commune happened a few years after the publication of vol. I of *Capital* and that criticism of the Lassalleans happened to dominate Marx's attitude to the conditions in which German Social Democracy was re-united. By doing some violence to biographical facts one can suppose that the recurrence of revolutionary utopianism subsequently faded away into a more optimistic attitude to the possibilities of gradualist

[3] See above, p. 227, note 24.

[4] Comp. *The Eighteenth Brumaire*, ed. cit., p. 131, and Preface to the German ed. of 1872 of the *Communist Manifesto*.

[5] Address of the Central Council of the League of Communists, March, 1850.

[6] Germany, Revolution and Counter-revolution, Chapter XVII, discussed by Lenin, *Sel. Works*, vol. VI, p. 218.

[7] This attitude has been directly reflected in Engels' articles in the *Neue Rheinische Zeitung*.

transition.[8]   Such an interpretation of the development of the founders of Marxism actually dominates a large part of the existing literature on the subject.[9]

But quite apart from their lack of foundations in historical evidence there is a *non sequitur* in such interpretations, the question how the working-class should acquire efficient military control of the State being different from what transformations of the State should be needed in order to make it an efficient element of working-class power.   Conquest of political power by armed insurrection may imply the need largely to change the structure of the State machinery still resisting the new rulers ; but this need not necessarily be realised.   A conception of revolution as replacement of one State machinery by an alternative one, originating from the Labour movement, may suggest the likelihood of violence—though conceivably on the defensive[10]—having to be applied by the Labour movement ; but this does not necessarily exclude an identification of the new organs of power with the sectional organs of the Labour movement which have developed comparatively peacefully within the womb of existing society.   The possibility that the T.U.C. might eventually form the new State machinery in Britain was seriously discussed in the Comintern.[11]   Any serious analysis of the problem of transformation of the State as we see it with the accomplished Marxist theory before us, must be a continuation of its systematic explanation.

[8] Nearly all the sharp statements made against Lassalleanism find their counterparts in criticism of the behaviour of German Social Democracy under the Anti-Socialist Law ; and the essentials of the 1871 attitude have been restated by Engels in his Preface to the re-edition of the *Civil War in France*, in the same year, 1891, when, in criticising the Erfurt Programme of German Social Democracy, his utterances on the importance of the democratic republic, since frequently quoted by Social Democrats, were made, and when (see below, p. 312) pending international issues were interpreted in a way that actually was bound to give grist to the mills of later Social Democrat supporters of imperialist wars.   Engels' Preface of 1895, to *The Class-Struggles in France* was falsified, for allegedly tactical reasons of preserving legality, but against the sharp protests of the dying Engels, by the leaders of German Social Democracy, and misused, in the altered form (see note 14 below) as " Engels' political testament."   Kautsky, in his *Way to Power* (2nd ed., p. 51) was the first to draw attention to that misuse ; but the exact content of the alterations was not disclosed before 1918.   For text and alterations see Marx-Engels, *Sel. Works*, vol. II.

[9] Characteristic is Masaryk's Marx-critique, section 142 (p. 522 in the German ed. of 1899), where Masaryk strangely enough uses volume III of *Capital*.   The following paragraph (143) is dominated by the falsification mentioned in the last note which Masaryk, of course, had to accept at its face-value.

[10] See below, pp. 261 and 324.

[11] True, Zinoviev, who spoke of it, in his capacity as President of the Comintern was later criticised for it, but it can hardly be asserted that that criticism in any way contributed to his fall.   Besides, Lenin's own attitude to the issue is up to our days, to say the least of it, regarded as indeterminate (see above, p. 242).

Revolution, in the sense of qualitative changes in social structure, is the very subject of Marxist sociology.[12] In the Marxist, as distinct from the anarchist scheme, such change presupposes change in the social function of the State ; and because class is the basic agent in Marxist sociology, revolution cannot be conceived except as the result of mass-movements conditioned by the class-structure of society.[13] Of these three characteristics the first, qualitative change in social structure, is open to rather varied interpretation : it is difficult to make a case in principle against anyone asserting that capitalism with recognised Trade Unions, a certain amount of " municipal socialism " (in the field of public utilities, etc.) and a recognised share of Labour in government, is something different in quality from that capitalism as described in Engels' *Conditions of the Working-class in England*. As we have seen in the last Chapter, the class-character of a State can be derived either from its economic functions, or from its origin in a revolutionary mass-movement. Thus the discussion of the meaning of revolution centres round the characteristics of the revolutionary mass-movements ; the element of State power enters that characteristic by defining those mass-movements that can be described as truly revolutionary.

Three basic attitudes are conceivable in this regard, and found ample representation within the modern Labour movement.

(1) The sectional mass-movement, as developed in the framework of capitalist society, may be described as in itself involving a qualitative change in the character of capitalism, and thereby also of the State the political representation of which is likely to be affected by the growth of sectional mass-organisation to an influential and recognised factor, so that merely political democracy is transformed into " economic democracy." This concept involves the rejection of sudden changes, " leaps " in the social structure[12] ; and its foremost representative, Bernstein, was honest enough to describe it, within a Labour movement dominated by the Marxist ideology, as Revisionism.

[12] See above, pp. 5, 8 and 18
[13] The possibility of "revolutions from above," does not fundamentally affect that characteristic ; those of them which are taken seriously in Marxist sociology appear as implications of an abortive mass-movement from below (see above, pp. 6-7). Naturally, the one instance of a "revolution from above" carried through by a revolutionary socialist state (the collectivisation of Soviet agriculture) is described in Soviet State ideology (*History of the C.P. of the U.S.S.R.*, pp. 304-5) as realising the demands, and carried through with the support, of a mass-movement from below.

(2) The sectional mass-movement, and its organisations, may be conceived as carrying through, at a certain stage of their growth, a change in government, which is regarded as the essential condition of transition to socialism, without this change being conceived as a replacement of the whole existing state-machinery by new organs originated from the revolutionary upheaval. The failure of attempts to repress working-class organisation may result in the decomposition of the repressive machinery.[14] But it is only since 1918 that the need for a specific fighting organisation, of a purely defensive character and subordinate to the struggle of sectional organisations operating within the existing framework, has been recognised amongst the defenders of this concept.[15] The purely sectional character of the attitude discussed is revealed by the fact that the conquest of power is said to be conditioned on the expected proletarisation, in the most literal sense of the word, of the existing lower-middle-classes, and by a criticism of Bolshevist practice on the ground that its framework lacked " proletarian purity " as well as because it deviated from accepted standards of sectional working-class organisation, such as traditional concepts of the tasks of Trade Unions. For historical reasons this trend, which, indeed, would be difficult to define except in opposition to the preceding and following ones, has been described as Centrism.[16]

(3) The change in the political regime conditioning the socio-economic transformation may be conceived as replacement of the

[14] This was implied in the original text of Engels' Preface to *The Class-Struggles in France* (8). The " corrections " made by the party-leaders resulted in elimination of the passages emphasizing the need for, and chances of, even armed resistance.

[15] The Linz programme of Austrian Social Democracy, of 1926, explicitly stated the inevitability of bourgeois attempts to prevent by force the peaceful conquest of socialism by democratic means. Such attempts might force upon the working-class armed resistance and the establishment of its dictatorship (at least as a transitory means of restoring and safeguarding democracy). The fighting organisation established by German Social Democracy, not on its own behalf but in the name of all the coalition parties (the others made hardly any contribution) never came into action, which is hardly surprising with such a political basis.

[16] The term has become current by the differentiation of the leading group within German Social Democracy (which itself shaped the term) since the Mannheim Congress of 1906, against the left-wing even more than against the (Revisionist) right-wing of the party, and by Lenin's writings during World War I, where it denoted those trends that without openly supporting their imperialist co-nationals rejected the Leninist policy of using the war-situation as an opportunity for revolutionary action. The progress made in the elaboration of the revolutionary theory from Marx to Lenin implies some ambiguity in the concept of " centrism ": Rosa Luxemburg's group was revolutionary in that it opposed the centrist concept that sectional mass-organisation as developed within the capitalist framework would be the successor to the former bourgeois regime, but itself would be regarded by Leninists as centrist

existing State machinery by a new one originating from the revolutionary mass-movement. This concept, which has been upheld in classic Marxist literature since the Paris Commune of 1871 and the Preface to the edition of the *Communist Manifesto* of 1872, implies a conception of the revolutionary mass-movement as different from the organised sectional movements normally working within the capitalist framework ; but this consequence, though not alien to the minds of the founders,[17] was not clearly drawn before the Russian revolution of 1905 when the specific character of the revolutionary mass-movements was emphasized by Lenin as well as by Rosa Luxemburg.[18]

A fourth conceivable point of view is represented by Blanquism which lies outside the Marxist framework even more obviously than does Revisionism : the revolutionary change, though possibly involving the whole political machine, is conceived as the outcome not of a mass-movement but of a well-organised conspiracy, mastering the technique of insurrection and appealing to no more than the sympathies of the masses on behalf of which it acts. This concept should be clearly distinguished from mere emphasis on armed insurrection as that stage of the revolutionary movement in which, and by which, the actual transfer of political power is carried out (which is the normal case for Marxism in general), or as a necessary step in the transformation of the exploited class of capitalist society into its potential heir.[19] Even for those defenders of the Marxist concept who, in the presence of a revolutionary situation, may regard even a defeated attempt at insurrection as a necessary and valuable lesson leading to later successes, insurrection would be senseless in the absence of a revolutionary situation. But in the Blanquist concept, the only objective condition regarded as necessary is a general state of society so desperate that a sufficiently strong elite finds it worth while to wager everything for the sake of its overthrow, and may expect mass-sympathies for its attempts at social reconstruction. As opposed to this point of view, Marxists

in as far as it opposed the concept of breaking up existing state-machinery by organised action and a centralist structure of the revolutionary party as necessary for such action (see below, pp. 257 and 263). As a source for this attitude, see for example, Stalin's letter to the Editor of *Proletarskaya Revoluciya*, of 1931 (in *Leninism*, ed. 1940, pp. 388).

[17] Otherwise it would be difficult to understand their repeated explanations of the declarations made by them on behalf of the International as necessary compromises with the sectional, especially Trade Unionist, point of view.

[18] See below, pp. 258-9   [19] See above, p. 48.

would emphasize the need for a truly revolutionary regime to operate upon the creative initiative of the masses, even if planned action of a minority played a decisive part in the conquest of power.

(b) THE REVOLUTIONARY SITUATION

In the Revisionist as well as in the Blanquist concept, though for different reasons, the conditions of the social transformation are identical with the existence and shortcomings of capitalist society. In the Marxist they are not. The concept of specific conditions confronting the working-class party with the task of assuming power is not absent from the more left-wing expressions of the Centrist attitude[20]; indeed, it can hardly be dispensed with unless the abstract concept of " proletarisation " characteristic for centrism is combined with complete neglect of the manifold agencies by which, in normal times, the bourgeoisie controls the minds even of rather destitute strata of the lower-middle-classes, so that the eventual achievement of a socialist majority in parliament as well as the ability of the workers efficiently to defend the constitutional rights of that majority may be taken for granted. However, in the Centrist outlook the concept of the revolutionary crisis is reduced either to forecasts about eventual economic depressions of overwhelming strength or to truisms such as that absolute Socialist majorities are unlikely to occur except in the aftermath of a great upheaval, such as a war. In the Leninist concept a much more concrete definition of the " revolutionary crisis " is called for ; the crisis would not fulfil its functions within that concept unless it implied a situation where not only the misery and the hopelessness of the prospects open to them within the existing society rouses the activity of the masses and their preparedness to make serious sacrifices for the cause of their emancipation, but also where prospects of success were opened by the evident inability of the present rulers to handle the situation, due to cleavages within their own ranks and between them and their former supporters. Without these changes in the objective situation, the entity of which is described as the

[20] Kautsky, *The Way to Power*, passim, espec. p. 105.

THE SOCIALIST CONQUEST OF POWER

" revolutionary situation," there can be, as a rule, no revolution ; but in order that an actual revolution should result from the revolutionary situation, to the objective changes implied in it a " subjective " change has to be added : the revolutionary class should be capable of revolutionary actions sufficient to overthrow the existing regime which, even in a period of crisis, would not automatically collapse. In this connection, [21] Lenin mentions examples of abortive revolutionary situations, in which revolution failed to take place because of the absence of the " subjective factor " : the Prussian constitutional conflict in the early 'sixties and the Russian political crises before the emancipation of the serfs and at the culmination of the terrorist activities of the Narodniks. All these situations have left distinct impressions upon the traditions of the respective Labour movement, and, perhaps, would hardly be commemorated unless those traditions involved recognition of their importance as well as criticism of their short-comings. But the correctness or otherwise of Lenin's illustrations hardly affects the validity of his general statement, which can hardly be questioned unless Marxism is misinterpreted in a mechanical way as denying the importance of ideologies and human efforts as the direct agencies of social transformation. The need to inculcate the working-class with the understanding of the conditions that both demand and enable revolutionary action, and the conviction that certain tactics, derivable from application of general Marxist principles to the concrete situation, fit the needs of such a situation, is the first and basic Leninist argument in favour of a revolutionary party representing the highest stage of class-consciousness which can be reached in these conditions. The first need, which implies leadership of a party in a mere propagandist sense, but not the second from which the need " to organise the Revolution " may be concluded, was recognised by non-Leninist left-wingers such as Rosa Luxemburg. [22]

In the Leninist concept, the decisive conquest is not regarded as a mere consequence of the workers' party's growth. Therefore, conquest by the revolutionary party of the predominant influence upon what has been called in the terminology of the

[21] The Collapse of the Second International, *Sel. Works*, vol. V. p.174.
[22] See above, pp. 230-1.

Comintern "the decisive majority of the working-class,"[23] a condition fulfilled at present in most of the Continental European and Asiatic countries, is in itself not regarded as a sufficient basis for the conquest of power, the more so as Leninism takes a more realistic attitude than centrism towards the chances of the lower-middle-classes becoming proletarianised, in the most verbal sense of the word, before the decisive revolutionary crisis.[23a] Extreme resistance of the bourgeoisie to the assumption of power by a socialist majority is taken for granted; and the mass-initiative of the working-class needed in order to solve the crisis in a positive way through the intermediate stage of "Dual Power" cannot be expected to arise except in a revolutionary crisis. Co-ordination of non-working-class with the typical sectional movements and offensive action directed at the destruction of existing State machinery need a well-organised revolutionary party spreading amongst the working-class a higher degree of class-consciousness than the merely sectional movement does, and co-ordinating its actions; and this connection between the function of Party and the concept of the revolutionary crisis is the place where the ways of Leninism and even left-wing social democracy parted.

A predominant symptom of revolutionary crisis is mass-activity exceeding the ordinary framework of sectional conflicts,[24] not only in its extent (which may be a mere function of the industrial cycle) but also in that it does not originate from the routine-activities of sectional organisation[24] and involves even the most backward strata of the working-class which in ordinary times are inaccessible to such organisation.[25] The element of spontaneity involved in such conditions has been elevated by

[23] The concept was first developed in Lenin's 'Left-wing' Communism, an infantile disorder (Sel. Works, vol X, pp. 127 and 136-7) in opposition to what were actually Blanquist (see above, p. 255) shortcuts to the task of basing Communism on broad mass-support. In later factional disputes within the Comintern it was applied in a double meaning; it might be directed against wishful thinking as to the chances of a Communist party overtaking Social Democracy but yet failing to command the support of a clear majority of the workers in the decisive industries to start a revolution, or else against too extensive an interpretation of the term "working-class" in that the workers of the large-scale industries were regarded as incapable of starting a revolution even if there was sound reason to expect broader support to come forward once working-class action was in successful progress.

[23a] See below pp. 332 and 341.

[24] To use a less careful terminology would beg the question discussed below in the text, whether mass-activity excited by an extraordinary situation is bound to by-pass the normal organisational channels.

[25] Which does not exclude their becoming organisable, also for normal trade-unionist purposes, in consequence of those spontaneous movements.

Rosa Luxemburg[26] to the true characteristic of the revolutionary situation ; but her attacks on the reformist bureaucracy dominating the German Labour movement as well as on the Bolshevist concept of Party tend to bias her argument on this point. Obviously, the ideal type of organisation reacting properly to all tensions arising amongst its members is a Utopia. Therefore, the rise of a revolutionary situation is bound to be signalised by a rise in the number of strikes and other spontaneous movements, that is, movements under *ad hoc* leadership. Quite apart from this, even in conditions more democratic than those of Tsarist Russia or Imperial Germany, numerous sections of the working-class are prevented by their economic backwardness and/or their ideology from entering trade unions in normal times even supposing that trade union leaders were more eager to organise them than were the German bureaucrats against whom Rosa Luxemburg's criticism was directed. But it is obvious nonsense to regard a revolutionary situation as characterized by the failure of existing organisations of Labour to organize those movements which the masses demand, whatever allowance may be made for the needs for a left-wing opposition establishing, in the face of the bureaucracy, the characteristics of such a situation. Even if the rise of mass-activity characteristic of a revolutionary situation comes as a surprise to the reformist leaders with an outlook dominated by everyday sectional contest, there is no sense in having a special Communist party unless it succeeds in leading at least the bulk of that activity and diverting it into the desired channels.

In the economic field, any group of workers awakening to new consciousness may start a strike, thus by-passing existing organisations. But in the field of political mass-strikes such spontaneity should be regarded as a sign of the short-comings of those organisations. True, in countries such as Tsarist Russia permanent leadership by the revolutionary organisations was technically impossible and their propaganda could not go beyond preparing the ideological groundwork for predictable situations in which it would have to be applied on the initiative of the workers themselves. " Spontaneous " mass-activity is also normal in situations of a clearly defensive character, such as the Kornilov-coup in Russia, 1917, or the Kapp-coup in Germany, 1920,

---

[26] In *Massenstreik, Partei und Gewerkshaften,* published 1906, as an attempt to explain the experiences of the Russian revolution to the German Labour movement.

when a certain reaction to a particular piece of political news can be anticipated in the general ideological preparation of the Labour movement. Instances when such reactions have to be specially ordered by the competent organs of the Labour movement even in very obvious cases such as the—very incomplete—general strike in Vienna, February 12, 1934, when it was already generally known that in Linz the guns were in action on both sides, are generally symptomatic of the absence of a revolutionary situation (not in the sense of general social tension—without which there would have been no shooting—but of serious chances for the working-classes to conquer power).

The typical case of a " spontaneous " political mass-strike is the full awakening of a labour movement hitherto suppressed as in Russia of 1905. Certainly it is characteristic of a revolutionary situation, but of the opportunity for a bourgeois-democratic revolution rather than for a socialist one which presupposes some preceding organisation of labour. Political mass-strikes— " spontaneous " or organised—originating as a reaction to bourgeois attempts at repressing an existing and organised Labour movement may help on the abandonment of such attempts if there is any fissure in the camp of the ruling class (or between it and its lower-middle-class support) which may be widened by evidence that the proposed policy is risky. Such failure, and the resultant rise in the prestige of the working-class party, may cause a general shift in political prestige and increase the hope of a peaceful transition, unless foreign support for the reactionaries is available.

The difference between those who envisage such a transition by spontaneous political mass-strikes, and those who base their expectations upon the current activities of sectional mass-organisation and its organised self-defence may seem important in practical politics. But unless the defendants of the former attitude accept an anarchist conception of the transitory period, they could hardly look lower for anything more than a ceding of power by the *bourgeoisie* to the sectional organisations of Labour, whether of long standing or established during the process of political mass-strikes. In so far, their concept approaches the centrist scheme of transition.[27] The Leninist concept of replacement of existing State machinery presupposes not only that the new machinery will rise from mass-activity

[27] See above, p. 254.

during the revolutionary upheaval, which would well fit into Rosa Luxemburg's scheme, but also at least the threat of organised military action to break up existing State machinery, which would exceed Rosa Luxemburg's conception of barricade-struggles as transitional steps in the process of the mass-strike,[26] presumably efficient because they would break up the internal coherence of the bourgeoisie's armed forces and its will to resistance.

There is common ground between Leninism and more moderate trends in recognising the moral importance of the workers feeling themselves on the defensive and being regarded as such by all the wavering strata of society, thus leaving to their opponents the responsibility for the outbreak of civil strife. " In order to obtain the power of State the class-conscious workers must win the majority to their side. As long as no violence is used against the masses, there is no other way to power. We are not Blanquists, we are not in favour of seizure by a minority."[28] There is no difference between this statement and that made by Engels[29] in 1892 and accepted by the Centrist leadership of German Social Democracy : " In this moment it is not we who are going bankrupt by the way of legality . . . please, shoot first, gentlemen bourgeois." Lenin would certainly have sub-scribed to Engels' further statement : " No doubt, they *will* shoot. One nice morning the German bourgeoisie and their government will get tired of looking, arms crossed, at the all-flooding tide of Socialism ; they will look for a refuge in illegality, violence. What will it help ? . . . The instantly overwhelming power of counter-revolution may delay the triumph of Socialism for a few years but only by rendering it, afterwards, the more complete and definite." As late as 1926 a similar attitude was accepted by so distinctly Centrist a party as Austrian Social Democracy,[15] and the Linz programme of Austrian Social Democracy served as the pattern for the treatment of the issue in the programme of the Communist-dominated Socialist Unity Party of Germany.

The Marxist-Leninist concept differs from the Centrist not by its expectation that civil war will become inevitable in con-sequence of the bourgeoisie's inability to accept peaceful transi-tion to socialism as long as there are chances of successful resist-

[28] A Dual Power, *Sel. Works*, vol. VI, p. 29.
[29] Sozialismus in Deutschland, in *Die Neue Zeit*, vol. IX/1, p. 583.

ance, but by its conclusion that the inevitable conflict should be
solved by offensive, or rather counter-offensive, working-class
action creating a new State-machinery and replacing by it the
former one. From this follows not only a different concept
of the forms of working-class organisation needed in order to
defeat the counter-revolutionary attacks, but also a very concrete
concept of the "acute revolutionary situation" as that moment
within the revolutionary crisis where offensive action is needed.
Engels, quoted by Lenin on the eve of the 1917 revolution,[6] had
described the needs of such a situation under the characteristic
heading that insurrection should be regarded as an art, subject
to specific rules related to, but distinct from, those governing
the art of war in general. In the enumeration of these laws the
characteristics of a revolutionary situation, and of the subjective
factor needed in order that it may result in an actual revolution,
reappear in a formulation modified by the different context : a
social phenomenon is no longer analysed as an objectively given
fact, but the rules governing the behaviour of those who intend to
bring that phenomenon to the culmination point are being
established as laws neglect of which is bound to result in defeat.
The disorganisation within the camp of the ruling class, and the
cleavages arising between it and its earlier supporters, which are
characteristic of a revolutionary situation, culminate at the
correct moment for the decisive blow. The rising mass-activity
appears as the element of moral superiority which should be
promoted by tactics aiming at continuously scoring successes,
however local and partial, and the "subjective element"
needed in order to produce actual revolution from the revolutionary situation culminates in the demand for continuous
offensive during the insurrection and for concentration of an
overwhelming superiority of forces at the decisive point. Thus
the general rules of warfare are applied to conditions where the
moral factor is of overwhelming importance and where the
opponent should be credited with a distinct technical and
organisational superiority. Insurrection is regarded as a form
of action with which one should never play, but which, once
started, has to be pursued without hesitation to the end. Such
an approach puts it into a category quite distinct from the other
possible forms of class-struggle which, whatever the immediate
outcome, are valuable just because they help the oppressed class
to acquire the consciousness and the organisational strength

necessary as a preliminary condition for the decisive struggle for political power. This distinctive function ascribed to armed insurrection contrasts sharply with Rosa Luxemburg's description of the political mass-strike as " the form of movement of the proletarian masses during the revolution," armed conflicts forming mere individual moments in the process,[26] and its description as an art subject to certain rules (and, of course, to be applied by an organisation knowing them) is in sharp contrast to Rosa Luxemburg's denial of the existence of tactical rules of general validity.

The differentiations within the orthodox Marxist (as distinct from the Revisionist, Centrist, and Blanquist) conception of revolution hitherto discussed may be regarded as mere differences in emphasis on various aspects of an identical process. Although the assumption of power by the new State machinery in a large country may be a matter of weeks, if not of months, and may be followed by further months of civil war and perhaps years of defence against foreign intervention, the political revolution is a well-defined event easily distinguishable from the changes in mass-activity which preceded, and the economic changes which follow it. The political revolution, though making the greatest demands upon mass-initiative, makes great demands, too, on organised staff-work, whilst during the preceding upheaval the " staff-work " of the normal sectional organisations works rather as a brake. From the revolutionary point of view, the function of some event—say, a large-scale strike, " spontaneous " and " unofficial "—may be very different in the first stages of the revolutionary upheaval, when it may mark the transition of leadership within the labour movement from coalition-partners of the bourgeoisie to consistent, even if badly organised, revolutionaries, and on the eve of the revolutionary crisis when it may be faced with a premature trial of strength. After the establishment of the new regime such a strike will be regarded by those interested in its stabilisation as a counter-revolutionary act, though some of the revolutionaries may still regard it as a somewhat violent form of working-class criticism of the elements of bureaucracy that have survived from the *ancien regime*. In the course of the life-and-death struggle of the new state misunderstandings on this point are bound to be settled, so that a clear division emerges between its supporters and its opponents (the latter including bureaucrats who compromise the new regime by treating the workers in a provocative way, and also demagogues who play on all existing grievances, legitimate or otherwise) ; but in the pre-revolutionary stage there is ample scope for argument even amongst sincere supporters of the revolution who on the one hand emphasize the need for disciplined and planned action, and those on the other who want the maximum encouragement of " spontaneous " initiative.

Perhaps, in our days, the whole argument about " spontaneity " is losing importance. The realisation of the Leninist scheme in a fourth of the world has made clear that socialism is a practical proposition, so that the workers need no longer assure themselves, by waves of "spontaneous" actions, that they are capable of managing without capitalists ; whilst, on the other hand, its implications on the international stage have rendered working-class revolutions hopeless unless they are well-planned and co-ordinated with what international support is available. We have now crossed the crucial ridge of the revolutionary period in the narrower sense of the word. This happened after the French Revolution with bourgeois democracy at least in Western and Central Europe. But it did not deprive the supporters of the Reform Bill and of the revolutions of 1830 and 1848 of the delusion that they were laying the foundations of a new world whilst they were actually harvesting the fruits of a battle already decided. In the one as in the other case the most important economic developments may still lie before us ; but this would not exclude the actual conclusion of the period the needs of which the political theory of Marxism had to serve.

The above argument about the dynamics of a modern socialist revolution (which, besides, has been derived from an avowedly bourgeois-democratic revolution lead by working-class parties, like the Russian of 1905-6) is distinctly post-Marxist : the distinction between sectional and revolutionary class-struggle was first clearly made in Lenin's *What is to be Done*, and most of the above argument started with Rosa Luxemburg's criticism of Bolshevism. Marx and Engels' utterances about the art of insurrection, the basis of their reputation as supporters of the concept of revolutionary crisis, originated at a time when criticism of the traditional concept of revolutionary conquest of established State machinery was certainly not yet in their minds.[30] In spite of his occasionally using the term " proletarian revolutions " in the plural,[31] Marx never experienced an actual proletarian revolution—unless the term is applied in order merely to denote that stage in bourgeois-democratic revolutions when their most consistent representatives have to rely upon working-class support, perhaps even when there are no other representatives of consistent bourgeois democracy except parties recruited from the working-classes, as was the case with the Paris Commune.

(c) PERMANENT REVOLUTION

Thus we find Marx's immediate contribution to the problem of the stages of the revolutionary process (as distinct from its sectional antecedents[32]) restricted to a scheme which deals with changes in class-leadership rather than in forms of class-action. Not only in name[32a] does the concept of "permanent revolution" directly continue the traditions of the great French revolution. It was evolved in the Address of the Central Committee of the League of Communists, in March, 1850, in order to denote the necessity of driving forward the revolutionary process by means of experience in incomplete attempts at realisation and by the logic of a situation which allows for no consolidation of a half-way house after the inherent though uncertain equilibrium of capitalist society has been destroyed, unless the equilibrium of a new and definite social formation is found. It was directed at the Communists of Germany, a country which, in the *Communist Manifesto*, was supposed to be economically ripe for a socialist revolution though because of its political backwardness the revolutionary upheaval was bound to start in the bourgeois-democratic framework. There is hardly any evolution in the forms of action (mass-demonstrations and armed insurrections were the generally accepted forms even of rather moderate bourgeois-democratic movements), but there is progress in the political slogans and in the allies whose support the working-class should use : from the general bourgeois-democratic framework to lower-middle-class radical democracy and finally, after all the other revolutionary parties have been compromised, to the establishment of its own rule, supported by the agricultural labourers (no longer by the peasants), and with the programme of action as

[31] See above, note 24 on p. 227.
[32] See above, pp. 225 ff.
[32a] It appears first in *The Holy Family* (M.E.G.A. vol. I/3 p.297) with reference to Napoleon I who accomplished terrorism by replacing permanent revolution by permanent war.

suggested in the *Communist Manifesto*. Because Germany was
supposed to be economically ripe for a socialist revolution, there is
no hint at supposedly necessary changes in the international
framework, which have made the term popular in our days in its
Trotskyist application.[33] The concept of at least the Western
capitalist countries forming an economic unit and of the likelihood of revolutions spreading from one to another of them
as experienced in 1848 was evident for Marx as for his liberal
contemporaries and needed no special proof.

While the *Manifesto* shows that revolutionary thought had
progressed far beyond the concepts even of the most radical of
the French revolutionaries, the development of revolutionary
action envisaged in the *Address* is very similar to that of the
French revolution when, by the mere dynamics of struggle, power
passed successively from one faction to another, each more radical
than the last : the revolution is described as " permanent " in
opposition to the demands raised by the moderates in every
revolution that, having achieved its alleged liberal, or *bourgeois-*
democratic purpose, it should be brought to an end, and order
(still a capitalist order) be restored. The scheme thus answers
the elementary question what should be the aims of the workers
when they begin to move within a certain situation which is
complicated by the co-existence of class-tensions between
feudalism and bourgeoisie as well as between the bourgeoisie
and the workers ; but it does not answer the question of how their
movement should develop even in the most simple type of revolutions, which seems not to have been a problem to Marx because
the forms of revolutionary action were given. The documents
of the League of Communists were re-edited by Engels up to the
last years of his life, the only self-criticism being with reference to
the obvious over-estimation of the revolutionary potentialities
of the situation of 1848 ; and right up to the very last period of his
life Marx did not cease to be interested in " non-typical "
revolutions.[34] So we have no reason to assume that he and
Engels dropped the concept of Permanent Revolution at any time

[33] In his Preface, of 1922, to his work on the 1905 revolution, and in most of his
subsequent writings Trotsky used the old-Marxist (pre-imperialist) conception of the
"international" unit (see below, pp. 283-4.) as an argument against the Leninist policy
of manoeuvring in order to see the Russian revolution through a complicated international situation, with the implication that the Russian revolution should make its
fate dependent on its success in initiating corresponding movements in other parts
of that unit (see below, pp. 295-7).

[34] See above, pp. 206-7.

during their lives, provided the situation envisaged for 1848 in Germany should be realised somewhere ; but all the concrete analysis available from the period after the conclusion of *Capital* deals with " pure " (or, as in the case of the Paris Commune of 1871, supposedly pure) working-class movements. The absence of such movements, during Marx's and Engels' lifetime, on any other but sectional lines, explains those classical statements, expecially of the later Engels, which may be quoted in favour of the Centrist concept.

The situation erroneously assumed to exist in Germany of 1848 was actually realised in 1917 Russia ; but the orthodox Marxist habit, meanwhile acquired, of looking for " pure types " had the result that, today, the term " permanent revolution " is currently associated with the views of those who deny the existence of conditions for such a situation in Russia, unless accompanied by a Western European working-class revolution. [33] Actually, the Russian revolution passed through the stages envisaged in Marx's scheme, but most of them were passed after the establishment of revolutionary State power. Even in June, 1918, the rural Committees of the Poor would hardly have taken action against the kulak-dominated part of the peasantry without the initiative and support of the working-class controlled State ; and the decisive step of collectivisation, taken in 1928-30, was described in official State ideology as a revolution from above, supported from below. [13] Thus " permanent revolution," that is, change in the socio-economic content of a revolution during its course in a backward country with great inherent possibilities, found its realisation ; and it may find further realisations in some semi-colonial countries. Perhaps even in the one or the other of the Western capitalist countries a temporary fascist dictatorship may force a Labour movement underground, and the latter may have to make a new start with purely democratic slogans from which quick progress to a typical socialist revolution could be made. But even without outside interference an antifascist revolution in a highly industrialised country could hardly be described as " permanent revolution " proper, because even a movement starting with the restoration of elementary Trade Union rights, etc., would essentially be working-class.

Thus the concept of " permanent revolution " is unlikely, in future, to provide any more answers in the search for the developing stages in a revolutionary movement of a distinct socio-

economic character than it did in its first, most important
realisation. Those who yearn for the creative play of mass-
initiative continued in infinitum without being polluted by the
self-assertion of a new-born state will hardly be satisfied by
the mere realisation that, by the logic of the conformation
under which it has entered the historical stage, such a state is
confronted with new, and continuously developing, tasks, and is
bound to make new and varying demands on the patriotic efforts
of its citizens. However important they may be as " midwives of
new societies," revolutions are not the normal and regular state
of society. The most that can be said of the orthodox Marxist
pattern of revolution is that its realisation in some parts of the
world has made and is further making an irresistible impact
upon developments in all countries. The validity of this pattern
of revolution is not refuted if, under its impact, other schemes
of transformation should also find some partial realisation.

(d) The Marxist concept of Party

The League of Communists for which Marx and Engels wrote
the *Communist Manifesto* had more in common with the party
based upon the teachings of *What is to be Done* than the fact
that, fifteen years after the latter was written, the Bolsheviks,
having assumed political power, resumed the old name of
Communists.[35] Each worked in a country ruled by a still
semi-feudal regime a bourgeoisie-democratic revolution against
which was obviously likely, and in each instance the young
and small working-class could hardly expect to play in that
revolution a part larger than that of the initiator and catalyst.
However, the working-class of 1902 Russia, as distinct from
that of 1847 Germany, had entered the scene with a chain
of large-scale strikes. Each party was composed of intellectuals
as well as workers, though, in the latter case, the status of

[35] Lenin suggested dropping of the traditional description of the Party as Social
Democrat, partly because that description was not clear and had been criticised already
by Engels in 1877 (quoted by Lenin, *Sel. Works*, vol. VII, p. 74), but especially
because of the War record of nearly all the Western Social Democratic parties.
However, the traditions associated with that description were so strong that, in spite of
the acceptance of Lenin's theses by the Party Conference in April, 1917, no change
in the description of the Party was made before the conquest of power, that is to say
during the period when the Bolsheviks tried to rally with other Social Democrat
groups prepared to accept their platform (in which they succeeded only with the
Trotskyists, accepted on the VIIth Party Congress, in summer, 1917). Only after
the dissolution of the Constituent Assembly, when a principal attitude to the issue of
proletarian dictatorship dominated the situation, the change was carried out at the
VIIIth Party Congress.

professional revolutionaries originating from a non-working-class milieu had to be specially explained[36] since the background of the movement was based upon the working-classes' exclusive claim to lead in the emancipation of mankind. This would have been impossible had not the *Communist Manifesto*, and the *Address of the International*, of 1863, influenced the minds of workers in Russia as well as in all other countries. Both parties grounded upon a strict conception of discipline and—apart from the practical needs of an underground movement—in both cases this discipline was dictated by the need of a young movement to prevent its doctrine from being confused with alien thought.

Both parties, apart from giving their analyses of the situation and the general tasks to be accomplished by the impending revolution, propose certain measures, " transitory " in modern Communist terminology, or to speak in the terms of the *Communist Manifesto* " measures which appear economically insufficient and untenable but which, in the course of the movement, outstrip themselves, necessitate further inroads upon the old social order, and are unavoiable as a means of efficiently revolutionising the mode of production." Evidently they are supposed, in consequence of the resistance likely to be met,[37] to imply further measures conducive to the desired aim. Mainly because of the analogies of the pre-revolutionary situation, the list of such measures drafted in 1848 fitted Bolshevist

[36] *What is to be Done ?*, ed. cit., pp. 137 ff. The issue, on a more sentimental basis, was not absent in the internal life of the League of Communists, as illustrated by Marx's frequent deprecatory references to " Knoten," that is to say, workers who by the mere fact of being such claimed superiority over the intellectuals. Within the framework of an actually sectional movement rallied round the statement that " the emancipation of the working-classes can only be carried out by the workers themselves " contradictions between the ideology of the movement and its actual need for intellectuals supporting it were unavoidable, and would be nourished by the attitude likely to be taken in conflicts between reformists and radicals by the majority of people of lower-middle-class origin. The issue may be theoretically settled on the level of *What is to be Done*, by the recognition that the worker as well as the intellectual, in order to become a revolutionary has to overcome the narrowness of his original outlook (Ibid, pp. 145-7) ; but even theoretical acceptance of the Bolshevist theory does not necessarily involve practical preparedness of all the persons concerned to avoid the use of un-Bolshevist argument say in factional disputes.

[37] Characteristic is the demand for Workers' Control, arising in every modern revolution out of the workers' opposition against their employers' belief that they are "masters in their own house," and applied in the Russian revolution as a device of either subjecting private entrepreneurs to a highly efficient supervision from below, supplementing that from above by the public planning organs, or (as actually happened) to produce a situation where their expropriation appeared as necessary self-defence of the State against law-breakers. On the experiences made with " transitory measures " during the Russian revolution see my *Soviet Legal Theory*, Chapter III, sections (a) and (b).

propaganda for the achievements of the 1917 revolution.[38] The authors of the Address of the Central Council of the League of Communists were conscious of the phenomenon of "Dual Power," familiar since the great French revolution, namely, the temporary co-existence of established State machinery and new organs created by mass-initiative ; but as to the tactics by which the transition of full power to the new revolutionary institutions should be achieved, we find in the *Address* no statement comparable with the later Communist demand that the Party should "organise the revolution." The address was confidential, and there would have been no reason to propose subordination of the envisaged Workers' Guards to the local organs of the Dual Power if the authors had envisaged them as acting under a central staff dominated by the Party's influence. However, direct initiative of the Communists in the organisation of certain forms of mass-activity was envisaged, though these passages may have been influenced by the authors' criticism of reformist opposition to "excesses" committed by the masses.

Even more impressive—because it was conditioned by more fundamental and less fortuitous attitudes—appear the analogies in the field with which we are immediately concerned in this section. The *Address* opens with a criticism of members who believed that, with the emergence of the revolutionary movement from the underground, the time for secret societies had gone and public activities were sufficient. In consequence, individual circles and local sections allowed their contacts with the Central Council gradually to die away, the workers' party remained organised in separate localities for local purposes, and thereby came completely under the domination and leadership of the petty-bourgeois Democrats. While advocating informal and temporary collaboration with those Democrats as long as they were in opposition to the reactionary regime, the *Address* firmly opposes organisational fusion with them in terms that could be easily quoted—and have been quoted—in factional disputes about the issue of the "united front" amongst pre-Hitlerite Communists. The authors of the *Address* suggested making the local sections of the Communists' League the central point for members of (obviously non-partisan) workers' associations in which the attitudes and interests of the proletariat would

[38] Comp. Stalin's report on the XVth Party Conference of the C.P. of the U.S.S.R. (1926) with the statement that "nine-tenths of these proposals have already been realised in our revolutions."

be discussed independent of bourgeois influences. This fits well with Lenin's statement "that (1) no movement can be durable without a stable organisation of leaders who maintain continuity, and (2) that the more widely the masses are spontaneously drawn into the struggle . . . the more necessary is it to have such an organisation and the more stable it must be (for it is much easier for demagogues to side-track the more backward sections of the masses)."[39]

If quotations are regarded as a sufficient proof, there is no sense in further questioning the point that the League of Communists, at least in the intentions of its leaders, was a Communist party in the modern sense of the word. The different attitudes which Marx and especially Engels[8] might have taken in later years would signify that a change had taken place either unconsciously (an unlikely assumption) or simply because they still regarded the pattern of their young days as fitting the needs of a revolutionary period, which unhappily did not exist, but would recur, so that it had to be shelved. In the 'eighties, Marx and Engels constantly expressed sympathy for the Russian *Narodniks* (whose attitudes were hardly palatable to anyone who regarded strict conformity with the level of mass-consciousness and mass-activity as a main Marxist virtue). In 1885, Engels re-edited the *Address* with a Preface in which he dissociates himself only from certain details such as the attitude to local self-government.

But we are less interested in the subjective feelings of the authors of the *Address* than in the implications of its formulations in the circumstances of its origin. However strong the criticism quoted above with which it opens, this criticism is uttered two years after the start of the 1848 revolution; and during the first of those two years the authors worked in Germany, editing a legal newspaper the influence of which on the general democratic movement was great, though it devoted only moderate attention to the specific interests of the Labour movement.[40] During that year there was some loose interconnection between the members of the League of Communists working in Germany,

[39] *Sel. Works*, vol. II, p. 138.

[40] At least this was Mehring's opinion. (See his Marx-biography, pp. 184-5.) The justification of such a criticism obviously depends on the assessment of the real strength of the German Labour movement in 1898. However, the authors of the *Communist Manifesto* had ascribed to it decisive importance in the events of a near future.

but no functioning national organisation. May not the cry for the latter—in circumstances when its establishment was incomparably more difficult than it would have been in 1848—find its simplest explanation in the facts described as its consequences, namely, in the members of the League coming under petty-bourgeois influences and appearing in public as mere representatives of that broad left-wing which had not made its peace with the powers that be as did the great bourgeoisie? The novelty would not have been the absence of a party organisation, but the resentment against it. The reasons for such resentment lay at hand : whilst in the ascending phase of the revolution even very radical propaganda could be carried through in a general " democratic " framework, in a period of reaction the fear of being isolated from those broader strata without whose support the members of the League would have ceased to be more than a few uninfluential individuals might result in those individuals ceasing to propagate Communism, as distinct from ordinary bourgeois democracy. The demand for the continuation of the propaganda society—which, with their own participation, had been allowed to recede into the background when conditions seemed to favour propaganda of Communist ideas even in a very loose framework—had to be explained by the authors of the *Address* in terms familiar to them and to the addressees in the immediate aftermath of a revolution the defeat of which was not yet realised, namely, in terms of actual revolutionary action that demanded organisation (especially in times when it was not produced by the mere play of mass-initiative).[41] It may be interesting to notice the analogies to, and differences from, what happened to Lenin's party during and after the revolution of 1905 : fusion with the Menshevik Social Democrats—in conditions where the latter formed the majority of the re-united party—was carried out in the ascending phase of the revolution, but the identity of Bolshevism as a distinct trend within that party was never allowed to drop, and the reorganisation of Bolshevism in an independent party was not carried out before 1912, when a new revolutionary wave was evidently rising. The reason for this different behaviour is quite simple : within a united Social Democratic party, even if dominated by the Mensheviks, Marxism in its specific Bolshevist form could be easily propagated, and the need for a specific Bolshevist party arose only when its own attitude

[41] See above, p. 260.

to tactical problems was likely to be tested in action ; but then it arose with all the seriousness demanded by Lenin's concept of Party as the organising centre of revolution, which had been absent with Marx. Within the framework of a broad Democratic party in post-1848 Germany Marxism could not be propagated in any form at all, for the simple reason that that party was a lower-middle-class party in obvious reality, not merely in descriptions by its opponents, as applied by modern Communists in order to denote the fact that Social Democrat parties represent the " lower " sectional stage in the development of working-class consciousness. When writing the *Address*, Marx actually defended the most general concept of a workers' party,[42] in the sense proclaimed later by the first International, and not, as did Lenin, a higher, revolutionary concept of class-struggle and Party against a lower, sectional one that had become a familiar phenomenon in social life.

If the German revolution of 1848 had lead to events comparable with the contemporary June insurrection in Paris, or at least with the part played by the Paris Commune in the crisis of 1793, the League of Communists might have entered the historical records as an organising centre of revolutionary action, though even in the former case the part played by it in the history of the Labour movement could hardly exceed that actually occupied by the Paris Commune of 1871. The fact that the 1848 Communist pattern corresponded to the needs of a democratic movement leading an underground struggle explains its easy reception in pre-Leninist Russia, and also the analogies between the Communist League of 1848 and the Bolshevist party of 1903. But a *fundamental* difference was caused by the fact that the former had done its work and had been dissolved into the broad stream of the sectional labour movement in which Marx's revolutionary attitude might have been lost, but which provided the only conceivable background for Lenin's distinction between the two grades of class-consciousness. Analysis of the background of sectional mass-organisation[43] seems to prove that even such organisation could not have come into being without the background of the political movement for democracy and the various

---

[42] Which, besides, is evident from the above quoted formulations of the *Address*. The "workers' party" the merging of which in the general Democratic camp could be complained of in 1848–50, did not exist in any organised form : it was a theoretical abstraction.

[43] The results of which I hope to publish in a later study.

reactions to it : Lenin was, I think, mistaken when assuming that the workers could automatically produce at least the " trade unionist class-consciousness."[44] Unless the impact of German Social Democracy and similar Western movements had brought Russian Economism and Menshevism[45] into being, the Czorny Peredyel[46] wing of the Narodniki movement would hardly have produced the background of sectional (" trade unionist ") class-consciousness against which Lenin could develop his scheme of a higher, revolutionary one. And German Social Democracy came into being just because the 1848/9 revolution had ended in capitulation of the bourgeoisie before the Prussian reality, so that what remained of bourgeois-democratic forces in the country had to back the young Labour movement. If there had been a revolutionary solution of the German problem, in 1848/9 or in the early 'sixties, the mass-movement of Labour might easily have developed in opposition to its " Utopian " predecessor to which it owed its very existence, as happened in Britain where the Trade Unions opposed the Chartist traditions. The type of pseudo-Marxism cultivated by German Social Democracy would therefore have failed to appear in Germany, and the message of Marxism would have had been carried on, on the Continent just as was actually to happen in the Anglo-Saxon countries, by small propaganda groups in opposition to the official framework of the Labour movement, until the Russian revolution had grown sufficiently strong to repeat the 1848 experiment in a national and international soil more fertile for its socialist elements.

It is impressive as a measure of Marx's and Engels' personalities that they did not hesitate to dissociate their historical prospect from an organisational instrument which could not produce real results beyond the bourgeois-democratic framework. As distinct from permanent conspirators like Bakunin they made no further attempts to frame such instruments for ideas whose realisation was bound to lie in the future. Yet they could not

[44] See above, pp. 228-9.

[45] Economists, dissenters from Marxism (corresponding to the German Revisionists) who denied the topicality of revolutionary action against Tsarism and intended to restrict the Labour movement to legal struggle for economic reforms ; Menshevists, that wing of the Russian Social Democracy, that, in opposition to the Bolshevists, aimed at a democratic mass-party not actively preparing the revolution.

[46] Redistribution (of land) without Compensation—description of the propagandist (as distinct from the terrorist) wing of the Narodniks whose members (in the 'seventies) " went to the people" and from whose ranks (with shift of emphasis from the peasants to the workers) Russian Social Democracy arose.

refrain from emotional outbursts of wishful thinking in their correspondence at the occurrence even of slight symptoms of a possible new crisis, and they paid tribute to " fellow-partisans "— of opposite factions—who attempted " to storm heavens," like the Paris Communards. The party, to which their allegiance belonged was " the Party in the great, historical sense," as distinct from " an organisation which died eight years ago, or an editorial board which broke up twelve years ago."[47] When the opportunity arose, they organised the International, as the platform where the ideas and experiences of the various national movements might be exchanged. Of course, they expected their own ideas to have ample scope on that platform and they tried to deny it to trends which they deemed disastrous for the Labour movement, such as anarchism. Later, when there was again an organised workers' party in Germany, they tried to keep it clear of trends which they regarded as treacherous, such as Royal Prussian Socialists of the Lassallean creed[48] and of capitulants who refrained from continued underground opposition to Bismarck's anti-Socialists law[49]; and in the critical situation which arose after the promulgation of that law they did not refrain from suggesting drastic measures against persons or periodicals whose attitude might misrepresent that of the Party.[50] The ample quotation of such utterances, current in Communist writings on the subject, can prove no more than should be obvious to any · serious student of Marxism, namely, that its founders were no liberal relativists and did not share the attitude current with right-wing minorities within the Labour movement (and their protectors) that all opinions had equal claims to be proclaimed on Labour's behalf provided only they were sincerely held by people who deemed themselves Socialists and paid their contribution to the Party's funds. But it cannot claim Marx and

---

[47] The remark was made, in 1860, in a letter to Freiligrath, the origins of which are explained in Mehring's Marx-biography (English ed., pp. 290–1). Certainly, in that situation, emphasis on orthodoxy would have contradicted Marx's tactical interest. However, Marx was hardly inclined to compromise on principles, and there are other utterances of his which well fit the above interpretation, such as the famous " Moi, je ne suis pas Marxiste."

[48] Marx's opinion on the point, as explained in his letter, has since been more than confirmed by the publication of Lassalle's correspondence with Bismarck (*Bismarck and Lassalle*, ed. G. Mayer, Berlin, 1928) characteristically encouraged by the upholders of Lassallean traditions within German Social Democracy.

[49] A very mild exposition of developments is given in Mehring's *History of German Social Democracy* (in German), vol. IV.

[50] Marx's and Engels' letter to the leaders of German Social Democracy, Sept. 1879, *Sel. Correspondence*, No. 170.

Engels for the Leninist theory of Party. Even Duehring's attitude which was criticised so forcibly, was described by Engels as the disagreeable by-product of a phenomenon in itself symptomatic of the party's progress, namely, of the German studiosus' conversion to Socialism,[51] and nothing more radical is suggested than the use of the Party's authority to exclude the theoretical output of such converts from the Party's central organ. As to the struggle against Lassalleanism, about which Engels had no reason to change his opinions,[48] it is characteristic that his publication of one of the fundamental documents of Marxism, Marx's *Critique of the Gotha Programme*, had to be carried out against the resistance of the Party-leaders (his and Marx's old fellow-partisans). All their lives, Marx and Engels never faced Lenin's central problem whether mere profession of a common political creed (as distinct from the conditions of common, disciplined action) formed a sufficient foundation for a political body. They were confronted with the much more elementary issue of whether the workers' party needed a distinct political theory, in contrast to a mere rallying ground, consisting of certain traditions and symbols. If they had attributed any fundamental importance to Party as distinct from other forms of Labour organisation they would not have satisfied themselves with merely private criticism of suggestions made in the name of the International to dissolve the Party in favour of the Trade Unions.[52]

These remarks are not meant to suggest that the founders of Marxism, in their later years, cherished the Centrist concept of Party—not to mention even looser ones—as opposed to what was later described as Leninism. They no longer regarded the League of Communists as a type of organisation appropriate to that stage of development ; but they never renounced it, and every word which Rosa Luxemburg uttered against Lenin's Jacobinism

---

[51] *Anti-Duehring*, ed. cit., p. 11.

[52] *Correspondence*, vol. IV, pp. 213 ff. Becker, President of the German language group of the International in Switzerland, had addressed, on the International's behalf, the Eisenach Congress of German Social Democracy (1869), at which the German section of the International became an organised party, with an address full of syndicalist and Utopian-internationalist utterances, culminating in the suggestion mentioned in the text. In their private correspondence (where it was not necessary to clear the issue of syndicalism) Marx and Engels dwelt upon Becker's usurping an authority not belonging to him, on his transferring a Swiss approach to nationalities problems to Germany, and his complete ignorance of the predominance of the issue of national unification (which certainly was a matter for a political party) in that country, but there is no word about the general nonsense implied in a concept of Party as an organ temporarily necessary until all the trades were well organised.

would have been regarded by them as directed against themselves. In spite of the Narodniks' rather unorthodox economic views,[53] Marx expressed a sympathetic attitude towards them which can only be explained by the activism of that first organisation of " professional revolutionaries." The concept of direct transition from pre-capitalist to socialist economics, discussed by Marx in that connection,[54] only makes sense if direction by a political organisation is supposed. The Leninist concept of Party is based upon the interpretation of ideologies as intermediate agencies moulding social life, which we found to be authentically Marxist. The Centrist concept of society as automatically shaped by economic developments, with Party as the mere political representation of a unit defined by its economic position, cannot claim similar authority.[55] But the distinction between the two degrees of class-consciousness, and all its implications as regards the concept of Party, never arose in the founders' minds, and could not because they never held the two links at the same time : when they were young, they held one which, according to the conditions of the times, was bourgeois-democratic in the best traditions of the French revolution ; when they were old, they held the other, which could not be inspected in the light of the generalisation of the revolutionary prospects, because the latter were absent in the Western countries where a Labour movement developed which at least claimed to be inspired by their ideas.

(e) VALIDITY AND IMPLICATIONS OF THE BOLSHEVIST
CONCEPT OF PARTY

Twenty years ago, most argument on the Bolshevist party still centred round the question whether it could retain power without dropping its basic programme. In that atmosphere, A. Rosenberg's statement that the Bolshevist concept fitted the needs of countries due for a bourgeois-democratic revolution stood midway between the self-assertion of the Communists who expected their pattern eventually to be realised all over the world, and that of their opponents who predicted from year to year the imminent downfall of the Communist regime in Russia. Today, there can be no question that, in a large part of the world,

---

[53] See above, pp. 190-1.   [54] See above, pp. 206-7.
[55] The connection between these two sorts of problems will be dealt with below, Chapter XV.

K

Communist rule has become the definitely established order ; and in the rest of the world, with the notable exceptions of the Anglo-Saxon and Germanic countries, Communism undoubtedly commands the allegiance of the majority of the " class-conscious " and organised workers. Even the fact that the world's largest industrial country is amongst the exceptions loses something of its impressive strength if it is realised that the U.S.A. has as yet no political mass-movement of Labour at all and that, once it should come into being (as happened in all the other industrial countries, and as Marxists, in any case, will expect) the chances for the emergence of a Social Democrat leadership are not great. The strongest possible tribute is paid to the Communist concept of Party by its opponents' reproach that it has absorbed the original concept of class-struggle in the service of which it originated—a statement which can be inverted as to say that the strength of the Communist parties has become the only form in which the power of the working-class over most of the World is exerted. In a sociological investigation we are not concerned with the question whether power is to be exercised, over the largest part of the World, by political parties which describe themselves as Communist and are closely allied with the U.S.S.R. : what matters for us is the characteristic of the type of rule to come. No undue reliance on descriptions of the Tito-regime by the Cominform is needed in order to realise that systems looking for independence both from the U.S.S.R. and the capitalist world may need even stronger internal discipline than those capable of operating upon International Communist support ; and nationalist regimes of the South American type may imitate the most disagreeable aspects of Communism whilst dropping its humanitarian approach.

We have seen that in any rational conception of " World Revolution " there will be, in different countries, examples of revolutionary as well as gradual transformation of society, and also instances of acceptance of basic elements of the new order by old-established ruling classes which otherwise could not hope to preserve their rule. The issue of the Bolshevist concept of Party, as opposed to looser ones, arises only where the transformation (revolutionary or gradual) is sought by the reformatory activities of the Labour movement and other social groups supporting it. The functions of a Bolshevist party are :—

(1) in terms of the *Communist Manifesto*, emphasis on the long-term interest of the working-class in thorough reconstruc-

tion of society as against the short-term interests of the members of the working-class themselves, which tie them to their own bourgeoisie or, in any case, prevent their joint action ;

(2) the co-ordination of the working-class movements with those of other groups opposing the existing regime, which cannot be understood except from a perspective broader than the sectional ;

(3) the need for planned co-ordination of revolutionary action in the narrower sense of the word ;

(4) the interests of the economic prosperity of the new economic system even where they have to be defended against the sectional interests of the workers as developed and conceived in the framework of the preceding, capitalist, society.

According to the traditional Marxist and also Bolshevist point of view,[55a] task (1) is supposed to be solved in due course by the logic of the capitalist system itself : the interest of the majority of workers in its abolition would overwhelm the short-term interests of individual groups of workers which might prevent joint action. Task (2) is evidently the reason upon which Rosenberg's argument which describes Bolshevism as characteristic of countries with important peasant, and/or nationalities, problems is based. Thus the discussion of the international validity of Lenin's argument on the need for a revolutionary and strictly disciplined party heading the transformation centres round the functions (3) and (4), namely, the need for breaking *bourgeois* resistance even by the application, or threat, of military action which is impossible without organised staff-work, and the need to enforce the economic needs of the new socialist system. The first problem coincides with the question whether compact *bourgeois* resistance to the socialist transformation is bound to emerge, a question which should not be answered mechanically for all countries. From the point of view of the individual countries where hopes for peaceful transition have not yet been refuted by actual experience, the whole argument depends on whether the traditional organisations of the Labour movement, which represent the only kind of democracy available to the working-class member of present-day society, provide sufficient leadership for socialist reconstruction.

[55a] In which what is described as " corruption of an aristrocracy of labour by imperialist extra-profits " is regarded as a mere partial and ephemeral phenomenon.

[10] See above, pp. 198–200, and below, page 318.

In the Centrist—not to speak of the Revisionist—conception[56] socialism is the fulfilment of the sectional aspirations of the working-class, because it is based upon organisations built up in order to defend the sectional interest. From this point of view, Bolshevism, with its demand for huge sacrifices if necessary in order to strengthen the new society, is a " dictatorship over the working-class " ; and it cannot be denied that if the working-class interest is described in terms of short hours, the transition of the U.S.S.R. from the seven-hour-day to the eight-hour-day implied a betrayal of the working-class interest. So also do most of the policies of the British Labour government. The very simplicity of the argument undermines its strength : It is possible to dispense with the services of a Bolshevist party for purposes (1) and (3) if conditions of extreme crisis convince the bulk of a working-class forming the majority of a nation that thorough changes are needed ; but under such circumstances an explanation of what the following reconstruction period will look like in terms of the realisation of all sectional aspirations would need a great deal of wishful thinking, to use a charitable explanation. As soon as the inevitability of conflicts between the national and the sectional interest in the transition period is realised, the differences *in this field* between socialist reconstruction in Russia and, say, in France or Britain are likely to be mere differences of degree. The argument under discussion can only hold its own with a considerable application of " ifs." It would have to be stated, say, in the following form : suppose economic developments in a country with a distinct working-class majority produce an overwhelming demand for nationalisation of the means of production, and suppose, further, that the activists of the sectional labour movement have correctly assessed the general conditions in the country and that the ruling class is not expected to resort to means of defence other than those familiar in every-day political conflicts, the establishment of a socialist regime is possible without the traditional sectional organisations of labour being subjected to leadership by an organisation representing a higher degree of political consciousness[57] ; and suppose the general resources and conditions of the country allow to a

---

[56] See above, p. 255-4.

[57] This statement is a paraphrase of the basic centrist assumption (see above, p. 254). It allows, of course, for the existence of a political party of labour carrying out the political side of the transformation, on the condition that this party represents merely one aspect of sectional organisation along with others.

considerable degree for the satisfaction of the familiar sectional demands after a very short transitory period, [58] such a political structure may continue even during the period of reconstruction. The reader may have noticed that the conditions described for dispensing with distinct party-leadership are considerably narrower than those established above [59] for the possibility of avoiding the violent breaking up of existing State machinery ; this is most natural since the very avoidance of such critical complications may suppose clever manoeuvering which would be inconceivable without organised political leadership. But the argument is not strict in that it proves the general necessity of a party of the Bolshevist type : the strength of the Bolshevist argument rests on the analysis of the concrete conditions of the countries in which the great transformation is likely to start [59a] and which should not be confused with an enumeration of all the countries eventually to be involved in a more than passive rôle.

This consideration defines the minimum of leadership needed by an organisation having the degree of political consciousness necessary for the success of a socialist transformation (and also the demands made upon political genius amongst the leaders of that organisation, which is another aspect of the same problem). It is not concerned whether leadership (some people would call it dictatorship) will actually be reduced to that minimum. Those sociologists who operate with a formalist concept of Power will assert that, if a certain amount of leadership is assumed as necessary, that amount will be extended to the maximum practicable without risking overwhelming resistance ; and they may hint at the ample opportunities for control of the individual which a socialist system of economics contains. We shall take up the last-mentioned issue in Chapter XVIII ; but the formal concept of Power, [60] once applied, should not be restricted to its institutional expression, such as the existence of a special " vocation of leadership," to use the description of the C.P. of the U.S.S.R. by the Webbs. It can flourish in an anonymous system based upon the formal equality of the supposed atoms in a purely competitive market society ; and it has been very seriously

[58] In the conditions of the Anglo-Saxon democracies, good results should be expected during the life-time of a single Parliament, or a Presidential term (if a stable Labour majority in Congress can be taken for granted, otherwise during the first two years of the term of a left-wing President).   [59] Pp. 241-2.

[59a] See section b of the next Chapter.

[60] Bertrand Russell, *Power, a new social analysis*, London, 1938.

asserted that the actual functioning of the alleged automatisms of such a society always depended on the proper working of anonymous leadership behind the scenes.[61] The question may be asked : is it likely that the power of individuals over individuals will grow excessive [62] once the phenomenon of leadership by a group identified with a certain social system (and therefore irremovable without destruction of that system) is introduced into recognised political ideology ?

In answer it must be admitted that, undoubtedly, the preservation of the system forms the supreme power-interest of the group which rules.   During the whole transitional period the new system remains exposed to competition and to possible intervention from abroad.   Such intervention probably has the advantage of starting from those countries where the old system was best developed and commanded superior technical resources.   But the new system is likely to be superior to its competitors where it can rely on mass-initiative in defence of what is regarded by the masses as their own cause.   The social interest in preserving and developing that asset is so enormous that an interest of the group in power will restrict   excessive assumption of authority by its individual members.   The history of the U.S.S.R., including the period since the purges (that is, since the needs of competing groups for mass-support ceased to be a factor), is full of illustrations for this fundamental fact.   For the duration at least of the transitional period we can safely state that the upper limit of the one-sided application of Power in the broadest, formal sense of the word is unlikely much to exceed the lower limit, which is defined above as a condition for the survival of the system. But no one can say today what amount of interference with personal freedoms regarded as normal in the comparatively stable period of the later 19th Century this will mean in concrete terms.

[61] E. H. Carr, *Nationalism and After*, London, 1945, pp. 13 ff.
[62] The so-called "leadership-principle," this is to say, the ideological demand for leadership by individuals, is a mere glorification of the lack of limitations upon such growth.

PART IV

THE CONDITIONS OF REALISATION

CHAPTER XIII

THE INTERNATIONAL FRAMEWORK

(a) THE ORIGINAL MARXIST CONCEPT AND ITS THEORETICAL FOUNDATIONS

The founders of Marxism expected that the proletarian
revolution would embrace in a comparatively short period all the
West and Central European countries[1] with fully developed
capitalist economics and a correspondingly strong industrial
working-class. These countries were regarded by contemporary
bourgeois economists as an economic unit whose consolidation was
assured by the removal of all obstacles to its complete realisation
by the progress of modern communications and of Free Trade,
whilst democratic revolutionaries in 1848 experienced a political
revolution embracing, or at least influencing, the whole area.
True, the critical historian writing *post eventum* may ascribe the
rapid spread of the 1848 revolution to its bourgeois-democratic
character in connection with the fact that, in the international
stage, the decisive break had been carried out half a century
before : when the socialist revolution did actually occur, in 1917
in Russia, apart from arousing sympathies abroad, as also the
French and American revolutions had done, it was no more
world-wide than they had been. Though the founders soon
realised that they were mistaken as regards the actual possibilities
of the mid-nineteenth century revolutions, throughout their
lives, which did not extend beyond the era of advancing Free
Trade, they retained their conception of the geographical basis
of the approaching socialist revolution. In their later years,
when the issues of a Russian revolution became topical, they made
due allowance for the possibility that a country with a strong
revolutionary movement, but as yet undeveloped in capitalist

---

[1] The inclusion of the U.S.A. was envisaged by Engels in the *Principles of Communism*, written in 1847, as well as in the letter to Kautsky, of Sept. 12, 1882. But the last chapter of vol. I of *Capital* certainly contradicts the expectation of a quick approach of the socialist revolution in U.S.A. as long as the possibilities of colonisation in the West were not yet exhausted.

industry and with strong survivals of primitive village community, might join in socialist reconstruction, provided that the community would still be in existence when typical proletarian revolutions in the West gave the necessary industrial backing.[2] They were far-sighted enough to realise that a socialist revolution in such an " international " framework was a matter for a minority of mankind ; Engels in his later years[3] envisaged the secession from the socialist group of nations, not only of the colonial countries proper, under a social regime the character of which could not yet be envisaged, but even of the dominions, to use the present terminology (though he expected that the power of example would in due course draw the colonial peoples on to lines similar to those of the socialist countries). Co-existence of a socialist and a non-socialist part of the world was evidently envisaged as a long-term affair ; and whilst attacking the idea of colonial wars to be fought by the new socialist regimes and of any attempts to force progress upon peoples reluctant to accept it, Engels envisaged the possibility of defensive wars of the socialist against non-socialist countries. This seems to indicate an approach to the problem as realistic as that of present Soviet leaders. Engels also appears to envisage the possibility of the emancipated colonies competing with their former masters with all the vigour of young capitalist lands based upon large undeveloped resources. In any case, the socialist sphere, for Engels, would have been no more world-wide than is the present U.S.S.R. with her sphere of influence. From the formal point of view, the whole dispute about the compatibility of " socialism in one country " with original Marxist teaching may be dismissed by the simple remark that Marx and Engles were bound to envisage socialism in a plurality of countries because the original realisation of socialism was envisaged by them in a region unhappily divided by historical developments into sovereign states, most of which were of the dimensions and importance of one of the medium or even minor Union Republics in the present U.S.S.R.

The formal issue may, indeed, appear unimportant once we leave behind the narrowmindedness of the Second International. Its members felt most happy in a framework of the Western and Central European labour parties, with representatives of questionable authority from Russia and U.S.A. trying to explain

[2] See above, p. 207.
[3] Letter to Kautsky, of Sept. 12, 1882.

indigestible factional controversies within uninfluential sects, and with the occasional coloured fraternal delegate—more likely than not to be a student of a Western university—receiving the tribute due to a symbol of ultimate humanitarian aspirations. But all the fundamental issues of the interpretation of Marxism are raised once we face the fact that Marx's and Engels' choice of the initial unit was dominated by the system of abstractions upon which their model of capitalist society was based. However helpful in illuminating tendencies prevailing throughout the capitalist world, these abstractions were bound to be ineffective in identifying concretely that group of countries where the first breakdown of capitalism was likely to happen. Having established mere general tendencies which, by themselves, could not produce a concrete revolutionary situation,[4] the founders of Marxism maintained the belief that pre-imperialist capitalism, as they knew it, was capable of producing such a situation. This means that they expected it in those countries where capitalism was best developed. Whilst they frequently realised the way in which complications would arise as the theoretical pattern had to be applied to reality, and whilst they drew sensible political conclusions[5] therefrom, they never considered whether theoretical " difficulties " discovered in that way might not represent the actual conflicts from which the crisis of capitalism was bound to arise. Erroneous conclusions as to the likely course of the breakdown of the capitalist system resulted from exaggerated emphasis put on the theoretical abstractions made in its analysis by the founders of Marxism, and by the classical economists whose general attitudes in this respect were accepted by them with insufficient criticism.

The first and most important of those abstractions is the very assumption of a purely capitalist world. With the classical

---

[4] See above, p. 180. In Bolshevist literature there is some dogmatical reluctance to face the fact that Marx and Engels were Utopians when even discussing the possibility of socialist revolutions immediately arising from pre-imperialist conditions (even Lenin in his speech of March 18, 1908, stated quite seriously that the Paris Communards, if they had avoided certain tactical blunders, might have been successful— evidently in the sense of a socialist revolution). Hence arose statements like those made by Stalin in discussing Socialism in One Country when he (*Coll. Works*, vol. IX, pp. 87–9) explained away the denial of that possibility by Marx by stating that it had been quite correct under pre-imperialist conditions, but had become obsolete with the development of monopoly-capitalism and the increased importance of the " law of uneven development of capitalism." (See also op. cit. pp. 158 and 659.)

[5] To which all the Communist attempts to find in classical Marxist writings hints at the concepts of workers' aristocracy and at modern Bolshevist tactics in the agrarian, national and colonial questions refer.

economists, it originated from inability to interpret the non-capitalist elements surrounding them otherwise than as abnormal in terms of a capitalist norm, because its growth provided the predominant issue of their time. Marx accepted their scheme to a large extent because this was the simplest way of refuting their assertion that the maximum improvement of social conditions would be achieved as soon as " unreasonable," pre-capitalist, obstacles were overcome. He was conscious of the fact that large parts of the world still needed a bourgeois-democratic revolution. He was also conscious of the problems involved in combing such revolutions with socialist ones in more advanced countries[2]; but he did not approach the problem of countries dominated by capitalism yet at the same time not predominantly capitalist in respect of the conditions of the vast majority of their population, so that the latter's awakening called for a bourgeois-democratic revolution in the presence of forces already driving beyond it. This seems strange in view of the fact that the *Communist Manifesto* owes its very existence to such conditions ; it seems as if Marx and Engels, when dropping the illusion of an immediately possible transition to a socialist revolution to which the *Manifesto* owed its existence, dropped too much, and neglected the likely results of a situation similar to that of 1848 Germany, should it arise at a time when the experiences of a large-scale labour movement—and their own teaching—should be available.

Secondly, Marx and Engels took over an abstraction from their classical predecessors according to which capitalist society was regarded as one interdependent unit the national divisions of which were bound to be overrun by its inherent dynamics. The liberal Freetraders had needed this abstraction in order to prove that the breakdown of some British industry under foreign competition was not detrimental to the national wealth, because the competitor successfully developing in some country more fit for the industry in question would create additional markets for other industries better fitted to Britain. Marx and the modern Labour movement in general[6] needed it in order to demonstrate the interest of the workers of one country in the successes of their class-fellows elsewhere. It is hardly necessary today to dwell

---

[6] The desire to prevent import of foreign strike-breakers dominated not only the attitude of the British Trade Unions to the International (Comp. Ryazanoff in *Marx, Engels Archiv*, vol. I, *passim*.) but actually formed the latter's main appeal to the masses. I have dealt with this problem in my (unpublished) Viennese thesis of 1922, *Socialism and the Trade Union Problem*.

upon the shortcomings of that abstraction ; but it should be noted that the rejoinder most current amongst bourgeois critics of Marxism is without fundamental importance : whatever allowance may be made for interests dividing the workers of one country from those of some other, there is no necessary conflict between specific national interests of the workers and those which the international Labour movement truly unite, nor do the specific interests of the national groups of labour necessarily coincide with those of their sectional opponents. British miners may well fight against the possible cuts in their wages resulting from the introduction of Polish miners (" national prejudice "), and at the same time oppose the Poles' anti-Soviet propaganda (" international class-solidarity ") ; but there is no basic contradiction between these attitudes.

The fundamental shortcoming of the abstraction under discussion is that it neglects what in modern Bolshevist terminology is called " the uneven development of capitalism," that is to say, the fact that the relation of strength between the different national units of a capitalist world is bound to be unstable.[7] Marx and Engels experienced the rise of the German and American industries to become competitors equal with the British, and regarded the destruction of the latter's monopoly as a necessary condition for the British working-class parting company with its own bourgeoisie[8] ; but in doing so they overlooked the possible growth of a " labour aristocracy " in Germany and U.S.A. More important, their analysis did not demonstrate what political implications such competition might produce, even in the pre-monopoly stage of capitalism, as soon as allowance is made for the possibility that a capitalist system might break down not in economic depression (which by its very nature is world-wide to some extent) but in consequence of failure in a war, perhaps undertaken just in order to prevent or end such depression. Even if in such a case economic destruction in both camps should be equally great, as it was at the end of World War I, the moral strength of the ruling class of the " victorious country " would be likely to have improved to such an extent that a socialist revolution in the victor country was a most unlikely event. The very fact that a revolution started in the defeated country might help the ruling-classes of its opponents to

[7] See below, p. 316.
[8] cf. Lenin's quotations from Engels in *Imperialism, Sel. Works,* vol. V, p. 98.

make full use of national prejudice accumulated during the war, and this might have limited the immediate results even of the from the Marxist point of view most favourable outcome of World War I : a socialist revolution in Germany, additionally to that which did actually happen in Russia.

The process of abstraction which overlooks the necessary inequalities in capitalist development whilst introducing the delusory expectation of a simultaneous revolution in all, or at least most, of the leading industrial countries, removes an alternative which has already proved important in the Russian revolution and may prove even more important in future colonial ones, namely, that a turn towards socialism should be enforced upon a bourgeois-democratic revolution in order to enable the revolutionary country to preserve its independence against the established capitalist powers. If the abstraction first discussed is dropped and foreign capitalist penetration proceeds to the full in a still predominantly pre-capitalist system, external defence against wars of intervention, with all its implications as to war-economics and enforced nationalisation, appears necessarily involved in an initially bourgeois-democratic revolution in a country of major importance.

The third fundamental, but unjustified abstraction made by Marxism in accordance with the classical economists, is the assumption of a homogeneous and completely coherent labour market, in which the laws said to dominate the movement of wages are bound to prevail in the long run. Apart from the second abstraction just discussed, there is no reason for the assumption that the Industrial Reserve Army, and those sectors of the working-class which are most exposed to its pressure, should develop equally in all the capitalist countries. Actually they are being concentrated in certain, colonial and semi-colonial, countries, and in multi-national countries the share of the various nationalities in the skilled, and comparatively secure, jobs is very different.[9] Clear realisation of this problem throws in doubt the concept of a mere workers' aristocracy amongst the leading nations being " corrupted " by imperialist extra profits and therefore likely to oppose revolutionary class-struggle.[10] It weakens the hopes of the Communist parties of the leading imperialist countries

[9] Comp. the sources quoted in my *Federalism in Central and Eastern Europe*, pp. 194–5, 297, 374 and 380, and Lenin, *Sel. Works*, vol. V, p. 291.

[10] See above, pp. 198-200.

to get, in due course, the support of the majority of their national working-class ; but it provides the key to the overwhelming importance attributed by Lenin, as distinct from Marx's and Engel's occasional remarks, to the colonial problem, and puts into clear perspective the main achievement of Leninism outside Russia, namely, the transformation of the international labour movement from a narrow-minded gathering of white workers predominantly of Western Europe into a body in which the coloured majority of the international working-class is bound to exercise its whole impact as soon as the initial backwardness of its organisation is overcome.

Lastly, though we owe to Marx the highly realistic analysis of the exploitation of the urban and rural lower-middle-classes in Chapters 36 and 47 of the third volume of *Capital*, his general scheme, because it is based upon the abstraction of " pure " capitalism, envisages the socialist revolution starting from a stage when at least the bulk of those lower-middle-classes, especially the peasantry, have been actually expropriated. In the *Address of the Central Council of the Communist League*, drafted at a time when the Junkers in Germany East of the Elbe were just finally expropriating the former poor peasant who might well have still responded to appeals similar to those used by the Bolsheviks in 1917, the agricultural labourers, and not the peasants, are explicitly described as the only support available to the Communists in the countryside. In *The Peasants' War in Germany*, Engels later approached a realistic discussion of the peasants' problem bound to confront a victorious socialist revolution, but he did not go beyond what Lenin would have described as a policy of " neutralisation." [11] The political reasons for such an attitude—mistaken as it obviously is in view of present East European reality—were implied in the obvious inability of the peasants to develop by their own efforts the organisation and political consciousness necessary to defeat a centralised political system. Engels, when discussing the German Peasants' War of 1525, has explained this inability in terms which could almost verbally be applied, say, to the Bulgarian peasants' resistance against the counter-revolution of 1923. A Labour movement thinking mainly in terms of propaganda might be able to leave to the future the concrete issue of how to reorganise the lives of a class which evidently was unable to produce the right conceptions

[11] See below, p. 328.

and to organise proper action by its own efforts. But if we remember that the East European nationalities issues, which we have to discuss in Chapter XV of this book, in their economic content are actually peasants' problems, we shall see that it was too abstract an approach to the peasant problem which obstructed the handling of the practical issues of the day. Engels' theory that in the event of a socialist revolution in Western Europe the colonies should be emancipated and left to their own presumably capitalist fates was mechanically repeated by those Bolsheviks who during World War I desired to restrict national self-determination to colonial peoples, while the subject nationalities of Tsarist Russia were to be satisfied with the promise of equal rights to be granted them by a successful socialist revolution.[12]

Taken together, these abstractions are sufficiently unrealistic to defeat the original Marxist concept of the regional basis from which the socialist reconstruction of the World would start. Certainly, no inherent laws of Nature set up the Western boundaries of the socialist section of the World just where they lay during the period between the two wars ; with better organisation and clearer political concepts on the part of the German revolutionaries, they might have been established from 1919 or 1920 onwards where they lie at present. And a German revolution brought about by internal efforts, even if followed by secession of the Catholic South and West, and by another Brest Litovsk treaty which would have appeased the Western interventionists by sacrificing the Ruhr, would not only have given a tremendous boost to socialist reconstruction in the Federation of Soviet Republics and conceivably spared its leaders much argument about the building of socialism ; it might also have been represented in State ideology as the Western support demanded by orthodox Marxism as a condition for the success of a socialist revolution in Russia. Nevertheless, the survival of the socialist part of the world would have been due to the space, military strength and immense natural resources of Russia, though the socialist rump of Germany might have played some part in the further development of socialist civilisation. Had World War I ended differently, no comparably strong socialist section of

[12] Comp. Lenin, *Sel. Works*, vol. V, pp. 379–80 (Annex). The argument was continued on the 8th Party Congress, in 1918, when the left-wing opposition demanded interpretation of national self-determination as to be exercised only by the working-class, self-determination of bourgeois nations being thus rejected. Comp. Ibid.,vol. VIII, pp. 344–5.

the World would have emerged, perhaps no socialist sector at all, because a French and even an English revolution would have been helpless against German and American intervention. Certainly Communist tactics in the post-1920 period were not beyond reproach ; but the mistakes made in Germany—the only major capitalist country where Communist tactics could influence a major decision—whatever may have been their importance for the eventual strength of the fascist regime, can hardly be supposed to have prevented an otherwise possible socialist revolution. The issue whether, after 1920, revolutionary possibilities may have been spoilt by avoidable tactical mistakes of Communist parties seems most interesting for some East-European countries and especially for China in the period of 1925-36. All of these countries have turned Communist in the aftermath of World War II. Had they done so already during the period between the wars, mainly the formerly semi-feudal or colonial part of the socialist sector would have been enlarged.

(b) MODIFICATION OF THE MARXIST SCHEME

The extent to which the Bolsheviks were dominated by the original pattern of Marxist thought is demonstrated in the development of their theoretical position. At first, along with all the other Russian Marxists they entered the historical scene in a dispute with the Narodniks on the inevitability of development according to that pattern for Russia[13] ; Lenin's *Development of Capitalism in Russia*, which actually laid the foundations for the study of economic systems penetrated by capitalist trends though not conforming with the capitalist pattern, was intended by its author as a proof of the validity of the classical Marxist scheme for his country. Next, the Bolsheviks argued with the Mensheviks as to the practical conclusions to be drawn from the fact that Russia was " not yet ripe " from the economic point of view and, therefore, needed a bourgeois-democratic revolution.[14] Finally, when assuming power and slowly learning that they were to remain isolated for at least another generation, they proved to their own dissenting factions and to the Western Labour movement that Russia, in due course, had become ripe for the development envisaged by classical Marxism. Up to the present day,

---

[13] See above, p. 191.

[14] Quite apart from this, the very process of the masses awakening in a still semi-feudal country implies some bourgeois-democratic stage such as from March to October, 1917.

Bolshevism has not recognised that the Marxist pattern, just because it is based upon the abstraction of "pure capitalism" (which is certainly necessary as a basis for the understanding of the more complicated reality), is utopian as to the immediate possibility of a socialist revolution starting from the countries envisaged by Marx and Engels.

But at least some approach to this conclusion[15] is implied in Communist tenets established partly by Lenin, partly after his death. Imperialism is interpreted as exploitation of the weaker countries by the monopoly capitalism of the stronger ones, and a "workers' aristocracy" corrupted by a share in those extra-profits is supposed in times of national prosperity to be capable of dominating the attitude of the bulk of the working-class. The emphasis laid in Comintern-theory upon the international importance of such traits of Leninism as its policies in the agrarian, national and colonial questions should have suggested that the chances of revolution were greatest where there was a coincidence of a development of capitalism sufficient at least as a starting point for socialist reconstruction, with the maximum development of those elements of tension characteristic of an impending bourgeois-democratic revolution. Such an interpretation is easy to grasp within the context of our analysis, but tends to refute the Comintern's assumption that only insufficient understanding and application of Bolshevist theory prevented the socialist conquest at least in some of the Western countries. More important, it implies the acceptance of the statement that, for better or for worse, the transition of world economics to socialism implies the transition of leadership in the international community to a new group of nations,[16] with others making the necessary concessions to their impact when it has grown sufficiently strong. It should be noted that, in the historical record, transition to a new mode of production has generally been

---

[15] Only an approach, because even Stalin's observations (*Leninism*, ed. 1940, pp.20-1) about the necessity for "breaks in the imperialist chain" arising at its weakest links still left the prospect of revolution in an imperialist country defeated in War, but preserving so much of its industrial potential that the right reaction of its working-class to the conditions created by defeat could secure it a leading part in socialist reconstruction. This prospect dominated the minds of most Communists in the post-1918 period ; it seems to have lapsed with the advent of Hitlerism to power. It can hardly be renewed any more, as a defeat of the U.S.A. in an intra-imperialist war is inconceivable, and the U.S.S.R. has already exceeded the industrial development of any other country.

[16] See below, p. 318.

associated with changes in international leadership, though the dominating ideas developed in the formerly leading group.

Our time, like all periods immediately following a great revolutionary wave, is characterised by a general rise of national self-assertion. Increased nationalism may be explained by the historian, even if a Marxist, as the rallying of the forces now re-aligned in the national sphere to fight out the issue on the international scene. However, recognition of the fact that the new concept of social order is mainly located in a certain group of nations would reduce its ability to bring into the new synthesis a minimum of the traditions even of those nations which originally opposed it. Therefore, the replacement of the original Marxist by a different international framework is not likely to be accepted in Communist ideology before the realities of the international situation are generally recognised and perhaps settled in a way allowing for international co-existence of Bolshevist and non-Bolshevist patterns of transition to socialism. Actually, the international influence of some political regime does not imply that it will be generally accepted any more than the period of British industrial hegemony carried with it general introduction of parliamentary monarchy (including a House of Lords) or a possible period of American hegemony would mean the general introduction of Federalism and the Presidential system of government.[17] On the other hand, the Soviet's original desire to comply ideologically with the most advanced pattern of Western progressive thought was, naturally, defeated daily by Soviet reality. The loss of propagandist appeal could be avoided if the claim for maximum realisation of the original Marxist pattern were dropped. However widespread the desire to see one's own hopes realised in some far-away country, Marxist propaganda in the old capitalist countries would not necessarily lose in impressive strength were it clearly stated to non-Russians, non-Chinese, etc., that the further evolution of their national ways of life cannot be simply derived from experiences made by civilisations with a completely different historical background.

[17] It is true, that international hegemony of some national system implies the likelihood of other national institutions being interpreted in its terms (or itself being suitably misinterpreted, as has been done since Montesquieu's days). Up to now, the Soviet itself has paid its tribute to this tradition by draping itself as a parliamentary democracy.

(c) SOCIALISM IN ONE COUNTRY

If the inherent limitations of the original Marxist pattern are realised, the change in Bolshevist ideology towards the concept of " Socialism in one country " loses the usually alleged character of a turn "from internationalism to nationalism," though it was bound to appear in that light to those participants in the discussions who were still dominated by the atmosphere of the Second International. In the historical perspective, it is likely to appear as a decisive event in the process of the awakening of the nations which needed and accepted guidance from more advanced ones and as the turning point from a sectional to a communal concept of socialism. From the point of view of the formal structure of the Marxist theory, no change in basic principles took place when the expectation that a revolution in some Western countries would provide the necessary industrial backing while the Russian village community turned to socialist co-operation gave place to the assertion that this backing had been provided by 35 years of capitalist and 10 years of socialist industrialisation of Russia herself.[18] This change should not appear as fundamental to minds accustomed to regard[19] as secondary the question whether the peasantry exploited by the national capitalism was located within the country, as in Tsarist

[18] This seems, to the retrospective mind, the naked economic content of the whole dispute about Socialism in One Country, apart from details such as the formation of a lever favouring collectivisation within the village in consequence of the dissociation of the original community into *kulaks* and *batraks*. Perhaps the importance of this moment for the definite success of collectivisation was so decisive as to render Marx's assertion of 1882, when it was absent, Utopian; though, on the other hand, the amount of dissociation suffered by the village community is certainly over-stated in official Bolshevist ideology in order to preserve continuity with Lenin's struggle against the *Narodniks* (see above, p. 191). In view of the weight carried by the proof of orthodoxy, the bibliographical aspect of the dispute was emphasised to an extent disproportionate to the discussion of the basic economic questions. See the note to page 134 of Lenin's *Selected Works*, vol III (Ibid., pp. 547 ff), which is translated from the official note to the Russian Collected Works and based upon Stalin's letter of October, 1931, to the Editor of the Journal *The Proletarian Revolution* (op. cit. pp. 388 ff). In view of Stalin's later (Ibid., pp. 658-60) recognition of his having developed a substantially new theory it is hardly worth while dwelling on this point. Lenin's text to which the note is made upholds the polemic against Trotsky's assertion that proletarian dictatorship (without the peasants) was needed in order to carry through even the bourgeois-democratic revolution, and also against the assertion of later Trotskyists that Lenin, in 1905, intended to stop at bourgeois-democratic achievements, short of a socialist revolution (to this point see also *Sel. Works*, vol. III, p. 145). But it explicitly contradicts the assertion of the authors of the note that Lenin, in 1905, envisaged the possibility of a successful socialist revolution in Russia without direct support by the European workers, who would " show us how to do it."

[19] As done by Rosa Luxemburg (see above, p. 194), as well as by Lenin (see above, p. 192).

Russia or, say, in the African colonies of the European powers ; but it is full of ideological implications as regards the very concept of socialism. As long as the latter was associated with the highest conceivable development of Western industrial society, it could be conceived in terms of maximum realisation of the sectional demands raised by the Western Labour movement with ample scope left to imagination as to the further achievements possible once " suplus-value " would be appropriated by the community and production planned. But the socialist character of industry established in Russia to make possible her transition to national planning even in agriculture had obviously to be measured by its success in achieving this aim (with due allowance for the needs of defence), leaving satisfaction of sectional demands to the second place. This would not have been possible unless the change had been carried out in a country where the backward conditions at least of the great majority of the working population were bound to be greatly improved by a policy of industrialisation even if temporary sectional achievements of a working-class minority were sacrificed to the needs of survival.[20] The contradiction between the demands necessarily made by a socialist community upon its members and ideological descriptions of socialism in terms of complete realisation of all the aims of the preceding sectional struggle is universal, but it may be particularly conspicuous in backward countries for whom socialist reconstruction is a necessary means of holding their own against the traditional rulers of the world markets.

Amongst Marxists of a country whose historic tradition was dominated by conflict between " Westernizing " tendencies and those asserting her distinct historical mission,[21] all those issues were bound to be discussed in terms of the enquiry whether Socialism (namely, that socialism as envisaged by Marx and the tradition of the Western Labour movement) was realisable in one

[20] As certainly done by the Russian revolution, at least since the completion of the First Five Year Plan. A policy so clever as the Bolshevist might be expected to combine, in peacetime, every increased demand made upon labour with some improvement at least from the point of view of subjective tastes. In 1930, the Five-day week, with the rest-day (every fifth) different for different workers (which, of course, implied disturbances of private life) was introduced, together with continuous working of industry ; in 1931 a general rest-day at least for the bulk of the workers was introduced, but merely every sixth day. Even in 1938 when, with open hints at the external threat, the seven-day week and the eight-hour day were re-introduced, things were made palatable at least for the religious-minded part of the population by the fixing of Sunday as the universal rest-day.

[21] I use this rather clumsy term in order to avoid implications of the term " Slavophil " that would not fit the modern framework.

country, especially in Russia. Stalin's answer to the problem is as original as any author's statements can be ; but in circumstances where reference to established authority was much more conducive to the general acceptance of the concept than the proof of its author's original genius, the isolated hints by his predecessors, which Stalin made his basis, have been enhanced to such an extent that what actually was Stalin's concept is ascribed to them.[18] Three different issues are involved and only the combined affirmative answer to each of them leads to Stalin's theory. In the attempt to prove orthodoxy it was hardly astonishing that Lenin's[22] affirmative answer to any of them has been used to prove that he foresaw the whole theory even at the time when, to any unbiased mind, the affirmative answer to one was combined with negative to the others. Of these issues the first, whether the Russian working-class, after having achieved the triumph of a bourgeois-democratic revolution, should continue to drive forward towards a socialist one, was answered by Lenin in the affirmative as early as 1905, but with the rider that its success would pre-suppose support from the Western working-class.[18] The second, whether success of the socialist revolution " in one or a few capitalist countries " was possible, was answered by Lenin in the affirmative in August, 1915, in his article on the slogan of *The United States of Europe.* But since this judgment was coloured by the revolutionary implications of the War, Lenin can hardly have held the opinion at an earlier period. At the time when the article was written the Russian armies had suffered decisive defeats and domestic political developments took place at home which reminded Lenin of those immediately preceding the 1905 revolution, and were regarded by him as evidence of a revolutionary crisis.[23] It is quite conceivable that he envisaged Russia as the country starting the socialist revolution ; but he clearly envisaged it as an incentive to a socialist revolution in the West and regarded it as topical since, in consequence of the War, the latter had become an immediate possibility.[23] Still paying

[22] There is no possibility of reference to Marx, though an affirmative answer by him to the first of those issues—only to that one—was conceivable if he had experienced the 1905 revolution and at that time preserved an optimistic attitude as regards the general development of the Western labour movement. In view of the narrow-minded distrust of Russia common to the Western tradition, efforts were already needed in order to recall Marx's very different attitude to Russian revolutionaries (see above, p. 206). Marx's and Engels' correspondence with Russian political activists has now been published in Russian by the Marx-Engels-Lenin Institute (Moscow, 1947).

[23] *Sel. Works,* vol. V, p. 141.

tribute to the concept of world revolution, he envisaged the mutual relations between the first revolutionary country and the rest of the capitalist world in terms which since have been frequently quoted on either side, in order to prove the impossibility of long-term co-existence of the two systems : " The victorious proletariat of that country, having expropriated the capitalists and organised its own socialist production, would *confront* the rest of the capitalist world, attract to itself the oppressed classes of those countries, raise revolutionary agitation against the capitalists and, in the event of necessity, come out with armed force against the exploiting classes and their states." Much, in the interpretation of this statement, depends on the accent : at its face-value, it does not necessarily imply more than a realistic approach to international relations in a world divided between two social systems, including realisation of the revolutionary country's propagandist advantages and of the use likely to be made of victory in wars which may have been purely defensive in origin. To " organise its own socialist production " is enumerated amongst the primary tasks of the victorious proletariat of the first socialist country, prior to playing its international part. However, there is no proof that Lenin, at that time, envisaged Russia as the country whose working-class was likely to assume that part. But in 1922, after the introduction of the N.E.P. and after he had succeeded in " stopping the retreat," Lenin stated that Russia " had all that is necessary in order to build a complete socialist society," provided she was not prevented from doing so by external intervention.[24] At that time (and also a few months later, when Lenin ceased working) conditions, especially in Germany, were still so unsettled that he might be forgiven for failing to reckon with the long isolation of socialist Russia from the capitalist world. However, the statement rejects a policy of retreat in Russia to bourgeois-democratic positions in consequence of the failure of the Western proletarians to join, and suggests a careful advance towards socialist economics. When the implications of such a course became obvious, the Stalinist solution of the problem lay at hand.

[24] Ibid., vol. IX, p. 403. The restriction made in the text is obvious, and has been elaborated by Stalin, op. cit. (1940), pp. 113 ff and 143 ff.

CHAPTER XIV

INTERNATIONAL POLITICS AND WARS

(a) MARX'S AND ENGELS' APPROACH TO THE INTERNATIONAL ISSUES OF THEIR TIME

By its appreciation of the international connections of the struggle of the working-class and by its interpretation of the issues of any other country in terms familiar to the politically interested worker, whatever his nationality, Marxism has become in our days the strongest incentive to an understanding of international relations. The one-sidedness of its interpretations, which is unnecessarily exaggerated in its current vulgarisations, is the current object of reproaches by students of international relations who are eager to emphasize the element of continuity, the importance of geographical factors, etc. ; and in times when revolutionary waves subside and even a Soviet Russia has to think in geographical terms of her security rather than in chances of security to be gained by the emergence of sympathetic regimes elsewhere,[1] the case of the critics appears strong. Obviously each side to the dispute grasps a mere facet of the complex reality. However, the facet emphasized by Marxism is the only one capable of explaining dynamic changes in international relations, and Marxism is by definition a system of sociology analysing the dynamics of social developments. So its approach is not exposed to inherent criticism, provided only it keeps to its own rules and avoids the elevation of a system representing the dynamics of a past period to a static standard for the evaluation of later ones. From the political point of view, the investigation of the objective social meaning of the assertion by some power of interests which are " purely " geographical or strategic in character is the only approach leading to a perspective broader than the simple assertion of the national interest of one's own country, or its ally. This is certainly an ideological approach no less than other approaches in which the ideological reasons put forward in

---

[1] Comp. my *Spirit of Post-war Russia*, pp. 96–7.

support of the respective national claims are emphasised ; but if one realises that the merits of ideological arguments such as national self-determination, emancipation of formerly oppressed groups, Justice, social order, etc., are bound to appear very differently from different social standpoints,[2] than one may prefer the essence of the thing to its appearances, and judge the merits of any conflict according as to whether its solution promotes that general trend which one regards as leading to maximum progress in all fields.

The founders of Marxism found a clear concept of international affairs elaborated by their bourgeois-democratic predecessors, and accepted it without fundamental corrections. Wars had already been described by Clausewitz, working under the impact of the French revolution, as a continuation of policies by different, namely, military means. For those who had experienced the anti-Jacobin wars and the Holy Alliance it was obvious that a country's domestic policies, that is, the attitude of its dominating groups towards the fundamental issues raised by the French revolution, prevailed also in its external policies. There was further the tradition of the Jacobin phase of the French revolution, prevalent in the circles in which the founders of Marxism moved, which seemed to prove that external war[3] threatening the existence of a revolutionary country was the safest means of driving the revolution forward and concentrating power in the hands of the most consistent of the revolutionary groups. There were certain flaws in those generalisations : it was not Ekaterina's Russia just getting over a rebellion of the serfs, but Britain (certainly the most advanced of the European countries, from the bourgeois point of view) which took the lead in the anti-Jacobin wars. After Napoleon's defeat the same Britain, though threatened at home by a democratic opposition stronger than in any other country, not excluding France, temporised against the Holy Alliance. Nor did the Wars of Liberation serve to strengthen the revolutionary forces, however much the need to hold their own against revolutionary France may have pushed Prussia and Austria in the direction of moderate

---

[2] I have discussed this point in *Federalism in Central and Eastern Europe*, pp. 472 ff and 520 ff, in the article, *Veto and Collaboration* in *The Fortnightly*, October, 1945, and in *The Spirit of Post-war Russia*, p. 116.

[3] Not even necessarily a defensive one. At least in the prevailing democratic tradition the fact that the Jacobins had opposed the Girondin war-policies of 1792 was neglected in favour of the more impressive record of 1793-5.

progress. However, the wars had been directed against Napoleon, the betrayer of the French revolution, and nationality itself was one of the principles raised by it. The part played by Britain might have been explained to European progressive minds in the second generation of the Nineteenth Century by the existence of many feudal survivals, and the Marxist development of this analysis would merely insist on ampler scope for commercial competition (in the anti-Jacobin period). If the scheme is taken as reflecting one facet of reality, with due allowance for the working of other continuous, geographic and strategic factors, it appears quite sensible : at the time when it was coined it had no serious competitor in the world of current ideas.

On the assumption that a bourgeois-democratic revolution was the predominant issue of the time—which was obvious to the early Marxists, even when they hoped it would turn soon into a proletarian revolution—the picture of European politics arising from the practical application of the scheme was fairly simple : on the one side stood the remainder of the Holy Alliance, the three Central and East European military and semi-feudal monarchies, with Russia, the only one of them not yet threatened by internal revolution, as their backbone. France had broken away by the revolution of July, 1830 (to be turned in 1848 into " the revolutionary Babel ") and Britain, under a moderately liberal regime, might be expected to offer moderate resistance to westward expansion of Russian influence. On the other side stood the forces of revolution in all countries ; but, with the exception of France, clearly democratic revolutionary movements could not continuously remain in the foreground : so a prominent part was to be played by national emancipation movements directed against the main enemy or its allies. In the foreground stood the Poles whose last stand (dominated by the squirearchy) against the partitions had paid its ideological tribute to the genius of the French revolution and who certainly opposed all the three reactionary monarchies. Next came the Italians opposing Austrian tyranny, soon to be joined by the Magyars. Western progressives preferred not to enquire too much into the democratic credentials of those national revolutionaries whose nations happened to be in the foreground of the general rise of nationalism just because they had never lost their national aristocracy (as Czechs, Slovenes and Ukrainians had done), and could therefore occupy leading positions on the political scene in an age when the masses did not yet count.[4] The Germans would join the ranks of the revolutionary nations as soon as their movement for national unification should oppose the traditional principalities including two of the reactionary Great Powers, Prussia and Austria. Amongst them, the German emancipation movement was certainly the only one which could properly be described as bourgeois-democratic ; partly because the Germans were by far the most developed and therefore they alone had a proper bourgeoisie, and partly because in the absence of foreign oppression and in the presence of a plurality of states ruled by nobles the national aristocracy would hold itself aloof from the movement for national emancipation and unification.

In all these regards Marx and Engels during and after 1848-9, that is, during the only period of their lives when they could influence a public larger than more or less convinced socialists, behaved like consistent liberal democrats. They opposed Tsarist Russia, to the point of advocating offensive war in which Germany " by liberating other peoples would emancipate herself "[5] ; they favoured the Polish cause, hoping that from common action against the common enemy a friendly settlement of Polish-German disputes would arise,[6] and they attacked all the allies of the common foe, along with its vaccillating opponents, whether Austrian Slavs or a British government refraining from energetic anti-Tsarist action. The current left-wing misunderstandings of the dynamics of the French revolution[3] were developed with remarkable consistency.[7] In opposing the moderate Liberals who disarmed the Poles lest they might retake the territories annexed by Prussia, Marx and Engels went to the length of offering the Poles Riga and Mitau in exchange for Danzig and Elbing, however questionable such procedure might appear from a modern democratic point of view.[8] They exhibited an anti-Slav tendency common in the

---

[4] See my *Federalism in Central and Eastern Europe*, pp. 5 and 155-9.

[5] Article " National Revolutions," in *Neue Rheinische Zeitung*, July 11, 1848.

[6] Article, " Poles, Czechs, Germans," in *Germany, Revolution and Counter-revolution* (Marx-Engels, *Sel. Works*, vol. II, pp. 86 ff.)

[7] In contradiction to Engels' later (see above, p. 284) recognition that progress is not an article to be exported by armed forces.

[8] Not necessarily from the rather narrow outlook of Engels' democratic contemporaries : it is quite conceivable that he took the German character of Riga and Mitau for granted. But the basic assumption was that the non-Polish peasants surrounding the Baltic towns and the Polish peasants surrounding Danzig and Elbing (Engels was conscious of the existence of both of them, see below, p. 308), did not count[6]. See also below, p. 303.

contemporary German liberal outlook which was not improved upon by theoretical attempts to deny the existence of the smaller Slavonic nations.[9] Lord Palmerston's alleged betrayal of the interests of the British empire by failing to defend the integrity of Turkey, was attacked by Marx, in strange alliance with Urquhart, though he confined[10] his stricture to " present circumstances," which was to mean " for the duration of Tsarist rule in Russia." All this is symptomatic of Marx's and Engels' conceptions of practical politics, and answers the frequent attempts to conjure up their spirits against modern Bolshevist essays in realist politics, but is hardly relevant for students of what actually survives of Marx, his theory.

The fundamental strains of present Marxist, which actually originated from pre-Marxist democratic, thought were already well elaborated on the eve of the revolution, without being appreciated in all their implications and potential contradictions. In a London meeting in favour of the Poles, November 29, 1847, Marx and Engels spoke for the German Democrats. Marx explained to the Chartists that Poland could be liberated not in Poland but by the triumph of the working-class in the leading countries, especially in Britain, and appealed to the Chartists to help the Poles not by expressing pious hopes, but by conquering their own domestic enemies ; whilst Engels stated that no people could be free whilst oppressing others, and that by helping the Poles to emancipate themselves the Germans would remove a main link that bound their country to the forces of reaction.[11] As the two appeals were made to Britons and Germans respectively, and only the latter shared in the oppression of the Poles, the basic problem of the national issues in the socialist movement[12] did not arise ; however, a modern Communist, when addressing Marx's audience, would presumably have preferred to speak about the Irish question rather than to state generalities about an eventual socialist Britain and its impact on the Polish issue.

The key to these contradictions is the failure of Marx and Engels to appreciate a national question, such as the Polish, as an issue of domestic class-struggle in the country concerned, which would not have excluded subordination of the local interest under a broader international, for example the interest of Polish

[9] See below, pp. 307–8 and 343–4.   [10] *The Eastern Question*, p. 27.
[11] *M.E.G.A.*, vol. VI, pp. 359 ff.
[12] See below, pp. 337-8.

minorities in Germany and German minorities in Poland under the supposed need of establishing a common German-Polish front against the Holy Alliance of the partition powers. However, in order to be subordinated to another, an interest has to be clearly stated and appreciated. Clear realisation of the class-content of the rôle played by the Poles in relation to Lithuanians, Ukrainians, etc., at whose expense Marx and Engels sought for anti-Tsarist compromises, or of the Sudeten-Germans in relation to the Czechs, would have lead the myth of the " progressive nations "[13] *ad absurdum.* However simple the statement " the Poles have to be supported because they oppose Tsarism, the main stronghold of European reaction," it would have appeared much less obvious if elaborated in the only terms fitting the demands of Marxist sociology : " in order to overthrow semi-feudal Tsarism, which threatens European democracy because of its yet unbroken ability to exploit the Russian, Ukrainian, etc., peasants for its purposes, the Polish aristocrats have to be supported in their exploitation of Ukrainian peasants." Only very occasionally did Marx and Engels realise the contradiction implied in supporting a semi-feudal group for bourgeois-democratic reasons. In a meeting, on February 22, 1848, commemorating the anniversary of the Cracow insurrection Engels stated that that insurrection, which he (like most of contemporary democratic opinion) interpreted as a triumph of the modern democratic over the traditional aristocratic approach, had removed the doubts of German Democrats as to the attitude of a reborn Poland towards a democratic Germany.[14] However, as regards the Poles' domestic structure, Engels[6] continued to regard as an open question their ability to progress beyond a semi-feudal state, based upon serfdom of the agricultural population. Had his policies in national questions been based upon the nation's likelihood of promoting domestic democratic

[13] I am not speaking here of nations regarded as progressive because they have taken the initiative in a social transformation regarded as progressive, from the point of view of those sharing certain common beliefs, as did the Dutch and English in the late 16th century from the Protestant standpoint, the Americans and French in the late 18th Century from the bourgeois-democratic, the Russians in our days from the Communist point of view. Neither the Germans nor the Poles played such a part, from the bourgeois, or the socialist, democratic point of view, in the mid-nineteenth century ; their triumph, in their existing social structure, over Tsarist Russia would have changed little in East Central Europe's social structure, unless it resulted in an overthrow of Tsarism by internal forces, an event which would have refuted the basic assumptions that "the Russians" were "reactionary".

[14] *M.E.G.A.*, vol. VI, p. 417.

progress, observation like the above should have been sufficient to prevent a socialist from reproaching the Czechs for lacking an urban bourgeoisie and for the allegedly artificial origin of their national consciousness from the efforts of a group of intellectuals. But Engels went to the length of pouring wily scorn upon the All-Slav congress in Prague, June, 1848 (which was connected with an insurrection of the Prague workers well in advance of other parts of Austria, and by no means narrowly nationalist[15]) because it was encircled and eventually suppressed by " another Slav congress," namely, Windischgraetz's army composed as it was of illiterate Slav peasants. What would Engels have said in 1871 of a Socialist who belittled the importance of the Paris Commune because it was encircled, and eventually suppressed, by another agglomeration of Frenchmen, namely, the Versailles army? According to the fundamental principles of Marxism, the existence of opposite tendencies within a nation is a mere consequence of its being in historical motion, whilst the absence of such cleavages is a proof of the respective nation's backwardness, even if the resulting attitude should fit as well into progressive concepts of international politics as did the anti-Russian tradition of the Poles in 1848. To deny the Czechs' historical future because they had been subjugated by the Germans, and revolted against that subjection,[8] was, to say the least, an expression of narrow-minded concentration upon urban civilisation[16] and neglect of the possibility that a nation which still had no national middle-class may eventually, in the very course of its struggle for emancipation, create one.

Many years later[17] Engels, when discussing the question whether the Polish Socialists should support the struggle for national independence, correctly formulated the Marxist answer

---

[15] See my *Federalism*, etc., and the sources quoted there. A characteristic expression of Engels' distrust of the left-wing Slav movement, from the *Neue Rheinische Zeitung*, 1848, is quoted by Carr, op. cit., p. 226. Marx's mentioning that article, as a valuable document, in a letter to Engels of October 7, 1868 (*Correspondence*, vol. IV, p. 106), together with Engels' article quoted below, seems to prove the Marxists continued adherence to the scheme of " progressive nationalities " as late as in the later 'sixties, and seems to me to refute Ryazanoff's assumption (in Gruenberg's *Archiv.*, vol. VI) that some of the cruder expressions of that scheme may be Engels' individual work.

[16] See below, p. 334.

[17] In his letter to Kautsky of February 7, 1882.

to the argument, proclaimed by himself in 1848,[18] that the emancipation of a backward nation was irrelevant in view of the prospects of international economic and social progress : no people lacking national independence could seriously discuss any problems of social structure, and an international labour movement supposed the collaboration of independent nations. Every Polish peasant and worker who awakened from apathy to political consciousness faced the fact of national oppression as a primary obstacle, without the removal of which no further progress was possible (as Engels explained, this was quite independent of the question whether, actually, national independence would be achieved before, or only in consequence of, the socialist revolution). Polish Socialists who did not regard the achievement of national independence as the chief plank of their platform[19] appeared to Engels to be mistaken as would be German Social Democrats who failed to start from the demands for repeal of the anti-Socialist law, for freedom of the press, of meetings, etc. But the argument is again made in connection with the importance of the continued partition of Poland as the main link perpetuating the Holy Alliance,[20] and Engels again emphasized his lack of sympathy with " the small Slavonic peoples, and relics of peoples which are separated by the three wedges driven into Slavdom, the German, Magyar, and Turkish", because of the necessary connection of their national aspirations with reactionary Pan-Slavism. He obviously failed to realise that his argument as to the national aspirations of the Poles did provide the proper socialist policies necessary to prevent the struggles of the Austrian, Hungarian and Turkish Slavs for national emancipation from being associated with Tsarist reaction.

However, Engels had meanwhile realised that Tsarism might break down before the future of the peoples of the Hapsburg

[18] He had gone to the length of concluding, from the failure of the 1848 revolution amongst the Czechs (he appeared immunised by wishful thinking against the similar failure of the Germans) that "henceforth Bohemia could only exist as a portion of Germany, although part of its inhabitants might yet, for some centuries (*sic!*), continue to speak a non-German language."

[19] Which eventually was the attitude of the (left-wing) Polish Social Democrats, against which most of Lenin's writings on the issue of national self-determination were directed.

[20] Which was obviously regarded as embodied in Bismarck's repeated attempts at preserving the " Three Emperors' Alliance." Engels may have been right in this regard ; but, in that case, he contradicted himself when suggesting, after the break down of those attempts, that Socialists ought to side with one fragment of that "Holy Alliance " against the other, now allied with the French bourgeois republic. (See below, p. 312).

monarchy could be decided. His statement that until that breakdown, disruption of the Hapsburg monarchy should be avoided in the international progressive interest, was only a paraphase of what Palacky, one of the Czech pioneers whom he had derided in 1848, had meant at that time when stating that Austria, if it had not existed should have had to be invented, and another of those pioneers, Havlicek—with rather more freedom from national sentiments than Engels himself showed in Czecho-German issues—had explained when stating that as long as Russia was a despotic country, the Western Slavs must unfortunately shun their own brother as their greatest foe, though they might well long for union with a free Russia.[21] Though it might have been more tactful to leave this argument to Slavs, who could make it more impressively, Engels would have been within his rights if he had merely stated that the national aspirations of the Slavonic peoples, large and small, should be realised within a framework dominated by the need to defeat Tsarism and Pan-Slav plans for world-domination " which are our, and the Russians', greatest foe". But even after the anticipated downfall of Tsarism, the smaller Slavonic peoples, though they were to be granted the right to secede,[22] were expected in these circumstances to petition, after six months of independence, for re-admission into the Austrian or Hungarian fold ; and in no case should they be allowed to interpret their independence as a right to interfere with the extension of the European railway-system to Constantinople ! It is indeed difficult to discuss such statements except as an example of the narrow margin dividing self-assertion of and make belief in regards to the historical mission of one's own national Labour movement[23] on the one hand, from the defence of the allegedly civilising functions of one's own country's imperialist expansion on the other. The All-Slav congress in June, 1848, upon which Engels had poured such scorn, had been convened by the Czechs as an answer to the invitation to elect deputies, sent by the Frankfurt National Assembly to the Bohemians as alleged German citizens, and to the acceptance of the invitation by the Sudeten Germans : it was intended thus

[21] Comp. my *Federalism*, etc., pp. 160-1.
[22] Engels formulated : " not before we can allow them (to secede)," which makes interesting reading in connection with his remark, in a nearly contemporary letter (see above, p. 284), that progress should not be forced upon colonial peoples.
[23] For another, and in its consequences more important repetition of the same mistake, see below, p. 312.

to counterbalance the importance of the Sudeten-German participation in the Frankfurt Assembly by reducing it to an expression of sympathy with their fellow Germans, legitimate in itself, but answered by the expression of corresponding sympathies with their fellow Slavs by the other nation inhabiting Bohemia.[15] On the basic platform of the struggle for their own nation's right to autonomous development, the left-wingers amongst the members of the Prague Slavonic congress opposed their co-national right-wingers who had just negotiated with the Court a settlement on the basis of the preservation of the Hapsburg monarchy, and also Tsarism which was the oppressor of the largest of the Slav peoples as well as the main backer of Hapsburg and Central European reaction in general, . True, they were defeated at the barricades ; but so, too, were in the next year those few consistent democrats in the Frankfurt Assembly who, upon the basis of *their* nation's claim to independence and national unity, strove to prevent its eventual realisation under the lead of Prussian reaction. From the point of view of Marxism, either side would regard its temporary defeat as a harbinger of eventual triumph, and might, indeed, hope that their own nation might play a leading part in the emancipation of mankind. Engels could not know that, whilst he and his fellow German leftwingers were wrong in their expectations, the Slav left-wingers in Prague were justified ; indeed, he could not even grasp such a possiblity within the framework of his basic assumptions. But he was not entitled to play the fortune-teller, and to turn his expectations as to his own nation's eventual achievements into a weapon against the recognition of other nations' claim to exist[18] and to play *their* part in the common struggle. His statement that an international labour movement supposed the collaboration of independent nations seems to have been conditioned by a rider saying " of such nations as actually fit into a pattern of international policies based upon the part actually played by the existing regimes in the various great Powers." In an article in *The Commonwealth*, of March 31, 1866,[24] Engels, in connection with the Polish question, went to the length of making a fundamental distinction between " the right of the great national sub-divisions of Europe to political independence," which was the accepted standard of democracy, and " the nationalities principle proper," namely,

[24] Reproduced by Ryazanoff in Gruenberg's *Archiv.*, vol VI, 1918.

the emancipation of what in Austria would be called the " non-historical nationalities." The latter principle was described as an invention of Tsarist propagandists applied in order to deny the Poles their right to territories inhabited by nationalities such as Byelorussians, Ukrainians and Lithuanians.

Such an approach to the national emancipation of peoples who temporarily could be misused by international reaction clearly contradicted the basic attitude of Dialectics. To quote Stalin[25] " all things have their negative and positive sides, a past and a future . . . and the struggle between that which is dying away and that which is born . . .constitutes the internal content of the process of development . . . Hence we must not base our orientation on the strata of society which are not further developing, even though they at present constitute the predominant force, but on those strata which are developing and have a future before them, even though at present they do not constitute the predominant force."

(b) THE MARXISTS AND THE WARS OF THE NINETEENTH CENTURY

In the issues just discussed Engels behaved as if Marx's and his own work on fundamental issues had never existed : but he got away with his mistake fairly lightly because, when working like any ordinary Liberal within a framework based upon distinction between " progressive " and " reactionary " Great Powers, his framework was obvious to all progressive thinkers of the day. Ten years after the defeat of the 1848 revolution, in a world dominated by counter-revolutionary forces, a new international tension arose from the contest for hegemony in North Italy fought out between bonapartist France and the absolutist Hapsburg monarchy which had been restored in immediate and avowed connection with Napoleon III's successful coup d'etat. On the face of it, there was little to choose between them ; and one of the immediate results of Napoleon III's success was the unification of Italy, which implied the emancipation of a recognized " historical nation " still subject to division and foreign oppression. But the conflict had its international implications, especially as to the internal situation of Germany ; and Marx and Engels were German democrats. The advocates of the Greater Prussian solution of the German question, amongst

[25] Op cit. (1940), pp. 595–6.

them (as could hardly be questioned since 1848) the bulk of the German *bourgeoisie*, were in sympathy with Napoleon III from whose success they expected a weakening of their main competitor for German hegemony. Such expectations were also shared by the Tsar because of his reliance upon Prussia functioning as his agency to punish Austria for her failure to support Russia during the Crimean war. Within Prussia herself, where for reasons of national sentiment active siding with France against Austria was out of question, the supporters of the Greater Prussian solution of the German problem, Bismarck and Lassalle amongst them, were in favour of neutrality, whilst circles more impressed by conservative solidarity with the legitimate Hapsburg or by anti-French sentiment favoured support of Austria, at least in the event of French successes that would threaten Austrian territories that belonged to the German League (as the Italian provinces in question did not). German left-wingers, Marx and Engels amongst them, viewed the issue from the point of view of the European framework in which German democracy was eventually to arise ; they regarded the defeat of Napoleon III (the oppressor of the revolutionary forces in what was regarded as the politically most advanced of the European countries) and the weakening of the position of Tsarist Russia as more important than a temporary setback for the potentially revolutionary Italian nationalist movement, in a war against the Hapsburg monarchy whose internal coherence was not estimated by anyone as considerable enough to survive a major war in its present structure. Therefore they were in favour of German support for Austria, even in an apparently non-German issue. A decisive part in deciding the Marxists' attitude[26] was played by the expectation, frequent in left-wing circles, that external war, fought against foes superior to the existing regime, would bring the revolutionary party to the foreground. In this case at least, their estimate of the implications of a major war seems to have been right : very incomplete defeat in a war concluded after the first indecisive battles was sufficient to break the ice of Austrian absolutism, and in Prussia,

---

[26] Comp. especially Engels' letter to Lassalle of May 18, 1859 (vol. III, pp. 184–5, in G. Mayer's ed. of Lassalle's correspondence). In this point there was no difference in basic attitude to the functions of War : Lassalle's argument, expressed in a letter originating at the same time (Ibid., p. 174, and again, p. 219) is based on the assumption (based upon an overstatement of the importance of the pro-Austrian faction within Prussia) that war would come in any case, but that it would not have revolutionary implications unless denounced by the revolutionaries to the peoples. Comp. also Marx-Engels' *Correspondence*, vol. II, p. 401.

even without war, during the years which followed the liberal opposition grew into a serious constitutional conflict. The Marxists were not the only people to realise the situation, and the conflagration hoped for was avoided by Austrians making peace before any threat to territories " essential for Germany's security" arose. So the situation grew to the very point where there was a distinct cleavage amongst German left-wingers whilst no obvious facts convinced either side that they had been mistaken.

In the dispute Marx showed an ability to assess the background and behaviour of personalities much superior to what is generally conceded to him. Of the people who took the opposite line, he described Mr. Vogt, one of the leaders of the South-German type of lower-middle-class democracy in 1848, who according to all his *antecedents* should have been a fanatic anti-Prussian, as a person corrupted by Napoleon III. Eventually, when the French revolution of 1870 opened the archives of Napoleon's secret service, Marx was proved to have been right. Against Lassalle, who had been taught in the Hegelian school to regard the Prussian state as the realisation of pure reason, Engels's polemic was in veiled and friendly terms, as a friend correcting a friend's mistakes. However, the dispute contributed its part to Marx's and Engels' later description of Lassalle as a traitor to the Labour movement, collaborating with Prussian reaction, in which case again they proved right.[27] The whole incident seems to prove the enormous importance attributed by the founders of Marxism to international issues as a test for the sincerity of revolutionary convictions. In backward countries needing the most elementary democratic reforms that test, indeed, could hardly be equalled by mere comparison between the demands for domestic reforms which were commonplaces amongst allegedly democratic politicians, nor between problematic tactics advocated in difficult situations.

In the Franco-Prussian war of 1870, again two reactionary regimes[28] opposed each other ; and again the success of one of them formally implied the reunion of one of the historical nations which was over-ripe, and likely to arise whatever the outcome of the next decision on the battle-fields. Had Marx and Engels thought that revolution in their own country was likely, they would have behaved like their friends, Liebknecht and Bebel, who, anxious for Prussia's defeat from the very start, opposed the war.[29] However, the chances of revolution in France, in the case of her defeat, were higher, and had been impressed upon Marx and Engels by their work in the International. Within a few weeks a French revolution happened. From that moment, there could be no further dispute amongst left-wingers[30] about France's fighting a progressive as well as defensive war against a reactionary regime which built its internal domination upon external conquest. The French left-wingers themselves during the first stage of the war[31] had taken an attitude which was formally identical with that of Marx (defeat of Napoleon III), though it was in fact identical with that of Bebel and Liebknecht (defeat of the oppressor of their own nation in order to grasp an opportunity for revolution).

In the *Manifesto of the International* issued at the beginning of the Franco-Prussian war, Marx and Engels had stated that " if the German working-class allow the present war to lose its strictly defensive character and to degenerate into a war against the French people, victory or defeat will prove alike disastrous."[32] The expected happened, and the historian's task is to discuss whether a war led by Bismarck could have been a defensive war at all, and whether a statement of its conceivably defensive character in a political manifesto was a suitable means of strengthening those who attempted to prevent it from becoming simple robbery, forcing upon the German people internal reaction by external conquest. If put in this way, both questions are easily answered even from a purely bourgeois-democratic point of view. The interests of the French and German labour movements were happily co-ordinated by an attitude that supported the former's demand for internal revolution as well as the latter's need not to

[29] It should be noted that, quite distinct from the bitterness with which they pursued the cleavages of 1859, Marx and Engels never questioned the purely tactical character of those disagreements and did not allow them to grow into a quarrel with their German friends, as opposed to the Lassalleans, who, for nationalist reasons well realised by Marx and Engels, were formally near to the latter's position. Mehring in his *History of German Social Democracy* has failed to realise that basic background of the issue.

[30] Even the Lassallean group, with its distinctly pro-Prussian bias, opposed the second stage of the war and the annexation of Alsace-Lorraine.

[31] During the second support of the defence of the revolutionary fatherland against the Prussian invaders was an obvious task.

[32] *The Civil War in France* (Annex) ed. cit., p. 69.

stand aside in the actual formation of the German national state, whilst opposition to specifically Bismarckian policies was amply testified by the Marxist policies during the second stage of the war. But an attitude that described the German bourgeois national state, whatsoever the methods which brought it into existence, as an achievement, was bound to lead to pitfalls as soon as that state collided with other states, bourgeois like itself (for, at the end of the 19th century, there were no more non-bourgeois states in Europe), though of different political tradition and structure. And Engels himself lived long enough to fall a victim to that pitfall, in spite of all that Marx and he himself had written about the danger implied in a schematic approach when the conditions on which the abstraction was based had changed.

In 1891, when the danger of a war between the Franco-Russian alliance and the Triple alliances became obvious, Engels [33] discussed the attitude of German Social Democracy towards such a war, the alignment in which was fundamentally identical with that actually realised in 1914 (when that article of his, not unnaturally, was amply quoted). He regarded even bourgeois France as progressive in comparison with the German Empire which remained semi-feudal, though dominated by the economics of the *bourgeoisie* ; but the position would be inverted once France should act as the tool of Tsarism, the backbone of European reaction. In that case, Germany would fight for her very national existence including also the existence of German Social Democracy and its opportunity to play its outstanding part within the international Labour movement. [34] In the case of a German victory annexations were inconceivable, for they would simply result in a further increase of the weight of the non-German Provinces which already burdened Bismarck's Empire ; but defeat might imply dismemberment. Accordingly, German Social Democracy would defend the fatherland against Russia and her allies, including France.

[33] In an article " Socialism in Germany," first written for a French Workers' Calendar, and reprinted in *Neue Zeit*, vol. X (1891).

[34] As against the misuse of Engels' already quoted attitude by the Social patriot leaders in 1914, it should be emphasized that in his article, amongst the tasks of German Social Democracy, the granting of self-determination to Alsace-Lorraine and to Northern Schlesvig, and restitution of Poland, for the betrayal of which the French bourgeoisie is reproached, are enumerated ; this even forms his basic argument against French and Alsatian patriots in order to convince them that they should not put their hopes in a war but wait till the assumption of power in Germany by Social Democracy (which Engels—op. cit., p. 584—expected within some 10 years) would easily solve all problems.

Attempts have been made to reconcile this point of view of Engels with later Bolshevist theory by asserting that it fitted the conditions of the pre-imperialist stage of capitalism when it originated. But such an argument confuses imperialism, as the highest stage of capitalist economic development (monopoly capitalism with a compulsion to export capitals) with imperialism as an aggressive foreign policy directed toward the conquest of empires. In the Leninist theory the two concepts are linked by the assertion that imperialism in the former sense necessarily implies imperialism also in the latter ; but in his *Critique of the Junius Pamphlet* (1916) Lenin himelf has recognised the occurrence of imperialist wars (in the latter sense) in pre-imperialist societies, especially in the pre-monopoly stage of capitalism.   It should be obvious to Marxists that a war fought in the 'nineties between Triple Alliance and Franco-Russian bloc would have been such a war on both sides.   The only debatable question is which would have been the best way for that war to have turned out from the point of view of the Labour movement.   The attitude taken by Engels is compatible with working-class internationalism if it is assumed that a German victory in such a war would create comparably favourable conditions for (a) a triumph of the impending bourgeois-democratic revolution in Russia, and (b) maximum development of the German Labour movement which would more than compensate for the thus reduced opportunities of the French Labour movement.   The first assumption was sensible, and was confirmed by the record of 1861,[35] 1905 and 1917. But the second supposed a very low estimate of Germany's military chances in such a war ; Engels actually expected it to result in a threat to her national independence and an opportunity for the German Socialists to save the fatherland by Jacobin methods.[36]   But if that assumption is to be dropped, Engels' tactics can only be defended on the basis of a conception of the socialist revolution as an automatic result of the strengthening of sectional organisations of Labour within a prosperous capitalist system,[37] so that the country with the strongest organisation of Labour, whatever its actual regime, thereby deserved victory in war.   Clearly, the last-mentioned concept contradicted not only the basic conceptions of revolu-

---

[35] When the mass movements leading to the emancipation of the Russian serfs resulted from defeat in such a minor war as the Crimean.

[36] See above, p. 299, and below, p. 320.

[37] See above, pp. 226–8.

tionary socialism as conceived by all left-wingers during World War I, but also assumption (a) : the Hohenzollern-regime, if strengthened—however temporarily—by external victory, would not have failed to intervene against an anti-Tsarist Russian revolution, and might easily have been successful. Thus it appears that since 1871 the original Marxist (that is, radical-democratic) approach to wars between major capitalist countries had outlived itself. All those countries—or, at least, either of the coalitions formed by them—contained certain elements of bourgeois-democratic progress (otherwise they could not aspire to Great Power status in the 20th century) : France and Britain had gone farthest in realising bourgeois-democratic political regimes ; Germany had the strongest Labour movement (and the most advanced social legislation) and fought Tsarist Russia ; the latter on her part supported the revolt of the smaller Slavonic nations against the Austrian empire which, itself, apart from fighting Tsarist Russia and being certainly progressive in comparison with her, had the merit of not being Prussia and of granting, for example, the Poles more comfortable conditions than they enjoyed in either Prussia or Russia. On the assumption that the working-classes had to decide their attitude to wars from the point of view of the bourgeois-democratic achievements defended by either side, the facts enumerated above (the number of which could easily be increased) provided as many arguments—or pretexts—for the identification of every national sectional movement with the defence of its own country.

(c) Lenin's conception of international relations during the imperialist period

The Marxist (or rather pre-Marxist) interest in wars as potential levers of revolution found still expression during the Russo-Japanese war of 1904, when nearly all Russian progressives desired the defeat of Tsarism as an opportunity for revolution, while amongst Western progressives there were strong sympathies with Japan, whose imperialist character (according to any standard) was hardly questioned. As long as a Russian revolution was generally considered as mainly anti-Tsarist, it might be popular with people influenced by the Anglo-Japanese alliance,

which was by no means inspired by left ideas. But in the general
attitude of the Second International, the Marxist concept of
revolutionary wars quite naturally receded into the background.
It was realised that the triumph of neither coalition in World
War I, the outlines of which had been growing clearly during
the preceding decade, could be regarded as promoting progress,
and the mass-parties of Labour tended simply to express the
common man's abhorrence of war in any form (at least before
he was exposed to the propaganda-machinery of a state at war).
The desire to give such feelings an expression more radical
and realistic than those available in bourgeois pacifism resulted
in the acceptance, by the Basle Congress (1912) of the International, of a Manifesto drafted by a sub-committee dominated
by the minds of Lenin and Rosa Luxemburg (Lenin being
supported by a majority of the Russian party, but Rosa Luxemburg heading a mere minority group within German Social
Democracy). Having their opportunity to formulate the document, the left-wingers did not fail to proclaim the principles of
revolutionary socialism with the maximum clarity for which the
approval of non-revolutionary Socialists—or, to use Lenin's
later expression, lower-middle-class pacifists—could be won.
World War I, the eventual constellation of which corresponded
exactly to that which the Basle Congress had anticipated, was
described not only as a crime, committed in the interest " of
capitalist profits, dynastic ambitions, and in honouring secret
diplomatic conventions," but also as a political and economic
crisis which should be used by the Socialists in order " to arouse
the people and to remove capitalist class-rule " ; and governments
were warned of the revolutionary dangers threatening them in
going to war. Lenin had no difficulty in proving, in 1914,
that such principles had been betrayed by those who had paid
lip-service to them in order to register their protest against the
war in the strongest conceivable forms. Their actual mood was
probably better expressed by the white-gowned girls who,
carrying a banner with the inscription " Down with the Arms,"
preceded the procession of the Basle Congress to the Cathedral,
offered as a meeting-place by honestly pacifist Churchmen.
Lenin, 1914, found no difficulties in proving that Social pacifism,
that is, abhorrence of war in general, including civil war, was
bound to result in support of Social patriotism, that is, support
of one's own government once war had broken out. To minds

afraid of the difficulties of revolution, there seemed to be no alternative except the choice between victory of one's own country, to be used in an enlightened sense according to the Social Pacifists' own ideology, and conquest by the external foe.

In opposition to this trend, Lenin developed his concept of imperialism. As explained in the Preface to his book, his theory is based upon Hobson's explanation of imperialism by export of capitals and Hilferding's analysis of monopoly capitalism, *Finance Capital*. Of the former, Lenin dropped Hobson's alternative of a non-expansionist capitalism, and of the later Hilferding's concept of a possible overcoming of the anarchy of capitalist production by monopoly-capitalist planning. Kautsky's concept of an " Ultra-Imperialism," that is, of the world-wide organisation of capitalist production by agreement between the capitalist monopolies, was answered by Lenin's statement of a general law of uneven development of capitalism, which would render any inter-imperialist agreement ephemeral and a mere prelude to new conflicts for the redistribution of the world.[38] The argument fails to answer the possibility of world-wide capitalist organisation in consequence of conquest at least of the capitalist world by the strongest of the monopolist giants ; and Lenin was careful enough to recognise the existence of a general tendency working in that direction and to direct his criticism of the concept of Ultra-Imperialism against its being regarded as relevant to the conditions of early 20th Century Imperialism. It was axiomatic amongst Lenin's Socialist contemporaries that world-wide capitalist organisation is impossible without a preceding chain of imperialist world-wars which created opportunities for socialist revolutions at least in some countries. Therefore acceptance of the concept of Ultra-Imperialism, Western Union, The United States of Europe, etc., is a betrayal of Socialist principles, especially in our days when its realisation presupposes destruction of a socialist system already in existence. Lenin's world of a plurality of imperialist giants fighting each other as well as the socialist systems which emerge from the breakdown of the weakest links of the imperialist chain[39] *is* the ultimate stage of capitalism in which the decisive battles for its

[38] *On the United States of Europe*, in *Sel. Works*, vol. V, p. 147.

[39] This formulation was first used by Stalin, in 1924 (op. cit., 1940, pp. 20–1), but it seems sufficiently backed already by Lenin's article, *Better fewer but better*, *Sel. Works*, vol. IX, pp. 398–9.

overthrow have to be fought out.[39a] There is no place for econo-mic " automatisms " producing the new society ; but if this is taken for granted, the analysis can produce no more than chances for successful revolution in some countries plus some general argu-ments as to the chances of the countries thus transformed to with-stand all attempts at intervention and to exercise a decisive impact upon the further developments in other countries.

In this strict formulation the concept was hardly palatable for a mass-movement which, apart from carrying on the traditional Marxist expectations of a breakdown in internal economic crises because of the anarchy of capitalist production, had a sensible abhorrence to conceiving its immediate chances of triumph as restricted to the consequences of such a horrible event as inter-national war, prevention of which formed its main *raison d'être*. Schemes of monopoly-capitalist organisation on a national scale as a more efficient means of fighting other national trusts on the international stage were derived from the regulation of capitalist economics on a war-time basis, the actual importance of which was exaggerated by Bukharin.[40] Or else they resulted from attempts of Communist authors to uphold the revolutionary prospect at a time when they failed to realise the approach of the Great Depression[41], however these schemes were generally rejected as heterodox and the characteristic of capitalism as anarchic on the national as well as on the international stage was strictly upheld. Nevertheless, these schemes appear much more sensible if interpreted merely to mean " even if some national capitalism should succeed in monopolist organisation on a national scale, the inherent contradictions of capitalist socidety would find new and sharper expressions on the international stage." There is nothing un-Marxist in conceiving internal contradictions of capitalism as ultimately realised on the international stage, and the importance of the Leninist theory of imperialism should be sought in that it closes the gap left in classical Marxist theory

[39a] In the last Soviet discussions on E. Varga's book on War-economics, the argu-ment has been re-stated by denying the possibility of a specific " State-capitalist " stage in the development of capitalism distinct from ordinary monopoly-capitalism (imperialism).

[40] *Imperialism and World Economics*, written in 1915, pp. 119-20, of the English edition. It should be noted that Lenin's Preface to the book, in spite of his well-developed tendency to take up individual arguments of Bukharin, contains no polemique against the statement discussed.

[41] Bukharin's articles of May, 1929, critically discussed in the note on pp. 395 ff of vol. V of Lenin's *Sel. Works*, see also R. Gerber, *Krisen und Krege*, in *Die Internationale*, July, 1928, in German.

by the extreme abstractness of its concept of the conditions for the final overthrow of capitalism.[42]

So once again we get a comprehensive picture of international relations differing from, but no less impressive than, the original Marxist—or pre-Marxist—scheme.[43] In our days, it is shared not only by Marxists, but even by their most bitter opponents.[44] On the one side we find the world of imperialism, dominated by giants whose numbers diminish as their method of competition, imperialist war, eliminates or subordinates the weakest of them. They are supported by all the vested interests even in countries subject to colonial exploitation, and also by what orthodox Leninists would call " the corrupted upper strata of the labour aristocracy," but what, in a more sober analysis, might be described as the necessary attitude of an essentially sectional movement of labour before the overwhelming force of circumstances turns at least parts of it into new, revolutionary channels. On the other side stand the revolutionary workers of all countries, headed by those countries where they have succeeded in establishing the new social order, and supported by all the oppressed peoples and especially the colonial peoples, whose emancipation, even if at first limited to a bourgeois-democratic revolution against the imperialists and the local feudal-lords supporting them, would undermine the economic basis of imperialism. Near the end of his life, when conditions of encircled Soviet Russia seemed difficult, Lenin went to the length of describing ultimate triumph as assured because Russians, Chinese and Indians, taken together, formed the overwhelming majority of mankind.[45] As early as in his criticism of Rosa Luxemburg's Junius-pamphlet, written in 1916, some scepticism as to the chances of a proletarian revolution in a prosperous imperialist country seemed to be implied in his remark that a formerly imperialist country, completely destroyed in preceding imperialist wars, might become the potential subject of a struggle for national emancipation.

Such remarks seem to indicate a conception of the ultimate historical decision as an upheaval of oppressed against oppressing nations. But this is not the only perspective envisaged by Lenin,

[42] See above, p. 180.   [43] See above, p. 300.
[44] Comp. the frequent statements of expectation that defeat of the U.S.S.R. would remove the threat of the colonial emancipation movements.
[45] *Better fewer, but better, Sel. Works*, vol. IX. p. 400.

and does not even comprehend the whole sphere allowed in his thought to the bourgeois-democratic element in socialist revolutions. There is nothing un-Leninist in the emphasis recently laid upon the bourgeois-democratic elements in revolutions against fascist systems even in distinctly monopoly-capitalist countries,[46] in view of the increasing association between monopoly-capitalism and more ancient forms of reaction, and of the obvious need of the Labour movement for a certain amount of civic freedom as a condition of rallying before it can turn into revolutionary channels. But application of this principle to fascism in general, including its possible extension to countries without feudal elements comparable with those existing in pre-1933 Prussia and Japan, would contradict the basic assumption of Leninism that imperialism is the ultimate stage of capitalism the only progressive way out of which is socialist transformation of society. On the other hand, no fundamental tenet of Leninism implies the need permanently to describe the relations existing between the socialist and the capitalist sector of the world in the terms[47] applied by Lenin when he first introduced the concept of socialist reconstruction in one or a few countries into an ideological setting still dominated by the desire for world-revolution. There is no need to belittle the chances of partial compromise and peaceful transition which may appear when the more progressive system can increase its relative strength against its potential opponents, its power of attraction towards its neighbours, and its ideological impact upon those forces within those countries which see alternatives to a desperate final struggle.

(d) Is the Leninist concept applicable to present international conditions?

Lenin's concept of international relations is impressive as a general abstraction which serves to establish general trends, as distinct from the assessment of the prevalence of the one or the other of the recognised trends in individual diplomatic situations (e.g., forecasts as to whether Mr. Chamberlain would succeed in continuing the policy of appeasement until after the inevitable German-Soviet conflict). Of much less

---

[46] Cf. G. Kozlov, *The German Robber Imperialism*, Moscow, 1944 (in Russian).

[47] Above, p. 297.

permanent importance than his general concept were the conclusions drawn by Lenin as to the principles that should govern the strategy of the revolutionary Labour movement in fighting imperialist wars. Of the three basic principles recognised by early Marxism,[48] the third, use of the war by the revolutionaries as an opportunity to take power in their capacity as the most consistent defenders of the national interest, was clearly inapplicable to a situation in which both warring parties were regarded as equally reactionary and in which resistance against imperialist war was seen as the basic task of the Labour movement. Such an attitude follows necessarily from the consideration that in a war between major powers no side could claim to represent bourgeois-democratic progress against the other any longer,[49] whilst the time when one Great Power should represent socialist progress against the others had not then arisen. But, clearly, with the description of either side's war effort as progressive action, in the course of which the most consistent of the progressive parties could obtain leadership, the main basis of the concrete Marxist policies in the wars of the 19th Century had gone.

Lenin closed the gap by applying, on an international scale, the concept of defeatism which was familiar to Russian revolutionaries. But, by its transfer to the international stage, the concept of defeatism changed its actual content. It had been sensible for Russian revolutionaries to hope for the defeat of Tsarist Russia, that is, for the victory of Britain, of Japan, or of whoever happened to fight her, with the prospect of taking power in consequence of that defeat and, at the worst, if the war should not end, subsequently to fight a revolutionary war for the independence of Russia under a transformed regime. But the basic assumptions of wholesale denunciation of imperialism and of international solidarity between the working-classes

---

[48] See above, p. 299.

[49] In his *Critique of the Junius pamphlet*, Lenin stated that reactionary wars, however characteristic of modern imperialism, were not the only ones to occur in the imperialist age. Even in the war of 1914-8, which was essentially a war between coalitions of imperialist powers, he did not claim that the war was equally reactionary from the point of view of each of the participant countries ; on the contrary, he deemed (*Sel. Works*, vol. V, pp. 196-7) that a Serbo-Austrian war, if taken in isolation, would have been a progressive war of national liberation, and the Belgo-German war, if taken in isolation, a legitimate war of national defence. But he demanded the subordination of such particularities to the basic character of the war which was bound to dominate the policies even of those members of the respective coalition who, if isolated, might have pursued other than imperialist policies.

of the belligerent nations would have been destroyed if Russian or French workers had regarded the triumph of imperial Germany as a legitimate implication of their revolutionary defeatism, or *vice versa*.

So the whole argument for defeatism as a socialist attitude valid for all the imperialist countries, depends on the existence of a third alternative, namely, of the possibility of the imperialist war being turned into civil war—national and international—between the forces of socialism and those of imperialism. This supposed a concept of imperialist war as a political and economic crisis of capitalism, implying opportunities of its overthrow. Such a concept had been evolved, 1909, in Kautsky's *Way to Power*,[50] which for that reason had evoked Lenin's sympathies ; and it had been accepted in the Manifesto of the Basle Congress. Supposing there were opportunities for the overthrow of capitalism in consequence of a war, then collaboration between national Labour movements aiming at the overthrow of their national bourgeoisie, and therefore prepared to regard its defeat as a suitable occasion for the revolution could proceed by the mere power of *example*, without any fantastic assumptions as to the possibility of well-timed action by an international conspiracy. It was fitting that the Labour movement of that country whose victory would be most undesirable according to recognised socialist standards, should take the lead in international defeatism.[51]

Lenin did not regard the correctness of the defeatist approach to imperialist war as dependent on the chances of actual and immediate realisation of the revolutionary alternative ; in reading his works dating from the first period of the war it is difficult to overlook the depressing impact which the moral bankruptcy of the Second International had made upon him as upon all other honest internationalists. When restating the presence of a revolutionary crisis produced by the War, he clearly stated that

[50] Ed. cit., pp. 102 ff, where also the connection between the political mass-strikes in Russia and the colonial revolts, which were bound to increase the internal contradictions of capitalism, and may result in collision between imperialists, is emphasized. In 1915, when the war analysed in 1909 was in actual progress, Kautsky retreated from his former analysis ; the main tenet of his *Internationalism and War* is the denial of the third, revolutionary, alternative and the assertion that the standard from which the national Socialist parties had to start was the decision whether they regarded the victory of their own governments, or of its external foes, as preferable.

[51] *On the Defeat of the own Bourgeoisie*, in *Sel. Works*, vol. V.

not every revolutionary crisis was bound to result in revolution, and that no Socialist could give a guarantee that World War I would result in socialist revolution. This question of fact was not decisive for him : provided, that in all countries serious efforts were made by socialist revolutionaries who were not afraid of being reproached for possibly strengthening the opponents of their own country by the unavoidable effects of their propaganda, and would proudly proclaim their preparedness to use external defeat as an opportunity for socialist revolution, such efforts would bear fruits, either in this, or in inevitable future revolutionary crises. In none of Lenin's writings during the War was defeatism interpreted in a more extensive sense : collaboration with an external enemy would contradict the Leninist concept of internationalism because it would counteract the attempt of the Socialists on the other side to defeat *their* imperialist government, and would give an efficient propaganda weapon to the latter, which would claim that its progressive character was recognised even by reasonable members of the enemy nation. The possibility of collaboration with a socialist enemy power had not then arisen. Defeatism, as explained by Lenin[52] is a mere ideological caution against the risk that Socialists might refrain from taking some steps desirable from the point of view of domestic revolutionary propaganda (such as Lenin's own return to Russia with a permit of the German General Staff) because they were afraid that such steps might be misrepresented as furthering the enemy's purposes. Revolution, even if purchased at the price of external defeat, was the only means to save the nation ; and at the same time when Lenin was elaborating the concepts of defeatist tactics he paid homage to his own nation's traditions in the famous article *On the National Pride of the Great Russians*. So far, Lenin's argument is faultless ; but it has become obsolete by its successful application in one major country.

The whole concept of international defeatism, as developed, presupposes that a war is equally reactionary from the point of view at least of both coalitions participating in it[49] ; but

[52] Only as regards Russia herself, Lenin, continuing the traditional line of democratic and Marxist argument, considered defeat as such as desirable (*Sel. Works*, vol. V, pp. 136 and 144) ; in his general argument he even conceded that *if* international co-operation in the broad sense *were* impossible, the Opportunists were right in many regards. In 1915-6 Lenin attacked the Tsarist clique for collaboration with Germany, and would have reproached any German Socialists collaborating with the Western Allies as being mere bourgeois democrats.

once we assume that socialism is to be realised in a historical process in which it is represented by one or more Great Powers opposed by others standing for other social systems, the progress of socialism is dependent upon the socialist powers' successfully playing the game described as power-politics. There was nothing astonishing in the attempt of the U.S.S.R., made during the first stage of World War II, to preserve neutrality whilst her own defence was prepared, while the imperialist conflict intensified beyond the point where a separate peace at her expense was likely and while facts would convince her own population that war was forced upon her by an obvious aggressor. But according to Marxist—and any realist—conceptions of international relations, this cannot impair the fundamental fact that every World Power is bound to be involved in every world war. Minor wars are hardly conceivable except as skirmishes between the minor satellites of the main power groups, the character of which would dominate the local outbreak, or, alternatively, as colonial and other wars for national liberation[49] a positive attitude to which is a *priori* implied in the socialist—and generally, in the democratic—outlook. It follows that, from the point of view of the basic Leninist interpretation of our age, the supposition of the Leninist policies during World War I, which described both belligerent sides as equally reactionary, can no longer correspond to social facts. Therefore, the defeatist attitude is inapplicable to one of them, whilst in the opposite camp it is bound to turn into active support of the " enemy " representing the progressive cause, or at least its socialist component. Whether Hitlerite Germany was to be interpreted as one of those possible setbacks in historical development that may put a bourgeois-democratic revolution back on the order of the day,[53] or simply as that of the imperialist powers whose internal regime was the most reactionary because she was most immediately bound to an attack against the U.S.S.R., the tactics applied by most of the Western Communist parties during the first stage of World War II resulted in that failure which is bound to crown the application of sacred formulas to a situation which no longer fits the basic assumptions to which they owe their origin. The injured spirit of History (or,

[53] An interpretation which certainly furthered the attempts of the U.S.S.R. to rally a broad " democratic front," but had solid foundations in the evident inability of a working-class deprived of any tradition of independent organisation and action immediately to proceed to the construction of a new social order based upon its initiative.

if the term is preferred, of Dialectics) was avenged by the fact that that last outbreak of orthodoxy, which had certainly fitted the interests of the U.S.S.R. during her neutrality, was followed by a situation where dissolution of the Comintern proved a helpful expedient in inter-allied relations.

Thus the formal structure of the Marxist approach to wars is returning to the classical Marxist—or rather pre-Marxist— pattern. The " revolutionary Babel," periodically arising (and vanishing) with the ups and downs of French policies, is replaced by the U.S.S.R., which because of its very stability is much less suitable a subject of revolutionary idealisations, whilst monopoly capitalism of the U.S.A. evidently pretends to the honours of the position of the late Tsar and his forebears (which does not imply the inevitability of actual war any more than did the war envisaged between the Western bourgeois democracies and Tsarist Russia). The first concept somehow worked from 1830 up to 1905, and there is no inherent reason why its modernised form should become obsolete any sooner. The third of the basic Marxist concepts,[48] preserved by Lenin merely in a secondary place,[49] is returned to the foreground because of the likelihood that working-class parties prepared to face the ultimate consequences of resistance in times of total war may prove the most efficient defenders of national independence not only in colonial countries rising against imperialism but even in well-developed capitalist countries allied with the U.S.S.R. ; even World War II has supplied more examples of approximations to the realisation of the Jacobin pattern of assumption of power by a revolutionary party acting as the defender of national independence, than were available before. True, in view of the horrors of modern total war no mass-movement of workers and peasants, certainly none that is based upon a country with a peasant majority, will forfeit the moral advantages of being on the defensive as recklessly as did the radical intellectuals competing with the national bourgeoisie.

The future fate of the concept is a matter of speculation on the future of international relations. If World War III, in the constellation envisaged, should become a horrible reality, the Marxist concept would have to stand its supreme test, though, a stalemate being the most likely outcome of such a war, repetitions of that test should not be excluded. If a catastrophe on that scale could be avoided, or if under its impact the socio-economic systems of the countries opposing the U.S.S.R. should be gradually assimilated to the needs of a new epoch so that the remaining differences would be of national tradition rather than of different stages of socio-economic development, complete integration would take place in both of the opposing systems. In such an event, the concept of international class-fronts cutting across the national power-groups would lose any objective meaning and appeal, though it might linger on for some centuries as part of the State ideology of both of the empires opposing each other, as did religious ideologies in a more backward stage of historical development.[54] But if the period of socialist transformations should be succeeded comparatively rapidly by a new wave of revolutions aiming at a further step in socio-economic development, as was the case with the bourgeois-democratic revolutionary period, the Marxist concept of international relations might experience a second revival, which would prove again that it is a mere implication of the revolutionary way of social transformation.

[54] See my *Federalism*, etc., p. 524.

CHAPTER XV

THE PEASANTS' AND THE NATIONALITIES' QUESTION

(a) THE IMPORTANCE OF THE AGRARIAN PROBLEM FOR MARXISM

Of the four fundamental abstractions of the Marxist scheme,[1] up to this point of our investigation we have eliminated the first and second : the assumption of a completely capitalist system of world economics and world politics, and the unrestricted interdependence of the national markets for commodities and capitals. Thus we proceeded from the original Marxist scheme of a socialist revolution starting in the most developed of the capitalist countries to another corresponding more to actual historical conditions. The other two abstractions: the equal impact of capitalism on the conditions of the working-classes of all nations and the complete assimmilation of the urban and rural lower-middle-classes to the predominant capitalist pattern, had to be touched on only occasionally, in order to get a realistic estimate of the popular support which the capitalists of the leading countries may reasonably expect in external crises. We now turn to the modifications which the pattern of socialist transformation, in those countries where it becomes topical, is likely to suffer in consequence of the dropping of the two last-mentioned abstractions.

The urban lower-middle-classes present no special problem of social reconstruction different from that produced by the presence of small capitalist entrepreneurs. A socialist transformation presupposes the predominance of large-scale capitalist enterprises and monopolies in industry, commerce and banking ; and thus nationalisation of the large-scale enterprises implies national control of those branches of economic life even though concessions may be made to ensure smooth transition and to avoid strengthening the front of reaction unnecessarily. But in agriculture recognition of peasant husbandry as a predominant and comparatively stable trait of pre-revolutionary society

[1] See above, pp. 285 ff.

implies far-going changes in the concept of revolution as well as in that of post-revolutionary society. As the peasantry is the main source of the labour force needed for an expanding industry, such recognition may also provide the key for the understanding of the great inequalities in the general development of various nations, and especially of the national differentiations within the working-class of a multi-national state.[2]

Marx's exposition of the theory of rent (part VI of *Capital*, vol. 3), opens with a refusal to regard the English type of land ownership and rent, upon which the analysis is based, as more than a model, and closes with a description of the alternative aspects assumed by the degeneration of agriculture in an alternative model, which is characterised by subordination of peasant land-owners in their capacity as sellers and debtors to the rule of capital. On one occasion,[3] the interposition of a group of typically capitalist farmer-entrepreneurs between landlords and working peasants is described as possible " only in those countries which dominate the world market in the period of transition from the feudal to the capitalist mode of production," i.e., it is a specifically British phenomenon. Even Marx's continued adherence to the model as such may be questioned in view of Engels' statement, in the Preface to *Capital*, vol. III, that Marx intended to rewrite the part on rent with Russia playing a part similar to that of Britain in the first volume " because of the wide variety of forms of land-ownership as well as of exploitation of agricultural producers prevailing in Russia." Every student of Russian conditions knows that amongst that variety the classical English model was conspicuously absent ; and it is left to his imagination to reconstruct a fourth volume of *Capital* in which a variety of forms of agricultural organisation would have to hold their own as equivalent examples of capitalist penetration of precapitalist forms of agriculture. Feudal latifundia in course of transformation into large-scale capitalist enterprise, village-communities in which the kulak's poor neighbour is gradually transformed into his labourer, free peasant settlers in colonial new-land, and Cossack farmer entrepreneurs would all find their place in such a picture. Certainly there would have been no need to bother about concepts such as " absolute rent " which occupy such a large part of Vol. III/2 of *Capital* as it stands.

[2] See above, p. 288.
[3] *Capital*, vol. III, pp. 428-9.

However, the preserved form of *Capital* was dominated by the Ricardian model which was an idealisation of the agrarian relations prevailing in 19th Century Britain, and thus that model was included in all current standards of Marxist orthodoxy. Kautsky, who followed the centrist pattern of thought according to which socialism would result from the predominance of a sectional labour movement within a purely capitalist society, elaborated a picture of agricultural developments in which concentration according to the pattern prescribed for industry would take place. David, speaking for the Revisionists, answered this scheme by a Utopia in which the middle-peasant grew prosperous and produced a co-operative socialism of his own, provided Social Democracy would help him to get protective tariffs, cheap credits, and would not trouble him by exaggerated demands in the agricultural labourers' interest. The latters' trade unions, growing important after the 1918 revolution, defended their own existence against the aspirations of lower-middle-class " Socialism " by defending the preservation of the large estates, even though in the hands of Junkers ; and at the Kiel party congress, 1927, an unholy alliance was concluded between the two trends by the acceptance of an agrarian programmé which would leave Prussian agriculture as it was. The kulaks were promised support (in David's sense), the Junkers—and their offspring who actually controlled the State machine of the Republic—were promised immunity until Kautsky's Day of Judgment, duly re-interpreted in terms of coalition policies.[4]   It is against the background of such an inevitable outcome of the lower-middle-class approach to the peasant problem, the first flights of which were easily distinguishable even in Engels' days, that we have to interpret his restriction of the possibilities of a positive Socialist policy, in the interest of the peasants, to tax relief, rent restriction, and protection against usury.[5]   In the framework of the analysis of the smallholder's needs given in *Capital*, vol. III, Chapter 47,[6] it is difficult to envisage, beyond the measures suggested by Engels, policies that would help the peasants without transforming them into a stronghold of bourgeois reaction. Even the division of the big estates amongst their labourers and the neighbouring small-

---

[4] On these issues see R. Gerber, *The Agrarian Problem in German Social Democracy*, Moscow, 1929 (in Russian).

[5] cf. his reference in his Preface to the 2nd ed. of the *Peasant War in Germany* (ed. cit., p. 19).

[6] Ed. cit., pp. 938 ff.

holders would be a distinctly reactionary measure in terms of Marx's analysis, at least for a fully developed capitalist country ; it could not be envisaged by Marxists except in connection with an actual socialist revolution which would subordinate the further development of the new peasants' economy to nationalised " commanding heights," such as banks, transport, large-scale trade, production of agricultural means of production, etc., etc. ; and its revolutionary importance would lie in its being carried through in violation of existing property rights and in its breaking the strongholds of reaction in the countryside. Actually such a policy was not envisaged by West and Central European Marxists before the acceptance of the 1928 programme of the Comintern.

The dilemma discussed above was not in the minds of Russian Marxists who envisaged a bourgeois-democratic revolution as the immediate task. Support of peasant demands the realisation of which would imply the growth of an agricultural bourgeoisie appeared as a legitimate price to be paid for the peasants' support in overthrowing Tsarism ; and the Trotskyist argument that such a policy would increase the difficulties of the eventual socialist revolution could be answered by demonstrating the prospect of a quick turning of the bourgeois-democratic into a socialist revolution even in Russia.[7] But it would be mistaken to attribute the difference between the positive attitude of the Russian, and the negative attitude of the Western Marxists to the peasant question merely to the demands of Marxist orthodoxy[8]; the positive attitude adopted by Western Communists under the impact of the Russian revolution failed to produce any noticeable results before a socialist transformation of national economy became a topical issue. As long as capitalism prospers moderately, the ideological dependence even of the poorer strata of the peasantry on bourgeois ideology is too strong for projects of agrarian reform other than those compatible with the preservation of the capitalist framework to appear to them as realistic.

But a totally different situation prevailed in Russia[9] where

[7] See note 18 to Chapter XIII.

[8] This difference dates only from the 1905 revolution ; earlier Russian Social Democrat attitudes to the agrarian question were restricted to suggestions of subordinate reforms as current also in the West. See Lenin, *Sel. Works*, vol. III, pp. 197 ff

[9] And also in some East European, and especially Asiatic countries where the (modern) Bolshevist approach to the peasant question has become almost a commonplace amongst progressives.

the imminence of an anti-feudal revolution was generally recognised. The actual difficulty, from the Marxist point of view, arose merely from the fact that the intellectual groups of revolutionaries who appealed to the peasants' support described themselves as Socialists and, under the general impact of a rising Labour movement, succeeded in convincing the peasants that a radical overthrow of feudal oppression should be described as socialism. Even in the Anglo-Saxon countries, radical liberal opposition to the pre-capitalist institution of rent has produced demands for nationalisation of the land (that is, of rent) which were described as " socialist " although private exploitation of the land (which implied capitalist profits) was expected to continue. There was nothing astonishing in similar descriptions being used in Russia where a radical land reform was evidently impossible without a violent revolution from below and where the ancient communal ownership of the village community appeared as a suitable starting point for rural socialism.[10] Most of the theoretical work of the early Russian Marxists—including Lenin's *Development of Capitalism in Russia,* the standard work for the application of Marxist economics to countries not typical of the Marxian model—was devoted to fighting that delusion and to demonstrating the progress of the modern social differentiations characteristic of capitalism within the village community. The traditions of that struggle may have been responsible for the slowness even of Russian Marxists in realising the needs of the peasant revolution growing before their eyes, and lingered on in a distrust of radical slogans applied in the direction of what was bound to be a merely bourgeois-democratic movement. Writing in 1907 for his own fellow-partisans, Lenin[11] had to attack Marxists who " while criticing the Narodnik theory overlook its historically real and historically legitimate content in the struggle against serfdom." The real effect of the revolution which the Narodniks regarded as socialisation would be that it would most thoroughly remove the obstacles to capitalist development, that is to say, backward smallholders as well as backward latifundia.[12] For this very reason Lenin supported demands for nationalisation of all land (including that held by the peasantry under various

---

[10] See above, pp. 190–1 and 206–7.

[11] *Sel. Works,* vol. III, pp. 178–9.

[12] Ibid., p. 240.

semi-feudal titles[13]) against the Menshevist programme (adopted by the Stockholm Party Congress of 1907) of municipal ownership of the land to be expropriated from the big estate-owners, and against those of his own fellow-Bolsheviks who suggested its division amongst the peasants.[14] Being unable to command even an impressive minority at the Stockholm Congress, he joined with the latter group. This may be explained by factional fellowship ; but it would have been inconceivable had he thought of nationalisation of land as a remedy for the hardships arising for the small farmer from his capacity to alienate his land. Nationalisation of all land, plus the equal re-distribution envisaged by the Social Revolutionaries, became practical politics in November, 1917.[15] In view of the quick progress of nationalisation, especially of the banks, the practical test of a capitalist agriculture free from rent has never been made in Soviet Russia. In the East European " People's Democracies " a compromise has been enacted[16] by which the land is granted to the toiling peasants, under safeguards for planned control of the " commanding heights " of economics by public organs. It remains to be seen whether the compromise, which has been envisaged as a comparatively painless way of transition to full socialism, will endure sufficiently long to be subject to economic analysis. The contributions made by the kollkhozes to the theory and practice of socialism belong to the structure rather than to the achievement of a socialist society, and may be left to discussion in the next chapter of this book.

A combination of a democratic, that is, anti-latifundia, with a socialist, that is, anti-capitalist, revolution was envisaged already by the authors of the *Communist Manifesto*. The replacement of

---

[13] His argument (Ibid., pp. 220–2) is solely based upon the prospect that nationalisation of *all* land, apart from implying that the feudal estate-owners would be dealt with radically, would clear the way for capitalist progress and (as distinct from municipalisation) concentrate the peasants' minds on the struggle for a democratic central government (Ibid., pp. 260 ff).

[14] That is, the slogan which since 1928 has become generally accepted amongst non-Russian Communists. But it should be kept in mind that Lenin's whole argument, in 1907, was based upon the fact that the peasants themselves preferred nationalisation to division of the land. In 1917, the nationalisation of *all* land—including the peasant-owned—was, for tactical reasons, *not* included in the Decree of the Soviet Congress, though presupposed by its reference to demands for nationalisation raised again by the peasants themselves.

[15] See my *Soviet Legal Theory*, pp. 40–2. The issue of rent had sufficiently dominated socialist literature to be mentioned in art. 17 of the Land Law of 1918, without any practical implications.

[16] Comp. for example, section III, and espec. arts. 15 and 19 of the new Yugoslav Constitution, reprinted in *Sovietskoe Goszudarstvo*, 1946, No. 9.

the British by the Continental pattern implies that the issue of rent, the full development of which supposes the existence of a class of capitalist farmers, has receded into the background as compared with peasants' demand for land, and for an organisation of transport, commerce and credit that would no longer serve as a means of their indirect exploitation. Some shift may take place from a first stage in which most of the peasantry is likely to support a struggle against semi-feudal latifundia, to later stages, in which the well-to-do peasant may be less interested than his poor neighbour in reforms likely to conflict with free disposition of property and free trade ; but there is no change in the fundamental attitude to private property. Because of the permeation of all vested interests, including the relics of feudalism, by finance monopolies, even the first stage of the peasant movement is bound to conflict with the main forces of the *bourgeoisie* (and, especially, with its main supporters on the international stage), whilst even in the later stages open conflict with the peasants' belief in property, and the consequent restriction of the agricultural support of the revolution to the actually proletarianised strata of the peasantry,[17] can be avoided. At no stage is the socialist transformation a purely working-class affair ; but the leading part played by the urban working-classes is even more strongly emphasized, because the reforms aimed at and achieved by their peasant allies would have no socialist significance unless the " commanding heights "—of an essentially urban character— were nationalised. This argument is completely independent of the violence or otherwise of the transformation, and of the statistics of the social origin of the party leading in it[18] : it would hold true even if in a country fitting the pattern discussed civil war (or its substitute, national resistance to a " Quisling " regime[19]) were completely avoided (which would not be easy as the existence of a considerable amount of feudal relics in social structure is supposed) and, consequently, if excessive application of " proletarian " ideology, distasteful to the non-working-class element of the electorate, could be avoided. But it should be

[17] As supposed in the scheme of the "permanent revolution," (see above, pp. 265-7), where bourgeois-democratic and socialist revolution are regarded as clearly distinct, though immediately successive, stages of the process.

[18] In a semi-feudal country needing a thorough revolution, such as Russia, the party leading the latter is likely to contain a considerable percentage of intellectuals, whilst a majority of those fighting for the revolution may be peasants.

[19] See my *Federalism*, etc., pp. 464-5 and 474.

kept in mind that the leading part played by the working-class is not a synonym of the workers' sectional interest : emphasis on the latter at the expense of the dominating need to win non-working-class support for the necessary transformation may defeat not only a revolution, by unnecessarily broadening the social basis of the " Vendees "organised by the vested interests, but even a moderate reform movement such as Viennese Social Democrats in the period between the two wars.[20]

(b) DEVELOPMENT OF THE MARXIST NATIONALITIES POLICIES

The most important implication of the positive approach to the peasant problem is an approach to the nationalities problems of the multi-national units of Central and Eastern Europe (and, a fortiori, of Asia) which must be completely different from the first Marxist statements which we have discussed.[21]   Internationalism means, primarily, co-existence of nations supposedly forming independents units[22] ; and all original Marxist argument as to whether the claims of some nationality to independence should be supported centres round the presence of the preliminary conditions for such independent existence.[23]   But, as was realised by Engels as early as 1849,[24] the Central and Eastern European nationalities do not form economic units co-ordinated with each other : in the typical case they denote social stratification within a single economic unit, the urban middle- and lower middle-classes (and that part of the working-class that originated from urban craftsmen) belonging to one nationality, the peasantry (from which, eventually, the larger part of the industrial working-class is recruited) to the other.   To side, in such circumstances, with one nationality against the other implied not merely, as the

[20] There was, in Austrian Social Democracy much less tendency to define the interest of the urban working-classes as opposed to those of the peasant than in other Centrist parties; Otto Bauer's *Kampf um Wald und Weide* (Vienna, 1925) represents the most realistic and positive approach to the peasant problem made by any non-Bolshevist Socialist, and coalition policies were described in terms of a necessary alliance " between workers and peasants." But so far as reality corresponded to such a description (as distinct from a coalition with the *bourgeoisie* dominating the Catholic party to which the peasants belonged) it implied dropping all serious efforts to support the poorest peasants and agricultural labourers against their well-to-do neighbours, whilst the constructive reform policy carried out in Vienna implied identification with the commercial centre which was regarded in the countryside as an exploiter. Therefore, in its struggle against " Red Vienna " High Finance could easily appeal to the provincial bourgeoisie's (including the *kulaks*) opposition to Vienna (in general), without any break in the reactionary front of the countryside.

[21] Above, pp. 301 ff.   [22] See above, p. 305.
[23] See below, pp. 343-4.   [24] See note 6 to Chapter XIV.

Marxists originally believed, siding with one national state, existing or coming into existence by a process of national emancipation, against another—an issue which might conceivably be decided according to the part played by those different national states in the great social issues of the time : it implied, primarily, taking sides in a domestic social conflict.   Engels[24] was naive enough to describe an eventual triumph of the Austrian Slavs over the Germans as a subjection of " the town to the country, and of trade, manufacture, and intelligence to the primitive agriculture of Slavonic serfs."   Certainly, because of the fixation of social in national divisions, the support given by the bulk of the peasantry to counter-revolution in Austria assumed a national aspect ; but to state this is merely another way of stating the need, from the revolutionary point of view, for a positive nationalities policy similar to that later applied by the Bolshevists, and certainly no argument for deploring the impending subjection of the top-dog to the under-dog.   The only mitigating circumstances which can be found for Engels' attitude is their proximity to the events which induced the early Marxists to expect a socialist revolution at a time when the working-class in East Central Europe had not yet been expanded by urbanisation of Slavonic peasants.   But to use that perspective as an explanation of an actually *bourgeois* attitude in the nationality question is merely another way of stating how completely Utopian it was.   At a later stage, when Central Europe was well industrialised and had a powerful working-class, such siding with the industrialised " historical " nations meant opposing those whose traditional backwardness was preserved by the fact that most of their members were restricted to the status of unskilled workers.[25]   Apart from neglect of the still important part played by those peasants who had remained in the villages, it implied a split in the ranks of the working-class by alliance of a privileged workers' aristocracy with the middle-classes of the ruling nation.   Up to our days, such an approach has continued to dominate the reformist attitude to the nationalities problem[26] ; and as long as one nationality in a

[25] See above, p.288.

[26] The most impressive examples, in our days, are provided by right-wing American (comp. Gunnar Myrdal's book, quoted above, p. 49) and South African trade unionists in their approach to the Negro problem.   Without external characteristics of the subject nation so impressive as colour, the approach mentioned has played its part in the Sudeten German issues, and apart from its contribution to the failure of Social Democracy in the Hapsburg monarchy, helped to bring National Socialism into being.   See my *Federalism*, etc., espec. pp. 198 and 304.

multi-national state is kept in a state of subjection and backwardness, the argument that the skilled workers' wages will be undercut by his uncivilised neighbour will not fail to be used with some appearance of justification.

The problem was realised by the founders of Marxism in connection not with the issues of East Central Europe—where opposition against Tsarism and its potential allies continued to dominate their minds as late as 1882[27]—but with the Irish question, which was topical in the milieu where they moved and not complicated by issues of international policies.[28] In 1848-9, Marx's and Engels' attitude to the Irish problem was restricted to opposing national hatred between Irish and English workers and especially " the prejudice which prompted the Irish people to confound in one common hatred the oppressed classes of England with the oppressors of both countries." They advocated a close alliance between the Irish national and the English Chartist movement, without envisaging political separation after the common triumph.[29] In the 'sixties they had realised that, for the time being, the British Labour movement was not Chartist, but reformist, and that such an attitude was based upon Britain's predominant position over against other nations. Ireland was a most obvious example ; the important part played by her in British domestic policies—and, perhaps, also Engels' private Irish connections—resulted in a very large number of statements on Ireland taking their place as contributions to the modern Bolshevist approach to imperialist policies made by the founders of Marxism. In his letter to Engels, of December 19, 1869, Marx dealt with the Irish question just as

[27] See above, pp. 305-6.

[28] The contribution made by the Irish issue towards embittering the relations between the two leading Anglo-Saxon nations forms a main additional argument in favour of the attitude described below, and is amply mentioned in the letter quoted in note 30 below.

[29] I cannot see more far-reaching conclusions should be drawn (e.g., as done in Bloom, *The World of Nations*, p. 38), from Marx's retrospective remarks in his letter to Engels of November 2, 1867. The only clear change to be observed in that letter, as against earlier and also later attitudes (see note 32 below) is Marx's preparedness to envisage a political separation of Ireland from England. But there was no enthusiasm for it—in Marx's letter of November 30, 1867, as well as in that of December 10, 1869, federation was envisaged, which was completely compatible with the relevant utterances of 1848 upon which my statement in the text is based (*Coll. Works*, vol. VI, pp. 652, 384, and 577). The real turn in Marx's attitude as expressed in the letter of 1869—which perhaps, on the basis of the letter of 1867, may be anti-dated to that year—does not concern the institutional forms envisaged for the cohabitation of the English and Irish nations, but the function ascribed to the latter's struggle for emancipation as a means to break, within the former, the political leadership of a reformist workers' aristocracy.

Lenin was later to deal with the emancipation of colonies : as a means of unseating the workers belonging to the privileged nation from their privileged position and to facilitate their progress toward class-consciousness. Obviously, such an appeal can only be directed to an advanced elite amongst the workers of the privileged nation which prefers the eventual fruits of increased class-solidarity to the continued enjoyment of privileges. As to the workers—and, indeed, all working members—of the oppressed nation the appeal can be broader, because their short-term and long-term interests co-incide. Starting from the co-existence of two working-classes, an English and an Irish, in every English town, Marx, in a letter of April 9, 1870,[30] stated that a decisive blow against the English ruling class, which would be decisive for the workers' movement all over the world, could not be delivered in England but only in Ireland.[31]   For the continued subjection of the Irish, who supplied a very considerable part of the workers for British industries, resulted in a division of the working-class in England : " in relation to the Irish workers, the English worker feels himself a member of the *ruling* nation and so turns himself into a tool of the aristocrats and capitalists *against Ireland*, thus strengthening their domination *over himself*." The Irish worker retaliates by turning "against the English worker as sharing in the guilt for the English domination in Ireland while at the same time serving as its tool."

The argument thus made is, primarily, an argument in favour of what was later known as the Bolshevist slogan of national self-determination : full recognition, by the traditionally ruling nation, of the right of the oppressed nation to secede, which might be followed, in this case, by federation on a voluntary

---

[30] To S. Meyer and K. Vogt, reprinted in Marx, *Sel. Works*, vol. II, pp. 645 ff.

[31] The reader may notice the difference in attitude to the statement, made nearly a quarter of a century before, that, in order to help the Poles, the British Chartists should, first of all, fight their own national oppressors (see above, p.302).   There is an obvious difference in that British sympathies for Poland were more likely than not to be reduced to cheap phrases, whilst concentrating the struggle of the British working-classes on the emancipation of Ireland would, indeed, mean tackling British Labour problems at the most difficult end (though the Liberals eventually, concentrated British progressive policies on the issue of Home Rule).   But the main difference is one of suppositions as to the comparative ripeness of the British working-class : in the earlier statement the latter is supposed to be capable of emancipation by its own efforts, in the latter such capacity is supposed to be conditional on the previous removal of ideological obstacles, such as are implied in the feeling of belonging to a ruling nation.

basis.[32] It was intended to bridge the gulf between the workers
(Bolshevists would add : and between the workers and part of the
peasants) within one economic unit, by removing the grievances
of the subject nationality. Here in a nutshell we find the two
principles of the modern Marxist nationalities policy : (1) no
nation should be subject to another, not only in its own interest,
but also in the interest of the oppressed classes of the oppressor
nation, for " a people, which oppresses others, cannot be free " ;
(2) social issues cannot be fought out without being cleared of
the racial antagonisms which divide the oppressed classes (within
a single economic unit) in the interest of their rulers ; therefore
it is in the socialist interest that the Socialists of the ruling nation
and, indeed, international Socialism in general, should press
for the most radical solution of nationalities problems which
may be needed in order to win the confidence of the workers of
the oppressed nations.[32] In the first application, which corresponds to the West European type of nationalities problems
familiar to the traditional liberal outlook, the traditional liberal
slogan of national self-determination implies the removal of supposed
anomalies in the structure of the community of nations, namely,
of multi-national states (or parcelling out of nationalities such as
the German and Italian) ; in the second, which was fruitfully
applied in the former Tsarist empire, it merely intends to enable
peoples of different nationalities to live side by side on more stable
foundations, which does not exclude the possibility that the
continued cohabitation of some scores of peoples of the U.S.S.R.
on a basis accepted voluntarily by them may have to be purchased
at the price of admitting the actual secession of a Poland or a
Finland. It may be questioned whether the Bolsheviks would

<hr />

[32] In his letter to Kugelmann, of November 29, 1869, Marx regarded the formation of such a federation as the obvious implication of an eventual repeal of the Union,
and in his critique of the draft of the *Erfurt Programme* (*Neue Zeit*, vol. XX/1) Engels
spoke of the desirability of federation between the English, Irish, Scots and Welsh as
opposed to his general preference for the unitary state with far-going local self-
government (amongst the examples quoted for which such recognised federations as
U.S.A., Canada and Australia figured).   Lenin's suggestion (*Sel. Works*, vol. V, p.
270) that Marx regarded federation, in the British case, as a mere unavoidable
compromise, can hardly be upheld against such statements ; on the other hand, it
would be clearly mistaken to regard the original Marxists as advocates of federation
in general.   They were still far from the Bolshevist attempts to raise national revolutions with the catchword of self-determination ; if they recognized an oppressed
nation's right to emancipation, they were prepared to go in constitutional forms as
far as necessary to win the respective nation's confidence : federation as regards the
Irish (who, at that time, raised no demands beyond Home Rule), secession (which
they hoped would be merely short-lived) in the case of the Austrian Slavs, after the
eventual fall of Tsarism.

have advocated the right of secession in a more than purely theoretical sense if the decisive parts of their country had presented such an intermingling of nationalities as, say, Bohemia.[33]

Both applications of the principle of national self-determination : as a method of actually clearing up the national chart of the world, and as a means of putting the continued existence of multi-national states on a voluntary and therefore more stable basis, can be pursued into modern Bolshevist theory. The first application is expressed in Stalin's definition, in 1913, of a nation in a way which presupposes its fitness to secede and to build an independent state of its own,[34] which was continued, in his speech introducing the 1936 Constitution, in the enumeration of the characteristics needed in order that a nation should be granted the theoretical right of secession,[35] though the demands made on a nation in order to qualify it for national autonomy had become much less stringent. The second application culminates in Stalin's[36] description of the class essence of the national question (in the U.S.S.R.) as the establishment of definite and correct relations between the proletariat of the formerly ruling nation and the peasantry of the formerly oppressed nationalities. It presents the exact opposite of Engels' attitude discussed above. From the point of view of democracy—which is different from the liberal idealisation of urban civilisation—it is certainly progressive.

Marx can hardly have realised all the implications of his handling of the nationalities problem in the Anglo-Irish case. Many years later Engels[27] still spoke of the whole problem as involving a few nationalities, the Irish and the Polish issue being the only important ones amongst those yet unsolved. It was not mere chance that Otto Bauer's book on the Nationalities problem, the first fundamental study of the awakening of the " unhistorical nationalities,"[37] appeared after the first Russian revolution

[33] By denying it in such circumstances they would not have incurred principal contradictions with its programme, which (comp. Stalin, *Marxism and the National etc. Question*, p. 50) demanded regional autonomy, with the implication of possible secession, for large units with a common economy, but possibly multi-national.

[34] See below, p. 339.

[35] See my *Federalism*, etc., pp. 392 ff.

[36] *Marxism and the National etc. Question.* p. 132.

[37] Kautsky's criticism of Bauer's book (*Nationalitaet und Internationalitaet*, Supplement to *Neue Zeit*, No. 1, 1908, espec. pp. 4 ff) fundamentally opposed that positive approach by favouring the absorption of the smaller and less developed nationalities into the larger ones, and his definition of nationality as community of literary language (see also *Die Befreiung der Nationen*, Stuttgart, 1917, espec. p. 32) forms a strict counterpart to the attempts of later Bolshevist nationalities policies (see my *Federalism*, etc., part III) to help the small and backward nationalities to build

had changed the former situation in which the Russian sympathies cherished by the Austrian Slavs had always been associated with domestic and international reaction. But as he shared the original Marxists' preference for large and viable economic units without sharing their appreciation of the revolutionary methods whereby such units might be turned into instruments of progress, his whole approach centred round the quest for a means by which the nations' legitimate claims for cultural development could conform to the preservation of the economic unity of the Danubian empire, and provoked Stalin's rejoinder[38] that national-cultural autonomy as advocated by Bauer would organise the nations under the leadership of the existing ruling classes. The Bolsheviks were certainly in favour of large economic units, but they were prepared to win support for the conquest of power within those units even at the expense of their size, the more so since the fact of a nation's owing its independence to the triumph of the working-class of the former oppressor state was the safest way towards turning, in due course, that nation socialist. But the emancipation of nations is of no value in itself: in his attack on Bauer's attempt to define nation in such a way that it would cover nationalities such as the Jews who lacked the most elementary conditions for separate political existence, Stalin[39] stated that Social Democracy " can reckon only with real nations, which act together in time of peace and in time of war, and therefore insist on being reckoned with."

When the Bolshevists had conquered State power, and Stalin had to organise their nationalities policies, the right of secession naturally receded into the realm of State ideology[35]; its actual importance was reduced to that of an expression of the need to organise the co-habitation of the peoples of the multi-national state in such a way that their specific national civilisations could prosper better within the union than within alternative dwarf-states likely to fall easy victims to the nearest imperialist aggressor. Within the framework of the multi-

national civilisations of their own. But it should be noticed that, in his writing of 1913 (l. c., p. 43), as distinct from his policies after the conquest of power (see note 42 below), even Stalin suggested solving the problems of the backward small nations of the Caucasus " by drawing them into the common stream of a higher civilisation."

[38] L. c., pp. 28–9 and 43.
[39] L. c., p. 13.

national state which, for the reconstruction of its economics and
culture, appealed to the efforts of scores of millions of formerly
illiterate peasants, the positive aspect of the nationalities problem
as a way to foment the awakening of those peasants was fully
realised.[36] The reserved approach to nationality as something
not just valuable in itself with which one had, however, to
reckon, was replaced by its description as the mould into which
the socialist content of the new civilisation had to be poured ; and
those forms would express the new content the more forcefully,
the nearer they were to the life of the peasant masses (which
implied every important variety of civilisation expressed by a
distinct national form). " Only if the national cultures develop
will it be possible to secure the real participation of the backward
nationalities in the work of socialist reconstruction."[40] Making
the local State and Party organisations " indigenous " by increasing the part played in their life by the formerly backward
nationalities, if necessary even by inducing the Great Russian
workers to assume the local civilisation and thus to raise it
to a higher level,[41] is regarded as a most natural means of
strengthening the U.S.S.R. and its social content.

Stalin has explicitly stated[42] that he regards Lenin's and his
own[37] former opposition to the development of new national cultures as conditioned by the capitalist character of those cultures.
It seems to follow that his whole polemic against Bauer's concept
of the Society To Come as multi-national, including the quotation
from the *Communist Manifesto* used on that occasion,[43] is obsolete,
at least for the first period of socialism.[44] For all practical purposes, we should regard the modern Bolshevist approach as a
consummation of the second of the two above-mentioned[45]
implications of the way in which Marx dealt with the Irish
problem, though it arose from the most radical consummation
of the first. Bauer was the first to realise that what appeared
to the original Marxists, and to their liberal contemporaries, as a
limited number of awkward issues disturbing mankind's social and
economic progress was, in fact, the form in which the broad

[40] L. c., p. 228.
[41] See my *Federalism*, etc., pp. 383–4 and 407–8.
[42] L. c., p. 227.   [43] Ibid., p. 29.
[44] But see below, Chapter XIX, pp. 420 and 428.
[45] P. 337.

masses of the East European peoples awoke to political consciousness ; but by fundamentally identifying the national with the
peasant, and the colonial with the national problem,[46] Lenin and
Stalin have raised the issue to the position of the key-problem
of contemporary history. Just as pre-1917 world economics was
dominated by the clearly capitalist sector, the transition to a
socialist pattern and at least the primary aspects of that pattern
itself are bound to be dominated by the direct opposition produced
within the capitalist sector, that is, by the industrial working-
class. But the very fact that the struggle between the two main
classes of capitalist society will be decisive in shaping the lives
of peasant masses far superior in numbers to capitalists and
proletarians together, prevents the transformation of that society
from corresponding to the cultural patterns developed by its
typical classes : neither capitalists can preserve, nor proletarians
overthrow the essentials of the capitalist mode of production without adapting society to the demands and outlook of the peasant
majority of mankind ; and liberal as well as proletarian internationalism are bound to give way to the fact that the peasants—
and the lower-middle-classes in general—are bound to think in
nationalist terms. When Marx and Engels answered the
national problems according to the pattern of 19th Century
urban civilisation, they were bound to be refuted by historical
events.

(c) Is there a Marxist concept of nationality ?

The first and most obvious conclusion from the record of
original Marxist policies on national issues is a rejection of the
current belief that Marx and Engels regarded such issues as
unimportant. The phrase of the *Communist Manifesto* that " the
proletarians have no fatherland, and they cannot be deprived
of what they do not possess " should be interpreted in connection
with the appeal made in the same document that, by the conquest
of political power, the proletarians should " establish themselves as the national class," namely, as the class determining
the nation's historical function. The sharpest criticisms which
we had to level against Marx's and Engels' nationalities policies
from the standpoint of their own general sociological theory,

---

[46] Interpretation of the colonial problem as, essentially, a peasant problem was
long since familiar to left-wing Socialists. See above, pp. 191-2, and 194.

concerned failures to apply the dialectical method to possible changes in the social structure and historical function of nationalities, with the danger of approaching nations as units with a stable function in the play of international politics. Certainly, Marx and Engels did not regard national self-assertion as the highest standard, and perhaps they may have regarded it as a distinctly undesirable one : we have no document from their pens which appeals so forcefully to their own nation's pride in its historical mission as did Lenin's *On the National Pride of the Great Russians* ; and we can have none because the conception of defeatism as a means of asserting the historical mission of one's own nation, which is so strongly expressed in Lenin's article, was strange to the founders' minds. Marxists who cherished internationalist standards but kept to the traditional Jacobin tactics of assuming power in the course of national defence obviously had to emphasize the merely secondary import- ance of nation, including their own, lest their tactics should have betrayed their standpoint and turned them into ordinary nationalists (as actually happened to the Jacobins). But there cannot be the slightest doubt that, in tactics, the Marxists regarded nations as the units : the only open question is whether they had a clear theoretical derivation of the essence and the interrelations of those units from their basic concept of class.

Virtually all the existing literature on the Marxist approach to nationality is devoted to the analysis of the attitude of the classical Marxists to distinct national problems ; and no clear and unequivocal approach to nation as such can be derived from such data. The conclusion may be described, according to the respective critic's tastes and sympathies, in terms of the Marxists' subordination of all national problems to the fundamental interests of the proletarian class-struggle, or in terms of simple political opportunism. The difference is merely one of politeness, as the fundamental interests of the proletarian class-struggle, in the international field, were mainly described in terms of Great Power relations. In its theoretical essence, the statement that the Marxists supported Poland because the Poles opposed Tsarist Russia cannot be distinguished from the statement that they regarded the Polish nation as progressive because its struggle for emancipation was directed against the stronghold of inter- national reaction.[47] But I should regard it as unjust simply to apply such a description to the original Marxists' attitude : they had some objective standard according to which they defined a nation's essence and historical function ; and its presence was revealed by the very attempts made to derive from it—sometimes in a rather artificial way—whatever conclusions were deemed to fit the predominant international pattern.

As we have noticed, in 1848 alleged inability of the Czechs to play an historical part of their own was explained by their predominantly peasant structure and by the absence of a national bourgeoisie. A few years later[48] Marx further elaborated the statement : their present historical development was attached to that of nations of different race and speech and they lacked even a national organisation within Austria, being divided amongst different Provinces. Unless this was intended merely to mean that the Czechs had no historical future because they were oppressed at that time (an interpretation which would do injustice to Marx even in his biased moments) the statement may refer (a) to the lack of a national bourgeoisie or aristocracy[49] in consequence of which the smaller Slavonic tribes should be considered as " appendages either to the German or Hungarian nations,"[48] or (b) to the lack of clear and viable limits of the national territory allowing for emancipation of the nation without the creation of new oppressed minorities. The argument is distinctly weak, because it neglects the possibility of creating a new national bourgeoisie from amongst the peasantry (as was actually to happen) ; and it is biased, because it describes the Austrian Slavs as a potential appendage to the Magyars who had no more substantial a bourgeoisie than the Slavs themselves (though they had a national aristocracy) and because it bypasses the fact that the Czechs, as a predominantly peasant people, shared the lack of clear territorial limits with the Poles who were supported for reasons of international policy, at least in public. But in a private letter to Marx of May 23, 1851, Engels expressed

---

[47] The naive assumption that the merits of a socialist foreign policy can be proved by tautological argument is shared by those recent Soviet theorists of international law who prove that the U.S.S.R. supports the claim to self-determination of all nations who stand for values held in common with the U.S.S.R.   See my *Soviet Legal Theory*, p. 286.

[48] *The Eastern Question*, p. 546, *New York Tribune*, May 7, 1855.

[49] The Provincial administration in the Hapsburg monarchy was based upon semi-feudal estates.   Even a nation with a strong bourgeoisie would have no share in it unless it had also an aristocracy of its own—or made a successful revolution, which would have overthrown the Provincial system.

his doubts as to whether the Poles, as distinct from the Russians
(and, of course, the Germans) were capable of developing a
national bourgeoisie[50]; and from the negative answer to this
question he concluded that the Poles, by being offered mirages
such as Riga and Odessa, should be played off against Russia in
order eventually (apparently after war had resulted in the fall
of Tsarism) to be defeated by joint Russo-German efforts. From
the point of view of those who still measure foreign policies
by the 19th Century catalogue of the "progressive nations"
this sample of macchiavellian policies has a very unpleasant
sound ; and one who shares Engels' basic standards would like to
have from his pen examples of similarly ruthless politics applied
to his own nation which, even during his lifetime, did not always
behave according to the proper standards of social progress.
However, support of a more than tactical character granted to
any nation was conditional upon its compliance with certain,
definite standards which were based upon social structure and the
implied ability of the nation to play a positive part in an era
of bourgeois-democratic revolutions. Apart from a common
language (which was so obvious that it had not to be explicitly
stated) and a common past (without which, according to Marxist
sociology, the common language could not have originated)[51] a
nation should have a common territory suitable for independent
existence and a national bourgeoisie, or at least the obvious ability
to create one. This characteristic, which can be distilled from
original Marxist statements on the different national issues, does
not fundamentally differ from that given in 1913 by Stalin,[52]
though the emphasis has been changed by Stalin's attempt[53] to
interpret virtually every national issue of his days in terms of
emancipation of a national bourgeoisie (which implied a positive

[50] Engels' doubts on the Poles' prospects were of a transitory character ; 30 years
later, in his letter to Kautsky of February 7, 1882, he recognised the Poles' as well as
the Russians' historical future.
[51] These two characteristics are recognised even with those nationalities, especially
the Czechs, who are described as "artificial" because of the absence of the two further
characteristics. The description of these nationalities as "hapless relics of former
greatness" ([48]), in any case favourably contrasts with Engels' description, in 1848 (see
note 6 to Chapter XIV), of the awakeners who made the Czechs, etc., conscious of
their past as "dilettanti."
[52] L.c., p. 7.   But there is a difference in that Stalin accepted from Bauer so
problematic an element as "national character" (see below, pp. 346-7) which the
original Marxists would certainly have rejected. But Stalin himself (Ibid., p. 15)
noted that the "national character" has no political implications whatever !
[53] Ibid., p. 13, for a criticism see my *Federalism*, etc., pp. 330-1.

approach to nations which Engels would have regarded as having no bourgeoisie and therefore no future). The progress made is evidently due to the meanwhile progress of the national movement (which had in the meantime forced even old Engels to correct his attitude to the Czechs' future[54]) as well as to Stalin's personal standpoint in a centre of national movements.

In Stalin's interpretation as well as in the classical Marxist one which we have reconstructed, nation is conceived as the subject of a political, bourgeois-democratic revolution. Bauer's approach to the theoretical concept of nation was dominated by the political purpose it had to serve ; and as that purpose did not include the formation of new national states his concept could be broader. Stalin, from his point of view, reproached Bauer with artificially constructing nations which did not represent raising *bourgeoisie* and, therefore, were not to be reckoned with in politics[39] ; but Bauer's definition is interesting just because it aimed at broadness, and thus exceeded the framework of a distinct stage in social development, namely, the bourgeois-democratic revolution. In aiming at the preservation and development of their nationality within the framework of the Hapsburg monarchy, which was to be preserved at least for the time being,[55] the Czech awakeners had defined nationality as community of language and culture.[56] Bauer continued to hold their attitude to the Danubian multi-national state at a time when they would certainly have dropped it[55] ; but it was clearly impossible for a Marxist who conceived civilisation as class-divided to speak of a community of culture. His Neo-Kantian approach,[57] and evidently also the impact of the Jewish problem, which has played rather disproportionate a part in the evolution of Marxist attitudes to the nationalities problem in Austria as well as in

[54] See above, p. 306.

[55] In 1865, on the eve of the definite settlement of the Hapsburg monarchy under German-Magyar hegemony, and certainly not uninfluenced by the emancipations of the serfs in Russia and the subsequent rise of the progressive movement, Palacky, in logical evolution of the attitude taken by himself and his friends before and during the crisis of 1848 (see above, p. 306), turned from the slogan that Austria, if not existing, would have to be created, to the other that the Czechs who had existed before Austria would survive her. See his *Oesterreich's Staatsidee*, 2nd German ed., Prague, 1886, p. 77.

[56] Ibid., pp. 12 ff, and *Politisches Vernachtnis* (Prague, 1872), pp. 32 ff.

[57] In the Preface to the 1924 edition of his book, p. xxvii, Bauer emphasized the connection between his former emphasis on national character (which, in 1924, was regarded by him as subordinate to his analysis of the historical growth of nation) and his then Kantian philosophy.

Russia,[58] induced him to define the characteristics of nation, shaped by the nation's past, as " national character." But this made things rather worse. Without distinct over-statements it is hardly possible to deny the existence of *some* elements of specific culture common to all members of a community which can be described as a nation in another sense than as a synonym of " subjects of a certain state," though these elements may change from case to case. In the case of fully integrated nations whose links with their past and their peasant background have not been completely destroyed (and *completely* urbanised parts of a nation, with a Hollywood-made civilisation, may be regarded as denationalised, whatever the potential appeal of chauvinist slogans on such masses) these common elements may be provided by *folklore ;* in the case of nations with a considerable level of popular education (Scandinavia providing conspicuous examples) they may be provided by elements also of the literary production accepted by the broad masses, and in the case of nations characterised by a certain religious tradition (the Croats or the Indian Muslims being conspicuous) by at least formal allegiance to a religious body.[59] Whatever community of character or " psychological make-up " there may be, it obviously must result from such elements of a common culture. To speak of the common psychological make-up of a large nation composed of the most different social strata contradicts the most elementary Marxist tenets according to which social psychology is conditioned by objective social life.[60] However, even Stalin was under the impact of the Jewish problem in the analysis of which

[58] See my *Federalism*, etc., pp. 220 and 329. In Russia even more than in Austria the Marxists' attention has been drawn to the Jewish problem in opposition to Jewish-nationalist attempts to split the Labour movement on racial lines, to which denial of the existence of a Jewish nation (Stalin, l. c., pp. 9–11) was the simplest answer. The Marxist attitude towards Czech nationalists who wanted to divide the workers within some factory along Czech-German lines could not differ from that taken towards Bundists who made similar divisions according to Jewish-Polish (or Russian) lines : but the tactical position was eased in the former case by the possibility of demanding (at least in the Stalinist interpretation of Marxism) a national home for the Czechs, where they would dominate the Trade Union movement, and the German minority would have to be satisfied with minority rights, just like the Czech workers in clearly Austro-German towns such as Vienna. When minorities are deprived of the grievance of repression, they are expected to be assimilated by their social environment, and so the specific Jewish culture comes to an end, though not the Czech culture.

[59] In the conspicuous Jewish case the impact of religious-custom, and of the specific ways of thought and argument cultivated within the religious community, evidently survives religious belief and formal adherence to the community. Apart from this it would be difficult to establish *any* community between an emancipated British or German Jew and, say, his Bjelorussian fellow Jew.

[60] cf. Kautsky's criticism of Bauer's book (in *Neue Zeit*, 1908).

the " national character " idea works to some extent,[59] and the bulk of the young and awakening nationalities who attracted Stalin's as well as Bauer's attention were predominantly peasant peoples living under fairly homogeneous social conditions. In the typical East Central European case where national and social divisions coincide, the distinct character of, say, the Czech (or Slovene) peasant and the German (or Italian) townsman was evident, and its derivation from rural or urban conditions is more real than from national differences in historical record, cultural consciousness, etc.

Socialists are naturally interested in those issues where national and social antagonisms coincide. " The great importance of foreign domination is that the distinct, national characteristics of the oppressor make immediately obvious, and therefore intolerable, any exploitation and oppression that could otherwise be understood only with considerable intellectual efforts."[61] On the supposition that the typical national revolutions of the 19th-20th Century are bourgeois-democratic, these typical instances of coincidence of social and national antagonisms are those in which an oppressed nation composed of peasants and unskilled workers strives for emancipation, that is, for the formation of a national bourgeoisie and intelligentsia and for the skilled and black-coat jobs in industry and commerce. In the language of Bauer, who has first analysed the process, they are striving to become an " integral nation." The very fact that the nation is not yet fully developed in the sense of the classical Marxist—and pre-Marxist—conception of the national problem makes the definition of nation appear much simpler than it actually is. The concept of " national territory " may have two different meanings : it may denote the territory essentially inhabited by some nation, but it may also denote the land used by a purely peasant nationality as its means of production, as distinct from some other nationality which has no comparable " territory," perhaps because it forms a privileged urban group, but perhaps also because it is mainly represented by industrial workers. As a rule, the difference would not be realised because the Bolsheviks would support the peasant majority (which would also supply a large part of the working-class) in its claim to determine the region's future, and would

---

[61] Bauer, op. cit., ed. 1924, p. 176.

appeal to a Great Russian working-class minority to help the use of the right of self-determination in the right direction (voluntary union with Russia) rather than to attempt to preserve the Great Russian character of the towns. But occasionally the principle would not work, or lead to direct conflict with the rights of a popular majority within the region.[62] Here we are merely interested in the theoretical aspects of the problem ; unless some mystical qualities are ascribed to the soil, which would be rather Physiocracy than Marxism, a group characterised by their occupations in the production process, if sufficiently numerous and if satisfying the other standards applied for the definition of nation, is no less a nation if it is composed of urban craftsmen and merchants than if it is composed of peasants, however important the difference may be for its prospects. If taken seriously, that is, as implying domination of the productive activities of some region,[63] the characterisation of nation by the existence of a distinct national territory implies not only the rejection of questionable nationalities such as the Jewish, but also the pitfall of the early Marxists who refrained from recognition of nationalities that had not yet become " integral " because they were denied access to the more important positions in economic life. On the other hand, the criterion of a " national character " will work well in those very cases where nationality is a synonym for a certain social position, as distinct from those where the presence of a well-developed nation is obvious. Czech and Irish peasants, Caucasian tribesmen drawn into strange industrial surroundings, immigrants to U.S.A. still resisting the maelstrom of assimilation, Jewish lower-middle-class people and intellectuals who overcrowd those occupations to which they are restricted by tradition and background, together with the opposites of all those groups who desire to assert their superiority : these are the typical bearers of well-defined " national characters," as distinct from Schleswig peasants and Berlin artists[60] both of whom, for different reasons, conspicuously fall short of what is expected of the tillers of the national soil, and the servants of the national art, respectively. What should be thought of a characteristic of nationhood which is best developed—or, at least, most con-

---

[62] See my *Federalism*, etc., pp. 333 and 393.

[63] As distinct from appropriation of the regional product, which may be partly in the hands of a small ruling class of different nationality, or of absentee landlords, or of the remote overlords of a colony.

spicuously present—in the isolated member of the nation dwelling abroad in strange surroundings ? Were Hess, Darée and Roehm actually the best characteristic Germans ?

In later years, Bauer[57] thought he could drop from his theory as unnecessary ballast the " national character "—which, however, together with language, had been his characteristic of nationhood—and he claimed as his actual merit the description of the historical process in which a nationality originally[64] composed of peasants becomes " integral " by forming its own intelligentsia, working-class and bourgeoisie.[65] Stalin's reluctant acceptance of the " national character " as one element of his definition[52] is accompanied by the remark that this character " is something indefinable to the observer, but in so far as it manifests itself in a distinct culture common to the nation it is definable and cannot be ignored." The most obvious conclusion for every theorist should be to leave that indefinable characteristic out and simply to state that nationality is community of at least some cultural achievements, language usually amongst them,[66] which are distinct from those of other parts of mankind and which have originated from community of past experiences.[67] Community of economic life and its preliminary condition in the modern world, community of territory, are

[64] As a rule—and quite typically in the European examples—this "originally" is relative ; the " unhistorical nation " which in consequence of former defeats has lost its upper strata, is in its revival inspired by memories of former greatness, usually exalted by the exaggerations of middle-class nationalism (on this point see W. Kollarz, *Myth and Reality in Eastern Europe*, London, 1945). To Marxists it should be obvious that the inspiration is not the cause of the revival, but a by-product of the process of the differentiation of the peasantry under the impact of capitalism. Nationalist ideologies are merely needed in order to prevent the absorption of the workers, capitalists and intellectuals into the nations traditionally commanding their new social positions.

[65] The basic concept of the "integral" nation is shared by Zionism, which attempts to heal the obviously abnormal structure of the Jewish people by ideological appeals to lower-middle-class people to turn into peasants and labourers. For purely ideological reasons, this has been attempted in a territory where the means available —for ideological and partly also for imperialist reasons—to soften the transition are applied to make life for a former Polish lower-middle-class man tolerable as a peasant not in Poland, but in a country with much lower standards. The successes achieved were possible because the lower-middle-class Polish Jew became a declassé in Poland and was afterwards largely annihilated. I cannot imagine Zionism outside Palestine surviving capitalism and fascism in the countries whence immigrants are recruited for more than one generation.

[66] To regard community of language as a characteristic necessary in *all* conditions—as done by Bauer as well as by the Russian Marxists—would occasionally result in regarding the Swiss as composed of four nations (see my *Federalism*, etc., pp. 219–20).

[67] See my *Federalism, etc.*, p. 332.

essential for the continuation of the national connection, that is, for the preservation of at least some of the cultural traits characteristic of the group, and the growth of some additional ones.

Some of the available forms may be bound to wither away even under capitalism ; some others—and this seems to be a main lesson of the Jewish tragedy — may be rescued from such a fate merely by repression which reasserts the cohesion of a group otherwise bound to be absorbed ; some may continue, and even flourish, in the social formation succeeding capitalism. However, the very concept of nation as a form available for capitalism (and socialism)[40] presupposes its pre-capitalist origin. There is an inherent contradiction between most Marxists'[68] attempts to give a definition of nation clearly and exclusively fitting the capitalist age[39] and the fact that their attempts to define the "interesting" nations have no sense except against the background of some broader definition of nation in general.[69] The contradiction can only be solved by clearly stating that nation, just because it is the form in which past social experiences enter the concrete shaping of later social formations, is something different from its impact upon any concrete social formation. Like society, productive relations, and the other basic concepts of Marxist sociology, nation needs a definition which is essentially formal because it has to fit more than one distinct social formation. A group distinguished from other similar groups, and united by certain common cultural traits originated from a common past seems the only definition sufficiently broad to meet those requirements.

There is plenty of historical experience backing such a definition. The concept of nation has no significance except in distinction from other nations with which there is regular intercourse : a primitive tribal community is no nation for the

[68] Kautsky (Die Befreiung der Nationen, p. 32), reproached Bauer for looking for a definition of nation in general, instead of modern (capitalist) nationality, and Stalin (l c., p. 11) went to the length of reproaching Bauer with " confusing nation, which is a historical category, with tribe, which is an ethnographical category." This is either a different formulation of Kautsky's reproach or it reproaches Bauer with nonsense which he has never uttered, namely, that the Jews, etc., were actual racial units in the biological sense. But see the next note.

[69] Occasionally (l.c., p. 12) Stalin, speaking of pre-capitalist conditions, refers to " nationalities which had been forced into the background " (which evidently supposes the existence of nationalities already before capitalism) and " had not yet been able to consolidate themselves economically into integral nations " (which may be associated with capitalism).

simple reason that such intercourse is reduced to occasional
border contacts. But if there is a common framework in which
such intercourse takes place—in the ancient world the large
multi-national empires, in the modern the world-wide interconnections of capitalist (and socialist) economics and politics—
it cannot be understood except as the product of an earlier
stage of social development. The expansive character of a
certain civilisation is expressed in the fact that groups formed
in an earlier stage of social development are assimilated to its
general pattern because this is the only way in which the existing
social relations, however transformed, can survive in the new
world.[70] The survivals of former tribal units, if their common
tradition is preserved by their common language or religion,
may form nations with a distinct function in the social division
of labour. The Jews, or the Helots in the ancient world,
the Negroes of modern America were and are *not* integral nations:
they owe their very existence to their occupying a certain and
well-defined place in the social scheme. Nations which are
already well-developed, such as the " unhistorical " nations of
the East Central European empires, may be reduced to such a
status by external conquest and the destruction (or absorption)
of their former leading strata, unless they succeed, like the
Japanese[70] in adapting their different historical background to
the need of holding their own in a world dominated by a different
mode of production, so that it forms the basis of a distinct and
integral nation from the very start. So also the nations shaped
or re-shaped in the capitalist world successfully[71] continue to
provide different forms into which the socialist content of the
next stage may be poured. The process may go on as long as
there is social change realised in an interdependent world by
peoples with very different historical backgrounds and cultural
inheritances. The different ways in which social change is carried
out add distinctly new features to the various national traditions,
whilst other traits are lost through assimilation within an
international cultural framework. Nation, though a form which
expresses traditions of the past, cannot continue to be relevant
except in a dynamic world ; only if the process of mutual

[70] See above, p. 7.

[71] Because their shaping has assumed the aspect of a national revolution which
may have been co-ordinated with the international socialist transformation, or at least
be conducive to the easy reception of its results.

assimilation were to be allowed undisputed sway (that is, if no new different traditions were created by new experiences common to the distinct groups) could it wither away.

The definition suggested has its difficulties. It only works clearly in the ascending curve of international integration : a multi-national empire dissolved into a plurality of national units might survive, if it were sufficiently solid to create common traditions, as a " world religion," conflicting with other " world religions " continuing the traditions of different multi-national empires, or at least different groupings within them. This may be regarded as a mere issue of terminology ; very large as well as comparatively small groups may be described as nations. It is of more importance that the suggested definition of nation is so broad that no single characteristics of the transmissable cultural heritage could be defined as in all conceivable cases essential ; a clear criterion so generally accepted as language may land us in difficulties.[66] But once the need for a broad definition of nation in general, and the impossibility of defining the type of nation fitting a certain stage in international social development except against the background of such a broader definition, is realised, the merits of precision in the definition of nation appear much smaller than usually assumed in Marxist literature. Bauer was certainly right when stating that the really important matter is the correct analysis of the processes going on in a distinct period.

PART V

THE SOCIETY TO COME

CHAPTER XVI

PLANNING AND EQUALITY

(a) THE WORKER'S RIGHT TO THE FULL PROCEEDS OF HIS TOIL

Nearly four hundred years passed between the days when Thomas More wrote his Utopia and Thomas Muenzer led the left-wing of the German peasants' rebellion and those when socialist reconstruction started in the U.S.S.R. During those four centuries capitalism, as a mode of production, was in the ascendant, but only during the last of them might it be described as dominating world economics. During the whole period revolting masses and humanitarian thinkers have protested against the misery and injustice involved in capitalism, but only during the last fifth of it has there been a scientific analysis of social transformation. And scientific analysis is closely woven with conflicting humanitarian protest in the attitudes to the coming of socialism, which are thus often contradictory in themselves.

As soon as the scientific system of the classical economists had been completed by Ricardo, it was applied by his socialist successors[1] in order to prove that entrepreneurial profits like all other kinds of unearned incomes originated from labour performed by persons other than those enjoying such incomes, and by Sismondi in order to prove the connection of periodic crises and mass-unemployment with the " underconsumption " of the working masses. Marx turned an abstract socialist Utopia which might serve to strengthen trade unionist arguments for reducing " exploitation " and " underconsumption " within the existing social framework into a realistic criticism of the failure of contemporary society to make full use of potential productive resources and no less realistic description of the tasks of the

---

[1] Especially by Hopkins, Thompson and Bray, whose merits were recognised by Marx (*The Poverty of Philosophy*, p. 60) in polemic against Proudhon's claim to have first put the theory of Socialism on such a basis.

society to come.   In his *Critique of the Gotha Programme*,[2] in refutation of the demagogic assertion of the workers' right " to the full
proceeds of their labour," Marx emphasized that in no society
can " the workers," that is, the sum of the individual workers,
dispose of the whole product of their labour amongst themselves
because of the need for reserves, for investment, for social services,
etc.   There is a capitalist argument of long standing against
socialism, which remains effective because of the continued use of
demagogy of the kind above mentioned : it is based upon establishing the minimal increase of the average working-class income
which would result from the distribution of the existing unearned
incomes, minus expenditure for investment, taxes and other costs[3]
which in any case would have to be paid for from the social
product.   It does not damage Marxism, whose founders claimed
that the criticism of capitalist society should be directed against
the anarchy and inadequacy of capitalist production rather than
against the inherent " injustice " of the distribution of the social
income[4] ; but it certainly hits the vague egalitarian propaganda
which is usually described as " socialism."   Half a century after
the publication of the *Poverty of Philosophy*, Rosa Luxemburg[5] still
had to state that the masses were drawn into the Socialist movement by their opposition to the " unjust "distribution of the social
income ; it was the party's task to endow them with the Marxist
insight to see that distribution was a mere function of the mode
of production the reshaping of which was the task of the Labour
movement.   But another twenty years later Otto Bauer,[6] when
introducing the liberal theory of Guild Socialism into a Central
European framework where opposition to war-time State-capitalist
regulations was still strong, actually stated that Marx had been
mistaken in over-emphasizing the element of planning and that
the mere achievement of social justice by removal of capitalist
privilege should and could be achieved whilst preserving the

---

[2] Ed. cit., pp. 15–6.
[3] A secondary counter-argument against this standpoint is based upon the fact
that the carrying out of socially necessary expenditure by capitalists out of revenue
which is regarded as their private property, grants them social power (say over
cultural institutions favoured by Maecenas), strengthens their prestige as a class (say
by associating necessary medical services with their "charity"), and secures public
attention for their prosperity.
[4] Engels' Preface to the ed. of the *Poverty of Philosophy*, ed. cit., p. 11.
[5] *Socialreform oder Revolution*, ed. quot., p. 34.   The word " unjust " stands in the
original in inverted commas.
[6] *Der Weg zum Sozialismus*, Vienna, 1919.

exchange of commodities produced by autonomous units of producers. Another ten years later, on the eve of the Great Depression, one of the leaders of the Guild Socialists[7] could state that what actually mattered in Marx's economic theories was the theory of surplus-value, or exploitation.

(b) DIFFERENTIATION OF INCOME ACCORDING TO THE WORK PERFORMED

In his *Critique of the Gotha Programme* Marx clearly recognised that socialist society could not work unless it distributed amongst its members the distributable part of the national income in accordance with the work performed by them even though such a mode of distribution may contradict moral standards legitimate from the humanitarian point of view.[8] Such criticism of the society to whose achievement Marx devoted all the efforts of his life was clearly inspired by his desire to preserve the case for the later transition to the higher, communist stage of society ; and even if we should regard such a prospect as Utopian it should be recognised that criticism of the description of the society to come as " just " and " egalitarian " promotes a realistic approach to its needs as well as positive efforts to reduce unavoidable evils to a minimum. Without a criticism directed even against an apparently just distribution according to the work performed by the members of society the case against that part of the capitalist profits actually consumed by the capitalists would have been much weaker too, because, at least in Marx's days, a very large part of the entrepreneurs actually performed managerial functions necessary quite apart from the capitalist mode of production.

Basic misunderstandings of Marxism are produced by the familiar sectional standards of the Labour movement. The assertion that an excess of the social product over that part distributed in one or the other way amongst the toilers is morally evil, and involves insufficiency of the markets for

[7] G. D. H. Cole, *Introduction* to Eden and Cedar Paul's translation of vol I of *Capital*, pp. xxii–iii and xxviii.

[8] Ed. cit., pp. 12–13, where Marx states that the right of each worker to equal pay for equal work done " is a right of inequality in its content, like every right. Law by its very nature can only exist in the application of an equal standard. But unequal individuals (and they would not be different individuals if they were not unequal) are only measurable by an equal standard in so far as they are taken from one *definite* site only . . . everything else (such as different physical strength and ability, size of the family to be supported, etc.) being ignored."

consumers' goods, may be ideological or even mistaken ; but it is an answer to the employer's plea that high wages would deprive him of legitimate profits and harm the men themselves by restricting the industry's competitive power. For this reason, these are the parts of the Marxist economic system that have been taken over by the sectional labour movement. So also objections to high differentiation in earnings according to different skill and productivity are not mere " lower-middle-class egalitarianism " (in which terms they are described in the U.S.S.R.) nor are they merely the resentment of the peasant just drawn into industry against the tempo of modern mechanized production. In every capitalist country they provide the natural reaction of the labour movement to the employers' attempts to split its ranks by attracting a highly qualified minority in key position and to make the less efficient worker redundant (and a potential strike-breaker) by luring his more efficient fellow into increased production. Phenomena such as " socialist competition " and Stakhanovism contradict the sectional labour movement's conception of ideal conditions of labour, which do not coincide with the maximum prosperity of a socialist state. The ideological impact of the sectional tradition was so strong that, in official Soviet propaganda, for a very long time increased productivity of labour, and increased investments which are conditioned by an increased " surplus-product " were described as mere long-term devices to increase mass-consumption, but in the discussions of 1936-7 the aim of the process of socialist reproduction was described as the creation of a communist society—which presupposes increased output of means of consumption, but also defence and social education —as distinct from the mere reproduction of the labour force on the basis of improving standards of life.[9] An increasingly realistic approach to the need of the socialist sixth of the world to hold its own and to overtake the capitalist world implied increase in the rate of investment.

Starting from a criticism of capitalist society, mainly directed against its lack of ability to satisfy the people's needs, Socialists soon find themselves measuring the problems of transition

[9] Academician Strumilin advocated in an article published in 1936 in the leading Soviet economic journals (*Planovoye Khozaistvo*, and *Problemy Ekonomiky*, No. 5) the last mentioned conception. But under the impact of a discussion (reported in German in my paper in *Zeitschrift fuer Sozialforschung*, Paris, 1938, No. 3) in his concluding article (*Problemy Ekonomiky*, 1936, No. 6) he accepted the first mentioned concept.

and of the structure of the order succeeding capitalism by the standard of efficiency. It appears a mere tactical question whether compensation should be paid for nationalised enterprises, that is, whether (under an efficient system of taxation) for one or two generations unearned incomes should be granted to their former owners. Preservation of small entrepreneurs in those branches of industry which could be better handled by them than by the young socialist State (which should rather concentrate its limited resources upon the " commanding heights of economic life ") would be distinctly preferable to wholesale nationalisation. But, unhappily, these are issues of social power more than of social justice; and as this is well realised by capitalists, the young Soviet republic is forced, by the logic of circumstances, to go further than was originally intended. Capitalists are expropriated lest they should find increased opportunities to finance White Guards, industries are nationalised sooner than desirable from the purely administrative point of view, lest production be stopped and the towns starved.[10] In order to justify the politics of sheer necessity in popular propaganda, "justice" is unearthed and egalitarian standards are proclaimed (besides, as there is hardly enough food to go round, there must be some equality, otherwise incentives for some would have to be purchased by physical starvation of others). But retribution follows the propagandist who describes what actually was a necessary concession to emergencies as an accomplishment of revolutionary principles : supporters of the revolution who conceived those principles in the egalitarian sense are disappointed when the emergency passes and there are more consumers' goods for everyone though they are more unequally distributed.

The increase in the rate of investment in the U.S.S.R. implied not only abolition of unemployment, but also shortage of labour. Accordingly, the incentives offered to more skilled and more efficient labour had to be increased. Even in early 1918, in the hey-day of the revolution, differentiations of earnings to a degree acceptable to the moderate Trade Unionist[11] were enacted. During the N.E.P., the proportion between the lowest (1st) and the highest (17th) wages (and salary) group was 1:4, and was

[10] See M. Dobb, l. c. (1948), Chapter IV, and my *Soviet Legal Theory*, pp. 43 ff, 89 ff. and 167 ff.

[11] 2:3 in the Petrograd metallurgic industry. 1:3 amongst skilled workers in the Post and Telegraph Services. See my *Soviet Legal Theory*, p. 45.

increased to 1:6 when the maximum compound allowance for
responsible work involving overtime was added.[12]   During the
first Five Year Plan the characteristic differentiation between the
respective remunerations of completely unskilled and highly
skilled work was 1:4 in the individual industries ; but the general
introduction of piecework, with remuneration for over-fulfilment
of the standard output proceeding on a geometric scale[13], made
differences between actual earnings much higher.   On the eve of
the last war, the proportion between the legal wage-minimum for
urban workers and the highest salaries enacted for the most
responsible workers in State, Science and Industry was about 1:10.
Further, premia are attached to the successful performance of
managerial as well as of technical and manual work.   Besides,
there is the Director's Fund to which a certain percentage of
planned profits and of economies resulting from reduced costs, and
a still higher percentage of profits reached above the planned
figure is allocated, and from which premia and improved ameni-
ties for the employees of the factory concerned are financed as well
as expansions of its activities in excess of the planned investments.[14]
From the point of view of socialist principles no issues other
than those involved already in different remuneration of workers
of different efficiency arise, though in this case the advantages
are shared by individuals who have unequally contributed to
their achievement.   In principle, this issue arises even with the
high earnings of individual Stakhanov-workers whose production
records obviously suppose smooth working of the whole factory
organisation without all those who have actually rendered the

---

[12] The latter amount—225 roubles per month—forming the maximum earning
allowed to Party-members.   Only non-Party specialists had higher contractual
earnings, and also the Party-member was allowed to retain 75 per cent. of royalties,
etc., earned apart from his salary.   Apart from this, there were also privileges for
valuable specialists in the field of housing, etc.

[13] See my *Spirit of Post-War Russia*, pp. 22 ff.

[14] The Fund, which was suspended during the War (perhaps because, at that
time, strict fulfilment of orders was regarded as more important than managerial
initiative, and also because expanded housing-plans, additional holiday-amenities, etc.,
were evidently not feasible), was re-established by a Decree, published in *Izvestia*,
December, 12, 1946. Fulfilment of all the three plans for production of goods (as to
quantity and quality), for lower production costs, and for making profits is a condition
for any allocation to the Fund.   The Fund is administered by the Director, in agreement with the Trade Union Factory Committee, and allocations for purposes other
than those of the enterprise and its workers are excluded.

success possible receiving special remuneration.[15] In the kollkhozes, where work is remunerated by a distinct share, depending on the individual members' efforts and on many factors independent of them, this element of inequality between equally efficient workers of one industry is most obvious. It is occasionally mentioned as one of the reasons why kollkhozes in their present shape should be regarded as a form of socialist organisation inferior to the State enterprise.[16] But it should not be regarded as fundamentally important once the description of distribution according to efforts as "just" is disclaimed.[8]

Unearned incomes are absent in the U.S.S.R. and, in view of the absence of differentiations according to sex, the differentiations amongst the earned incomes just mentioned would be rather less than is usual in this country. The system of piece-work and premia available in the most diverse walks of life would increase the actual differentiation between the lowest and the highest incomes observable amongst the urban population, but it need not create anything like class-differentiations : high incomes on the basis of " progressive piece-work " are more easily accessible to the manual than proportional premia to the black-coat worker (with a few exceptions, such as renowned artists and technicians). On the other hand, in the absence of unearned incomes taxation is not shaped with the intention of reducing the incentive to earn higher incomes, and the differentiation between real incomes may even be increased by non-monetary benefits in the field of housing, holiday-making, etc., granted to the efficient worker, with cars for higher employees. During the war the system of social differentiation according to the responsibility of the work done was taken to the length of introducing special officers'

[15] Complaints, levelled by would-be Stakhanovites of lack of facilities, such as ample supply of tools, raw materials, and auxiliary labour, that would have enabled them to establish some production record, as well as criticism of factory managers who disorganised the general production of the factory by paying excessive attention to increasing its prestige by enabling some Stakhanovite achievements, were frequent during the hey-day of Stakhanovism. Apart from the public interest, the private interests of the persons concerned were also involved in a country where most industrial labour is paid by piecework so that interruptions of the average worker's work by absence of raw-material diverted in order to enable the Stakhanovite's smooth working may result in the former's not fulfilling his plan, and therefore earning less. These were growing pains of the Stakhanovite movement ; but the principal point made by us in the text remains valid even when the position is inverted and the average worker, though to a lesser extent, shares in benefits accruing to the factory collective as a whole ([14]) because of its overfulfilling the plan.

[16] Stalin, op. cit. (1933), p. 238 ; see also the above, p. 150, quoted Soviet arguments on value and rent.

clubs and orderlies, institutions which formerly were regarded as alien to the spirit of the Red Army.

Such facts illustrate the extent to which the anti-egalitarian tendencies have developed. This inequality is not more than is usual in Western countries (within the realm of earned incomes) and hardly more than would be familiar to the Western Trade Unionist movement if it had to cover all earners from the last unskilled worker to the first technician of the country managing a giant factory as the Soviet Trade Unions do. But it is more than is allowed according to the ideological standards of a Trade Union movement actually restricted to the manual workers. The actual difference lies in the basis of the existing differentiations : a Western Trade Unionist can hardly fail to observe the absence of differentiations according to race and sex in the U.S.S.R., but he may be less satisfied with the fact that such differences as are current in both countries between the least qualified sales assistant and the university professor may occur in the U.S.S.R. between the least skilled worker and some Stakhanovite neighbour of his in one factory or mine as well. The basis of such an attitude is demand for some sort of common Labour front against an opponent which is assumed to exist no longer in the U.S.S.R.

(c) PLANNING AS THE MAIN ARGUMENT IN FAVOUR OF SOCIALISM

The realisation of socialism in the U.S.S.R., a backward country whose peasant population needs high incentives to acquire industrial skill,[17] has taken from the idea of socialism much of its former egalitarian appeal, whilst its triumphs in the field of planned economics are conspicuous. Under the impact of two world-wars and the implied necessity of directing war-economics, planning has become popular in the Western world also. During World War I this tendency hardly exceeded the importance of an attempt to make Germany's State-capitalist measures (which were conditioned by her strong bureaucratic tradition and by her very difficult position even during World War I) popular with right-wing Social Democrats. But during World War II, which was preceded by the American New Deal, intensive planning of the distribution of available resources became necessary in Britain at a time when she was allied with the U.S.S.R. and the " red " bogey was temporarily shelved. Keynesian economics

[17] But we have seen, in Chapter XIII, section b, that such a country was most likely to start a socialist transformation, and, in Chapter XV, that other peasant nations are most likely to follow it.

had broken the familiar academic and deflationist line of resistance and appeared to offer an approach, through national planning of investments, which would overcome at least the worst anarchy of capitalist society and secure full employment without that restriction of the individual's (including at least the larger entrepreneur's) freedom implied even in the more moderate concepts of N.E.P. or nationalisation of the "commanding heights." To that intellectual climate we owe, in the philosophical field, such works as Mannheim's *Man and Society in an Age of Reconstruction*, in the economic field the study, prepared by The Oxford University Institute of Statistics, on *The Economics of Full Employment*, and on the borderline between the economic and the political field Lord Beveridge's report on *Full Employment in a Free Society*, free being regarded as a synonym of preserving at least a considerable amount of freedom of capitalist enterprise and the assumed freedoms of the individual. Although that trend has actually become the ideological guiding line of the British Labour government it is difficult to say anything about its further chances ; very little further support from non-Socialist quarters is likely since in U.S.A. the New Deal has given way to a renewed cult of " free enterprise " and Soviet socialism has become " Public Enemy No. 1 ".

However, we have to deal not with an ephemeral ideological constellation, but with a fundamental problem of social transformation. Both the Marxist and the Keynesian approach are directed against post-classical[18] academic economics. In the " vulgar-economic " system (to use Marx's terminology) it is asserted that by the play of free competition in a capitalist society those goods which best fit the consumers' demand are produced with a minimum of production costs. Under the further assumption that every supply creates its own demand, that is, to use Marx's interpretation of that approach, that commodity exchange can be analysed by an abstraction which omits the fact that it is commodity exchange,[19] it follows, in a purely tautological sense, that there can be no unemployment except that which is

---

[18] The difference between the definitions of " classical " economists by Marx (*Capital*, vol. I, note to p. 53) and Keynes' *General Theory of Employment*, etc., note p. 3, respectively, is illuminating : Ricardo forms in the former the conclusion, in the latter the starting point, so that the development described by Marx as " vulgar-economic " appears as " classic."

[19] See above, p. 165. A corresponding criticism of the basic approach of traditional economists has appeared in academic economics as late as in Keynes, op. cit., pp. 19–20.

due to the occasional misdirection of investments, and is bound to be corrected by the very play of free competition. Recent academic economists have translated into learned terminology the average employer's conviction that the workers' failure to accept such wages as are compatible with the conditions of the market is the only obstacle preventing his employing all of them and yet making a moderate profit. Some have gone to the length of accounting for the unemployment, during the Great Depression, of nearly half the working-classes in Germany and U.S.A. in terms equally applicable to the marginal housewife's failure to accept part-time work because the trouble thereby caused in her household exceeds the pleasures of the marginal enjoyments which, from her earnings, could be added during the family's holidays.

The Marxist counter-argument originally started from the obvious theoretical simplifications of the vulgar economist pattern[19] and even more obvious contradictions to reality, which invite ideological explanations.[20] Against the alleged necessity of free competition to minimise production costs and to fit output to consumers' demands, it may be stated that capitalist monopolies actually succeed in rationalising production, and also the consumers' demand, by influencing public opinion and by distribution machinery, in such a way that the average housewife is likely " freely to choose " such commodities as the monopoly happens to produce.[21] In both directions, socialist economics can be at least equally efficient. Reduction of production costs to a minimum is actually achieved in the U.S.S.R. by a system of incentives not fundamentally different from those applied in large-scale monopolist organisations. As an instrument creating and satisfying the average consumers' needs in those very fields where they are in the process of development, socialist State industry is superior to private monopolies, as can be easily grasped by a glance into Soviet shops dealing in books, cosmetics or pharmaceutical articles. It is superior even to " co-operative socialism " which bases its whole approach to the problem of planning upon satisfaction of consumers' demands by consumers'

---

[20] Which have been given, in a most impressive way, Ibid., pp. 32-3.

[21] The last-mentioned part of the argument, though implied in all the Marxist statements on the dependence of distribution on production, has actually been developed in recent Marxist less than in non-Marxist progressive literature, perhaps because of the former's obsession with rather scholastic issues.

organisations,[22] because it does not have to reckon with consumers' demands shaped by private monopolies' interests and because the survival of its distributive system does not depend upon high dividends.

The Soviet successes, in the peace-period following the first two Five Year Plans, and in every period of peace which may be allowed to the U.S.S.R., are favoured by continuous economic expansion in a country where such expansion involves a quick rise in mass-demand for non-essential goods, and some leadership as to the way in which such demands should develop. This implies a continuation of what in capitalist countries would be called " a sellers' market." From the socialist point of view, this makes it the more desirable that the seller should be identical with an organisation standing for the social rather than for private interests. Certainly, the cheap supply of books, in the U.S.S.R., is in the interest of the government. Mass-output of political literature in the U.S.S.R. does not provide in itself an argument in favour of socialism, unless the question is begged and socialism, or at least democracy in a conception implying mass-interest in politics, is supposed to be desirable on its own merits ; but, certainly, the mass-output of crime-stories forms no argument in favour of capitalism. Nor does a price-policy aiming at maximising profits made in the production of essential drugs, and taxation of the female part of the population by the pricing of cosmetics, even if fittingly combined with a propaganda that enforces the payment of the tax by creating the suitable " public opinion " amongst prospective consumers. We are here concerned with the fact that a socialist state (not only the U.S.S.R.) is likely to use the decrease of overall production costs facilitated by mass-output of political literature in order to supply books of educational value cheaply, whilst private entrepreneurs

[22] We are not speaking here of the part played by consumers' co-operatives in the distribution of the products of a nationalised economy, which is a practical question and has been answered in different ways in different stages of Soviet development, but of the concept (see also below, p. 372) of approaching a higher and planned social order by development of such co-operatives with corresponding increase of their own production of commodities to be sold in their shops. The merits of co-operation in the first, narrower, sense are most evident in time of excessive shortage of goods. The manager of a village shop who stores pins when his customers need nails is sacked quicker if employed by a consumers' co-operative then if he belongs to a complicated State machine, the local members of which may share with him a common need to take a charitable view of each other's shortcomings. But this does not necessarily mean that he—or his employers—are more far-sighted than would be a well-managed set of State shops if, say, the merits of various pharmaceutic preparations for the various accidents occurring in the countryside are in question.

will cash the profits made from the sales of crime-stories or, conceivably, spend part of them upon increasing their prestige by producing such political books as *they* feel desirable. A socialist State may be interested in some proceeds from taxation of luxuries, but this interest is not likely to overshadow the public interest in improving the morale of all groups of workers and in promoting their physical health. Issues of a different character will arise at a later stage of development when elementary mass-needs whose social value is obvious, are satisfied, and further differentiation in the satisfaction of recognised needs will be demanded.[23]   But it is likely that early socialist triumphs will take place in those very countries where conditions similar to those characteristic of the U.S.S.R. prevail.

In the conditions of comparative scarcity with which the U.S.S.R. has to reckon, satisfaction of consumers' needs is a question of deciding priorities ; and this decision is a political one.   Planning is carried out by special organs which, on the basis of the general order of priority (as to productive investments, consumers' needs, defence, etc.) as established by the leading State organs, elaborate various possible alternatives of the general plan.   The largest enterprises which are under the direct jurisdiction of the Union Ministries get their plan tasks directly allotted in the national plan.   But it is generally regarded as most important that plans should be addressed to concrete people and organisations who would thus know exactly what is expected from them.[24]   As to State and municipal enterprises, differences in importance decide only the place in the planning hierarchy where such concrete allocation of their plan task is made. Collective farms are allocated a certain minimum of deliveries due in the way of compensation for the services of the State-owned Machine Tractor Stations, and as a tax.   Kollkhoz-deliveries exceeding that minimum (partly dependent on decisions in the field left to the kollkhozes' autonomy) and the output of small craftsmen and their co-operatives have to be calculated in a way similar to that applied in capitalist countries by government statisticians ; and similar incentives are available to influence those " autonomous " decisions in the direction desired. Excessive use of the influence of the Communist *nuclei* in the

---

[23] See below, pp. 386-7.
[24] See above, pp. 154-5.   Cf. G. Sorokin, *Socialist Planning of Soviet Economics*, Moscow, 1946 (in Russian).

kollkhozes in opposition to the average members' interpretation of their interests would soon destroy that interest, unless their suggestions could be backed by hints at premia, tax reliefs, etc., offered by the State.

Every variant of the plan is supported by elaborate balances, not only of man-power and of the consumption of some essential raw-materials (as for State-supervised capitalist economics, as in Britain), but also of the anticipated purchasing power of town and countryside respectively and the available means of satisfying that demand, The financial balance appears merely as the concluding element in which all the implications drawn from the more essential balances find expression.[24] Thus the political organs, when deciding between the variants, can do so in full knowledge of all their implications ; if the plans are properly elaborated and proper provision made for the necessary reserve funds against unexpected contingencies, diversion of productive resources to the detriment of the most essential needs, as well as " bottlenecks " of undue dimensions, may be avoided. There may be shortages of labour, of imported raw-materials, etc. and it may be even said that the presence of a situation in which decisions of fundamental character between priorities would have to be made in whatever economic system, makes for an obvious advantage of a system in which such decisions are clearly made from the point of view of the public interest and all available national resources are applied in order to produce what is deemed most essential.[24a] However, today at least, the appeal of socialism is based upon conditions in which comparative satisfaction of the most essential needs is regarded as the decisive test of an economic system, not only in the U.S.S.R. but also in this country.

(d) Different approaches to Planning

Like Marxism, the Keynesian theory denies that effective demand is assured by some mechanism as soon as economy in the application of productive resources is safeguarded by the play of free competition. The growth of that theory coincided with the dropping of the Gold standard in Britain, with the New Deal in U.S.A. and with the achievement of full employment by German War economics. Theoretical consciousness, as expressed in the

[24a] Cf. Dobb l.c. (1948) Chapter 1.

Keynesian theory, was conspicuously absent in U.S.A. (where the quick collapse of the New Deal was certainly promoted by its artificial fitting into a traditional Free Enterprise ideology). On a much lower level of abstraction it developed in Nazi Germany, where the issue was tackled on a financial rather than upon an economic level even in the more serious of the available theoretical analyses.[25] However, in the field decisive from the Marxist point of view, which is production, the American (T.V.A.) and the German practice in planning far surpassed the British. Whilst the obvious needs of a prospective debtor-country had rendered control of foreign trade and exchanges familiar phenomena, the merits of private enterprise in domestic production were still supposed to be evident, and even much later were identified with Freedom by leading Keynesians such as Lord Beveridge. Lord Keynes himself saw " no reason to suppose that the existing system misemploys the factors of production which are in use."[26] Even distinctly left-wing Keynesians such as Mr. Kaleczki[27] speak with favour of "deficit spending" by public expenditure for social services and of transfer of parts of the national income to the poorer strata of the community with their higher propensity to consume, and criticise methods aimed at the stimulation of productive investment by private entrepreneurs, without regarding as fundamental the issue whether the direction of productive investment necessary in the public interest could be achieved by encouraging private investment, or by nationalising

---

[25] In 1936 Nonnenbruch, the main economist theorist of the Nazi party, published his *Dynamische Wirtschaft*. The main thesis of the book (and of his articles in the *Voelkischer Beobachter*) is the statement that the " liberalist " circulation between commodities and money, which implies unemployment, if there are no markets for the commodities, was being replaced, in the National Socialist state, by a new one in which deficit-spending creates additional employment and thus increases revenue. The analogies to the Keynesian theory are obvious, but so are also the differences : Keynes (for instance, *General Theory*, p. 303) argues about " true inflation," that is, about a state of things in which monetary expansion would increase output no longer (because there are no more unemployed productive resources) but merely increase prices, whilst the Nazi (evidently arguing against Schacht, etc.) tries to establish that deficit-spending would ultimately result in elimination of the deficit. Nonnenbruch is not even interested in the issue whether the expenditure creating additional employment is more or less rational (see below) ; for it is silently supposed that expenditure in war will increase national wealth by the successful outcome of the war and the implied appropriation of foreign wealth. Full employment—round which the Keynesians thought centres with some one-sidedness (see below, p. 368)—appears to the Nazi as a by-product of the pre-war effort, desirable because of its strengthening influence upon the home front.

[26] L. c., p. 379.

[27] In his contribution to *The Economics of Full Employment*.

the spheres of production where such investment is needed.[28] The whole approach to the volume of employment as the basic issue that matters implies acquiescence in the way in which productive resources are usually employed in a capitalist society[26] as well as dealing with unemployment as a specific grievance needing special remedies, which invite combination with remedies for other grievances such as shortages of housing, milk for children, medical services, etc. Such an approach fits the familiar " left-wing " ideology, at least in countries with traditions of gradualist reform ; but it contradicts the basic needs of the situation in which Keynesian economics would have a chance to inspire practical politics, namely, of a situation demanding reconstruction of the foundations of national economics in a country where socialisation of new investments, but not expropriation of existing ones may appear feasible without class-conflicts strong enough to interfere with the nation's acting as an entity on the international stage. In such a situation, the opponents of the nationalisation of investments, who certainly would include the financier, and the bulk of the industrial monopolist interests, would be exposed to the reproach of betraying the national interest to foreign financiers, whilst attempts of parts of the working-class to carry out a distinctly Marxist policy (even of a moderate character, without preposterous attempts at wholesale nationalisation) would be rejected as splitting the national front. In such a situation, it would not be justified to regard pyramid (or house-) building, armaments, or the reduction of the deficit in Britain's balance of trade as equivalent methods of putting the multiplier into action : in certain regards its working would be most undesirable, whilst in those spheres where maximum efforts should be made, not the mere employment of a maximised labour force but its maximised output should be achieved. There may be spheres where the fulfilment of the second condition may be incompatible with the preservation of private ownership of the industries where the investment is made, coal-mining being only a species amongst them. The incompatibility may be caused, as in the example just mentioned, by reluctance of the labour force to make the necessary efforts under a discredited system of owner-

---

[28] Ibid., p. 49. Slum clearance, etc., are described as typical instances of public investments. Expansion of existing equipment at a high rate is described as a specific condition demanding specific controls " not unlike those used in war time," and " only after the process of capital expansion has proceeded sufficiently far is a policy of full employment of the kind described possible " (Ibid., p. 43).

ship and management ; but it may also be caused by the doubts of the workers whether the existing owners will apply the new investments in the way they want, or their fear lest sacrifices made by the whole community may make some groups of owners too powerful. " Socialisation of investments," and gradual depreciation of investments made by private persons, imply a choice of alternatives : whether expropriation of members of the community will be carried out in favour of the community or of certain monopolist groups whose power would be increased by the rentier's euthanasia. The latter alternative would correspond to a fascist system[29] ; if it is rejected, " socialisation of investments" in a situation where investments have to be directed into the " commanding heights of production " would lead to the nationalisation of those heights. The specific weight of the nationalised sector would grow because an increasing number of industries would have to undergo the procedure and because the specific weight of the nationalised industries would increase because of the investments concentrated upon them. For reasons just explained this would be a step *beyond* the Keynesian position which, in itself, not only is not a variety of planning, but even supposes a situation where planning of productive resources appears unnecessary.[28] It would be a different kind of N.E.P., originating not from self-restriction of a state nationalising industries in order to clear class-relations (and therefore likely to be carried by the logic of class-conflict further than intended,[10]) but as a condition attached to the development of industries the need for the development of which could hardly be denied while the advocates of subsidies to private investors may fail to rally such mass-support as would make resistance to nationalised investments practical politics. In such an event, the " euthanasia of the rentier " may imply the euthanasia of private enterprise— or, to put it in a more positive way, the opportunity for society to dispose of such services as private entrepreneurs may still be able to render for so long as they remain helpful. Private entrepreneurs, too, would be spared much evitable hardship in such a situation and society may be able to dispense with emergency measures. But it would be erroneous to describe

[29] Of course, we are not speaking about its description in State ideology, which is a matter of tradition and political tactic. The economic foundations of fascism are already implied in the familiar device of war-economics in capitalist states which consists in letting some private monopolies fulfil some " public task " which further strengthens their position towards their less privileged competitors. See below, p. 374.

such a society as " free " if freedom is regarded as a synonym for free enterprise.

In my opinion, such a situation is the only one in which Keynesianism can get its practical test (though as a mere transition stage) whatever left-wing Keynesians may feel about a situation in which expansion of existing equipment at a high rate rather than increase of mass-consumption forms the starting point of the whole experiment. In U.S.A., with her highly developed economic resources and her international position which would be safe even with a much reduced rate of productive investments, the economic consequences of policies seeking full employment mainly by increased mass-consumption might be less detrimental than in Britain and other European countries ; but in such circumstances it is also impossible to see what factors would force acquiescence upon those social powers which broke the first New Deal. And a nationalisation policy carried out in order to break political resistance to a " full employment " policy would no longer be Keynesianism, not even in the mere economic sense.

Within the Marxist camp, with the receding of the egalitarian approach, wholesale nationalisation, as distinct from that of the " commanding heights " of economics, has lost its *raison d'être* unless it is necessitated by the political situation, and especially by sabotage on the part of the remaining entrepreneurs. The best chances of avoiding such complications would be given in a situation where nationalisation of the " commanding heights " of economics appeared as directed against the owners of those enterprises not as such—that is, in terms of the capitalist ideology, as successful and efficient entrepreneurs—but as betrayers of the national interest because Big Business had assumed a Quisling rôle in an international conflict in which the socialist interest could be identified with the national interest. So the lower-middle-classes and those few entrepreneurs who had defended the national interest could be successfully integrated into the new society. The attempt to introduce socialism in this way is actually being made in the East European countries, and might have had chances even elsewhere had growing international tension not put a premium on desperate resistance to policies of nationalisation.[30] Even in those cases where actual relations

[30] I have dealt with that eventuality in Chapter IX of *Soviet Legal Theory*, in the atmosphere of 1944 which was more hopeful than today for the future of international relations.

of power excluded the possiblity of civil war, those social facts which had turned the leaders of the capitalist hierarchy " Quislings " in the past international conflict might range part of the remaining middle-class elements on the side of the opponent in some further conflagration in which their own country would now be identified with the international anti-capitalist interest. The fear, on the part of the rulers, that something of this kind might happen, as well as artificial stimulation of every internal friction within the socialist (or semi-socialist) system by its external opponents may eventually render impossible the continued co-existence of socialist (large-scale) and private (small-scale) enterprise in some countries, however undisputed its merits be from the socio-economic point of view. But the situation might be different in cases where the " socialist sector " had started from a mere desire to preserve public ownership of investments made by public efforts, plus the elimination of private ownership in a few key-industries where it had proved conspicuously inefficient. There would be friction in some industries where private and public enterprises would compete ; and as the whole hypothetical case pre-supposes the respective countries' need to free themselves from " Free Trade " and its natural protectors, encouragement of such friction from abroad would not be lacking. However, if controls of investments and foreign trade are firmly handled, and occasional incidents of distinct mismanagement of private enterprises are answered by nationalisation under conditions unfavourable to the former owners, nothing worse than further reduction of investments in the private sector, with the implied quicker rise of investments in the nationalised sector, is bound to occur. As no large-scale industry without continued investments is conceivable, the merits of " free enterprise," which may be enhanced in State ideology as much as desired, may gradually recede to the level of the Soviet private dressmaker's no doubt justified assertion that she can satisfy the cultivated consumer's taste in a way superior to the dress-department in the State Univermag, though more expensive. There may even be important fields (such as the stimulation of agricultural efforts by restoring peasant ownership of the land with due regard for co-operative marketing of the product and for some State supervision in exchange for State subsidies) where " private enterprise " would rise above the present level. All this would not prevent it from being reduced to a special aspect of the use of managerial premia. It could be prolonged (1) until in every field of social production the superiority of the large scale (and therefore State owned) enterprise was conspicuous ; or (2) until the incentives offered in the huge administrative machinery of nationalised enterprise to the gifted manager's ambitions had drained the private sector of every available talent ; or finally (3) until the progress of nationalised economy should actually reach a stage where conspicuous inequality as an incentive to productive efforts should be needed no longer. There is no proof that the third reason for a disappearance of the " private sector " would be realised first, and that therefore the " injustice " of that specific aspect of managerial premia that were called " entrepreneurial profits " would have to be solemnly proclaimed. In every other development of the relation between the private and public sectors they would simply wither away.

At this stage of our investigation, it may be helpful to represent diagrammatically the very different policies (and theoretical approaches) current in our days under the heading of " Planning." The vagueness and problematic nature of the term has been expressed in Mannheim's description of planning as a " reconstruction of a historically developed society into a unity which is regulated more and more by mankind from certain central positions" [31] the last link of the phrase being perhaps more realistically [32] translated into " certain social groups formed in certain ways and controlling the key-positions of social life." Planning thus embraces all approaches in which the interplay of the economic forces (apart from natural or external catastrophes, for which provision has to be made by the establishment of reserve funds) is itself conceived as controlled by the policy applied. [33]

[31] *Man and Society in an Age of Transition*, London, 1940, p. 193.
[32] See also Ibid., pp. 74-5.
[33] Comp. Ibid., p. 152. Mannheim is not consistent in his definition of planning because he regards it essentially as a transition process. Thus he comes (p. 193) to a definition of planning as " foresight deliberately applied to human affairs, so that the social process is no longer *merely* the product of conflict and competition "—a definition to which, if not every intelligent businessman, every large-scale combine, or the Russian right-wing Communists of 1928 who regarded Soviet Planning as operating within a basically anarchic market could subscribe. The foundation of Mannheim's attitude is philosophic : the regulation of an actually organised society, as distinct from the planning process, would, to him, be administration. The triumph of planning is, to him (Ibid.) the end of " history, the unforeseeable, fateful dominance of uncontrollable social forces." Engels (see above, pp. 91-2) derived the derivation of causal laws of society from the present anarchic and molecular character of social processes ; however, he did not hold that, with the achievement of a society in which causality would work through human consciousness, history would come to an end ; on the contrary he held it would at that very point become history proper.

Radical syndicalism, which poses merely the egalitarian issue
and leaves it to the workers controlling their respective factories
to deal with each other according to market principles, does
not belong to the planning ideologies proper ; nor does
Keynesianism itself so far as it deals merely with the incentive to
invest and the propensity to consume, the concrete aspects of
production and consumption being regarded as secondary.
But moderate forms of syndicalism, such as Guild Socialism, which
provide for some central planning agency based upon the co-
ordination of the individual guilds, belong to our scheme, as does
also the above envisaged variety of N.E.P. (or " mixed economy")
starting from the implications of control of investments. The
various schemes of planning, in that sense, can be classified
according to the starting point, though eventually in nearly
every planning ideology full control of the whole system of
national economics is envisaged. The schemes start either
from distribution, by Co-operatives or by Public State Trade ;[34]
or from production (which may be planned by capitalist monopolies, by Trade Unions, etc., as envisaged in the moderate forms
of syndicalism, or by the State, in the Marxist pattern) ; or,
finally, from investments controlled by the State. Of all these
" pure types " only the Marxist pattern has won actual and predominant importance. But there are certain combinations of the
different approaches, which are most easily illustrated in a graphic
scheme on the opposite page.

In this scheme, connections compatible with, but not necessarily characteristic of, fascism have been shown by dotted lines : it
is not defined by the justification of its claims to have met the
peasants' difficulties or to have made public investments in
fields other than war-preparation.[25] But fascist claims that their
economic policies are based upon actual sectional mass-organisations (co-operatives, trade unions, etc.) should be disregarded : if
attempts made in that direction (in Austria, and to some extent
also in Italy) had been crowned with more than nominal success,
they would be separated from " Economic Democracy " of the
German reformist pattern[35] (which also failed) by a mere different
political terminology. Fascism is defined as connected with the

[34] Such schemes had been elaborated, by Neurath and Wissel, during the German
" Socialisation " debates of 1918–9.
[35] In the current use of the term by right-wing German Social Democrats and
Trade Unionists. Analogies with some forms of Guild Socialism, and moderate
forms of fascism (see below in the text) are obvious.

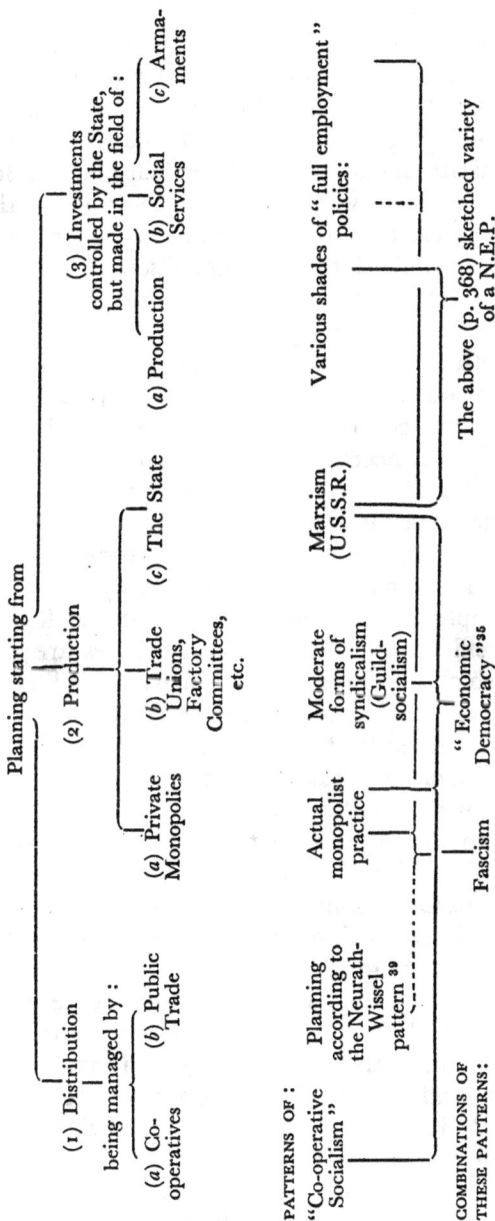

Planning starting from

(1) Distribution being managed by:
- (a) Co-operatives
- (b) Public Trade

(2) Production
- (a) Private Monopolies
- (b) Trade Unions, Factory Committees, etc.
- (c) The State

(3) Investments controlled by the State, but made in the field of:
- (a) Production
- (b) Social Services
- (c) Armaments

PATTERNS OF:

"Co-operative Socialism"

Planning according to the Neurath-Wissel pattern [39]

Actual monopolist practice

Moderate forms of syndicalism (Guild-socialism)

Marxism (U.S.S.R.)

Various shades of "full employment" policies:

"Economic Democracy"[35]

Fascism

COMBINATIONS OF THESE PATTERNS:

The above (p. 368) sketched variety of a N.E.P.

N

State merely in the latter's capacity as a controller of investments, not of production (which is supposed to be regulated by
the monopolies, under supervision by a State controlled by
themselves) ; and a case can be made for explaining the failure
of " Economic Democracy " and the connected patterns by
failure to decide the question " Who is to plan in Whose interest ? "
Nor are kollkhozes mentioned because their place in Soviet reality
is as an organ through which the State co-ordinates the initiative
and private interest of the producers with its own planning
influence ;[36] only the latter is under discussion. But the origin
of the policies by which economic activities are co-ordinated, is
only *one* aspect of planned economics : if our scheme had been
concerned with the scope granted to the initiative of the members
of the society and to the way in which incentives to produce are
applied, we could construct various types of socialist economics
which would not necessarily be unrealistic (in the sense of
" Economic Democracy " etc.) because only one of them fitted
the specific needs of the U.S.S.R.

So far, we are confronted with two alternative prospects for
the growth of a planned society : planning by private monopolies
with an example already tested in Germany at least as regards
its military efficiency, where the monopolies are co-ordinated
by a State which also directs investments for military and other
public purposes ; and planning by the State (which, because of
the resistance offered by the supporters of the other alternative,
could hardly operate unless based upon working-class support)
as the main owner of the means of production. Of the basic
standards from the development of which this chapter started,
Equality, at least for the present stage of development[8], has
been reduced to the demand that inequality of income and social
status be correlated to different personal shares in the national
productive efforts, or to state it in other terms, that there should
be no unearned incomes. Of the two alternative main patterns,
the State-controlled one is the only one that can (and, in view of
its supporters, ultimately must) comply with that standard, whilst
the other is bound to appeal to a property-owners', and perhaps
even rentiers', ideology. Amongst the possible variations of
the State-controlled pattern those in which control is loosened in
the interest of " freedom " run the risk of admitting unearned
incomes because they work with units so autonomous that

[36] Stalin, *Report on the XVIIth Party Congress*, op. cit., (1940), p. 418.

amongst the apparent differentiations of income resulting from greater ingenuity and effort, chance, changes of taste, etc., cannot be easily discerned.[37]

Planning, as a recognised standard for the evaluation of social systems, is the antithesis of the anarchy of the allegedly free society of competing private entrepreneurs ; and it depends upon the concrete origins of a social experiment how far this antithesis will be emphasized in State ideology. It was duly advertised in German fascism which based its mass-appeal upon the bankruptcy of " liberal " economics when they were in fact already trust-ruled ; but I should not wish to deny to possible American experiments their proper description because they are likely to be started on behalf of " free enterprise." From the Marxist point of view, planning in itself is an achievement, if not the main achievement, of the Society to Come ; but again undue stress should not be laid on the terminology likely to be applied if the above discussed variant of a Keynesian approach to Marxist policies should be realised. In actual social reality it seems obvious that free competition has outgrown itself ; so the actual issue in our days (or of the period following the next depression in U.S.A.) is not whether there will be planning or not, but "Who shall plan according to What interests? " (which will certainly be elevated to the dignity of the national ones). Thus the whole issue seems to centre about the social foundations of the planning State. For this reason the issue of equality, in the sense of rejection of unearned incomes, is still topical, independent of the importance of such incomes for the distribution of the national income, and even of the question whether or not their larger part is taxed away (provided that there still remains social prestige and influence) : a state in which all citizens do not enjoy an equal start in social and political life cannot plan for all.

(e) The incentive to work, and the two stages of a Communist Society

In capitalist society, there is a well-established mechanism of incentives and deterrents that keeps economics going, normally with that minimum of external (legal) compulsion which, in the

---

[37] This holds partly true even as regards the kollkhozes where distinctions between prosperity due to increased efforts of the members (including more efficient management) and advantages offered by natural conditions appropriated by the kollkhoz (that is, rent) are difficult to make, and even more difficult to account for in actual economic intercourse, without destroying the incentive to invest parts of the earned income in as rational a way as possible. See above, note 94 on p. 150.

ideology of that society, is described as Freedom. The existence of the " industrial reserve army," to use the Marxist term, [38] makes starvation or, under conditions of modern Welfare policies, mere subsistence under most undesirable conditions the alternative to acceptance of what employment is available, and to compliance with such discipline as the employer deems fit to enforce in the interest of production. It enables the starting of new enterprises in spite of the reluctance of workers to leave moderately satisfactory employment. Within the labour force employed, increased efforts are encouraged by piecework and other methods of payment by results. Professional proficiency as well as obedience to entrepreneurial (or managerial) authority may be remunerated by promotion which, in due course, may lead to the ranks of the black-coated workers ; and increased social prestige falling upon the black-coated-workers from what Veblen has called " the leisured class "increases the authority of the existing social system (represented in the factory by employer or manager) as well as making a step up the social ladder more attractive. Obstacles to the rise of the individual worker—such as lack of education, manners, etc.—may strengthen the desire to give his children a better start than he himself enjoyed, which presupposes at least his continuous employment at reasonable wages, and compliance with entrepreneurial demands. In the managerial class (which includes the small and medium entrepreneur) efficiency is rewarded by increased prestige and power (whether in the shape of promotion to more responsible posts, or by the rising importance of the enterprise) at least as much as by increased money income. But still, at least for public opinion, prestige and power are symbolised by individual disposition of capitals, in the extreme case by retirement from actual managerial work into the finance oligarchy (which merely deals with combinations of capitals, not with production as such) if not into the leisured rentier class.

In order correctly to appreciate the criticism to which those incentives may be subjected from the point of view of Marxism, we have to start from the basic assumption that moral standards cannot exceed a social framework conceivable at the time when they originate or, to put it differently, that " mankind

[38] " Absence of Full Employment " is a much less happy description, because it concentrates attention upon marginal phenomena. Marx's argument on the dynamic of capitalist development centres round the reproduction of the industrial reserve army on an enlarged scale.

always takes up only such problems as it can solve, since . . . the problem itself arises when the natural conditions necessary for its solution . . . are at least in the process of formation."[39] Relevant criticism of the incentives working in a capitalist society has to be based upon the proof that their working contradicts the social needs of our days. The very existence of the Industrial Reserve Army implies a vast amount of human misery and an equally gigantic waste of possible human efforts in order to achieve results which are partly undesirable in themselves (such as subordination of the worker to his employer's private whims and a general servile attitude) or which can be achieved in much less painful and more useful ways. Its opposite, the existence of social groups receiving unearned incomes and enjoying social prestige for this very reason, proves harmful because it causes waste of human efforts upon the administration of such incomes and the satisfaction of the needs of their receivers, and because it promotes social attitudes harmful to the prestige of useful labour. The social prestige which the leisured shed upon the black-coated-workers class implies reduced prestige of manual work. Social status achieved by any but one's own social achievements (for example, by being the wife of a person holding a position of high responsibility and prestige), deprives society of the effects of legitimate ambition as an incentive, say, for some women to acquire prestige and status by efforts of their own ; and inequality of chances according to social origin and position is bound to result in direction of individuals to activities other than those for which they are best fitted. This would be undesirable from the social point of view even if the misdirection should be effected merely by influencing the individual's surroundings and desires, so that he would not have the feeling of frustration.[40] In capitalist society, differentiation of earned incomes according to efforts made (directly on the job, or indirectly in acquiring the skill needed for it) is a main incentive to efficient work ; but its efficiency is reduced by the interference of social graduations of different origin and by the realisation by organised workers that it should be resisted as a potential source of unemployment. In Marxist literature[41] it is recognised that this incentive is most important

[39] Preface to the *Critique of Political Economy*, ed. cit., pp. 2–3.

[40] We have, intentionally, formulated the standard applied in so broad a way that it hits not only actual capitalist society, but also possible reforms within it, and inconsistencies in its socialist successor.

[41] The decisive passages are *Critique of the Gotha Programme*, pp. 12–4, and *State and Revolution*, Sel. *Works*, vol. VII, pp. 87–8, based upon the former.

during the first stage of communist society (called " socialism ") ; and the present U.S.S.R. may be regarded as the field where it is more consistently applied than anywhere else.[42] The higher stage of communism has occasionally been described by Lenin as " a system under which people become accustomed to the performance of public duties without any specific machinery of compulsion, where unpaid work for the common good becomes the general phenomenon[43]." The argument was made in connection with the " Communist Saturdays " (sacrifice of the weekend for socially useful work without remuneration) and provided another example[44] of Lenin's tendency to seek solutions of the problems of the coming (stabilised) society in phenomena characteristic of the revolutionary upheaval (in this case, even in reactions to national emergencies familiar also in non-socialist societies, if sufficiently integrated). Also in *State and Revolution* [45] Lenin relied on the preparedness of people voluntarily to work according to their abilities without asking the " Shylock-like " question whether their neighbours have worked as much for the same remuneration. The distribution problem appears to be settled on the basis of Utopian assumptions as to the eventual level of production or a glorified rationing system including all reasonable enjoyments of life and enforced by educated public opinion.

But differentiation of incomes works also as an agency which, without interference of compulsory machinery, distributes such goods as are scarce in relation to potential demand. Marx's argument against the justice of that distributive agency is based upon considerations of different sizes of families and different fitness of different individuals for work which, in our days, could be dispensed with in ways familiar to every moderate *bourgeois* reformer. In the present U.S.S.R., care for the family is regarded as an incentive to work, but no one regards such a state of things as satisfactory or definitive, and the public responsibility at least for larger families and for children of unmarried mothers is recognised to an extent far exceeding the maximum achievements in *bourgeois* countries.[46] As to the individual's varying fitness for

---

[42] See above, p. 358.
[43] *Sel. Works*, vol. VIII, p. 239.   [44] See also below, pp. 395-6.
[45] L. c., p. 88.
[46] See my *Spirit of Post-War Russia*, pp. 59–60, my *Changing Attitudes in Soviet Russia*, vol. I (*The Family*), pp. 367 ff, and Alva Myrdal, *Nation and Family* (London, 1945), pp. 135 ff, 325–6, and 416.

well-paid work, in discussions of an evidently remote state of social evolution at least as much allowance should be made for progress of scientific advice in the choice of profession, rehabilitation of invalids, etc. (fields unknown in Marx's days) as is usually made in Marxist literature for progress of technique of production beyond all experience. However, only in a very primitive conception of the aims of the Labour movement can distribution issues be identified with maximised earning powers.

From the point of view of a movement directed against the needy conditions of the masses it is obviously objectionable that even the inefficient worker (or someone who is an idler because of psychological failure to adapt himself to his social surroundings) should be denied enjoyments deemed necessary for civilised life; but the Socialist movement is also directed against the misdirection of human tastes and efforts. Much can be said against the intrinsic value of many things upon which income augmented by greater efforts is spent. In many cases the only justification (short of the completely relativist standpoint) of the production of many things upon which income is spent lies in the fact that their availability works as an incentive to increased efforts in the production of more valuable things, and that the level of mass-tastes may gradually be improved.[47] Even if there is agreement as to the desirability of granting every member of society, independently of his efforts, the standard of life generally accepted as desirable,[48] most people would regard it as fair and reasonable that people with greater demands should pay for the satisfaction of their personal wants by special efforts.[49]

Even if an efficient and skilful supply of labour should be available in a communist society without monetary rewards because of the progress of social education, the prestige earned by efficient work in every field, the satisfaction of ambitions

[47] For the corresponding problem in the U.S.S.R., see my *Spirit of Post-War Russia*, pp. 49 ff.

[48] It hardly needs to be specially stated that that conception need not coincide with some "subsistence minimum" in the physiological sense. For the analogous problem in a capitalist democracy see Lord Beveridge, *Report on Social Insurance and Allied Services*, paragraphs 300, 307, 373, and 455.

[49] This argument can also be stated in terms of "value". Unpromising as such an enterprise would be in view of the shortcomings of the Marxist theory of value in the very field concerned (see above, pp. 128–9), it would also fail to hit the characteristic situations in which the problem arises: a society which—or at least important trends within which—disapprove of football-pools or even of drinking, is not likely to produce them unless those interested in their supply react to it with *more* than the equivalent labour effort. But it is interesting to notice that in the case under discussion the "value" argument is not meaningless, though inaccessible to exact definition.

by promotion for good work, etc., the above argument would hold true as long as social labour remained scarce in relation to the maximum output of commodities and services of any kind for which there is demand (independent of consumer's price)[50] and to the demand for increased leisure-time which was regarded by Marx as an essential condition of freedom.[51] The formula " He who does not work neither shall he eat," which turns against the enjoyers of unearned incomes their attitude towards the Industrial Reserve Army, should indeed become obsolete in a socialist society grown upon its own foundations which could afford to regard the idler as an isolated pathological case ; and differentiations in income as current in the present U.S.S.R. should be regarded as evidence of the needs of socialist revolution in a backward country rather than as characteristic of socialism, in whatever country it may be established. But even from the purely economic point of view no society can grant to its members, regardless of their individual contribution, satisfaction of all their needs, unless social needs are strictly limited either because of their being standardised (by education and by the pressure of public opinion), or because society has become static to such an extent that after satisfaction of the existing needs all further (probably slow) progress of productive forces may be entirely devoted to increased leisure.

(f) INEQUALITY OF INCOME AS A MEANS OF DIRECTION OF LABOUR

A subsidiary argument is based upon the methods applied in the direction of labour to localities and industries which do not attract sufficient prospective workers.[52] In capitalist

[50] The evidently preliminary condition, that social education and the pressure of public opinion prevent waste of goods distributed gratis (or at a purely nominal price) can be made because we are discussing Marx's conceptions of a communist society firmly grown on its own foundations. Obviously the issue is in no way connected with the question whether, in order to check efficient production, there should still be cost-accounting (see below, p. 387).

[51] See below, p. 411.

[52] The problem is usually discussed as a question as to how a socialist society would manage to direct workers to dirty and unhealthy professions. Those opponents of socialism who use the argument either neglect the fact that socialist society could apply the incentive of higher earnings even better than capitalist (because it would not have to overcome social prejudice) and because it could much more easily close down industries which are disagreeable but not essential to society, or are naive enough to overlook the fact that they are arguing not merely against socialism but against full employment in general. Being usually employed in rather healthy and comfortable conditions, they state that the society defended by them cannot survive without driving people by the scourge of starvation into unhealthy jobs. The advocates of socialism, on the other side, usually evade the problem by wishful thinking as to technical improvements which would render the unhealthy jobs obsolete. There is some truth in the argument, but it is quite inconceivable that in a non-static

society the problem is additionally complicated by social prejudice originating from its structure[53] which makes essential occupations such as mining even less attractive than they ought to be because of the great physical demands, the unhealthiness of work, etc., or by traditions of backwardness and lack of personal freedom which reduce the appeal even of quite healthy and interesting occupations such as agriculture and nursing. But it is somehow solved with the help of the Industrial Reserve Army, though the very absence of full employment and the risks implied in settling in a new place further complicate the problem by causing reluctance of workers to accept employment which otherwise might well appeal at least to the more enterprising amongst them. In a few industries where conditions are distinctly unhealthy but where the demands made on the workers' skill are incompatible with their being recruited from the ranks of the Industrial Reserve Army, excessive wages are expected to compensate for a low expectation of life and health, and the capitalists selling the more expensive and less rational forms of amusement may be relied upon to popularise the attitude necessary to back that incentive.

If full employment is achieved in a fascist system, comparatively willing labour for such jobs where it is needed will be attracted by a combination of ideological appeals based upon a militarist conception of the nation (which fits the main directions in which direction of labour is needed in such a system) with promise of higher earnings at least for the key-workers, while direct compulsion, especially applied to " undermen " belonging

society at any time jobs could be made equally attractive. For example, the very fact that man is exploring new aspects of nature to which his own biological nature is not adapted, e.g., nuclear phenomena, implies grave dangers to health which cannot be overcome except in a process of trial and error ; and while in every dynamic society there will be scientists prepared to risk becoming invalids and dying early in order to advance that knowledge for the progress of which they are responsible, it would be completely unjustified to expect the average worker to approach the risks involved in the production of atomic energy in another way than he does silicosis—the main difference being that the latter, as distinct from the former, is better explored and more subject to control. If it is stated that jobs regarded as unhealthy or disagreeable for other reasons, may be combined with better conditions of life, increased holidays, etc., this involves acceptance of the argument made in the text, namely, that the solution of the problem presupposes inequality of income : if in the hypothetical communist society everyone should have a claim to the holidays he deems desirable and useful to his health, no one could be attracted to the mines by the promise of longer and better paid holidays.

[53] See above, p. 377.

to " inferior races "[54] will supply the bulk of the " hands." A socialist system, of the type at present existing in the U.S.S.R., will refrain from a militarist formulation of its ideological appeal,[55] chiefly because it discourages that personal initiative of the workers which is cherished as a main advantage of socialism. Though such a society may apply compulsory labour as a means of re-educating elements not fitting into its framework and, perhaps, also as a means of directing part of the labour force into places where it would not otherwise move,[56] it is likely to refrain from any ideology which would permanently keep the labour thus won in the lower grades of the social scale and thus waste their potential energies : they will be encouraged to undertake skilled and efficient work in the same way as other workers. In the earlier stages of Soviet development, latent reserves of unskilled labour were available because of the insufficient development of the productive forces in agriculture, so that mere technical progress in the latter field resulted in an abundance of kollkhoz labour ; at present[57] the supply of all kinds of labour to places where it is needed for new industries has to be secured by encouragement of mass-migrations. Skilled labour is attracted by higher remuneration, partly, since 1940, by the direction of the

[54] Applications of similar procedure are familiar in the colonial policies of long-standing capitalist democracies, so that the novelty is actually restricted to the transfer of South-African practices to the European continent (perhaps the main reason for which it was deemed " un-Christian "). It should be stated, in defence of the Nazis, that their procedure was the consistent, and perhaps unavoidable, outcome of an attempt to defend that very concept of European superiority upon which some concepts of " Christian civilisation " are based. See my Federalism, etc., pp. 451–5. For the definition of the practice described it is, of course, irrelevant, whether the scourge is applied in order to drive the workers to the place of employment, or " merely " in order to raise a poll-tax from the natives in order to force them into " voluntary " employment on long term-contracts, and afterwards to keep them properly disciplined.

[55] Apart from military purposes proper, where such methods are applied by every state and where, indeed, the sacrifices demanded are so high that appeal to other than ideological motives would result in a most undesirable structure of the army. Formulation of the ideological appeal in terms of patriotism is current in the U.S.S.R. more than elsewhere, but is always regarded as complementary to the material incentives. In 1936 women were appealed to to go to the Far East, in order to help to solve the well-known difficulty implied in the inequal numbers of men and women in pioneer countries ; but the differences between the wages-scales valid there and in the old industrial districts respectively were not hidden from them. So also, during the war, the U.S.S.R. found nothing strange in encouraging high output in war-industries by appeals to the individual's interest in high earnings as well as to his patriotism.

[56] Starting from ordinary journalism and (as evident even from Mr. Dallin's Forced Labour in Soviet Russia, New York, 1947, Chapter XI) from the not quite uninterested complaints of ' Soviet dumping,' the assertion that the Soviet State approaches the problems elsewhere solved by the Industrial Reserve Army by " forced labour " has entered a high percentage of the writings on the U.S.S.R. current in

graduates of the public technical schools (just like young doctors and some engineers) to their first job. Such a formation of " labour reserves " is regarded as so important that not only theoretical standards of equality of opportunity have been subordinated to them,[58] but even compulsory powers of recruitment for the new technical schools have been kept in reserve.

A socialist system is likely to supplement the offer of higher remuneration for jobs in themselves not sufficiently attractive by ideological appeals explaining also to the other members of society (at whose expense the higher wages are paid) the need for excessive remuneration in comparison with similar jobs in other industries where there is no shortage of labour. According to the laws of probability, the promise of high earnings (and, in many cases, also of higher social prestige) will attract the number of young people demanded by the plan to those jobs where shortage of labour is felt, whilst still leaving to the individual youngster the choice of a less well-paid profession or job, for non-material reasons.   It will also as a rule encourage compliance with scientific advice as to the choice of profession, or rehabilitation, without compulsion having to be applied. As long as we regard development of personal initiative and choice as a merit of socialism we must regard the direction of

this country (not to speak of U.S.A.). Perhaps it might be sufficient to notice that the term of " labour reserves," the importance of which is continuously emphasized in recent Soviet documents (comp. for example, Zhdanov's speech on November 7, 1945, reproduced in *Bolshevik*, 1945, No. 22), is always applied in relation to the reserves of *skilled labour* the recruitment of which (see below in the text), whether compatible with ideal socialist standards of equality of educational opportunity or not, certainly does not direct the alleged victim to a place in society inferior to what he would otherwise get. As to the some hundreds of thousands of individuals who have been actually resettled by the G.P.U. and its successor, it is obvious that, in the conditions of 1931, a former kulak had no other chance of getting a new start in life than by becoming an industrial worker, and that the Soviet authorities were eager to give him this chance where new factories had to be built and little alternative supply of labour was available. Nor were the Volga Germans, removed during the war from their former settlements, likely to be given new land just in those parts of Siberia which were already well populated. Compulsory labour is mainly applied in the timber-industry of the North and in a building force for waterways, the strength of which can be gathered from the fact that the Soviet never could start more than one major canal project at one time. It should not be denied that, as in other factories promotion earned will most easily be enjoyed at the place where it has been won, in this case, by the former convict becoming, as a free worker, a foreman who has to train newcomers in the job. So far, his direction to a certain place and occupation will remain definitives.

[57] For the change of the position in consequence of the collectivisation of agriculture, see Stalin, op. cit (1940), pp. 369-70.

[58] In 1940, abolition of free higher education for other than the more proficient youths was combined with the establishment of public technical and military schools which thus provided the only opportunity for children who had neither the special gifts which become evident in examinations, nor well-to-do parents, to acquire a professional qualification enabling them to earn a higher income. A certain part of

labour by inequality of income as far superior to any alternative. For apart from all "liberalist" ideologies, a society which risks losing a few workers from essential jobs to other work of their own choice will get stronger individual efforts, more inventions, and candidates better fitted for responsible posts amongst those who have chosen the essential job for themselves. But this supposes the continuation of inequality of income for other reasons : if a society should actually live up to the standard "from everyone according to his abilities, to everyone according to his needs" it would have either to ascertain the individual's abilities in some way independent of his individual tastes,[59] or to rely upon the likelihood that its ideology should induce a sufficient number of people to volunteer for the least desirable jobs. Therefore we have above described this whole argument as subsidiary. On the other side, whilst strengthening the case for the continuation of some inequality of income, it weakens the "justice" of such inequality in terms of the society to come : inequality of rewards applied as a means of directing labour would favour not only anyone who accepts a more dangerous or disagreeable job, but also everyone already employed and at home in a factory which happens to expand quickly but is situated in a far-away province so that newcomers have to be attracted thither by higher earnings. Whilst the first kind of inequality, in terms of socialism, may be regarded as "just," the latter is not ; and in order that it should pass without provoking serious criticism, the general level granted to everyone who conforms to the social standards of honest work should be so high that the needs, upon whose satisfaction the incentive is based, may be regarded as luxuries or "fancies" appealing to some, but not provoking a feeling of grievance amongst the many who do without them.

the pupils of those schools later, after having shown practical gifts as well as theoretical interest, get higher education in the technical institutes of the industries in which they happen to work, and many of them in due course may be promoted to positions of higher responsibility. They may not have been socially discriminated against ; but even if the share of graduates of the technical schools in the intake of the institutions of higher education should be higher than the 5 per cent. reported by Ashby (*Scientist in Russia*, London, 1947, p. 72) society may have been deprived of some potential artists or scientists unlucky in the choice of their parents and with the kind of gifts that prevented them from being *otlichniki* in school. Worse misdirection, perhaps, occurs as regards those children of well-to-do parents of average gifts who, in due course, may become average, or slightly under-average, doctors or teachers but who would have been more efficient, and more happy, average workers had not their parents' ambitions (used by the State as an incentive to work for those parents by concessions to the middle-class scale of social values) resulted in their being directed towards occupations of higher social prestige though (in consequence of the Soviet system of remuneration, see above, p. 359) not necessarily higher earnings.
[59] Which would not necessarily mean "in opposition to his wishes," because a society may be so static (as the mediaeval was) that most of its members feel integrated "in their proper stations."

(g) THE HIGHER STAGE OF A COMMUNIST SOCIETY

A socialist society such as can be derived from the Marxist criticism of capitalist society, if fully developed and freed from the needs of a struggle for survival,[60] would be characterised by the complete absence of unearned incomes, the obligation of all its adult members to do some work accepted as socially useful,[61] the equality of opportunity to qualify for such a position as each is fit for, and the absence of differentiations in income other than those necessary to encourage increased efforts in social production and the acceptance of jobs which in themselves are regarded as less desirable. With the increasing productivity of labour the minimum of enjoyments regarded as due to every member of such a society will increase so as to include all the generally accepted cultural values, and incentives to work based upon the alternative loss of that standard of life will be dispensed with ; and with the rise of the general cultural level skilled and professional labour will lose much of its scarcity value. Eventually it may be possible to dispense completely with higher remuneration for scientific, artistic, and similar work which is attractive in itself to those who perform it, to regard excessive effort in manual work as not so useful to society that it should be encouraged by higher remuneration, and to render exceptional especially unattractive kinds of labour the disutility of which[52] could not be compensated for by improved conditions of employment. If the socialist society is organised on democratic lines and sensible to tensions arising from big differentiations in income, progress in all those directions towards the increasingly egalitarian character of the society is quite conceivable, and if the national income greatly increases in consequence of planned economics and of the completely changed attitude of the individual to his work; the equalisation of incomes may be approached. However, unless society should become static (which would

[60] The first condition dispenses with discussions of the kollkhoz in any other capacity but as one of the possible solutions of the problem of autonomy of the productive unit (see below, pp. 407-8), of consideration of the problem of rent (see above, p.156), etc. ; the second allows us to by-pass such phenomena of present Soviet life as restriction of the individual worker's right to change his place of employment (see below, p. 400), or of the equality of educational opportunities ([58]). But it should always be kept in mind that an international constellation which prevents the U.S.S.R. from conforming with an ideal pattern of socialism also implies the reasons why socialism triumphed in Tsarist Russia, and may triumph in other countries. However, Marx, whose argument we are discussing, did not deal with a mere transitory condition.

[61] Which does not necessarily mean " work in a public enterprise or institution " ; the attitude of society to education of children in the family home is in no way prejudiced by our definition.

also put an end to its tendency to equalisation because the hierarchy of productive functions established at the time of stabilisation would become static too) there will be a certain tendency for social needs, including the need for increased leisure, to outrun any conceivable progress in social production. If, for some mystical[62] reason, the coming society should grant to every one of its members an equal share in the total social output, there would be only three alternatives. Either (a) that share covers just the minimum (and maximum) of enjoyments socially accepted as desirable, which amounts to a rationing system (mitigated to some extent by the introduction of " points "), or (b) it allows for some, but not all of the " luxuries " or " fancies " known in the society under discussion, or (c) it allows for all of them in all conceivable combinations. Alternative (a) would correspond to a rather static, and certainly not very free, society. Alternative (b) would involve, from the point of view of some members of society, shortages which would not be recognised as such by other members, and thus invite the suggestion that those interested in the production of the disputed goods should make an additional contribution (which should not necessarily take the shape of smokers growing tobacco). Alternative (c) would correspond to the higher stage of communist society in Marx's sense, which does not necessarily protect it against the criticism by a majority of its members that achievements regarded as questionable by them are purchased by a common sacrifice of alternatively possible leisure. Society will be confronted with the alternative of enforcing, presumably by public opinion, very strict standards as to the choice of profession, the efforts to be made in it, and as to the needs whose satisfaction is deemed reasonable, or of continuing *ad infinitum* to allow its members freedom of choice in all those regards at the expense of at least potential inequality of income, though on a continuously rising level. The slogan from everyone according to his abilities, to everyone according to his needs may be inscribed on the banners of that society[41] in the most literal sense, namely, as an accepted ideological standard : everyone will be expected to put

---

[62] For people living in the 22nd and 23rd centuries, apart from a few students of what will then be called " mediaeval ideologies," will simply be incapable of grasping why incomes should be equal on principle or not graded according to age, family-status, efforts, or something else. The last-mentioned criterion of gradation will have at least the support of memories of a comparatively recent past, when Stakhanovites or successful scientists were celebrated as " heroes of socialist labour " and accordingly remunerated.

all his abilities at the service of society, and social distribution will be measured by the opportunity granted to every member of society to satisfy with reasonable efforts every need accepted as reasonable by given social standards. As production rises every demand raised by part of the members of society and, at first, satisfied with considerable efforts will in due course, unless proved unreasonable, come within everyone's easy reach. But this will be all : short of a new static age, individualisation of needs, which has been regarded by Marx[41] as implied in human personality, will imply some individualisation of efforts. The minimum effort demanded from every individual (apart from pathological cases) will be brought forward by some agency bringing pressure upon the individual, though the threat of starvation working in the capitalist and in the lower stages of the socialist society, as well as compulsion by the law working within the latter,[63] may, in due course, be completely absorbed by less formal pressure of public opinion.

Accountancy can be dispensed with at no stage of human development unless society were prepared to forego the advantages of large-scale production. In order to demonstrate the social relativity and conditioning of the offence of theft, and in pursuing the more poetic than rational suggestions of their ancient forerunners, Utopians such as Fourier have envisaged a society where everyone would simply enter the public stores and carry away what he needed. But, apart from public utilities, transport, and some commodities which cannot be stored without risk of waste, no serious argument can be adduced in favour of such a mode of distribution, even if society could regard the individual member's share as unlimited : every housewife knows that when she goes shopping more time is needed for ascertaining her wishes and handing over the commodity in the shape desired (services which should be reasonably performed even in a communist society) than for writing and paying the bill, which may be worth while even if in the Society to Come merely the efficiency, though not the honesty, of shop-assistants will need checking. If one wishes a model of society which is not too Utopian with virtually free distribution of goods, it may be imagined as paying almost equal salaries to all its members and a slightly reduced stipendium (because of the special needs implied in work) to all

---

[63] See below, p. 400. For the corresponding approach in Welfare economics in a capitalist society see paragraph 373 of the Beveridge report quoted above.

those who are not expected to work, say, because there are legitimate reasons for their non-participation in normal work (some artists, etc.). Some of the goods and services offered by the community may be supplied gratis (as school-milk is supplied today to British children), others may be supplied at prices which are amply covered by income even if consumed in maximum quantities, and there may be a social convention that the unused parts of the income are deposited (without interest, of course) so that the planning organs have sufficient statistical foundations for their work. All relevant issues of Marx's " higher stage of communist society "[41] can be discussed within this model by asking how far society can proceed in establishing the level of desirable consumption, in abandoning the material incentive to work or wage-differentiation as a means of directing labour by bringing even the lowest wages to the level of desirable consumption, and in dispensing with pricing as a means of enforcing economies in scarce goods ; and how far the savings habit, transformed from an expression of individual thrift into one of society's resources, will supersede spending habits which may survive from the days of " conspicuous consumption " as well as from those when the Stakhanovite's expenditure was regarded as a symbol of his production achievements.

Nor need we include, in a serious discussion of the possibilities of a communist society, Utopian forecasts as to a possible withering away of the separation of mental from physical work, that is, of the division of labour, in those very fields where highest specialisation is demanded, say between the surgeon and the nurse. The social cleavage may wither away, partly because of reduced claims of the *intelligentsia* in general to social superiority, partly because the nurse, in her leisure-time, may be a renowned artist or politician. But this is something very different from retrogression in the technological division of labour : every step of scientific progress, in fields where division of labour even amongst the present specialists is unavoidable, reduces the prospect that those doing the operative work under the scientists' supervision, however the demands made upon their own skill and education may increase, can take more than the intelligent layman's interest in the scientific aspects of their work.[63a] But certainly it does not

---

[63a] In recent Soviet writings (cf. K. Ostrovitianov in *Voprosi Ekonomiki*, 1948, No. 2, p. 21) the prospect of an eventual withering away of the division of labour, especially as regards the intellectual professions, is clearly rejected.

follow that in every conceivable society they should receive lower material rewards than those who do the more interesting work associated with greater personal prestige.

So we can do without the more Utopian of Marx's forecasts about the higher stage of a communist society, however easy it is to explain their origin after what we have learned about the origin of Utopian concepts in general.[64] Having received, from Feuerbach, the humanitarian approach as a consummation of liberal and pre-liberal ideals[65], Marx spent his life in fighting the lower-middle-class approach according to which society would be "just" when it conformed with the small craftsman's conception of "just exchange"; and when he directed his criticism against the Lassallean authors of the Gotha programme he was certainly convinced that he was dealing with a slightly improved re-edition of Proudhon. His whole emphasis in the argument is directed against the implications of an idealisation of the economics of the first stage of socialist society in its attitude towards State and Law.[8] Well-elaborated patterns of the " higher stage" familiar to Marx's contemporaries had been produced by the classic Utopians from which Marx differed in means though not in ends. Fourier had stated that the Society to Come would demand work from everyone according to his abilities, and grant the enjoyments of life to everyone according to his needs; and probably Marx never realised that that formula would involve him in contradictions with, or possibly within, his own concept of Freedom.[66] But the proper Marxist conclusion from the criticism of the alleged justice inherent in the lower stage of communist society would have been the simple statement that with its achievement the history of human society would not come to an end. The fact that some concrete assertion about the subsequent stage was ready-made in the shape of the Fourierist Utopia should have raised Marx's distrust: according to his own theory standards of Justice are conditioned by the stage of social development from which they originate.

Marx's error is explicable by his very attempt at a realistic approach. As opposed to the wishful thinking of those who carried over into the coming society the sectional Labour movement's approach to piecework, etc., he understood that socialist society, during the first stage of its existence, might need those things

[64] See above, pp. 73-5, and 89.
[65] See above, p. 39.   [66] See below, p. 412.

even more than its predecessors; but that he also grasped their contradiction to Labour's general standards as well as to ordinary humanitarian conceptions growing under its pressure. Meanwhile such conceptions have in capitalist states undermined the application of the principle " He who does not work neither shall he eat " to the Industrial Reserve Army, with implications remarkably parallel to those drawn within the socialist system.[63] Within the U.S.S.R., the Fourierist principle " From everyone according to his abilities, to everyone according to his needs," as received by Marxism as a description of the highest aim of social reconstruction, was confronted with the need to prove against " world-revolutionary " adventures (or defeatism) that the Union by its own efforts could achieve the highest aims of mankind.[67] Accordingly, progress of socialist reconstruction beyond the stage where the sheer threat of starvation serves as an incentive to production was described as the gradual realisation of the higher stage of communist society. In this connection, free distribution of some commodities, the circle of which would be gradually widened, was suggested, starting with bread and similar mass-products essential for subsistence. From the economic point of view, such a policy would not differ from the granting of a subsistence-level to everyone even in a reformed capitalist country (under the assumption that social education has made sufficient progress in the U.S.S.R. to prevent waste as efficiently as is done elsewhere by the consideration that that part of the dole spent on the most essential goods cannot be spent for other purposes).[68] In either case it is supposed that the cultural demands not included in the free minimum are strong enough to work as an incentive even when the sheer threat of starvation has been removed, which implies that in neither case are all human needs satisfied independently of the work done. I cannot see that any but propagandist use could be served by introducing a social subsistence-minimum, by a method which implied dropping the elementary standard of

---

[67] See my *Spirit of Post-War Russia*, pp. 118–9.

[68] To some extent distribution in natura is right when misuse of the minimum by the beneficiaries (or their parents) for purposes other than intended has to be avoided. Children's milk as distributed in the schools of this country is a conspicuous example. But as long as considerations of that kind can be of any importance as to a mass-commodity of generally recognised usefulness (and free distribution of other commodities would not be relevant for the characteristic of social organisation), the question of transition to " the higher stage of communist society," however gradual, does not arise.

accountancy at a time when it is most needed. Perhaps because these difficulties were realised, in the more elaborate statements about the eventual transition from socialism to communism,[69] free distribution of individual commodities has been reduced to the status of one of various possible transition measures, and great emphasis has been laid on Marx's statement—made, it is true, in another connection[70]—that Communism should be regarded not as a condition to be established but as a social movement aiming at changing present conditions. In this connection, possible transformations of Soviet society which actually would imply no more than the dropping of its still existing non-socialist elements, such as transition from the Artel to the agricultural Commune[71] as main form of the kollkhoz, have been given place of honour. Such an attitude merely expresses, in the forms of traditional Marxist phraseology, what the sober sociologist may express in the statement that " the higher stage of a communist society " cannot be sensibly defined except as a generalisation of one of the possible trends in the development of a socialist society, idealised because it corresponds to the ideological environment in which the modern Labour movement came into being. So far as a realisation of that trend, on the production side, is possible, it will be realised by a gradual rise in the subsistence level granted and by a withering away of the legal methods of enforcing the individual's participation in social production. On the consumption side, it would be preceded by a standardisation of consumers' needs, in the ideal case with a tendency of the graphs of the income actually granted to everyone and of the maximum demands imaginable by anyone to approach each other. Whether they should meet elsewhere than in infinity is a question which must be left to metaphysical speculation.

[69] Comp. M. Rubinstein, On the problem of the technical basis for transition from socialism to communism, in *Bolshevik*, 1938, No. 20, espec. p. 42, and G. Gak, From Socialism to Communism, in *Pod Znamenem Marxisma*, 1939, No. 9, espec. pp. 41–2. Both in Russian.

[70] See above, p. 56. The statement, in *The Holy Family*, is directed against definition of Communism (as a distinct social movement) by a certain Utopia rallying its supporters, not against investigating, as in the *Critique of the Gotha Programme*, what kind of communist society would eventually result from its activities.

[71] That is a form of kollkhoz where the individual member's income entirely depends on his share in the co-operative income (without an " auxiliary private economy "), which must not necessarily exclude gradation of that share according to the work done. In this case, as in that mentioned in the preceding note, the different meanings of Communism, Commune, and communist society allow for confusion of issues.

CHAPTER XVII

STATE AND LAW IN THE SOCIETY TO COME

The Utopian element in Marxism which we have touched in the description of the higher stage of the communist society is becoming very clear in the concepts of the future of compulsive social machinery[1]. In this field, the origin of the idealised concept of the new society from a consistent development of all the ideas that brought its predecessor into being is conspicuous ; and the social mechanism enforcing this consistency was described when, in Engel's letter accompanying the *Critique of the Gotha Programme*, the influence of anarchist competition upon the formulation of the Marxist ideas on State and Law was mentioned. Marx and Engels were not afraid of denouncing competing sects as talking pure nonsense, if they found reason for such procedure : when combining, in their relations to the anarchists, sharpest political criticism with an acknowledgment of the community of ultimate ideals[2] they did so because they honestly believed, in conformity with all contemporary progressive thought, that a society the achievement of which was worth the most strenuous efforts should be the most consistent consummation of the liberal ideals. They had shown that the liberal concept of emancipation from legal restrictions of human freedom was formal in that it brought into being a society in which the legal restrictions were replaced by the no less brutal working of anonymous economic forces,[3] and they were realistic enough to see that those forces could not be broken except by political and legal machinery adapted to that purpose. But they never dropped the basic attitude that compulsive machinery as such was evil

---

[1] We apply such a general term in order to avoid tautological argument See note 3 to Chapter XI.

[2] In Lenin's State and Revolution (*Sel. Works*, vol. VII, pp. 95 and 109), this tendency is even stronger, but may have a tactical background : in the international Labour movement of his days anarchism was to some extent supported by workers who by denouncing the State in principle expressed their disapproval of reformist compromises with the existing state. Lenin thus regarded anarchist workers as potential recruits for the Third International who by patient explanations should be taught the Utopianism of their claim for immediate abolition of the State, including the State of the victorious working-class.

[3] In their early days they had expressed this juxtaposition, in the terms familiar to earlier Socialists, as one between " political " and " human " emancipation. See above, p. 37.

and should not be accepted except as an evil temporarily necessary.

But, on the other hand, they did not avoid confusion between the consistently liberal (or anarchist) attitude according to which State is evil because it restricts the freedom of the individual, and the attitude of the proletarian class-struggle, with which they identified themselves, according to which State is evil because and in so far as it oppresses the working-class and protects a social order implying exploitation of man by man. During a revolutionary upheaval, when the broad masses of the working-class rise and participate in the exercise of such compulsion as they deem necessary, they do not realise the existence of a State distinct from their own activity. Engels paid tribute to the Communards' sacrifice (which Marx and he, sensibly enough, had tried to prevent as long as they had any chance of influencing events) by stating that the Paris Commune of 1871 was no longer State proper.[4] More distinctly, Lenin found in the very identification of the repressive machinery with the masses of the revolutionary class, at the very height of revolutionary repression, the elements of the eventual withering away of the need for compulsion.

However, Marx, Engels and Lenin, though they might occasionally dream of short cuts to the ultimate realisation of Freedom, were realistic politicians. Emphasis on the necessarily evil character of State as such was conditioned by the concrete circumstances of the polemics to which the *Critique of the Gotha Programme* as well as *State and Revolution* owe their existence : as against the reformist idealisation of the existing state as a potential lever in the emancipation of mankind (which, with the Lassalleans, was a direct prolongation of Hegel's glorification of the Prussian state as " the reality of the moral idea ") it might be helpful to emphasize that State as such, including even that to be established after the socialist revolution as a necessary means of facilitating the coming of communism, was evil. " As long as the proletariat still *uses* the State it does not use it in the interests of freedom but in order to hold down its adversaries, and as soon as it becomes possible to speak of freedom, the State as such ceases to exist."[5] Such re-statement might be politically important as a warning against hesitations

---

[4] See above, p. 244. Marx and Engels knew very well the internal history of the Paris Commune and could not doubt that lack of disciplined and organised action was a main reason of its fall.

[5] Engels' letter to Bebel, accompanying Marx's *Critique of the Gotha Programme*.

in the use of political power once grasped, which would only prolong the misery (including political repression exercised against whole groups of the population) brought upon mankind by the continued existence of class-divisions. But, as we have seen in the last chapter, Marx and Engels were at pains to explain the injustice (as seen from higher humanitarian standards) of the legal standards expected to be applied in a socialist society long after class-divisions, and class-repression, would have gone.[6] Absence of any compulsion by specific social machinery was, for them, a fundamental characteristic of truly humanitarian society.

Three basic elements have to be distinguished in that attitude : (1) Compulsion, in itself, is the opposite of Freedom, though compulsion against a few may have to be applied in order that the many can be free, that is, can develop their personalities.[7] In the transition stage, with which we are no longer concerned here,[8] such compulsion has to be applied against the vested interests upholding private property in means of production ; in a completely developed socialist society it has to prevent idlers and other anti-social elements from disorganising production (and also, as long as inequality of income is necessary, to protect the resulting, unequal property rights in means of consumption). Whatever allowance may be made for the effects of the social education of people growing up in a socialist society, for the withering away of a " Shylock-like " approach of the individual to his fellows,[9] etc., it is impossible to imagine, except under clearly Utopian assumptions, a social order in which the element of compulsion could be *completely* dispensed with. The only assertion that reasonably can be made is that, in a society without class-divisions and with guarantees for the welfare of all its members sufficient to prevent an economic urge towards violations of the established order, the compulsion still necessary can be carried out by the pressure and the indefinite sanctions of public opinion. But, in principle, public opinion is an agency enforcing a certain behaviour, not different in principle from other agencies such as the threat of starvation, or special

[6] Exaggerated formulation of this idea has been further elaborated by Lenin, into the concept of a " bourgeois state without a bourgeoisie." For a criticism see my *Soviet Legal Theory*, pp. 30–3.
[7] See below, p. 409.
[8] For the concept of the dictatorship of the revolutionary class as a means of breaking existing class-privilege, see above, pp. 239–40, and 245.
[9] See above, p. 378.

repressive machinery working according to certain rules (laws). Besides, none of the other agencies would work without *some* backing by public opinion : in comparison with capitalism a communist society would be characterised by the restriction of the number of cases in which compulsion has to be applied as well as by the growth of public opinion into a force so homogeneous that there would be no more loopholes through which to escape from its pressure (and therefore no more need to supplement it by the working of other agencies). The former, but not the latter aspect of the development could be described as progress in Freedom.[7]

(2) As distinct from pressure by public opinion, the very efficiency of which implies that the overwhelming majority of those subject to the social order do not regard it as restrictive of their freedom, compulsion exercised by a special machinery established for that purpose[10] is evident. Therefore the breakdown of that specialisation in times of revolution may be regarded as in itself promising a quick " withering away of State " : it is assumed that the enormous political activity developed by a very large proportion of the common people during the revolutionary upheaval will continue (and even increase until a virtual identification of the rulers with the ruled takes place), while the repressive functions of the new state " wither away " step by step as it succeeds in abolishing class-divisions. Both assumptions are not only Utopian, but also contradictory : it is characteristic of a revolutionary upheaval that all human energies are diverted into a certain channel in order to create the preliminary conditions for other activities (to speak in the language of the masses, in order to enjoy the fruits of the revolution[11]), though it should not be denied that after a successful revolution which has raised the general cultural level and given the masses a real stake in the State, there will be more continuous mass interest in the *body politic* than before. That concentration of mass-interest upon politics happened just because an obvious need to defeat a powerful internal enemy was felt : as soon as that task is fulfilled, mass-participation in the working of the repressive machinery will " wither away " much quicker than its repressive character. A state originating from a great

[10] See Engels' definition quoted above, p. 393.
[11] For a discussion of the resulting tension between the masses (and those leaders who represent their interests) and those who keep to the traditional revolutionary scale of values see my *Spirit of Post-War Russia*, pp. 20, 65 ff, and 180 ff.

revolution tends to establish its authority like any other[12]—
or perhaps even more, because the very essence of authority has
been questioned during the revolutionary process. This is
quite independent of the extent to which it has succeeded in
winning popular support, or even in reducing its own individual
officials to ordinary clerks deprived " of every shadow of
privilege of every semblance of ' official grandeur'," a demand
of Lenin's to which every sensible American *bourgeois* would
subscribe.[13]

(3) Unless fantastic assumptions are made as to the possibility of carrying out the greatest experiment in large-scale
social organisation without adequate centralised machinery,[14] it is
obvious that the organisation shouldering the task of planning
and administering social production, which in the post-revolutionary period is identical with the State, will never " wither
away." The only things that conceivably can wither away
are its repressive and compulsory functions. Engels had this
in mind when, many years after the *Communist Manifesto*[14a], he
foretold that with the abolition of class-divisions the government

[12] Characteristic is Mr. Shvernik's statement, in moving the change of the description of the highest administrative state organs from " People's Commissars " to
" Ministers " (1st session of the Supreme Soviet of the U.S.S.R., March 12–19th, 1946,
Official Protocol, p. 85) ; the old description had originated during the period of formation of the Soviet state, when the old State machinery was destroyed, but the new one
not yet stable and still in a process of formation, which was concluded only when the
constitution of 1936 came into force.   Now it was necessary to apply the terminology
generally applied in political practice (that is, in the practice of the existing, bourgeois,
states), in order to make the position of the highest Soviet state organs clear.
[13] Lenin, *State and Revolution*, l. c., vol. VII, p. 42.   The argument is preceded by
the statement that on the basis of large scale capitalist production the great majority
(Lenin did not wish to overstate his case) of functions of the old " state power " have
become so simplified and can be reduced to such simple operations of registration,
filing and checking that they can be easily performed by every literate person for
wages not exceeding those of other workers.   The argument is sound against the cult
of the state official traditional on the continent, and certainly conforms with the need
of the Soviet state not to lure the most promising youths from productive engineering
etc., into " more respectable " office jobs, as most Central and East European states
did.   So far, the Paris Commune of 1871, to the traditions of which Lenin appealed,
was quite all right ; but the argument does not carry any of the far-going conclusions
drawn from it by Lenin.   Certainly a revolutionary state does well in entrusting
responsible functions to ordinary working-class people who, during the upheaval,
have proved their capacity for mass-leadership : but not because the clerical functions
in the State machinery are similar to those daily exercised in any major commercial
enterprise (it is a pity if workers risen from the masses have to be wasted on such jobs)
but because sound judgment and capacity of mass-organisation are qualifications
superior to bureaucratic routine which can be acquired in due course.   The issue of
social inequality is not based upon civil servants being better paid than people doing
comparable work, elsewhere, but upon the scarcity of highly skilled labour, including
(but not mainly) that needed for the higher grades of the civil service.
[14] Cf. Lenin's statement in *Can the Bolsheviks retain State Power* (*Sel. Works*,
vol. VI, pp. 265–6) that the organisational machinery developed by capitalism should
be made still bigger and still more comprehensive.   14a. See note 3 on p. 237 above.

of persons would be replaced by the administration of things and the direction of the processes of production.[15] But such " administration " and " direction " is always directed towards *persons*. It may be accepted by them as technical advice the reasonableness of which is taken for granted because every executive worker trusts the social organs sufficiently to believe that his superiors will be appointed because they understand their job. Or else such advice will be carried out because of the worker's conviction that possible disagreements about the technical soundness of an order are better ironed out at the next production conference, and that the homogenity and discipline essential for large-scale production should not be undermined by such disagreements. But in the background of technical advice stands discipline, and ultimately the question as to how it should be enforced. It may be enforced by the anonymous pressure of public opinion (which may err considerably), it may be enforced by some machinery established in order to settle disputes of that kind ; but there is no reason to assume that the rights of the individual dissenting from his superiors would be better granted if this machinery should be identical with, or controlled by, the same hierarchy to which those superiors belong, as distinct from a different body which is supposed to be neutral in the dispute. Whether such a body is called a " court " or something else is a matter of political terminology ; and the question how far it should be led by general rules and by the merits of the individual case respectively is one of the basic issues of jurisprudence in general. Marx's statement that " unequal individuals (and they would not be different individuals if they were not unequal) are only measurable by an equal standard in so far as they are . . . taken from one *definite* side only . . . everything else being ignored " fairly represents *one* side to that dispute, but there is another side which finds some backing in Soviet experiences in the extreme identification of legal with ordinary social machinery (that is, the production hierarchy).[16] No legal theorist (nor all of us together) can hope to make more than a limited contribution to the solution of one of the most complicated problems of human organisation ; but if the restriction of unreasonable compulsion exercised against the individual is taken as a standard for measuring the value of solutions, as Marx does,

---

[15] *Anti-Duehring*, ed. cit., pp. 308–9.
[16] See my *Soviet Legal Theory*, pp. 161 ff, and 269–70.

no *a priori* case can be made against the preservation, in any coming society, of special machinery for the settling of disputes and of at least general principles according to which that machinery has to work. The whole argument in favour of protecting the economic organisation of society (" bourgeois society " in the Hegelian terminology) against interference by " political " machinery allegedly purely compulsory, is ordinary liberalism ; what really matters is not the point to which division of labour between the different branches of the social organisation should be preserved in a socialist system,[17] but the extent to which the latter can keep its compulsive powers in the background (these are not necessarily less severe if they include instead of prison and fines social boycott) and enforce its needs by convincing its members of the propriety of the rules with which they have to conform.

Since 1938, it has been asserted in the U.S.S.R. that the State, though, as regards its domestic functions[18] bound to wither away with the achievement of a communist society, would continue to exist even in a communist society as long as the latter were threatened by capitalist encirclement. Such an assertion, made in the official ideology of a revolutionary state facing supreme dangers, may invite an explanation of its historical background rather than scientific criticism, and its first part seems already on the way of being dropped altogether.[18a]   In the development of Soviet ideology, it followed the disputes on the possibility of building socialism in a single country, during one stage of which the opposition has asserted that it was possible to start the building of socialism in a single country but not to accomplish socialist reconstruction as long as that country remained the only major socialist state[19] ; and it coincided with an obvious desire to strengthen the authority and prestige of Soviet state machinery[12,18a] which had not exactly been confirmed

---

[17] It is hardly necessary to emphasize that a division of labour involving the continued existence of a profession of lawyers able to restrict the part played by the ordinary man or woman elected as a member of the " court," or whatever it is called, is incompatible, not only with socialism, but with democracy in general. But the specialists bringing forward technical argument irrefutable by ordinary commonsense are much more likely to originate from the ordinary technical hierarchy, to hope for the abolition of which is sheer Utopianism. See above, p. 388.

[18] From which in Marxist theory (see above, p. 234) the whole concept of State is derived. [18a] Cf. Vyshinsky's remark (in *Sovjetskoye Gossmdarstvo i Pravo*, 1948, No. 6, p. 10) that it is not in the interest of the Soviet State to devote theoretical interest to the problems of its eventual withering away.

[19] Comp. Stalin, op. cit. (1940), pp. 157-8.

by Lenin's forecasts of its obsolescence.[18] Logically, it is unnecessary from either point of view : Lenin's statements in *State
and Revolution* on the eventual withering away of the State in consequence of the achievement of the higher stage of communism are
extremely careful, emphasizing the protracted nature of the
process and the impossibility of making any forecasts as to its
length and concrete forms.   In the only sensible conception,
the growth of the higher stage of the communist society has to
be regarded as *so* protracted a process that, to anyone who
believes at all in a trend of human society towards socialism
and the possibility of establishing peaceful co-operation between
socialist states, ample scope is left meanwhile for the ending of
the isolation of the U.S.S.R., and for whatever functions the
Soviet state machinery has to accomplish. Stalin's juxtaposition
of the internal repressive functions of State, which would wither
away with the gradual achievement of communism, and the
external protective ones which should continue as long as the
capitalist encirclement continues, is unjustified : those internal
repressive functions of State that could wither away in any
conception of communism not based upon pure Utopianism[20]

---

[20] To define the higher stage of communism from the distribution point of view
would evidently (see above, pp. 386–8) lead to periods to be measured, if at all, in
centuries ; free distribution of *some* commodities would not affect the need of the State
as an agency protecting private property in those means of consumption the interest
in acquiring which would remain a main incentive to work.   I use this occasion to
note the difference in the treatment of the issue between this and earlier works of mine.
In *Soviet Legal Theory* (p. 31) I discussed my classical Marxist sources which, for their
part, dwelt on the current bourgeois argument that *some* excesses of individuals
are likely to need repression in nearly every society ; in *The Spirit of Post-War Russia*
(pp. 118 ff.) I noticed the parallelism between the above (pp. 390–1) discussed Soviet
proposals for some (as I now think, clumsy) methods of granting everyone a subsistence
minimum with parallel phenomena in capitalist countries, and stated that there was
nothing Utopian in such proposals as such, though it was another question whether
their achievement would coincide with Marx's and Lenin's concepts of a communist
society.   At present, mainly under the impact of considerations about the economics
of higher stages of a socialist society I am inclined to regard these two aspects as
rather irrelevant.   If one conceives with the Communist Manifesto, and at least some
trends in recent Soviet ideology, withering away of State as withering away of some
functions of a machinery which, with changed functions, is bound to continue in-
definitely, it matters very little whether the treatment of, say, occasional sadist offenders
be carried out by that machinery or directly by the public psychiatric services.   For
theoretical definitions it is obviously irrelevant whether private property protected by
such machinery should be property in bread, butter, imported fruits, or motor-cars
(from the humanitarian point of view, the difference would be enormous and would
provide a strong argument in favour of the " lower stage of communist society " even
if the higher should remain a Utopia).   What really matters to the average member of
a society is not the description of the treatment of some sadist criminal, nor even of
some impostor who embezzles public funds in order to influence a girl by the luxuries
he can offer to her, but the amount to which the existing compulsory institutions
enter his and his fellow's orbit, be it even merely as a necessary deterrent.

are those enforcing the citizen's participation in the production process (directly, or by preventing alternative, criminal methods of securing his living) ; but the demands which must be enforced by the State, whatever the means, are closely dependent on its external security needs. Indeed, the strongest defence of the U.S.S.R.—and of socialism in general—against the reproach that it simply replaces the threat of starvation, as an incentive to work, by the Criminal Code, is the observation that those measures which point most definitely in that direction[21] were obvious consequences of the external threat, enacted after full employment had been established for about a decade without the need to resort to such measures. On the other hand, the need to use the Criminal Code to reinforce the demands for diligent fulfilment of duties which may elsewhere be backed by the mere threat of losing a much desired and socially secure job (as those of civil servants, employees of nationalised railways, etc., are on the Continent) had made its impact upon the Soviet Penal Code long before the external threat had reached its climax.[22]

I should not regard such a development as characteristic of socialism in general, though it may be characteristic of socialism where the need for quick industrialisation exaggerates full employment into distinct scarcity of labour, perhaps combined with such a scarcity of other than the most essential commodities that few privileges can be granted to the average diligent worker who holds his job.[23] The Criminal Code directly enters the field of labour relations where the threat of dismissal has lost its deterrent force, and before new moral incentives have developed sufficiently to secure the discipline needed in the social interest ; but it remains efficient (though in the background) even where such a development has been avoided : it supports the inequality

[21] December 28, 1938, loss of status in social insurance and of dwellings offered by the employer was prescribed as a consequence of dismissal for disciplinary reasons or for other change of employment unless agreed with the management, and June 26, 1940, the last mentioned action (and also repeated lateness at work) were made criminal offences. August 10, 1940, criminal responsibility was introduced for small-scale thefts and for hooliganism committed in the factories, which were formerly dealt with by disciplinary action by the management, in some republics, such as Georgia, by Factory Fellowship Courts. During the War itself, severe sanctions were enacted against leaving Essential Work—as was done also in other countries.

[22] See my *Soviet Legal Theory*, pp. 117, 128, 162 ff, and 229 ff.

[23] This was the main reason for which the initial, economic, sanctions against change of employment without sufficient reason ([21]) proved inefficient. A place in a barracks can be found everywhere if hands are needed everywhere ; and the key-worker would not forfeit his present privileges unless he had made sure that the new employer would grant him at least equal ones, and also manage the matter with the authorities.

of income (and property in consumers' goods) upon which society relies as a main incentive to work and it bars easy ways to such enjoyments which otherwise might appear attractive to the less stable members of society as long as they are surrounded with glamour, and perhaps even with social prestige. Marxists, who emphasize the social background and conditioning of crime, should realise that the mere existence of social inequality preserves a potential cause of many anti-social acts against which protection by compulsory machinery is necessary. If we regard inequality of income, at least for a very long period, as the least undesirable regulator of productive activities,[24] and the preservation of special machinery for the management of disputes, if reasonably handled, as the least undesirable regulator of the compulsory element inherent in every social order,[25] the " withering away of State " recedes into the background of Utopia or, at least, of a future so remote that it is not worth while arguing about the international constellation likely to exist at that time.

[24] See above, p. 386.   [25] See above, p. 397.

CHAPTER XVIII

THE INDIVIDUAL AND COLLECTIVISM

(a) CONCEPTS OF FREEDOM

There is no Freedom in general ; every demand for Freedom is actually the demand for the removal of certain restrictions which have become obsolete. Such demands may be backed by rising social groups just because they deem that removal of existing restrictions on free choice is bound to result in " free " acceptance of what is reasonable according to the spirit of the age. Bourgeois society, and Liberalism as its most highly developed ideology, owe their origin to such demands for its free development. From the sociological point of view—as distinct from that of the verbal interpretation of the generalisations made in such connections—it is obvious that such demands for the freedom of development of bourgeois society and its ideological foundations do not imply the demand for freedom to overcome it. The demand that everyone should be free and encouraged to read the Bible in order to convince himself, by his own efforts, of the true essence of Christianity as defined by a particular Protestant sect did not imply the demand of freedom for the authoritarian Roman Church, and occasionally not even the demand for freedom for competing Protestant sects which might mislead the Christian's sound judgment. Certainly it did not imply freedom for the godless who questioned the authority of the Bible as an ultimate source of truth. Nor does the freedom granted to every citizen of a bourgeois democracy to suggest whatever policies he deems fit in the communities' interest imply a right to undermine the foundations of society. The issue is veiled by abstract generalisations current with liberal framers of constitutions (as distinct from the Protestant reformers, who found nothing inconsistent even in burning atheists at the stake) as to the right to advocate *every* idea, and therefore any conceivable change. But the real justification of such freedom, from the point of view of the liberal bourgeois, lies in the alternative danger lest legitimate party-strife over reforms conceivable within the framework of bourgeois society may be restricted by vested interests which complain of any moderate reform as an alleged interference with fundamental property rights,[1] perhaps also in the prospect of opening some harmless outlet to potentially revolutionary tendencies. If the freedom of dissent granted within a definite constitutional framework actually involved freedom to change the foundations of society, it would imply the obligation of a minority supporting the existing foundations to submit to a majority decision interfering with what they are bound to regard as the foundations of social ethics, and thus also of the obligation to submit to majority decisions. No serious sociologist has alleged the existence of such an obligation.

The demand for freedom has promoted social progress during the last four hundred years (and, in addition, during an even shorter period in the development of the ancient world). But if the demand for socialism, that is, for a fundamental change in the foundations of present society, is based upon that tradition, such extrapolation can involve only formal characteristics (which are also the only characteristics common to all the different stages of the demand for freedom of bourgeois society) namely (a) the statement that existing freedom is insufficient, in that existing institutions prevent considerable masses of the people doing what they may reasonably want to do in the present stage of social development, and (b) the demand for freely reasoned decision (as distinct from authority accepted *a priori*) as the criterion of the legitimacy of the origin of the new social institutions (which, being institutions, themselves present barriers to some hypothetical, but at present latent, " freedom "). Unless the demand for Freedom should imply the rejection of Democracy, that is, of the right of the majority to shape their social environment, Freedom cannot be defined by some catalogue of natural and inalienable rights, (that is, by idealisation of certain features of existing society opposed to any fundamental alterations) but only by the criterion that social institutions should enable the maximum possible development of every individual's personality.[2] From this point of view it is obvious to Socialists that capitalist society is unfree because it fetters the development of the personalities of the great majority of mankind (and also distorts the development of the individuals belonging to the privileged minorities). The answer

---

[1] The Viennese Social Democrats were actually repressed, in 1934, for being " housing Bolsheviks," but have since managed to agree with the Catholics who repressed them upon a common policy against actual Bolshevism.

[2] S. and B. Webb, *A History of Trade Unionism*, ed. 1920, p. 757.

that such fetters as exist[3] are economic, not political or legal, is disposed of from the Socialist point of view, as being formalist and as implying the preservation of anonymous economic fetters which are protected by the existing legal order.

More difficult than this negative argument seems the positive proof that a socialist society, which ends the existing freedom of some individuals to direct and to dispose of the efforts of others, would be free in that it removes existing restrictions on the activities of the majority of men, and enables them to share in those social decisions which determine their fates. The Socialist answer to this question has been prepared by the whole course of German classical philosophy : if one maintains a scientific explanation of the World and therefore cannot ignore the objective causation of human actions, Freedom is but the consciousness of what is necessary, which implies ability to foresee the outcome of one's actions. So far as such freedom is restricted by the still insufficient state of scientific knowledge, Freedom is realised by the progress of science ; but so far as the social institutional element is concerned, the "leap from the realm of Necessity into the realm of Freedom" depends upon the establishment of a social order in which objective needs will be realised no longer by dependence of men on anonymous social forces, or the commands of superiors who are obeyed because they wield power, but will be carried out by people who understand those needs and take their full share in shaping the necessary course of action.[4] In this sense Engels spoke of the eventual " withering away of the State " as the process in which rule over persons would be replaced by administration of things. This forecast need not be interpreted in a more Utopian sense than that, because of the abolition of class-divisions and the reduction of social power to the enforcement of rules of behaviour the rationality of which is realised by the large majority of those subject to them, the administrative-technical aspect of human institutions will eventually replace the political one.[5]

[3] In the ideal type, apart from " democracies " such as South Africa, the Southern states of the U.S.A., or Greece. Certainly, apart from the argument made in the text, the question arises whether the " ideal type," even if restricted to some countries, or to some minorities in some countries, would be realisable in the world unless those countries (or minorities within some countries) were favoured by economic privileges which could not be upheld except by overt inequality, or pseudo-democracy, working against other parts of mankind. This argument, though apparently left-wing, is actually implied in the current statement that " democracy," " liberty," etc., best prosper amongst trading nations.

[4] Engels' *Anti-Duehring*, pp. 311-2.   [5] See above, pp. 396-7.

(b) ECONOMIC DEMOCRACY AS A CRITERION OF SOCIALISM

This definition is usually resisted by individualists because it implies the impossibility of realising Freedom except for a collective in which the individual would be merged. Socialists reply that the individual's dependence on the collective is a given fact, indeed the elementary condition of human civilisation ; but that collectives may be distinguished according to the opportunity which they provide for their individual members to understand the collective's needs as actually identical with those of the bulk of its members (which is impossible in a class-divided society) and to participate in shaping that action which results from common understanding of the common needs.[6] These are objective criteria, which should not be confused with the success or otherwise of propagandist efforts to bring about identification of the worker with the system under which he works. In fascist systems the workers are told that the enterprises left to the private entrepreneurs' " trusteeship " actually belong to the nation, and social reality is measured, by fascist sociologists, by the effects of such propaganda. But the essential point as to the ownership of Soviet factories is not how far Soviet propaganda is successful in inducing Soviet workers to identify themselves with those who issue the orders which they have to obey : sociology has to investigate what chances such identification has to continue over a long period without being refuted by facts. The advanced worker will feel it incumbent on him to make suggestions as to the organisation of production and welfare, and to see that such suggestions are followed up unless refuted by reasons which he understands as distinct from submission to paternal authority ; and the bulk of the workers would reject, or soon terminate, identification with a system where their efforts would have effects opposite to those intended (for example, a Western worker may render himself, or at least his fellows,

---

[6] Naive misunderstanding of this fundamental point is evident in observations such as that made by G. Williams, (*The Price of Social Security*, International Library for Sociology, etc., 1944, pp. 165–6) that the question whether the Russian workers actually owned their factories was irrelevant ; essential was their belief in their ownership, and their resulting behaviour, but this should be achievable also in what (with the usual Western suppositions, see above, p. 402) is called a " democracy." Such remarks inevitably result from an exaggerated functionalist approach in which the social content of institutions is dispensed with. If someone wants to induce the British workers to a similar feeling of identification as in the U.S.S.R. he would probably have to realise even more economic democracy, because without it large masses of the British workers would not accept the assertion that they had their full say in " their " factories.

"redundant" by his own excessive efforts, German workers, by trying to secure the victory of the "master-race" and its chance to exploit "undermen," actually brought their nation under the control of armies of occupation). Thus interpreted, socialism has a clear and unequivocal criterion to distinguish it from fascism and similar methods of planning from above (which may involve a considerable amount of nationalisation[7]). Socialism is a system of collective organisation of economics based upon mass-organisations of a sectional and functional character,[8] the members of which therefore can participate in the shaping of the concrete decisions on the management of economics, as distinct from fascism (however called) in which mass-organisation merely serves to support authoritarian decisions by the government, and therefore is of a distinctly military and hierarchical type. This criterion is quite independent of the number of political parties recognised in the state in question, but it is deeply involved in the issue of how far democratic institutions can grant the individual worker his say in the shaping of the production process which of necessity absorbs the larger part of its energies.

This issue grows in importance the more, with the progress of the modern conveyor methods, etc., the working process itself, for the great majority of the producers, is deprived of any variety and of most of the opportunities to develop personal initiative. It cannot be solved by mere economic democracy in the sense that the worker, *qua* citizen of a socialist state, participates in such economic decisions as are left to open discussion (the number of which would certainly increase in a state freed from such emergencies as hitherto have dominated the life of the U.S.S.R.). Such extension of political decision to economic issues is important in the negative sense that anonymous economic powers thwarting democratic decision are eliminated, and in the positive sense that with the absorption of important issues into the political orbit of all, the number of citizens actively participating in shaping the political framework is bound to grow. Thus in all fields where no specialist knowledge is needed the bureaucratic method of recruiting the political hierarchy (which, in a socialist state,

[7] Whilst, on the other hand, socialism is not necessarily bound to 100 per cent. nationalisation. See above, pp. 369-71.

[8] This should not be regarded as an argument in favour of Guild Socialism and against centralisation of decisions : it is merely demanded that the organisation should enable its individual members to have an efficient say by confronting them with questions within the reach of their understanding and experience.

largely coincides with the economic) may be supplemented, and gradually replaced, by voluntary efforts reflecting the mood of those whose activities are being organised. But Lenin's demand that every washerwoman should be able to participate in governing the State should not be interpreted in a Utopian sense to mean that at any time every washerwoman, or even every textile worker, will find the satisfaction which the production process denies to her, in voluntary participation in political life. Such a Utopia is of questionable value—at least for those who take the description of Man as a political animal in not too verbal a sense, unless the mood of a revolutionary movement, whose justification lies in the very need for a revolutionary transformation, is carried over into the times when that need will have been satisfied.

However, if we define Man as a conscious animal, we cannot accept as satisfactory a position in which the majority of people participating in the production process can take no other share in that process beyond fulfilling mechanical tasks alloted to them, whatever the extent of their identification with the machinery allotting the tasks and with the purposes thereby served and whatever their chances to enter the higher ranks of that hierarchy if they have the necessary gifts and ambitions. Present socialist experience does not yet supply a satisfactory answer to the problem. Trade Unionism, in the sense of sectional mass-organisation defending the workers' interests against the management, after the abolition of class-differences is bound to dwindle to the position of a democratic machine for reducing frictions ; as a participant in the production drive, which is its present main function in the U.S.S.R., it is evidently bound to a transitional situation in which that drive is accepted as a condition of national survival. Its remaining function as self-government in welfare-matters, however strongly developed, strikes only at the fringe of the problem. The present kollkhozes, whatever the limitations to which their autonomy is subject by the needs of planning, are probably the nearest approach to economic democracy existing anywhere ; but it should not be forgotten that that autonomy is the reverse side both of far-going dependence on factors partly independent of human wills, and of failure to come up to such standards of equality as are otherwise recognised within the system. [9] Perhaps kollkhoz democracy works well

[9] See above, p. 150.

just because the commanding position of science in agriculture is not yet so undisputed as to prevent the average worker with good production experience from arguing an effective case even against the specialist ; but, clearly, the problem wins its main importance just where the labour process has been deprived of any individual choice and other than purely mechanical responsibility. Clearly, it cannot be solved by Utopian expectations of an eventual withering away of the division between manual and intellectual labour.

Socialism allows a problem excluded by the basic concepts of capitalist society to be put on an institutional level, but as yet it has no answer to it. We cannot conceive a modern society without a distinct production hierarchy, and—least of all from the Marxist point of view—we cannot prevent that production hierarchy from being a hierarchy of social prestige and power. Short of Utopia the best one can expect is a social order in which that hierarchy is not the only possible one, so that ample opportunities are opened to the individual's interests and ambitions. This argument evidently leads to the leisure problem which we have soon to discuss. In the present stage of transition, socialism derives its claim to represent a new stage of freedom from the mass-interest in the transition as such, as preceding struggles for Freedom have done. In so far as they can participate in reshaping the production process—or, more correctly—its social framework—modern men are free. This is a purely dynamic concept and we cannot look beyond it[10] ; but it is sufficient to prove the importance of the institutional forms in which that dynamic is realised.

(c) FREEDOM AS ACTIVE SHAPING OF HUMAN LIVES.

The whole social life of a state like the present U.S.S.R., is dominated by the desire that citizens should become efficient and intelligent workers, taking as active a share as possible in public life. With an outspokenness that sounds provocative to Westerners interested in Art for Art's sake, and in terms that proudly proclaim the belief that human life can be moulded and mastered just as Nature can, Soviet writers are hailed as " engineers of the soul." If some of them forget their mission, they are reminded that " the policies of the Soviet system are the foundation of its life," and that that system " cannot allow its youths to be educated in a spirit of indifference towards its

[10] See above, note 33 on p. 371.

policies, nor should they be allowed to drift, deprived of guiding ideas."[11] In all countries, such an enormous amount of general educational work has still to be carried out that, if the desirability of the social system supported by public educational activities is taken for granted the largest part of public attempts to shape the individual citizen's way of life may pass with little controversy. What criticism may be normally levelled against them will be based on undue concessions to existing mass-taste[12] rather than upon the impact of elements of State ideology controversial even amongst the supporters of the existing system. The obvious propagandist advantages as well as the economic consideration that centralised mass-production will provide a maximum of cultural services at minimal costs have rendered such state-sponsored services common even in typical bourgeois-democratic countries such as Sweden and Britain, and objections to the working of such services are usually restricted to ideological details. But there is, in Britain, little argument about that vague religiosity, opposition to which is not " respectable " ; and there is, in the U.S.S.R., no argument about such tactful rationalist implications as may follow from due emphasis, in Adult Education, on Darwinism, etc. Most of the public cultural services will pass without any controversy, especially if the alternatives (such as letting their tasks be fulfilled by private monopolies, or, say, allowing children to go wild) are distinctly unattractive to a big majority of the population. Therefore their natural bias will not be regarded as a restriction of Freedom as conceived in the society in question. In a socialist system it will be claimed that public cultural services make the worker not only more healthy, efficient and contented than is possible in capitalist countries, but also more capable of making his contribution towards shaping the social framework within which he works. Therefore, they help to realise Freedom. Freedom thus defined is to be found not only, and not even mainly, in the leisure-time devoted to the citizen's private interests, but in the production process itself and, even more, in that part of his leisure which the citizen devotes to unpaid civic activities, making his contribution towards the understanding and the realisation of what is necessary.

[11] Resolution of Central Committee of the C.P. of the U.S.S.R. on the literary periodicals *Zvezda* and *Leningrad*, of August 14, 1946.

[12] Comp. also my *Spirit of Post-War Russia*, p. 49.

This trend in modern socialism, and modern life, is well-defined and not Utopian at all. But there is a second way to define Freedom, and it, too, has made its contribution to shaping the Marxist outlook. When making their contribution towards freeing society from feudal fetters the classical economists refuted the delusion that such freedom meant, even for the capitalist entrepreneur, freedom to do what he liked : the objective laws of social life would enforce a certain, socially beneficent use of that freedom. All Marxism rests upon the basic assumption that there are such laws which may be realised and consciously fulfilled, but can never be dispensed with. " For ever, even when exchange value will be abolished, the time of labour needed remains the creative substance of wealth and the measure of costs involved in its production."[13] Whatever the social structure, Man's struggle with Nature will remain the realm of necessity.[14] It will increase with the increase of human needs, but increasing productive resources will increase the possibility of satisfying those needs.[15] The character of this necessary labour is fundamentally changed by its being restricted in time, by its being done for the benefit of the workers themselves and forming the basis for leisure to be enjoyed by them, by the abolition of social antagonisms[13] and by the increased control of Nature.[15] However, Marx is not satisfied with this part of the argument[16] :

[13] *Theories on Surplus Value*, vol III, pp. 305-6. The argument, which evidently provides the background for the next quotation (from *Capital*) is even strengthened by the connection in which it is made : Ricardo is praised for having dealt with the problem of necessary labour from the highest standpoint possible on a bourgeois basis : he wanted to reduce the working class, about the unavoidably hard conditions of whom he cherished no delusions, to as low a percentage of society as possible. In comparison with this, socialism means some necessary labour, that is drudgery, but also some leisure, that is freedom, for all.

[14] A contradiction in terms to Engels' statement above⁴ quoted is obvious, and becomes even more evident in the just quoted paragraph from *Theories on Surplus Value* where " labour performed under the pressure of an external purpose " is described as " necessity or social obligation, whatever description is preferred." Engels—but also Marx in many other statements—found in that " description," that is, in different attitudes to necessary social labour, the " leap from the realm of Necessity into the realm of Freedom."

[15] *Capital*, vol. III, Chapter 48, pp. 954.

[16] Popper (op. cit., p. 96) gives one-sided emphasis to the second part of the argument (now following in our text), partly because of neglect of the parallel in *Theories on Surplus Value*, partly because of his failure to quote the passage in *Capital* (¹⁵) upon which his own argument rests in all its essential aspects. There is dualism in Marx's point of view, but not, as Popper seems to think, in the popular sense of matter plus soul (Hegel was not such a fool as to conceive Man as a purely spiritual being). Marx's dualism lies in his having two different concepts of Freedom, namely (1) (which he shared with Hegel) that necessary work should command such a spiritual attitude that it could be regarded as conscious, and therefore free (2) that necessary work should occupy as small as possible a place in human life.

" The realm of freedom actually begins only where drudgery, enforced by hardship and external purposes, ends ; it thus quite naturally lies beyond the sphere of material production proper."

Beyond that sphere begins that development of human faculties which constitutes an end in itself, the true realm of freedom.[14] It can flourish only on the basis of that realm of necessity and the shortening of the labour day is its fundamental pre-requisite.[15] Leisure-time of which one disposes oneself is true wealth, needed for the enjoyment of the products of one's necessary labour as well as for free activities not dictated, as labour is, by the necessity of an external purpose.[13] I think there can be no doubt that Marx found the merits of the Society to Come in such a free play of human activities rather than in abundance of all conceivable consumer goods. Our interpretation of his concepts of that society should be subject to this fundamental consideration which is an original derivation of his own[13] rather than to his occasional repetition of the current Fourierist formula " from everyone according to his abilities, to everyone according to his needs".

At this point, where we appear to touch fundamentals, I should like to make two cautioning remarks. (1) Marx's argument if seen in the context of his work,[13] has a sectional background : it is derived from the workers' protest against drudgery implied in labour in a society in which they do not work for themselves. Since the days when it was made, under the pressure of the sectional labour movement working hours have been reduced to such an extent that there is no longer such a strong *prima facie* case for the assertion that they imply a distortion of human personality. It may be asserted that the whole argument would lose its strength in a changed social framework in which working hours not only would be made more agreeable—as can be done even in a capitalist society—but also would form the basis for the development of so important an aspect of the citizen's human personality as his having his say in the direction of the national productive efforts. It should be noticed that, at least on the Continent, the pressure of the Labour movement which enforced shortening of the working day was caused by its realisation that such a shortening was a preliminary condition for the average worker's ability to take part in its activities and therefore a pre-requisite of further progress. For this reason, not because of any abstract concepts of human personality, " class-conscious " labour movements, like the

Austrian, found achievements in this field more important than higher wages.

(2) Marx describes the Society to Come as characterised by the free play of human activities ; but the criticism of the way in which today the individual's tastes and leisure-time activities are shaped by capitalist interests is no less important an element of Marxism, as distinct from Liberalism. Certainly, the cultural activities in the Society to Come may be conceived as those of individuals who spend their leisure in isolation (or in small groups of friends) after they have given society its due during the hours of necessary labour. Such an interpretation is possible, and compatible with Marxism. But there is also an alternative interpretation familiar to the activist of the modern labour movement (and especially to the Socialist worker whose leisure, spent in the struggle for the emancipation of his fellows, is really that part of his life where his personality can be developed) : Leisure-time activities are cherished because they are not performed under external pressure, and because a large variation between them, according to the individual's tastes, is possible ; but they are valued as a social activity serving social purposes, and free in the sense that, during those hours, the individual makes his own, individual, contribution to the formation of social life. That attitude is bound to wither away once the great transformation is achieved and social activities cease to be the worker's single and predominant higher interest ; but so may also Marx's attitude which corresponds to an even lower level of social development, when the worker's life was sheer drudgery.[13] It is impossible to give a definite answer to such questions, concerning a still remote future ; but it is quite conceivable that it may be found in a synthesis. Many of the eventual objects of leisure-time interest may actually lie outside the sphere of social organisation, they may indeed become more individualised ; but the way in which those interests are pursued may be influenced by the fact that for a considerable period they had been regarded as a social activity pursued with the main intention of rescuing necessary labour from the realm of drudgery. Obviously it depends on such considerations whether the men of the future will find anything objectionable in society, or public opinion, taking a strong interest in influencing the direction of artistic, scientific (so far as these lie outside the production interest) and similar interests.

(*d*) CONFORMITY AND VARIETY IN A SOCIALIST SOCIETY

In attempting an approach to this question we have to distinguish two different aspects of the problem, namely (a) the extent to which centralised and planned economics is compatible with free choice of its individual employees as to the direction of their leisure-time activities, and (b) whether the agency which may bring about a socialist, and eventually a communist society is bound to mould public opinion to the exclusion of individual tastes in private matters. The first aspect of the problem does not merely concern socialism, but is raised by the very fact of monopolist organisation dominating the supply of commodities and services essential for the satisfaction of cultural needs. At least for the broad masses of the people " free choice " is already restricted to the " free " decision to satisfy, in a way accessible to the common man's purse, a need made sufficiently popular or fashionable by the propaganda of the entrepreneurs. True, unless conditions have grown so tense that legal repression, or at least ostracism by respectable public opinion, is applied against " un-Ruritanian " thought and ways of life, some loopholes are left to the dissenter because of the continued prevalence, in theory at least, of " free competition." If a socialist society, once fully established[17] wishes to preserve and extend to much broader strata of the population such freedom of choice as had been available before, it would have to apply specific devices. In present society, definite agencies prevent, for example, the few individuals who are in actual control of some academic senate, and who are more likely than not to represent a past stage in the development of scientific thought, from barring academic expression to new trends, provided the latter keep within the generally accepted framework. To a reasonable extent this is achieved by the general acceptance of conventions as to (1) the desirability of progress as such (which would certainly be shared by a socialist society, as a guarantee against technical stagnation), (2) the conditions with which a novel scientific approach has to comply in order to be regarded as serious, and (3) the disapproval of decisions made by external pressure (from

[17] As long as there is some N.E.P., there is also a private sector in cultural life, which is more likely than not to represent social trends opposed to the transformation. So there is also some likelihood that the eventual end of the N.E.P. will leave those cultural trends encouraged in the " private sector " in a rather hopeless position, with little popularity and small chances of getting public support without which they could no longer survive.

State, Maecenas, political parties, etc.). Every one of these conventions, in itself, is rather vague, and in isolation not sufficient to be effective. The opponents of, say, a new scientific approach will deny that it is progressive and that it can be taken seriously, and if they enjoy *too* much independence and " autonomy " stagnation may result. However, they are exposed to some pressure from outside, by the State and by various other organs of public opinion competing with them,[18] whilst those exercising the pressure have themselves to comply with the accepted conventions (for example, not to support, or to oppose, academic appointments suggested for all too obvious political reasons). There is no reason why it should be impossible to solve by similar devices of professional autonomy influenced partly by the State and other bodies of interested citizens,[19] problems such as the granting of a wider field of opportunity than at present in the U.S.S.R. to journalists, artists and scientists dissenting from the prevailing trend. This should be possible as soon as the new society has ceased to need to regard every cultural activity as part of its struggle for survival.[11] This once taken for granted, progress and variety are likely to be regarded as desirable for political and economic reasons, unless society should be controlled by some agency, characterised by a certain general approach to life so all-embracing as to leave no scope for the individual's choice, and so deeply rooted that it would not be relaxed when the emergencies that brought it into being had gone. It is at this point that the second of the above-mentioned aspects of the problem comes in.

[18] The reader may notice that we do not mention private individuals or pressure groups. To state that, say, the progress of modern medicine is safeguarded against professional narrowmindedness of the doctors in existence and in positions carrying influence within the profession by the freedom granted to Christian Scientists, or to enterprises producing homeopathic medicines and their advertisement, is pure nonsense.

[19] This argument should not be confused with Mannheim's (*Man and Society*, pp. 110–1) suggestion of " secret societies," or " orders," where discussion should be completely free under guarantees that all suitable persons were admitted, but public discussions of issues arising within these bodies prevented before competent and specialist opinion on the issue has been cleared (which may mean its complete prevention in those fields where specialist judgment is relevant). Something of that kind is common to all existing social systems, not only to One-party-dictatorships where the need for discussions in an " inner circle " unfettered by ideological dogmatism but bound by collective discipline to defend the accepted decisions before the broader public in terms of the State ideology, is obvious and generally recognised. In every democratic system, whatever the number of parties admitted and the legal freedom granted to the dissenter, membership of the inner circle of some powerful body has to be purchased by not making use of the freedom to dissent in public.

From a formalist approach to Power as the only relevant social agency there follows the popular conception of a socialist society controlled in every regard by the heads of a political machine wielding apparently unlimited economic power. The argument appears strongest in those cases where socialism is introduced by dictatorship of a revolutionary party, perhaps acting for a long period under the emergencies of domestic and external conflict ; but it is generally applied to socialism, however it may have originated. Suppose that Power has some inherent tendency to be applied without limitations (so that, eventually, every group not kept by proper balances in its place, would enslave, mutilate or kill all other men), then the very success of socialist planning, namely, the absence of agencies capable of disorganising production, would imply the passing of all limitations to Power. But, at least in a modern state and economy, as distinct from the abstractions of formalist sociology and some historical examples drawn from the decomposition of feudal society, the group wielding " power " is not composed of a few few humans being exposed to all conceivable psychological temptations, but forms a large agglomeration of people linked by common beliefs and interests (amongst which the interest in preserving " power " that is, the social order underlying their common concepts, is predominant) and exposed to all influences originating within the vast machine which they have to work. The comparatively small group which, in every social structure, formally or actually controls that agglomeration, is subject to the laws governing its behaviour ; and the danger that a highly centralised organisation may actually be defeated because of some mistakes made by a few leading individuals makes for even sharper control of their behaviour. If the basic ideology underlying the regime is based upon hierarchical subordination and acceptance of authority as such, some merits may be found in the very fact of regulation, and a pragmatist philosophy will make every value dependent upon its serving the desired end ; but if increasing mass-activity (and conviction of the masses having their own say) is regarded as a fundamental element of the strength of the regime, regulation for regulation's sake will be looked upon as producing unnecessary friction.

Up to this point, our argument has been valid for socialism in general. In view of the obvious fact that at least in some countries socialism is being brought about by a revolutionary dictatorship, and that Marx regarded such a mode of transition as typical, we have to ask whether there are any inherent needs for unlimited expansion of the scope within which such power is exercised. Beyond emergencies, with which we are not dealing here, such unconstrained needs would have been found within the conception of the dictatorship itself.

Dictatorship of the most consistent of the revolutionary parties, when needed in order to save a revolution which is in danger, needs no further theoretical justification than that revolution itself : an argument based upon the advantages of socialism in comparison with capitalism, if sufficiently strong and especially if linked with hints at the actual limitations of the freedom available in capitalist society, is actually also an argument in favour of the restrictions of freedom which are necessary in order to bring the new society into being. The theoretical importance of statements about the eventual withering away of State, Utopian as they are in their verbal content, lies in the fact that idealisation of the necessary compulsion is rejected. Thus, Rousseau's use of the term *volonté general*[20] was a fiction applied in order to bridge the gap between his liberal-democratic foundations and the totalitarian claims of the public interest which he tended to establish. Marxism[21] clearly describes as such whatever limitations of the individual's freedom are found necessary. In the honest upholding of such descriptions, not in attempts to prove that Utopia is being realised,[22] lies mankind's hope that the Society to Come will find in its own ideology the tool for effecting the gradual withering away not of its social order, which is a Utopia, but of attitudes which, however necessary for human progress, represent only one side of human life. The problem of the prospects of variety and individualisation in the coming society lies in the question whether the members of that society will value such variety in itself. At present, in devoting

[20] That is the best realisation of the public interest accessible in the circumstances to the most advanced minds. The term is frequently confused, even by those who claim to follow Rousseau, with the *volonté des tous*, that is, the prevailing trend of public opinion, from which liberal-democratic ideology derives the legitimacy of government. The confusion—which is a contradiction in terms—is contained in the use of the term " volonté " for two completely different things.

[21] See above, pp. 393 and 410.

[22] This — from the point of view of the basic attitude of original Marxism—is the dangerous aspect of the attempts to demonstrate that even in the isolated U.S.S.R. *some* State functions could "wither away." Evidently, "withering away of the State " is here taken as a synonym of " integration of society " which is something quite different. But see note 18a to the preceding Chapter.

himself to the cause of the emancipation of his class, every worker can find a fullness of life denied by capitalist society to nearly all of those of its members who duly fit into its recognised pattern ; and in accepting a discipline serving the needs of that struggle, he transforms the hard necessities of life into limitations willed by himself. There is nothing problematic in such an atitude from the point of view of those concerned, unless it is either exaggerated so as to restrict the community's ability to form a reasoned opinion about its task or prolonged into social conditions where the needs to which it owed its emergence have disappeared.

The comparison between present-day Communism and the early Church has frequently been made. Unless *a priori* value is ascribed either to liberal or to ecclesiastical dogma, it is difficult to see why either party to the comparison should resent it. Men make great efforts, involving the possible sacrifice of their lives, because they are upheld by the consciousness of belonging to a community called to realise the highest values. Such a community claims a certain authority for its basic tenets and for the organs deciding on its behalf on the application of those tenets to concrete issues. Such claims are quite independent of the presence or absence of political power to enforce them ; the need for homogeneous action or even simply for the symbols of unity will prevent permission of dissent within the membership on what are deemed essentials. The habit of discussing fundamental problems by ascribing one's own point of view to the authoritative source of the common creed is much older than the Marxist responsibility for a great state (which, in due course, found the relative inflexibility of its basic ideology rather embarrassing). In a community facing tasks regarded as fundamental, nearly every aspect of life will be judged in its relation to the essentials it stands for. Therefore it may be described as totalitarian without implying that it enforces its views on matters only indirectly connected with essentials upon outsiders, or even upon members without ambition to conform to the highest conceivable standard. But there is a likelihood that, in every issue, there will be a definite solution which is correct from the community's point of view. It may change in the course of time ; and the objective needs of society will, within the community, find expression in different applications of the basic tenets ; but once a certain solution is agreed, it is likely to be upheld for the time being, by the whole authority of the common faith. The implications of these general observations upon the degree of individualisation possible in a society brought about by something like a world revolution of the original Communist pattern seem obvious. But the foregoing argument is a mere extrapolation from conditions and attitudes prevailing at specific times, namely, when the religious foundations of the ancient world, or the preservation of capitalism today, are the crucial issues amongst those who are most strongly impressed by those conflicts and their implications. In historical reality, socialism if it should become worldwide reality, cannot be brought into being as a mere result of Communist efforts any more than feudalism, as a predominant pattern of civilisation, could have been brought into being by the Church's influence upon the Germanic tribes, or capitalist civilisation by bourgeois-democratic revolutions of the classical French (or French plus American) type. There will be whole national civilisations which, at the best, will only take over certain aspects of socialist countries representing the "classical" type into their internal development, and even in the U.S.S.R. selected non-Communist elements of the national past will be admitted into the integration because of the sheer necessity of establishing national unity in a hostile world.[23] The most for which the successful ideology can hope in such circumstances may be a general tendency to express very different elements of the synthesis in its own terminology. The awareness of the imperfection of Man is at present expressed in the Christian world in terms of a myth written some three thousand years ago by an author who probably intended to illustrate the jealousy of gods[24]; the relations between Thought and Nature were discussed for some centuries between Nominalists and Realists in terms of an awkward comment on Aristotle which the Church, in its earliest days, would have firmly rejected as alien to the Christian outlook; and the Mikado as well as the aspirations of workers rebelling against capitalist society find expression in bourgeois terms. From the point of view of the preceding as well as of the subsequent social formation such terminological forms of expression may appear strange; from the point of view of the

---

[23] Comparisons in this point with mediaeval societies are misleading because the specific claims of theological ideology prevented the synthesis from taking a shape other than reception of non-Christian elements into Church-dominated ideology.

[24] The narratives of original sin, and of Babel, are both originated from the so-called L-source of the Pentateuch whose author's tendency has been interpreted as very similar to that of the authors of the Prometheus-story.

people who use them they are quite adequate, and human lives are not at all dull because perhaps some later generation may describe all the conflicting trends as hardly distinguished varieties within a species recognised as only one amongst many possible others. From the Marxist point of view, with which we are here concerned, it seems obvious that the objective needs of a socialist society, discusssed above, will find expression in whatever terminology may have originated from the process of transition and reintegration. Should such needs include admission of a remarkable degree of variety,[25] whilst State ideology measures everything by its conformity with the communal interest, ways and means will be found to prove that both are completely compatible and that even the dissenter fulfils a public duty. If a communist society should become static, it would have at the disposal of its ideology the tools needed to explain such behaviours as necessary because of its stagnation. But this would be a development opposed not only to the liberal elements in Marxist ideology —which we may regard as irrelevant for the assessment of its general trend—but to the very dynamics of the process to which it owes its origin.

[25] See above, pp. 413-4.

CHAPTER XIX

NATIONALITY AND INTERNATIONALISM

In itself, Marxism is no more or less internationalist an ideology than Christianity, Liberalism, or any other ideology claiming to be true in a sense broader than the pragmatist sense of serving the needs of a certain nation.[1] The Victorian age with its outlook based upon universal Free Trade has left distinct traces in Marxist ideology, including dreams such as those of an eventual disappearance of national differences and of a universal world language replacing the existing ones. Whatever lip-service may still be paid to such concepts,[2] it vanishes in importance before the reality of the creation of scores of new national civilisations and the revival of other scores of existing ones threatened with extermination by the progress of capitalism. From the democratic point of view, Socialism looks well in the company of the awakening peasant masses of "backward" peoples and their entry into the current of modern economics in cultural forms appealing to the common man's background.[3] In constrast, its association with the Liberalism of the Free Trade era during the growth of the Labour movement was less beneficial. During the whole history of the Marxist movement, the trend that emphasized the need for national emancipation and independence as a condition of efficient common action for higher aims common

[1] In theory, it is possible to construct even a fascist ideology with an international appeal ; and references to the growth of "brother-movements" in other countries are most common in the propaganda of fascist parties in the stage of formation, or in phases (or directions) of policies of a fascist state when (or where) emphasis on the desire for world domination has to be avoided. However, it is impossible to build the ideological appeal of fascism on another basis than one's own nation's calling ; and while ambitions expressed will differ as between Slovak, German or Japanese fascists, according to the realities of the respective nation's position, not even Slovak fascists can manage without appealing to slogans distasteful to their Magyar "fellow-fascists." Within the truly international movements mentioned above, conflict between different national sections is always regarded as a deplorable and, in principle, avoidable incident.

[2] Comp. Stalin, *The National Question*, etc., ed. cit., pp. 224 ff. The whole argument is direced against Great Russian and German chauvinists within the Labour movement, who from the ultimate prospect of a withering away of nations derive a demand for subordination of nations subject to that "historical nation" to which they happen to belong.

[3] See above, pp. 337-8.

to all nations [4] was opposed to another trend which regarded those higher aims as a suitable pretext for neglecting the nearer, national ones, [5] though its representatives occasionally proclaimed in the name of internationalism the duty of smaller and inferior nations to submit to leadership by the working-class of their nation. [2] It should be further noted that the International originated, apart from the desire of British Trade Unionists to prevent undercutting of their wages by foreign strike-breakers and the left-wing desire to encourage anti-Bonapartist opposition in France, as the consecutive link in a long chain of attempts by British democrats to organise co-operation with refugees representing the oppressed " progressive nationalities " as accepted by contemporary left-wing opinion. [6] Even Bakunin, whose followers became the main supporters of the a-national approach, had started his career as organiser of a left-wing national movement, true, of the Slavonic nationalities that were not accepted as " naturally progressive." [7]

Socialist concepts of the Society to Come as international, that is, as being based upon the friendly collaboration of different nations, [3] are extrapolations from conditions supposed to be normal in the movement that brings socialist society into being. The argument is not quite conclusive : even assuming that friendly collaboration between the various national labour movements is bound to prevail as long as the threat of common enemies overrules any differences in national interest, such differences may emerge as soon as the new society has ceased to be a contested issue on the international stage. But unless it is overstated in a Utopian way, so as to exclude any major difference of interests between countries, the argument is maintained by the Marxist explanation of imperialist wars by economic motives, an explanation which would cease to be valid in a socialist society, and by the evident successes of Marxist nationalities policies. As the new society will find itself confronted with all the possibilities of mass-destruction evolved by its predecessor, it is quite sensible to assume that consciousness of its common origin may have more persistent

[4] See above, p. 305. [5] See above, note 37 on p. 338.
[6] Comp. Th. Rothstein's article, *A Preamble to the History of the International,* amply quoted in G. M. Stekloff, *The First International,* English ed., London, 1927, espec. pp. 22 ff. The analogies include such details as the selection of the meeting-room traditional for such events. In the *Address of the International* the connection is preserved by the famous phrase about the Pole and the Magyar who could not be emancipated unless the worker was emancipated everywhere.
[7] See above, pp. 306-7.

implications than the corresponding phenomenon in mediaeval Christianity which hardly exceeded a *treuga dei* and some rules of chivalrous warfare. However, the whole argument supposes that the new society would have grown everywhere in the world from common efforts of co-ordinated Labour movements or, at least, that the influence of such movements would be strong enough to prevent socialist societies grown from antagonistic sources[8] from following courses inherently hostile to one another. The concept of the society to come as internationalist, in a more than Utopian sense, is bound to the international character of the Labour movement in so far as the latter is not merely sectional, but an actual factor in bringing the new society into being.

Now this international character is threatened whenever in international conflicts the national Labour movements take sides against each other. This is something very different from taking sides against a certain party to the international dispute : we have learned, in section (b) of Chapter XIV, that, at the time when the International originated, such taking sides was regarded as the most natural of policies. But in the interest of international solidarity it must be supported by the opposition movement within the state discriminated against and be followed, if this state is actually defeated, by a policy which prevents at least that opposition from resenting the part taken by the international labour movement during the war. Such standards were actually preserved by the original Marxists in their attitude towards conflicts between the leading West European nations from the common efforts of which the socialist transformation was expected.[9] But contradictions were bound to arise as soon as the safe ground of every nation's right to independence was left behind. On the assumption that Engel's forecasts underlying the description of some nationalities as " historical " and of others as bound to linger on and in due course to be absorbed with the progress of capitalist civilisation[10] had been correct, his distinction between the rights of " the great national subdivisions of Europe " and " the nationalities principle proper "[11] would

---

[8] See above, p. 325.

[9] This holds true for the hypothetical war-situation of 1859, in which Engels (letter to Lassalle of November 22, 1859, ed. Meyer, Vol III, p. 240) argued against Lassalle with reference to the support of his anti-Bonapartist war policy by the French opposition, as well as for that of 1870–1 (see above, pp. 310–11). In the hypothetical situation of 1891 (see note 33 to Chapter XIV) Engels, in any case, started by explaining his attitude to the Labour movement of the nation discriminated against in the concrete situation.

[10] See note 18 to Chapter XIV.   [11] See above, p. 307.

appear compatible with Stalin's later distinction between
" nationalities " and " integral nations."[12] However, Stalin
did not deny that the former might become " nations with which
the modern labour movement would have to reckon," and did not
orientate his policy in such a way that mistakes in the assessment
of the chances of some nationalities to form a working-class of their
own[13] would result in driving that working-class into the arms
of their national bourgeoisie (as did forecasts by the followers
of Engels that the Czechs could not expect a historical future).
There is no Socialist dogma according to which just those
nationalities existing at present should necessarily participate in
the building of the new society : some, whose economic functions
have gone in the modern age[14] may be absorbed, and others who
take the wrong side in international conflicts[15] may suffer
enforced assimilation. The fates of these peoples will be
interwoven with the present international transformation just
as it formed a distinctive trait of preceding ones. However, all
forecasts that international conflicts will be avoided because
of the Labour movement's share in shaping the new order are
based on the supposition that there could be no serious and
continuous conflicts between the Labour movements of those
nations that eventually will form parts of that order.

As long as the predominant interest of Socialist internationalism is defined in sectional terms of avoiding the import of
strike-breakers, or of commodities produced under sub-standard

[12] See above, p. 350. It is not clear to me whether there was any connection
between Stalin's and Engel's use of the distinction. The latter was unearthed in a
paper by Ryazanoff published three years after the publication of Stalin's article, also
in Vienna where Stalin's paper had originated. If such a connection should exist,
the change of function of the juxtaposition as described in the text, with a Russian
author of Stalin's standing, would have to be regarded as intentional. Ryazanoff
gives no comments but does not hide his disapproval of Engels' attitude.

[13] To which he was certainly not immune. See above, p. 339. But it should
be noticed that his mistakes (which, therefore, were comparatively harmless) arose
from underestimating the speed of social developments, namely from the expectation
of a comparatively long bourgeois-democratic development, during which the
mountain tribes of the Caucasus would be absorbed by the Russian, Georgian, etc.,
nationalities ; a socialist revolution, with a quickly following industrialisation even of
the most backward areas, was indeed the only contingency that could preserve such
tribes and transform them into " integral nations." Engels continuously worked
on overstatements of the step of the socialist transformation (see above, p. 334); but
this made the mistake no less harmful when, unexpectedly, a Czech working-class
emerged to resent Greater German ambitions of its German fellows.

[14] See above, pp. 349-51.

[15] During the last war, some Autonomous Republics of the U.S.S.R., the predominant nationalities of which had shown propensity to collaborate with the invader,
were abolished, which presumably implies a policy of absorption.

conditions of labour,[16] it coincides happily with the above defined conditions for an eventual peace-order (the sociologist of ideologies would say : the concept of such an eventual peace-order is an extrapolation of the actual sectional interest in preventing mutual dumping at the expense of labour). In principle, imports of unfairly cheap commodities from China or Japan are just as bad as those from France or Germany and cheap labour from Ireland would be even worse than a limited supply from Poland. So there are no limits to the sectional interest which every worker may have in being organised and feeling himself connected to his fellows everywhere by mutual solidarity. But the position may undergo a great change as soon as issues involving the conquest and still more[17] the preservation of political power arise and the lower-middle-classes, both urban and rural, are assessed as relevant political forces alliance with whom may be more important than the sympathies of some foreign Labour movement of questionable strength. This is not, as frequently asserted, a mere example of power-politics on the part of some socialist state. There may be a clear Soviet interest in keeping the frontier of the Soviet security zone on the Oder, whatever may happen in Germany ; but there is also an international Socialist interest in not making unnecessarily difficult the task of Polish Socialists who have to build the new society on the foundations of a not very favourable national tradition. All Socialists, including sincere Socialists in Germany, are strongly interested in avoiding a situation in which internal weakness of Polish socialism might encourage foreign intervention and thus produce World War III. But there are also other Socialist, and even national Soviet interests concerning the implications of the Oder frontier on German domestic politics. The task of correctly assessing their respective weight may be difficult ; but it is simply nonsense to assert that the interests of any group of workers (who themselves may be exposed to nationalistic ideologies of a distinctly anti-Soviet colour) should necessarily take precedence over those of the peasants (who may have a national tradition that attracts them into the socialist orbit). As long as sharply contrasted social systems oppose one another on the international stage, each of them, by following the course determined by its basic tenets, may

---

[16] See note 6 above, p. 286.

[17] Because in the struggle for power the specific weight of the politically conscious workers is much higher. Once a state is established, the morale of one soldier is, in principle, as important as that of any other.

NATIONALITY AND INTERNATIONALISM

win sympathies amongst those sharing those tenets, even in countries whose national interests are overruled ; radical land reform in Eastern Germany, carried out against the will of the Western allies, may form at least a partial compensation for the Oder frontier. But such ways of combining concessions to national aspirations of one country with the preservation of some sympathies in the other are (a) open only to states, as distinct from socialist movements disposing of nothing but their sympathies, and (b) they are bound to a stage of international development in which there is still not merely ideological, but actual difference between the policies pursued by the competing states. There would be no point in the combination of Oder frontier with land reform if the latter were supported by the Western allies as well who, because of their geo-political position, might still defend German interests against Polish aspirations. It follows that (a) the combination of the international socialist interest with the specific power interests of certain socialist states, far from being unnatural as asserted by those who deplore the " degeneration " of Utopia, is the only condition in which at least *some* solidarity of the Labour movements of nations whose immediate interests appear as opposed to each other can be preserved in spite of the likelihood that the national interests of some Labour movements will be prejudiced by the inevitable compromises with others ; and (b) that this ground for the preservation of the international solidarity of the Labour movement will come to an end when, in some way or other, the basic principles of the new order have been generally realised. As this may easily happen without a break in the different national traditions of at least the major powers, and without dropping the ideological differences whose mere economic background would have vanished, it is at least conceivable that mankind may enter the socialist stage of its development without having achieved a common standard overruling all differences in national interests.

In Marx's days, the case for a conception of the international Labour movement as one unit, for merely tactical reasons operating in different national fields and ultimately called to establish a world-state, rested on a threefold basis : (1) the conviction, based upon the quick and unfettered expansion of world trade, and expressed as early as in the *German Ideology*, that external economic pressure would bring about the failure of any communist experiment not embracing all the leading industrial nations (2) the realisation of the speed with which bourgeois-democratic revolutions had spread over Western and Central Europe (3) the need to prevent the import of strike-breakers.[6] None of these arguments holds true very consistently in our era of large-scale economic units protected by high tariffs and State regulation of external trade.[18] But there is another argument which in classical Marxist documents was conspicuously absent,[19] but which has become the main support of internationalism since modern war became too vast to be regarded as a mere incident occasionally implied in the clearing of national problems : the abhorrence of war. The hatred of war provided the moral backing of the Second and, in a more rationalised form, of the Third International. It has certainly not ceased to be an efficient force because of the mere fact that in World War II the forces of progress were clearly associated with one of the struggling parties, and identified with its war-effort. But internationalism was re-interpreted when those forces were rallied, and won their most spectacular successes, in national resistance movements the aims of which did not necessarily always coincide. The transfer of Socialist ambitions to their national realisation, not the dissolution of a very narrow organisational form, nor a transitory stage in the development of Great Power relations, has raised Socialist internationalism from the organisational level of the Third International to that of international fellowship between people holding common standards, which is not a privilege of Socialism.

This may appear as a short-term argument not very relevant for our discussion of the ultimate prospects of a world-wide socialist society. But the same objection also holds true as regards the tendency to answer the threat of destructive world-wars by some type of world-state, ultimately a world-wide federal organisation. Elsewhere[20] I have attempted to demonstrate that federal organisation is impossible unless the partners agree upon all basic issues of social organisation. In a period

[18] There may be a sensible basis for I.L.O.s and similar institutions ; but the comparison between such realisations of sectional internationalism and the original inspiration of the International provides the strongest support for the argument made in the text.

[19] For it would have prevented recourses to the Jacobin tradition of conquest of power by the most consistent revolutionary party in consequence of a war-emergency from being exalted into a recommendation of wars not immediately implied in the revolutionary struggle (see above, pp. 309 and 313).

[20] In my *Federalism*, etc., espec. the last chapter.

of struggle between opposing social systems federalism may conceivably provide an organisational form for one or both of the parties to the dispute. But its application for that purpose is extremely unlikely : it is not likely to commend itself to a world power which is prepared to take the lead in defending the traditional order and to shoulder " the white man's burden " but is resolved to preserve its hegemony within its orbit and to protect its industrial interests against the competition even of its allies. Nor is a world power bound to the principle of equal rights for all member nations of a federation, but eager to uphold its national integrity, likely to enter any federation with partners of equal strength. Neither the U.S.A. nor the U.S.S.R. will wish the distinctly national character of its civilisation to be submerged. But however the problem of the internal organisation of the parties striving for the coming social order will be solved, it is simply impossible to imagine various nations federating for joint defence without envisaging some potential aggressor, or for granting each other economic preference without envisaging any competitor. If a federation is intended not merely to improve the chances of survival and prosperity of its members in competition with other parts of the world, but to form the future organisation of international solidarity, it loses all that might otherwise make for its internal coherence. From the point of view of the defenders of the traditional order it is possible to conceive their alliance as nearly universal, because of the prevalence amongst the existing states of units supporting their outlook. From the point of view of those striving for a new social order it is not. If the present trend of the socialist countries to emphasize the appeal to the broad masses of their nations continues, as indeed it should in times of increasing international tension, their international system is bound to assume the shape of a plurality of states, perhaps multi-national federations characterised by certain distinct types of civilisations, linked with each other by relations of alliance and perhaps such economic agreements as may be desirable for large-scale planning. If the number of component units should be comparatively small—which is likely if the nations with the greatest numerical strength should eventually be found amongst the supporters of the new order—in no stage of the development need there be any strong demand for a " world state " : the economic arrangements necessary in order to rationalise production on a world-scale could be made between

" independent " units. This procedure would hardly meet more organisational difficulties than co-operation of representatives of the most different civilisations within a " world-government, " and would provoke less antagonism caused by self-assertion of the different national types of development. If very different types of the new society should co-exist after a gradual withering away of international conflicts still describable in terms of class,[21] the ideological demand for a " world-state " might easily have become obsolete to such an extent that it could no longer seriously affect the organisational forms used by all nations for their common purposes. Should the Marxist forecast of a withering away of the repressive functions of State, in any non-Utopian sense,[22] prove correct, it is easily conceivable that the remaining functions of State would be so clearly differentiated according to different national traditions that their merging in a new unit would appear as a very unintelligent way of achieving what could easily be achieved by some agreements between the existing ones.

So we remain confronted with the final problem of whether national differentiations are likely to wither away in a world-wide socialist system of economics.[23] For a very long period the cultural awakening of strata inaccessible to any civilisation which does not appeal to their specific traditions and outlook is bound to make up for the gradual withering away of fundamental differences between the social systems in which they live. But at some point a certain cultural level must be taken for granted everywhere, and much of the further progress will consist in the reception of cultural achievements of other nations (at present restricted to a comparatively small part of the *intelligentsia*). The orthodox Marxist case is the assertion that, in such a stage, national differentiations, forming a " superstructure," will wither away because the economic foundations would have

---

[21] This would not exclude a preceding period during which frictions between systems no longer fundamentally differing in social structure might be described in traditional terms just as, for quite a considerable period, the commercial conflicts between the growing capitalist states were described in terms of religious conflicts.

[22] See above, pp. 399 ff.

[23] Cf. Bauer's op. cit., pp. 101 ff, Kautsky's *Die Befreiung der Nationen*, pp. 35 ff, and my *Federalism*, etc., pp. 222-3. Stalin's attitude, in 1913, sharply opposed to Bauer (*The National, etc., Question*, pp. 28 ff and 51 ff) has since developed towards a removal of the issue from the realm of Utopian forecasts. There is no clear contradiction in terms. Formally, Bauer, Kautsky, and the Stalin of 1913 all discussed issues of the Society to Come. But they would never have discussed it with any comparable fervour, had they not actually discussed the fates of the Austro-Hungarian and Russian multi-national states during the next generation or so.

become fairly homogeneous. But this supposes social evolution coming to a standstill once socialism (or " the higher stage of a communist society," or whatever definition is preferred) is achieved : any further evolution of society is bound to be affected by whatever differences in the starting point have been caused by the different ways in which it was reached.

Here we may conclude our analysis : Marxism is a theory of social dynamics, and nothing else. It is impossible to prove its basic tenets except by proving the advantages of choosing the development of productive resources as the independent variable amongst the various interdependent factors in social evolution. If we assume for a moment that society will become static, it is no longer possible to state that economics provides the content to be filled in various cultural " forms." Nor is it possible on that assumption to state anything about the character of the society to come—except that, on pain of starvation, it can never restore private property in means of production. If we drop this assumption, as should be natural for Marxists, we have also to drop Utopian extrapolations of the liberal ideals from the consistent consummation of which Marxism as an ideology is derived, though it did not originate as a social force in this way. The higher stage of the communist society, the withering away of the State and of nation, are parts of the tribute paid by the founders of Marxism to what one of them has described as the evil of system-building.[24] For sociological reasons system-building may be an unavoidable by-product in the formation not only of philosophical schools, but also of mass-movements. But it is not that part of Marxism which will survive.

[24] Engels, *Ludwig Feuerbach* etc., pp. 23–9.

CONCLUSION

In making an appreciation of Marx's work, we appear merely to have established a different aspect of its historical limitations. He has disentangled the philosophical structure built by Hume, Kant and Hegel from idealist metaphysics ; he has moved progressive thought from the quest for realisation of abstract ideals to the concrete investigation of the ways in which human lives are moulded by institutions, and institutions transformed by human action. He has led the modern Labour movement, which would nevertheless have grown without his work, to the task of becoming not merely a representative of the interests of the underdog, but the agency of the impending transformation. Marxism is no more original than the Aristotelian system, that other synthesis which succeeded in transferring to a civilisation to come the achievements of a passing epoch. In either case it is not difficult to trace the origins of each element of the synthesis ; but by doing so we hardly approach the function of the given element in its new connections. Our appreciation of the Marxist system does not even depend upon Marx's own ability completely to assess the new meaning which the concepts assumed in his hands : no genius stands so much above his time that he can exactly state whether terms honestly borrowed from other thinkers are used in the same sense as they used them.

Marx has completed the economic theory current in his day, and he has succeeded in turning it into a theory of the growth and fall of capitalist society. But he has not succeeded in presenting a working theory of the functioning of the capitalist system. The theory with which he worked was an abstraction based on that stage of historical development when the society of small commodity-producers was dissolved into a capitalist one ; and he was at his greatest when he turned the Labour movement from longing for ideals of Justice abstracted from an idealised past to the concrete task of shaping the future. He had fewer delusions about the Society to Come than any of his contemporaries in the progressive camp ; however, the task which we tried to tackle in the last part of this book consisted mainly in disentangling his basic and original contribution from a shell of 19th Century liberal ideas. He was the first to find a realistic approach to the interpretation and transformation of political institutions ; but however lucid his concept of class as a means of interpretation was, it largely evaporates as soon as we follow it up in the fulfilment of the historical task it had to serve. It is not difficult to appreciate the historical meaning and the historical justification of the statement that " the emancipation of the working-classes can be the work only of the workers themselves " ; but it is difficult indeed to connect with this phrase an unequivocal meaning once we follow up, as Lenin did, Marx's criticism of a purely sectional, " trade-unionist " workers' movement and his sober appreciation of the relations of the necessary policies of a socialist State to the sectional demands and ideologies which have helped to bring it into being.

Like all really great men, Marx was an optimist, and he saw realisations nearer than they were. When trying to find in international politics the concrete agency which would let loose the accumulated internal contradictions of capitalism, he was on the right track and much superior to his liberal and anarchist contemporaries who dwelt in an a-national Utopia ; but he was not just at his greatest when, failing to understand the ultimate aspects of capitalist society from which the break-down would start, he analysed international policies from an ordinary liberal point of view. In all these regards his work was fundamentally improved upon by his Bolshevist successors ; but however strongly the latter may claim continuity with Marx's work it is difficult to overlook the extent to which their work, at least since 1917, has been conditioned by the specific national framework in which Marx's thought found its first realisation. But even a course of events which would justify Lenin's most realistic assumptions as to the way by which the new society would come into being would render Bolshevist theory no more identical with original Marxism than Christianity and Islam are identical with the Aristotelian system (and its Stoic successors) because they were the concrete historical forms in which the heritage of Hellas was to exercise its impact on further developments.

In comparing the foundations of Marx's thought with the terms in which it is relevant in our days, we juxtapose thought and realisation—an antagonism implied in the very fact of realisation, and a proof of thought's capacity to transform reality. But more than this : the intellectual framework in which Marx worked can actually lead to a system which, however adapted to factual changes such as the progress of capitalism into the imperialist stage, the start of the socialist transformation in some individual country, the evolution of " ordinary " *bourgeois* counter-revolution into fascism, etc., still preserves the essential evaluations from which Marx started, as distinct from another system which is more likely to satify the needs of the world in which his thought is being realised.   In issues such as the theory of value we may understand the permanent content of his thought better than he could himself, unfettered as we are by assumptions which he regarded as indisputable ; in others, such as the European and colonial national questions, we may drop the attitudes of the 19th Century Marx in favour of those which a 20th Century Marx would have been bound to assume if he had consistently pursued his basic attitude ; but in some regards we cannot preserve that basic attitude when pursuing Marxism into realisation.   The Trotskyite who asks whether the realisation of " the first stage of a communist society " as observable in our days leads towards, or further away from, the Marxist concept of the second and higher stage, is much more easy to refute in the political than in the spiritual field. Marxism is not the first revolutionary ideology the Utopian elements of which might serve as ideological weapons against its possible realisations ; but by stating this we have not yet answered the question whether Utopia represents at least the asymptote towards which reality is gradually moving.   During the last half of a millenium this has been so : many of the Utopias of one century have turned out to be idealisations of the actual political tasks of the next, and commonplaces of the following one.   There is no reason why transition of international leadership from one group of nations to another, however many details are modified, must necessarily bring to an end this line of development.   But there is also no *a priori* ground why the line of development which started with the formation and emancipation of the middle-classes and ends with the abolition of private enterprise and private property in means of production will continue straight into the centuries to come.   However this basic question may be answered, it should be obvious to modern Marxists that the man Marx, a son of the 19th Century, was bound to generalise from that line and in his thought to prolong it, *ad infinitum*.   We cannot be Marxists in that sense without belying the basic Marxist statement that human thought is conditioned by the actual structure of human society.   On the other hand, we cannot now refuse the basic Marxist statements any more than a serious physicist can be a non-Newtonian, with the further great difference that, in the field of sociology, more generations must pass before an Einstein appears. He will not come before Marx's work has born all its historical fruits.

BIBLIOGRAPHY

A special book would be required in order to give a somewhat complete survey of the works of Marx and Engels, and even of merely the more important of the books dealing with their work. I restrict myself to some suggestions to the student who wishes to follow up some of the issues discussed in this book, with due consideration for the state of present literature on the subject in the English language and for the obvious need to concentrate English studies on Marxist problems on the essentials rather than on details, treatment of which would require acquaintance with a host of specialist literature of very mixed value. There is a lot of important literature on the subject in the Russian language, but, quite apart from the linguistic difficulties, it is hardly accessible to more than a few individuals amongst my readers. So I have restricted myself to a few suggestions which I feel relevant for a proper criticism of my work. Only in order to prevent the enormous amount of German literature on Marxism from being lost, not because I would ascribe any special value to one amongst the many existing bibliographies (the most complete one, and the only of academic standing, has been published by the Marx-Engels-Lenin Institute in Moscow), I mention R. L. Prager's *Marx, Engels, Lassalle, Ein Verzeichnis ihrer Schriften und der Werke ueber ihre Ideen*, Berlin 1924. A number of important historical studies have been published, before and during World War I, in the *Archiv fuer die Geschichte des Sozialismus und der Arbeiterbewegung*, published by K. Gruenberg in Vienna, and in the *Marx-Engels Archiv*, a few issues of which (in Russian and German) have been published since 1927 on behalf of the Moscow Marx-Engels Institute.

Below I give (a) the more important of the works of the founders of Marxism with preference for editions easily accessible to the English reader and amongst them for those which I found most suitable as reference for quotations, (b) books in the English language which I deem helpful for the appreciation of the founders' teaching, especially in those fields where the latter is spread over a number of not always easily accessible works, and (c) books interesting from the point of view of the further development (notwithstanding the fact that most of their authors regarded themselves as orthodox Marxists) and criticism of Marxism.

(a) MAIN WORKS OF MARX, ENGELS AND LENIN

The Collected Works, edited by the Moscow Marx-Engels Institute, are complete only in the Russian language. I restricted myself to quotations from the edition in the original language of Marx's and Engels' writings, noted as *MEGA I*, the available six volumes of which cover the period up to March 1848. By *Correspondence*, I refer to the Marx-Engels correspondence, which is available, in the original language, as part IV of *MEGA* (in four volumes). Partial editions of the less known of Marx's articles after March 1848, only a few of which are available in the below-mentioned English collections, have been published (in the German language) by Mehring and Ryazanoff. The specialist may, in such cases, prefer to have first a look at the (complete) Russian edition of the Collected Works, complaints about the linguistic qualifications of which I have never heard.

Capital has been referred to in this book for Vol. I in the photostatic reprint of the first (1889) English edition, published London 1938, for Vols. II and III in the Kerr-Sonnenschein editions of 1907 and 1909. A good German edition was published in 1933 by the Marx-Engels-Lenin Institute.

The *Theories on Surplus-Value* are not available in English (a fact which better than anything else illustrates the present state of studies on Marx in the Anglo-Saxon world). I quote the German edition, Stuttgart 1923.

Contribution to the Critique of Political Economy, translated by G. Stone, 2nd edition, New York 1904.

Engels' *The Condition of the Working Class in England in 1844*. English edition by Sonnenschein, 1892, last reprint 1943.

In the Marxist-Leninist Library are available :

Vol. 1. Engels' *Anti-Duehring*.

Vol. 2. Engels' *Ludwig Feuerbach* (including Marx's Theses on Feuerbach).

Vol. 3. Marx's *Letters to Kugelmann*.

Vol. 4. Marx's *Class-Struggles in France*.

Vol. 5. Marx's *Civil War in France*.

Vol. 6. Engels' *Germany, Revolution and Counter-revolution.*
Vol. 7. Engels' *Housing Question.*
Vol. 8. Marx's *Poverty of Philosophy.*
Vol. 9. Marx-Engels, *Selected Correspondence* (part of their mutual correspondence, and selection from their letters to other partners, not without bias, but extremely valuable).
Vol. 15. Marx's *Critique of the Gotha Programme* (with accompanying correspondence).
Vol. 16. Engels' *On Capital.*
Vol. 17. Parts I and III of the *German Ideology* (complete in *MEGA* 1/5).
Also Engels' *Dialectics of Nature*, ed. Haldane-Palme Dutt, London 1941.
A collection Marx-Engels, *Selected Works* (quoted : *Sel. Works*) contains in Vol. I, apart from reminiscences of Marx (including Lenin's article) and some important letters, the *Communist Manifesto, Wage Labour and Capital, Value, Price and Profit;* in Vol. II the works on the German and French events of 1848 ff, apart from other works which I have preferred to quote from the separate editions in the Marxist-Leninist Library.
Other English editions quoted :
Marx, *The Eastern Question*, ed. Aveling, London 1897.
Engels, *The Peasant War in Germany*, ed. Ryazanoff, London 1927.
Engels' article *Der Socialismus in Deutschland* has been published in *Neue Zeit*, Vol. X (1891), his *Critique of the Erfurt Programme*, ibid., Vol. XX (1901).
K. Kautsky published in 1935 in Prague, under the title *Aus der Fruehzeit des Marxismus*, his correspondence with the founders (in German, two vols.).
Lenin's *Collected Works* are complete only in Russian (and German), the English edition in progress. Reference has been made only for works which are not available in the Selected Works (*Sel. Works*).

(*b*) Some Books in the English Language on Marx and Engels.

S. F. Bloom, *The World of Nations, a study of the national implications in the work of Karl Marx*, New York 1941.
Maurice Dobb, *Marx as an Economist, an essay*, London 1943.
Sidney Hook, *From Hegel to Marx, studies in the intellectual development of Karl Marx*, London 1936.
K. Korsch, *Karl Marx*, in Modern Sociologists, London 1938.
Gustav Mayer, *Friedrich Engels*, English edition, London 1935.
Franz Mehring, *Karl Marx, the story of his life*, English edition, 1936.
G. Plekhanov, *The Fundamental Problems of Marxism* (Marxist-Leninist Library, Vol. 14).

(*c*) Works Interesting for the Development and Criticism of Marxism.

Otto Bauer, *Die Nationalitaetenfrage und die Socialdemokratie*, 2nd ed., 1924.
E. Bernstein, *Evolutionary Socialism*, Engl. ed., London 1907.
E. v. Boehm-Bawerk, *Karl Marx and the close of his system*, English edition, London 1898 (the classical criticism from the academic economist point of view).
The best criticism of the Austrian school (and academic economics in general) from the Marxist point of view are : N. Bukharin, *The Economic Theory of the Leisure Class*, English edition, London 1927, and G. *Eckstein's* articles (in German) in *Neue Zeit,* Vols. XXII/2, also XXVIII/1.
L. v. Bortkiewicz, *Zur Berichtigung der Grundlegenden Theoretischen Konstruktion von Marx*, in Jahrbucher f. Nationalkonomie & Statistik, Vol. XXXIV (1907).
N. Bukharin, *The Theory of Historical Materialism*, 1921 (in Russian, German and French).
E. H. Carr, *Karl Marx, a study in fanaticism*, London 1934.
—— *The Twenty Years Crisis*, London 1939 (2nd ed. 1942).
—— *The Soviet Impact on the Western World*, London 1946.
C.P. of the U.S.S.R., *History*, short course, English edition 1939 (official publication, now completely included in Stalin's collected works. Chapter IV/2, Dialectical and Historical Materialism, has been included in Stalin's *Leninism* as early as 1940 and appears to be a continuation of much earlier work of his).

H. Cunow, *The Marx'sche Geschichts- Gesellschafts- und Staatstheory* (Problems of Marxist Sociology), 2 Vols., Berlin 1921.

Maurice Dobb, *Political Economy and Capitalism, some essays in economic tradition*, London 1937 (referred to as *op. cit.*).

——, *Studies in the Development of Capitalism*, London 1947.

——, *Soviet Economic Development since 1917*, London 1948.

Rudolf Hilferding, *Das Finanzkapital*, reprinted Vienna, 1927.

J. A. Hobson, *Imperialism*, London 1902.

Karl Kautsky, *Die Agrarfrage*, Stuttgart 1899.

——, *The Economic Doctrines of Karl Marx*, English editions, London 1925 and 1936.

——, *Der Weg zur Macht*, 2nd ed., Berlin 1910.

——, *Nationalitaet und Internationalitaet*, Supplement to *Neue Zeit*, 1908, No. 1 (a criticism of Bauer's *op. cit.*).

——, *Die Internationalitaet und der Krieg* (Separate print from *Neue Zeit*), Berlin 1915.

——, *Die Befreiung der Nationen*, 2nd ed., Stuttgart 1917.

——, *Die proletarische Revolution und ihr Programm*, 2nd ed., Stuttgart 1922.

——, *Die materialistische Geschichtsauffassung* (2 Vols.), Berlin 1927.

L. A. Leontiev and others, *On the teaching of Economics in the U.S.S.R.* (Engl. transl. from *Pod Znamenem Marxisma* 1943, No. 7-8, in the American Review of Economics, 1944, No. 3.

Rosa Luxemburg, *Works*, ed. Froehlich (in German, incomplete. The publ. vols. comprise Gewerkschaftskampf und Massenstreik, and Against Reformism).

——, *Organisationsprobleme der russischen Sozialdemokratie* (translated from *Iskra*) in *Neue Zeit*, Vol. XXII/2 (1904).

——, *Die Akkumulation des Kapitals*, 2 Vols. (the 2nd her answer to the critics of the book of 1915, written 1914), Berlin 1921. An English edition is being published by Routledge-Kegan Paul (London).

——, *Die Krise der Socialdemokratie* (The Junius-pamphlet, Engl. translation, New York 1919, and Lenin's criticism in Coll. Works, Vol. XIX).

Karl Mannheim, *Ideology and Utopia*, English edition, 1934.

——, *Man and Society in an Age of Reconstruction*, London 1940.

T. G. Masaryk, *Die philosophischen und soziologischen Grundlagen des Marxismus*, Vienna 1899.

Franz Mehring, *Geschichte der deutschen Sozialdemokratie*, 4 Vols., Stuttgart 1893 (2nd ed. 1903).

Natalie Moszkovska, *Das Marx'sche System, ein Beitrag zu dessen Ausbau*, Berlin 1929.

——, *Zur Kritik moderner Krisentheorien*, Prague 1935.

A. Notkin and N. Tsagolov, *On the Problem of Economic Balances* (Russian), in *Planovoye Khosaistvo*, 1936, No. 7.

K. Ostrovitianov, *The Basic Laws of Development of Socialist Economy*, Engl. translation in *Science and Society*, Vol. IV, 1945).

——, *Socialist Planning and the Law of Value* (Russian), in *Voprosi Ekonomiki*, 1948, No. 1.

Joan Robinson, *An Essay on Marxian Economics*, 2nd ed., London 1947.

Arthur Rosenberg, *An History of Bolshevism from Marx to the first Five Year Plans*, Engl. ed. 1934.

Rudolf Schlesinger, *Soviet Legal Theory, its Social Background and Development*, London 1945.

——, *The Spirit of Post-War Russia, Soviet Ideology*, 1917-46, London 1947.

Joseph V. Stalin, *Marxism and the National and Colonial Problem*, Engl. ed. 1940.

——, *Leninism* (referred to as *op. cit.*) eds. of 1933 (in 2 Vols.), and 1940 (since reprinted).

——, *Collected Works* (in Russian, in progress).

P. M. Sweezy, *The Theory of Capitalist Development, Principles of Marxist Political Economy*, London 1946.

Leo Trotzky, *1905* (especially the Preface of 1922).

——, *Permanent Revolution* (Russian), Berlin, 1930.

Michael Tugan-Baranovsky, *Theoretische Grundlagen des Marxismus*, Leipzig 1905.

N. Voznesensky, *The War-Economics of the U.S.S.R.* (Russian), Moscow 1947.

437

INDEX

For Product Safety Concerns and Information please contact our EU
representative GPSR@taylorandfrancis.com
Taylor & Francis Verlag GmbH, Kaufingerstraße 24, 80331 München, Germany

www.ingramcontent.com/pod-product-compliance
Lightning Source LLC
Chambersburg PA
CBHW072104270326
41931CB00010B/1455

* 9 7 8 0 4 1 5 6 0 5 0 0 7 *